GERTIGSTRASSE 56

A WARNING FROM THE PAST FOR THE FUTURE

Hamburg, Germany

At the start of the First World War, Rudolf Stender (senior) has no alternative but to leave his fifteen year old son as breadwinner and man responsible for his family. In the midst of the Stender family's struggle to survive hunger and poverty, *Werner* is born. Now there are five siblings for Auguste to care for. During 1917, the responsibility of provider for the home falls on Ernst's shoulders when Rudolf (junior) is conscripted into the army. After 1918, the German population experience many turbulent years. Violence and fear pervade the streets of Hamburg and starvation is inflicted on the underprivileged during the financial crisis of the 1920s. Rudolf (junior) is not idle during this period. With others, he tries to improve the living and working conditions of the poor.

Finally the upsurge of fascism threatens to destroy Germany's democracy. Difficult decisions are made by Rudolf, Ernst and *Werner.* All three siblings risk everything by joining different sections of an anti-fascist resistance movement in order to try and stop the right wing extremists of the Nazi Party. Two of the brothers are arrested by the Gestapo, tortured, imprisoned in Fuhlsbüttel Concentration Camp, and then sent to trial for High Treason against the State. *Werner's* commitment to fight fascism continues much later in Czechoslovakia and Rudolf joins the International Brigade, fighting in the Spanish Civil War. Where will it all end?

This is a novel about the true story of the author's family. Ruth Stender has researched the information over many years, using family letters, archive material and listened to her father *Werner* who is now aged 99 years.

GERTIGSTRASSE 56

A WARNING FROM THE PAST FOR THE FUTURE

RUTH STENDER

Matador
9 Priory Business Park
Kibworth Beauchamp
Leicestershire LE8 0RX, UK
Tel: (+44) 116 279 2299
Email: books@troubador.co.uk
Web: www.troubador.co.uk/matador

ISBN 978 1784623 760

British Library Cataloguing in Publication Data.
A catalogue record for this book is available from the British Library.

Printed and bound by CPI Group (UK) Ltd, Croydon, CR0 4YY
Typeset in 11pt Aldine by Troubador Publishing Ltd, Leicester, UK

Matador is an imprint of Troubador Publishing Ltd

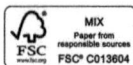

This book is dedicated to my father, Werner Stender.
He is a loving, family man and a courageous, honourable person.

Preface

"Gertigstrasse 56" really came into fruition when my father reached his retirement age and decided that unless he wrote down a short version of the family history, then all the suffering and risks the three brothers took in the fight against fascism would be lost forever. A few years later, he mentioned that he also had a few documents and letters to add to this short history. This was a complete understatement when to my amazement he produced document after document from a very large suitcase which was full to the brim with paperwork including personal letters; and then he brought out to me boxes of important information. My enthusiasm was fired as I could not believe the information my father had kept. I started retracing Rudolf, Ernst and Werner's lives including visiting various archives until I had so much information that I felt humbled into realising that the rest of my life would now be destined with passing on this information to as many people who are prepared to listen. It is a frightening prospect to take on as I have never written a book before.

I would like to emphasize, that this would never have been written without the support of my father. All the personal letters, reports, archive material both personal and official have been translated for me by my father and I am honoured and proud that each chapter has been checked by him for any inaccuracies.

This book is naturally dedicated to my father, Werner Stender and to his two brothers, Rudolf and Ernst. Without the sacrifices they and many others have made for this world, there would not be any such material for me to write about. Over my period of research I have made many friends from overseas as well as here in England and once again a big thank you for their encouragement.

There are only a very few fictitious first names used for trivial purposes to make the three brother's life story's "flow" for the reader.

I feel that I must explain the aims of the majority of the resistance workers within the Hamburg area who fought alongside the Stender brothers. All three of the Stenders were socialists in their outlook. They believed in the rights of the working class people to have a decent life, with freedom, justice, the opportunity to enjoy a reasonable existence with honest hard work and the ability for society to help the less fortunate. They wanted a "world without fascism". There is a letter written to Rudolf's son from someone who fought alongside him in the International Brigade. He finished the letter explaining that Rudolf's life *"was fighting for peace, freedom and socialism"*.

There is no point when reading this book in making modern day assessments using the knowledge of hindsight. The period in Germany 1918 – 1939 was extremely turbulent. Violence was answered with violence. It is almost incomprehensible to imagine the situation in Hamburg during those times of hardship and fear. All the three brothers wanted was a better world for the ordinary citizen to live in. I hope that I will open the reader's eyes in order to understand how the Stender family coped with this traumatic period of modern history.

I have narrated the story as accurately as can possibly be related. I have details of Rudolf's life in the Soviet Union from 1933-1936, which includes information he gave to the soviet authorities about his earlier years in Hamburg and finally of his time in Spain. I obtained this paperwork from the RGASPI Russian State Archives and I am grateful for their help.

I have been extremely fortunate that my father (Werner Stender) still talks to me about his brothers and also his own life. Also his sister, Lotte and Ernst's daughter Gretel have provided me with as much information as they can about the brothers but the rest concerning Ernst as well as Rudolf has been discovered through reading several 'staged' court trials of not only Ernst and Rudolf but also their resistance friends.

I hope that you will enjoy this book as well as learn about the experiences of my family. It is also a warning from the past for the future. I sometimes wonder though, have we learnt anything from this past? There are so many similarities from the last century which we seem to be ignoring in this century.

"He who controls the past controls the future and he who controls the present controls the past." (A quote from George Orwell's book "1984")

In 2012 the statement below was written by my father, Werner Stender, born 21st December 1915

"In order to understand this book and the struggles three brothers took against the evil leading to fascism, you have to understand the social and political situation in Germany at that time.

It started with the end of the First World War when the Treaty of Versailles was signed; the resulting rising of the right wing organisations, the murder of Karl Liebknecht and Rosa Luxenburg who were leaders of a working class political party, unemployment increased and money became worthless in the 1923 inflation. There was the rise of Hitler and his National Socialist German Workers Party (NSDAP also known as the Nazi Party) and by the end of the 1920s, early 1930s, unemployment reached six million. Germany stood on the eve of social upheaval.

The SA storm troopers attacked more and more people in the working class districts, murdering trade unionists, social democrats and the communists. The social democrats formed the Iron Front and the communists, the Red Front Brigade in order to defend the working class districts, but they were not united to fight the common enemy.

The critical point was reached in early 1933 when the ruling class and big businesses such as Krupp, Thyssen etc decided to put Hitler in power to prevent a social revolution. After the fire which destroyed the Reichstag, all progressive organisations were outlawed and the leaders arrested and murdered. Concentration camps were opened and mass terror started in preparation for World War Two. Employees at rearmament factories worked different shifts during the day and overnight.

During this time we three brothers were actively engaged in fighting against fascism in order to warn the German people of the danger of a world war to come. The three of us were not alone in our fight – we had comrades who fought alongside us, many of whom never saw the freedom and social justice they yearned for.

As a result of these problems, we ended up being catapulted into different experiences having been tortured, sentenced for High Treason against the

German Reich and as a result imprisoned in concentration camps. Between us, we experienced life in Soviet Union, resistance work in Czechoslovakia, the Spanish Civil War, internment in Vichy France, internment in England and Canada, enforced enrolment of the terrible Bewährungsbataillon 999 (known as the 999 Punishment Division) In general we received terrible treatment from the Gestapo and Nazis.

This book is to help you understand the sacrifices so many people took to give you your freedom today. It is also to make you aware of similar dangers in the future so that this never happens again."

Acknowledgements

My parents, Werner and Joan Stender, without whom I could not have written this book

Gretel Witt who wrote and gave me a short story about her life during the 1930s and 1940s. She also spent many hours providing me with her personal recollections of our family during this period.

Penny Cole-Baker who has continually supported me in my quest of writing this book. She has spent many long hours reading my story and providing constructive comments. She joined me at the National Archives where we spent many hours researching material.

John Cole-Baker who has helped me with some translations and being very patient listening and helping me.

Margaret Ferrett, my cousin, who spent time with me in Spain and France visiting places relevant to Rudolf's life and we spent many hours in various archives.

Dagmar Schörnig who provided her time and energies with me in my research in Germany, especially in the German Archives. Ernst Schörnig with his support to both of us.

Christine Meier from Hamburg who has become a very good friend of mine over these last few years. She has encouraged and helped me as well as spent many hours with her anti-fascist friends promoting the local history of the resistance movement in the Winterhude area of Hamburg

Jarrestadt Initiative; an exceptional group of people still fighting fascism A special thanks to Andrea Krieger

Christiane Chodinski and her colleagues at the VVN-BdA in Hamburg. (Anti-fascist movement)

Ursel Hochmuth for her knowledge and support helping me with archive work and help, as an author, of how to prepare my work

Gunda Ostericht; her father was a fellow resistance fighter and has provided useful information

Herta Rebstock; who was part of my father's resistance group

Walter Beyer; who was part of my father's resistance group. We spent many hours after the war, learning about life in the movement after my father had to leave Germany.

Orda and Horst Petersenbeyer: (Walter Beyer's daughter and husband) who provided us with Walter's life story.

Irene Peffers who has continually supported me in my quest including visiting the National Archives

Dr Christian Hannen, Hamburg University who gave his time willingly in my research concerning Fuhlsbuttel

Gail Malmgreen Tamiment Library-Robert F Wagner Labor Archives, New York University

Sarah Morris, for her help with regard to the chapter on the Spanish Civil War and upon initial completion of the book

Jim Carmody and Marlene Sidaway from the International Brigade Memorial Trust (IBMT)

Grit Ulrich, SAPMO, Berlin Archives for researching family letters in the Archives

Irina Hood who translated the Russian documents for me

Alban Sanz who helped me with information about the International Brigade and the Internment Camps in France. He also had immense energy tracing many web sites. A man of many talents and to whom I shall always be grateful!

Stephen Pearson for resolving my formatting and publishing problems plus being very patient with me!

Holger Witt (grandson of Ernst Stender) and Sandra Witt (great granddaughter of Ernst Stender) for resolving some outstanding queries and their support towards the completion of the book.

Contents

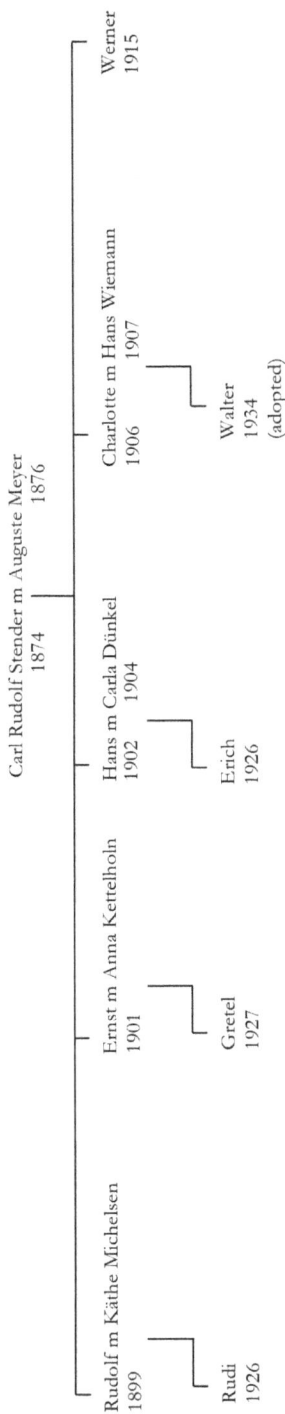

Family Tree

Carl Rudolf Stender m Auguste Meyer
1874   1876

Rudolf m Käthe Michelsen
1899

Ernst m Anna Kettelholn
1901

Hans m Carla Dünkel
1902   1904

Charlotte m Hans Wiemann
1906   1907

Werner
1915

Rudi
1926

Gretel
1927

Erich
1926

Walter
1934
(adopted)

CHAPTER 1

Introduction

A cold wind howls through the cobbled streets of Hamburg totally impervious at anyone's attempt to keep warm. To top it all, sleety rain adds to the feeling of chill. Perhaps it is winter's last attempt to remind people of the season they had thought was over.

A man pulls up his collar to try and keep warm and dry but to little effect. He glances nervously to his left and right as he hurries along the street. The little shops were fairly busy considering the weather conditions and above the stores are four floors of flats. As he glances up at them, he notices that the windows were all tightly shut. He checks these windows more thoroughly to see if anyone is watching him, but can see nothing unusual.

How on earth has it come to this when German is fighting German? How has the population let such an evil man as Hitler and his fellow henchmen of the National Socialists gain power? All these thoughts race through his mind. It is 1934 and a time when many of his fellow resistance fighters are being arrested, many of whom will never be seen again, so it is vital to keep his wits about him. He reaches his destination where his fellow resistance worker is waiting for him.

There is something wrong. He studies his comrade's face which is anxious and deathly white. His colleague's eyes dart nervously from side to side. The approaching man's body feels his muscles tense. This is not the usual casual but attentive behaviour of Fritz which always makes him blend in with other pedestrians. What is wrong? He glances around to see if they are being watched.

Fritz nervously shifts from one foot to the other and then recognises his comrade approaching but there's still a distance between them. He knows that he just can not betray a colleague to the Gestapo. He has no alternative. He's already suffered mentally and physically under torture by the Gestapo and regrets terribly that he has given them even this small bit of information of this secret meeting. He mustn't betray the organisation.

The Gestapo had concealed themselves in alcoves and doorways and with their SS back-up are ready to pounce on the approaching resistance fighter as soon as they know who it is.

A bus rattles along the cobbled street trying to catch up for lost time. It had been caught up in a traffic jam earlier on its route. Visibility had deteriorated for the driver as the sleet became horrendous but he is worried about being reprimanded when he reaches the bus station.

Without any further hesitation, the captured fighter steps off the pavement and he knows no more as first the bus knocks him over and then the wheels of the vehicle complete the job.

The contact watches in horror at the scene but quickly pulls himself to his senses. The Gestapo suddenly appear from the doorways in the attempt to stop the suicide. A furious group of Gestapo look around to try and surmise whom they are looking for and stop a few people who have been innocently walking along the pavement.

Adrenalin steps in along with his need to survive. The resistance fighter puts his head down, quickly crosses the road and disappears in the crowd.

CHAPTER 2

1914

Rudolf's story

"It's finally happened" I announce to my friend as I turn the corner into the cobbled street of Gertigstrasse. "I'm no longer a child and now I can prove how hard working I am. With a bit of luck as well, I can make some real money after my apprenticeship. And then I will be able to help Mama and Papa so that our family can enjoy life more".

My friend slaps me on my back and laughs. "You are so keen to get out into that big world aren't you Rudolf. Let's hope that it'll make things easier for you and your family."

We smile nervously at each other trying to look adult now we're about to leave our childhood. However, there is a mixture of feelings lurking in my mind as I have just finished my school days and I know that my life is about to change forever. I'm fourteen years old and will be expected to be a breadwinner along with my father. I have enjoyed school as there had been so much to learn and I hadn't been idle. I love maths, history especially social history and any physical activities. If I have any spare time, I can carry on studying at home. Perhaps I can borrow some of Ernst's school books when he brings them home at the end of the school day.

In the meantime this is my chance to be a man, like Papa, and help my family. Papa always works long hours. My beloved Mama is the centre of the family, never complaining and always supportive. I will make them proud of me.

I'm about to pass Papa's little shoe shop on my way to the main flat which is above it and to find Mama but notice my father busy in the little workshop to the right of his shop. The shop is below tenement buildings and has to be entered by stepping down a couple of steps from the pavement; therefore it's easy to look down into the premises. Papa is sitting by the window to get the best light to repair and also make shoes but he looks tired.

"Hello Papa" and then I gasp as I enter his work room. "Good heavens where have all these old shoes come from?"

Ernst, my younger brother is already standing next to Papa busily helping him. Ernst will be thirteen tomorrow and has managed to get home from school before me.

Looking up from the work bench my father's face suddenly lights up. "Hello Rudolf, how was your last day at school?"

"It was really strange" I reply absent-mindedly picking up and putting down some of the shoes on the bench. "For the first time ever, our teacher was full of fun and laughter and rather than have lessons in the true sense of the word, he spent more of his time trying to give us as much advice as possible to help us succeed in the years ahead. I never realised that he could be like that but I think we all appreciated his behaviour and encouragement." The heel of the lady's bootie in my hand looks really worn at the edge. "But why have you got all these shoes to repair all of a sudden?"

"I've been fortunate that the Schmidt family have decided to have nearly all their shoes repaired ready for Easter and they've asked me to do it. It'll help us enormously at the moment as we really need the money. The only problem is that they want them repaired by tonight".

He'll never do this in time if I don't help. I'd prefer to go out with my friends to celebrate the end of my school life, but that thought makes me feel guilty. I can't let Papa down so I resign myself to a change of my plans.

"Thanks son" acknowledges Papa with a smile. That's the most emotion Papa will ever show us. He's never the tactile parent – that's Mama's prerogative! After a few minutes with all three of us working as a team, Papa asks "How does it feel to be a young man now?"

I quickly look up from my work. I notice that Papa has a little twinkle in his eye. I can't help smiling back at him. We are just so lucky that we are such a close family. Ernst and I are very different in character and yet so close. We never really have to say anything to each other as we always know what the other is thinking. Our parents are very caring and compared with so many of my friends they will listen thereby trying to help their offspring. There is Hans who is three years younger than me and finally my dear sister Lotte who is only seven years old.

Mama must have been so pleased when Lotte was born having had us three sons. At last she will eventually have some help in the home and not be so outnumbered with all the men around.

It must have taken about another hour with all three of us working away at the repairs, but Ernst and I chat to each other about our day at school whilst Papa quietly listens to us. I know that he is proud of his family. He never speaks much, but his silence is a contented silence interrupted by telling us of an amusing situation which happened in his shop that day.

"Well that's all finished" Papa sighed with relief. "Thank you sons, but now I think we deserve to go for our evening meal. I'll just walk round to the Schmidt's flat and deliver the shoes and then we had better get home before Mama starts scolding us for being late".

"We'll just have a quick wash and change of clothes Papa before we have our meal". Ernst and I share a bedroom behind the shop. Mama and Papa's rented flat is not big enough for all of us as it has two bedrooms.

After Papa locks up the shop and heads towards the Schmidt's flat, Ernst with a worried look on his face remarks "I've noticed that Papa looks so drawn and tired when he thinks we're not watching him. I feel so bad that I can't start work yet and help the family financially as you are about to do".

"Whatever happens, you mustn't feel guilty. Ernst you are very intelligent and you must take every advantage of learning whilst you can. I will soon be bringing money home to help their finances. I know that as an apprentice I won't be earning much to start with, but I'm hoping that when I am qualified, then this will change their lives for the better. Make use of your last year at school. Anyway" I tease "I need you to carry on at school so that I can borrow your books". Ernst laughs and I slap him gently on his back. A play fight inevitably starts but as I emerge to breath I yell "Come on Ernst; is it you or me to start washing first?" And with that, I rush out into the scullery aiming to be the first. After all I am the oldest!

The scullery is also used as our washroom. If we had not been so fortunate as to have the flat above, this would have been the main kitchen. However Mama uses this room as the laundry room.

Poor Mama has a hard life. Once a week the floor is covered with dirty washing and here she stays all day washing item after item until eventually she finishes. She always looks so exhausted. The sink has a washing board and some sort of plunger which she uses for the washing. However, we are luckier than most as we have a very small garden where on a day when it does not rain, Mama can put the washing outside. The other women in the flats are very envious as they have no choice but to climb the four flights of steps to the attic to hang their washing up there to dry. The apartments are built as a quadrangle and due to the height of the building our yard is always in the shade, apart from in the high summer. As a consequence our washing sometimes takes a long time to dry. And then there are those pesky rats resulting in poor Mama scurrying around the garden with a broom trying to catch one of them. They are attracted to the food which has been put down for the chickens. If only I can make Mama's life easier.

Ernst must have been following my thought patterns as he starts talking about Mama. "It's nice you know that Mama has Lotte around for female company even though she is still very young. I'm sure Mama still misses her mother even after these two years. She was such a support for her and I'm sure she had a tough life as well but had Mama's love and perseverance. When I think of it, the women seem to have a harder life than the men. I shouldn't admit this should I! I will be able, hopefully to go out and earn money, but poor Mama spends her life looking after us" he remarks.

"You think too much Ernst" I tease. "You know Mama loves keeping "her men" happy. She is in her element fussing around us." Ernst smiles and I continue. "Seriously though, our family is the most important thing to her and she's our rock. One day let's hope that we can support her more so that she can have some treats in life. Come on, hurry up otherwise she will not be very happy with us for being late".

We leave our their tiny flat and out of the front door which leads straight into the street, turn left and I push open the big heavy door of

56 Gertigstrasse. It is still quite chilly as we climb the short flight of steps and open the inner door to the entrance hall. Papa has left the front door to the flat slightly open. There is a lovely feeling of warmth as we enter and the smell of coffee had reached the entrance all the way from the tiny kitchen at the back of the apartment. Bread and cheese has already been placed on the dining table in the lounge. Lotte skips around the table having seen us arrive. She flies up to us and demands a hug. She has a way of destroying our image of trying to be "grown-up". Money or no money, we really are lucky being so close.

"Ah there you are" beams Mama as she brings in the scalding hot coffee pot. "Hurry up and sit down. Just think Papa, you'll have competition now with another bread winner in our family". Papa laughs.

She turns to me as she is about to pour the coffee into the cups. "How does my eldest son feel now that he is no longer a school child, but a grown man?" I can see on her face that she is so proud of me. I know that compared to my other siblings, I am the strong-willed one. I have worked hard at school, but I have been so eager to learn a trade in order to try and improve our living conditions. I hate seeing my parents struggling to make ends meet.

Papa looks long and hard at me. "Son, I know that you will work really hard at your apprenticeship, but I hope that you will keep your head down and learn your trade well. I'm sure you will see many things which will make your blood boil. There will be many injustices your employers will mete out to you and your work mates, but remember, you need to learn and to get your qualifications. You are very capable, but you have a tendency to be hot headed at times. They will not tolerate anyone who expects decent working conditions. Believe me; I have seen other people losing their job for very minor reasons."

"I know Papa. I haven't forgotten what happened to Wolfgang in the flat next door. Do you remember? He asked for overtime money for all the extra hours he was expected to do and in a factory with such terrible lighting that it was dangerous working on those machines. Without a moment's hesitation, he was sacked. Have you heard the latest news? His father lost his job last week when he was badly injured operating those heavy machines late in the evening? I can't believe that his employer was so hard and callous towards the family. That's two breadwinners from the same family. I don't know how they're going to live now."

"That's how life is for people like us son" sighs Papa.

"But it's not right Papa" I reply.

"That's enough of this conversation" remarks Mama. "We should be thinking about tomorrow as it is Good Friday and Papa for a change will not be working. You have just finished your school life Rudolf and tomorrow it's Ernst's thirteenth birthday. We have to think about the good times now".

Lotte and Hans clap their hands in joy. "Mama what will be happening tomorrow then?" asks Hans.

"Well I am sure that your two older brothers will want to celebrate with their friends' tomorrow morning. However, I have been baking… "

Unanimously we all give a huge cheer. "I thought that I could smell some lovely cakes Mama" says Hans gleefully.

"Yes and tomorrow late afternoon, we shall be enjoying them along with our extended family as they are all coming over to celebrate the joint occasion." She turns to Ernst and I and adds "I hope that you two boys have practised some music on the mandolins so that all of us can sing and be merry."

"Oh lovely" chirps Lotte and once again skips around the table.

The weather the following day is absolutely perfect for our friends to explore the Stadtpark which has only just opened. Papa had told me that around 1900 the Hamburg Government pursued the idea of a recreational area for the rapidly growing population and they had set aside 148 acres. This green oasis so the officials boast is accessible to all "walks of life". Even us I chuckle to myself. The Stadtpark is now our favourite place to meet as it has such a vast expanse of parkland, sports area, woods, gardens, canals, large pool for people to paddle and a huge lake.

Unfortunately as it is only April, swimming is not considered, but we have nearly a whole day to be with our friends and have fun. Ernst being only a year younger than me always joins in at such occasions. However this is an extra celebration being his thirteenth birthday. We are up early and out of the flat to join our friends who were also keen to celebrate the ending of their school life.

By four o'clock we run home in order to quickly wash and change our clothes and then dash round to No. 56. As we walk through the doorway of our upstairs flat, we are greeted by as many of our family who can possibly squeeze in our home. It seems as if they are all talking at once as the noise is immense, but this is not an unusual situation when our family have a get-together. Tante Miele comes over and gives me a hug. There is happy banter between my parents and their siblings and it is lovely to see my cousins again. Mama brings in cakes she had baked and coffee. I'm amazed to see such a quantity of food. Knowing my Mother, she had been saving for weeks so that Ernst and I could have a day to remember.

Finally when all the food has been devoured the conversation quietens down. To the pleasure of everyone in the room Ernst and I bring out our mandolins. One of my relations has brought their accordion and before we know it everyone in the room was in full volume singing accompanying our playing. Music has always been an important part of our existence and as often happens, the lounge windows which are just above the main street are open and to our amusement, we can hear people singing to our music as they pass by. What a wonderful day it has been. Mama and Papa have really put everything into this event but to do it, they must have made so many sacrifices.

When everyone finally leaves, I turn to Mama and give her an enormous hug and swing her around and around. It is so wonderful to hear her laughter as she finally pushes me away and tells me not to be so silly. Papa smiles from ear to ear – I know that he feels that it is worth every bit of the struggle to see the family so happy.

Ernst and I help clear the flat up for my parents as they both appear exhausted. Lotte looks as though her little eyes will not stay open any longer so she is gently pushed towards her bedroom which she shares with Hans. Ernst and I wish them all a good night's sleep and wander downstairs and outside into Gertigstrasse heading towards our little flat behind the shop.

The reality of my new life starts immediately after Easter. I've managed to get an apprenticeship at Maihak which is located in Semperstrasse. It isn't that I dislike working as I'm totally enthralled at the thought of learning a new skill as a lathe operator and I love making things using my hands. The hours are very long though and at first I find that I am expected to "fetch and carry" for everyone whereas I want to work on the lathe. However as my experience increases, I am left to labour on my own with my engineering tools.

I feel really grown up when my work colleagues start asking me to join them after work. We settle ourselves around a table in a local pub and soon the discussions become very heated as they discuss the social and living conditions that are inflicted on us. I have already formed my own opinions about the injustices of the employers against the working class. I notice that some of them are surprised how well informed I am and able to speak quite well on these subjects considering my age. We work harder than ever before and yet receive no increase in money and no holiday or sick pay was forthcoming. Some of my colleagues are finding it difficult to continue with this pressure which is inflicted on all of us and as a result they have some health issues. To everyone's horror these particular people are starting to lose their jobs and are being replaced by other people desperate for work and are willing to do more for less money.

I'm going to join the Social Democratic Youth as I feel that this is the only way we can try to resolve the social and working conditions of people of the working class such as ourselves. If we do not stand together, then we will be "walked over" for the rest of our lives. Papa, Ernst and I are sitting in the lounge. Papa is enjoying a cigarette after our bread and cheese supper so I take this opportunity to explain my latest idea.

"I have found at last other people who are feeling the same as me. In fact I've been distributing leaflets in my factory both legal and illegal documents and now I'm trying to increase the wages for us apprentices. It's just not right expecting us to work for next to nothing. I know we're learning a skill, but we need to survive financially. There are a lot of families who rely totally on an apprentices wage packet."

Papa who is also a social democrat agrees with me but is worried about my involvement fighting against injustices. One evening he sits and quietly talks to me after our evening meal.

"I must ask you Rudolf to be careful. I feel that black clouds are just over the horizon and it is quite likely that I will be "called up" to fight in a terrible war. I've been a Reserve since 1895 so it is very likely I will become involved. If this happens, you will be the only working man to care for our family. Ernst still has another year of schooling to attend, so I will be relying on you to be in charge."

"Is this impending threat anything to do with the assassination which took place of Archduke Ferdinand, the nephew and heir of the Emperor Francis Joseph of Austria?" asked Ernst. "I was reading in the papers that Austria has declared war against Serbia. How will that affect us? Anyway Papa, you are no longer very young so surely you will not be expected to go and fight?"

"I have a nasty feeling that our country will get dragged into this. There is a long history to this but so many European countries have signed Treaties promising to help each other. Russia is bound by a Treaty to Serbia and Germany is allied to the Austro-Hungarian Empire. Kaiser Wilhelm and his "cronies" are frustrated in their desire to carve out a grand imperial role for Germany. I don't know if you are aware that they have been building up both land and naval forces which has been financed by big business and we will just be pawns in their need to become richer. As for my age, you mustn't forget that as I am in the Landsturm Infantry[1] Reserve and I am Class One at shooting, I am sure that I will be conscripted into the army. Age does not seem to count at such times. We will wait and see, but until we know for definite, I think we should keep this conversation to ourselves and not worry Mama".

As I walk home a couple of days later, Papa's conversation reverberates in my mind. It's 1st August and the headlines in the paper state "Germany declares war on Russia". So our safe albeit poor little world is over.

Three days later, another newspaper headline states "Great Britain declares war on Germany". I rush home to find Mama and Papa who are looking at each other in horror, the newspaper in Papa's hand.

---

[1] Older class of reserve soldiers

"So you've seen the headlines" I exclaim.

"It'll just be a matter of time now before I will have to go and fight" Papa replies forlornly and then he follows up the statement with "so you must prepare to be the man of the house"

Mama being her usual positive self comes over to me and gives me an embrace saying encouragingly "I know that we can rely on you Rudolf so Papa must not worry about us but he must try and keep himself safe"

However I can see Mama's eyes were not saying the same thing as she knows that Papa will fret about us and in turn she will be anxious about his safety.

"Auguste, don't worry about me as I will keep my head down ALL the time" teases Papa to Mama. Once again, I can see that both are keeping a brave face on things.

I 'devour' the newspapers each day as the situation is indeed deteriorating in Europe. France decides to turn on Germany in revenge over their defeat in the 1870s of the loss of the coal rich territories of Alsace and Lorraine and being forced to pay reparations and the siege of Paris when the citizens were starved into surrender. It brings back all my history lessons at school when Bismarck had wanted to create a unified Germany and thought nothing of the misery he would cause in invading other countries. The result of what had happened forty three years ago, along with our greed for a "Greater" Germany has now started another war.

Father has been right all along. Our Kaiser had been determined to establish Germany as a great colonial power at the turn of the century. He wanted territories in the Pacific and also Africa and yet why did nobody try and stop him? I really ought to take politics seriously now as without the masses being aware of the situation, we will all suffer.

The following day, my father closes his shop early as he and Mama decide that we should have an official photograph taken of our family. Papa had said that it was to record the fact that now there are two men working in the family, but somehow I have that uneasy feeling that he is worried that this might be the last photo of our complete family. We are instructed to dress in our best clothes. Ernst and Hans dress themselves in their Sunday best which is young sailor's uniforms. Mama wears her best white blouse with her dark long skirt and Lotte ties her hair with ribbons making her hair into long bunches down each side of her face and she wears her special dress. Papa and I both have suits on which we keep for Sunday best and bow ties. How impressive we all look. Mama and Papa sit formally at a tiny table and the four of us stand around them. We are all asked to look serious, which is not our normal family demeanour, but this is the expected pose for formal photographs[2]. It is important to preserve a memory of our complete family especially with the political situation threatening the stability of our future!

That evening, Ernst, Hans and I decide to cool down by going for a quick swim in the canal which is just behind our quadrangle block. We aren't the only ones who have thought that this would be a good idea. Several of our neighbours' offspring are there and I have to say it is wonderful to just forget all the approaching worries and run down the road and plunge feet first into the water. This is so much more fun than taking our turn in the bath tub in the kitchen!

Summer ends and Christmas draws near. Already there are families in our district losing their fathers, brothers, and sons. The details of their deaths are never really explained. Then the dreaded letter arrives at our house for my Papa to report for duty on 12th December 1914.

"Don't fret Auguste, I'll be back in March for a week when my training will be finished. You never know, the war might be over by then" he says trying to reassure Mama.

I can't help but have the ominous feeling this event will change all of our lives. The day comes and we all gather together in 56 Gertigstrasse first thing in the morning to wish Papa a fond farewell. I am to become the "man of the house" at the age of fourteen.

Mama has always been our "rock" but just for a short while after father walks out of our home, her sadness with a tinge fear flickers into her face and then it's gone. Stoical is I suppose the best way now to describe the expression on her face. Lotte even at her tender age

----

[2] Picture at the end of this chapter.

can see through that expression as she rushes over to her to give our mother a reassuring hug.

"We love you Mama. We'll look after you". Mother laughs at this, blows her nose and hurries into the kitchen to prepare some food for us.

Looking at me with concern Ernst says "I'll have to do some growing up quickly now".

I can't help smiling at that. Ernst has always been the quiet sensible one of us, although he has always looked to me to make any final decisions. Somehow, we will get through this so that when Papa comes home, he will be proud of his family.

Ernst's story

We try to cheer Mama, Lotte and Hans up over Christmas. We play music, sing all the songs we love best and eat the food that Mama has been preparing during the last few weeks, but somehow it is not the same without Papa.

"Let's hope that this will be the only Christmas when we are apart" comments Mama.

1914 Left to right Hans, Mama, Rudolf, Papa, Ernst, Lotte

Gertigstrasse 56 taken at the end of the 20th Century

CHAPTER 3

1915 – 1917

Ernst's Story

The year 1915 arrives and the bitter weather of winter progresses but somehow we manage to get ourselves into a new routine. Hans, Lotte and I work hard at school and Rudolf carries on learning his new trade. Finally the great day arrives in March when Papa walks through the entrance of our flat.

"Papa" chirps Lotte with delight. "You're home". Knocking Papa off balance, she throws herself into his arms. He bursts into laughter.

"I'm only here for a few days I'm afraid. I've finished my training so I have some time to spend with you all".

"Then we shall try and be together as much as we can" I remark with determination in my voice.

Mama nods in approval. Over the next few days, Hans, Lotte and I make sure to head straight home after school and I am pleased to see that Rudolf seems to have cancelled his meetings after work and is home on time. Finally the day comes when Papa packs his bags and the following morning was gone before we had woken. I am disappointed at not seeing him off, but I can understand why he had done so. It would have been too much for all of us seeing him in his uniform going off to battle. Why does he have to go when he is forty years old – far too old to be considered a fighting soldier? Before he went he told us that he had been put into the 1st Company, 2nd Landsturm Infantry Battalion with other 39-45 year olds who have been called up to replace the losses of the winter campaign.

I feel so guilty that Rudolf works hard to bring home his pittance of a wage. I am so proud of him. He's only 15 ½ years old and has worked for over a year as an apprentice. In that time he's had the courage to stand up for better wages for apprentices in his firm and now he's become the Socialist Youth Movement Cashier and a delegate at the Stadt Conference in Hamburg. I don't think Rudolf knows the meaning of the words "relax" and "idleness".

As spring moves into early summer, Lotte pulls me aside one evening. She had become very reserved since Papa had left but I had presumed that it was because she was missing him so much.

"Ernst, I'm really worried about Mama. She is getting dark rings under her eyes, always looks tired and she's even been sick in the morning. Do you think that we should get a doctor for her?" she asks.

Lotte is such a loving, caring sister and acts far older than her years with regard to picking up emotional or relationship problems. However, even Lotte's maturity could not help foresee the thoughts which are now racing through my mind. I had to find an opportunity of speaking to Mama alone when Hans and Lotte have gone to bed. First Lotte and at long last Hans, retire to their bedroom. I follow Mama into the kitchen.

"Forgive me Mama, but I have to ask this question. Are you pregnant?"

Mama stops tidying up and looks at me with apprehension. Then with a sigh she nods and sinks down onto a kitchen chair.

"How are we going to cope? I can't tell your father whilst he's out fighting. I'd never forgive myself if he became distracted and as a result was killed. It's almost like a repeat of my mother having me so late in her life, only I am nearly 39 years old whereas she was 42."

Poor Mama – I walk over and give her a hug. She is right, as we are struggling at present, but I can't say that to her.

"Well she was three years older than you so you should find it easier" I bluff with my total lack of knowledge about giving birth at such an age. "Look Mama, Oma was a tower of strength to you and she brought you up to become a strong and caring mother. I don't know what any of us would have done without your support. You will do this again for my new brother or sister except this time we are all here for you. Anyway Lotte will be nine years old soon and she seems to have developed into a quiet and loving girl and I bet you that she will be "over the moon" at having a new brother or sister to care for."

She squeezes my hand I suppose in gratitude, that I'm not upset.

A few weeks later, Mama decides to tell the family. Sure enough, Lotte is so excited at the thought of a new brother or sister to love. I try to avoid Rudolf's anxious look as in a way this responsibility falls on his shoulders until Papa will be demobbed.

Rudolf has received a slight increase in his wages which will help us enormously but he is becoming involved with the Social Democrat Youth Movement so it is really up to me to spend more time with the family to support them emotionally. I'm busy studying to take my final exams at school, but I manage to catch up with the conversations Rudolf has been having with his work colleagues when we went to bed in our basement bedroom. He and I are now working as a team, which makes me feel really proud as he is treating me as an equal. We really have to behave as adults now even though we are only fourteen and fifteen years old. Also Rudolf had received a slight increase in his wages which would help enormously.

It is a hot day in August 1915 and it is our school summer holidays. Although I have been helping Mama in the shoe shop, she encourages me to take some time off to see my friends in the Stadtpark. When I return at the end of the day, everyone in the room looks really excited. Papa has sent some post to my mother. She hands me the postcards. On the back of one of them is written

"2nd August 1915

My dear Gusta

At the moment I am again doing guard duty. I have already stood here for two hours but it is something different. I am sending you a picture. I hope that you can see me. Otherwise everything is all right. Greetings and kisses (this is probably your dream) Rudolf. I hope to see you again soon."[3]

I had to smile at the "Gusta". It shows that Papa is relaxed and cheerful as he always calls Mama that as a sign of his fondness for

---

[3] In italics, letter translated from father

her. I turn the card over. It said "Brüssel-Laeken 1915". There is a crowd of elderly men in light coloured uniforms with dark hats. All are holding bicycles and it looks as though they are either in barracks with high walls surrounding them or a hospital[4]. Rudolf peers over my shoulder.

"What on earth are they doing? What are the bikes for?"

"I've no idea" said Mama "but at least I'm happier with these two photos rather than the one he sent me in May. Do you remember that photo when he was dressed up and standing to attention holding a gun with a bayonet attached? That really frightened me".

"I can only presume that they've finally realised these are elderly men and not fit for serious fighting" said Rudolf reassuringly. "It's unbelievable that anyone would recruit that generation, especially when the war started only a year ago. Whoever is in charge really hasn't thought very hard. Our so called enemies must be having a real joke about the German Reich when they see the ages of our soldiers."

"German imperialism is not only sacrificing the young generation" I murmur and then add quickly to Mama "but Papa seems to be safe for the moment so don't worry".

Changing the subject quickly I ask her "When are you going to tell him about the pregnancy as reading this card, it's obvious that you still haven't done so yet!"

"I've been thinking long and hard about that" she answers thoughtfully. "I've decided not to tell him until the baby is born. I really don't want him worrying about me and how we are coping. It's not fair on him".

Although it seems a harsh decision I can understand that a letter telling Papa that he will be a father again would be a shock. She always thinks of everyone else before her own welfare. It was up to us to try and support her. Unfortunately it's impossible for us to help with the shop what with Rudolf working and the rest of us at school. How difficult is a pregnancy? So many of my friends have seen their mothers' struggle when they are having babies and some do not

---

[4] See photo at the end of this chapter

survive but on the other hand others cope. Mama is old though to be pregnant. If only we had someone to advise us.

We decide to ban her from fetching the coal from the attic this coming autumn and insist that Hans should collect it morning and night. The coal which is delivered for us goes the same way as for the other tenants, by being hauled up by a pulley which is situated at the top of our tenement block. This way the deliveries cause no dust or dirt inside. At the top of our flats and up four flights of stairs there is an attic where the coal is stored in individual locked compartments.

We have the most incredible tiled stove in our flat which takes a lot of room all along the wall between the lounge and bedroom from the floor to ceiling. There are smaller versions in the second bedroom and in our basement flat, so it was quite a task fuelling them. For the moment at least, we can help Mama keeping these alight when we have money for the coal.

As autumn departs Christmas is only a few days away. Poor Mama really is finding these last few weeks a struggle, but we all try to help. Finally the great day arrives. When I return home from school, there is a sound of yelling from the lounge. I have vague memories of the cries of pain when Lotte was born but being older and no Papa, it's far more worrying. Thankfully the local woman who helps with the births in our neighbourhood is here to help. Will Mama survive this ordeal? At long last we hear the cry of our new brother or sister from where we'd all been seated in the kitchen. We look at each other with relief. The lounge door opens and Frau Bräun calls us.

"Would you like to meet your new brother?" she asks. Lotte rushes ahead of us and there is the most wonderful sight of seeing our beaming but exhausted mother and tucked neatly in a blanket in a box by her side is our little brother, fast asleep.

"What do you think of our little Werner?" she asks as she holds out her hands to greet us. Oh if only we could be as strong in character as Mama. She's had to cope with so much without Papa and yet she still thinks of us.

"Werner?" queries Hans.

"Yes, I've decided to call him Werner as your father chose that name if Lotte had been a boy".

"Good idea" Rudolf and I answer in unison. We look at each other and burst into laughter. All the worries of the last months have just melted away. Lotte just can't stop herself and she picks little Werner up to give him a gentle kiss on his forehead.

"Hello little brother" she cooes at him.

"Now it's time for the difficult job, Mama. Papa needs to know that he has another son". I smile at the thought of my mother trying to compose that letter and also my father's face as he opens that letter. What a Christmas present for him!

As for us, Werner is our Christmas present too. With mother being pregnant and trying to look after the shoe shop without help plus coping with all our washing and feeding four hungry children I know that money has been extremely tight. Hardly any profit has been made at the shop so how will we survive especially now we need extra food? However I'm lucky that both Werner and Mama have survived and to our knowledge so has Papa. With our music, we will have some pleasure during this festive period.

This is something many of our friends could not say as they had lost either their father or their brothers or for some of my friends have lost both due to this wretched war and which our leaders have started! That makes me feel guilty that our large family is still intact. Haven't our leaders and "betters" got any shame sending so many of our country's men folk to their deaths fighting for things we do not comprehend? We realise that we might be too young to understand totally world politics, but thanks to Papa and his friends, we have been listening to their conversations to learn of the situation affecting all of us.

Both Rudolf and I have seen the impoverished families who have been left to fend for themselves when their men have been conscripted into the army. How can anyone avoid noticing that when the men folk are initially sent for their training for three months, the food for the new recruits is insufficient? The only decent meal they are given is the mid-day meal. The Reich expects every family to provide extra money for food in order that the men can fight for their country and homeland.

Rudolf and I speak often to each other when we are alone in

our basement flat. We didn't want to worry Hans and Lotte, but just like many other families in our situation we have even less money for us to survive. For so many people buying new shoes or even repairing them is a luxury. Poor Mama is struggling so much now that Papa's shoe shop is not doing very well and it's not her fault.

In April, my turn would come when I could go out and earn some money albeit a small amount with my apprenticeship. Straight after Christmas, Mama opens the shop and I am able to be with Rudolf during any spare moments I have helping with minor shoe repairs if these are required but lately this happens rarely due to the growing poverty of the working class. Thank goodness Papa has taught us basic repairs, but we miss his expertise.

Whilst Mama's busy in the shop, she also struggles to look after little Werner and also care for us. Lotte is brilliant becoming a second mother to Werner. She seems quite happy spending her time apart from her schooling with him. Their bonding to one another becomes very close and Mama I know is relieved that between us all, we are pulling together as a family.

Then we receive a letter which I can see is upsetting Mama. I'm almost too frightened to ask what is wrong as her hands are shaking as she holds the piece of paper. Surely it's not Papa who has been hurt or even worse. I call Rudolf who is in the next room. By the tone of my voice, he arrives almost immediately, looks at my horrified face and then at Mama's white, strained face. Rudolf now looks as scared as me but he takes charge, putting his arm around Mama's shoulders and starts reading the letter.

"It's from Papa's sister" Rudolf says. "Oh Mama I'm so sorry" says Rudolf squeezing Mama with affection.

"What's happened Rudolf?" I ask feeling really scared now.

"It's your namesake Ernst – our Uncle Ernst[5]. He was killed in action on 4th February fighting for our fatherland."

---

[5] Ernst Gustav Stender (Opa's brother born 8th April 1879 and died 4th February 1916. Ernst Gustav Stender (brother of Rudolf, Hans, Lotte and Werner) who was born 13th April 1901.

Silence reigns in the room for a minute of two with all of us in a state of shock. Mama breaks the stillness.

"He was thirty six years old, just five years younger than Papa. These men are too old to fight battles. Shall I write to your father and tell him or should I wait until he gets home. He'll be devastated to hear this news as he was so close to him. That's why you were named after him Ernst. He was such a lovely man and now he's gone, just like so many other good men."

She thinks for a moment and then decides that it is best to leave this devastating piece of information from Papa as she is so frightened of the effect it will have on him. We can do nothing to help Mama. I know she's in shock about Uncle Ernst but she must be thinking of our father. The reality of this war hits us hard. We love our Uncle Ernst but we're all fearing the worst now for Papa. Oh this terrible war which has made our father leave the safety of our home. We must try and behave normally for Mama's sake. Life is so hard for her.

My school finally comes to an end in spring 1916. I had enjoyed my time at Barmbeker Strasse School and I'd even learnt to play the violin there but now I have my future career to consider. Thankfully my prospects are mapped out with an apprenticeship as a dreher (or lathe operator) at the engineering firm Heidenrich and Harbeck. Although, like Rudolf, my wage is virtually non-existent, they will help increase the amount coming in to the family coffer.

Like Rudolf, I join the SAJ[6] hoping that we can contribute towards improving conditions for the working class population eliminating the terrible poverty here but we are both becoming concerned that the organisation seems to be run be people who do not understand the urgency for change. They just do not seem to have the same aims as the youth. Finally with great frustration on our part, our youth movement is dissolved. So much for the rights of the working class Rudolf mutters to me in disgust but very soon afterwards, he comes home smiling from ear to ear.

---

[6] Sozialistische Arbeiterjugend

"We've solved our problem with not having an organisation which suits our beliefs. My friends and I have formed our own organisation and I've been asked to be the leader."

"That's some responsibility Rudolf – are you sure you want this?"

"Oh yes as this means we can go forward doing something positive. We can begin taking action against the present government by demonstrating etc but we'll no longer be restricted by people in the SPD who are not prepared to fight for the working class."

True to his word, Rudolf starts taking part in as many illegal demonstrations and action as he can, fighting for the disadvantaged people of Hamburg.

As the months progress, Mama became desperate to find money to feed us. Forever proactive, she decides to take some new shoes from the shop and go out into the countryside. She is extremely resourceful and would barter them for milk, meat, flour, fruit and vegetables. She did the same with some reasonably valuable coins from my father's cupboard. The most important thing for my mother was to keep us all alive but eventually there were no more shoes and coins to sell!

At the beginning of October 1916, Papa is finally allowed home on leave and he can finally meet little Werner at last. I can see the pride in his eyes as he looks down on his little son. But there is also something else in his demeanour which worries me. The spark seems missing as it has with all those men I had seen coming home without limbs. What horrors have they endured? How can he react so badly with Mama when he walked into his shop to find the shoes had gone? Didn't he realise that we have so little money to survive on? Mama just had to tell him straight that in order to feed us this had been the only option. He is silent on hearing this.

Poor Papa then has to return for duty on 10th October 1916 knowing our home life is not at all good. His nerves are beginning to become frayed and he is still in shock at losing his brother. He can't help his family and he is seeing things on the battlefield that no man should ever see. Rudolf also noticed the change in our father. Added to this helpless torment, anger is erupting in Rudolf seeing the deteriorating state of our glorious nation and the conditions of the ordinary working class families. But what can we do about it? We are not even seventeen and sixteen years old. What a nightmare.

Yet another Christmas comes with no extra food on our plates, but thank goodness we are all still alive. We cheer ourselves up with playing our mandolins and we can't help laughing at our little Werner who crawls around the room, stops and waves his arms up and down with excitement at the sound of the music and our singing. He is such a lovely child, but his physical development is worrying us due to the poor diet.

In March 1917 my world is shattered when Rudolf receives his conscription papers. Surely I won't lose him to this terrible war. I just couldn't bear that! He's just finished his apprenticeship as well so his future life has the possibility of being reasonable. What if all his future is wiped out in one second with just one bullet?

Late in the evening, when we are finally alone in the basement flat, we sit down at the small kitchen table and Rudolf speaks seriously to me giving me final instructions with regard to my responsibility of becoming "Head" of the family. It's a frightening thought that at the age of nearly sixteen, if Papa and Rudolf do not return from the war I was the oldest male of our family. I wouldn't let him down and he knows that. There are times when we just do not need to speak as we understand each other so well.

Finally he says to me "I'm going on to the next stage of my life. I have no choice but to go and fight, but you know Ernst, I'm going to put this to good use because who knows if I will need it later to overturn this government. Our leaders and Kaiser Wilhelm have no feelings for the likes of us. It'll be up to us to put Germany on the right track whichever country wins this war. I intend to learn as much as I can whilst I'm away and then if I'm lucky enough to return, I will give my heart and soul to fighting for a "free and socially just" Germany. These people who are in power now are backed financially by big business so they are only interested in selling arms to the State for financial gain for themselves. People have a right to live to a reasonable standard of living, to work and receive a decent wage enough to feed their family. This selfishness has got to stop."

I grip his hands and we both lock our eyes together in agreement. He also told me that he'd resigned as leader of the newly formed organisation. It just wouldn't be fair on anyone if he'd stayed in charge whilst away at war.

Life seemed so desolate after he'd left. Hans joins me in the basement flat and little Werner finally has a bedroom albeit sharing with Lotte who is so pleased at having him with her. Mama just laughs watching Lotte fuss over her little brother. It is such a help for her having my sister around. She has grown into a lovely "little Mother" and little Werner simply adores her although he is really struggling health wise due to the lack of nourishment.

Life is difficult during the summer, but somehow the warm weather makes up for it. Rudolf arrived home on leave for a few days which is marvellous. He has brought a picture of himself taken in his new dress uniform[7]. He looks very impressive as he has been put into the Prussian Guarde Kürassier Regiment, Berlin. His helmet has an eagle on the top looking as though it were just about to take flight. (Usually the helmets have a spike on so this is something special). He also wore metal body armour strapped on his upper torso, had huge cuffs to his gloves, and his boots went up to the knees of his trousers. All very impressive but Mama I know thinks he's just too young to be dressed in such a way. She makes no such comment to him though.

I can see that Mama didn't know what to say looking at his picture. She'd seen the damage mentally and physically to the men who had gone to war. Also there has been three years of observing the wounded coming home or her friends receiving the dreaded letter of "regret". Rudolf also has been watching her face and understood her reaction. He put his arm around her and promises that he will do his best to return home to all of us. She smiles at him, but really nothing more needs to be said. We all know the risk and in a way Rudolf is excited at this new world opening up for him. He's always enjoyed physical activities and death seems unlikely to all of us of our age.

---

[7] Photo shown at the end of the chapter

Hans returns to the first floor flat for these few nights so that Ernst and I can have this precious time alone together. That night, Rudolf again reiterates to me his intentions to fight for the working class when he returns.

"For some unknown reason I've been put into the premier fighting division of the German Army so they have given me specialist training. As this division is considered one of the best at attack and defensive fighting, I know that I will see a lot of action. I have no choice of my destiny, but I will put that right if I return Ernst. If you get any chance not to be conscripted because of your bad back, you must take that opportunity as the family need you. Both Papa and I intend to return, but you never know. In the meantime, I'm relying on you to keep me informed about the youth movement."

I nod in agreement and give him a hug. For a few seconds I can feel his body respond to my affection but Rudolf is not as sensitive to emotions as me. He always seems to have a mission to succeed being so politically motivated.

Autumn arrives which shakes us into the reality of our situation. We do not have enough money to buy coal to heat the flat and with the rain pouring down day after day, it feels damp. Mama has been going into the country to try and collect wood, but we still do not have enough to keep warm.

Little Werner's health becomes worse and finally develops double pneumonia. Mama calls the doctor and without any hesitation, the doctor insists that he should be taken to hospital to recover. Poor mother protests on hearing this as she does not want to part from him but was told that Werner does not have enough fat in his body and with pneumonia; he needs to be cared for professionally/medically for a while.

Mama is beside herself with worry at losing Werner, but she reluctantly agrees knowing that it is his only chance of survival. She spends a long time comforting Lotte who in the end also accepts the situation that for her little brother to survive, she must just look forward to his return. I take Lotte over to the Stadtpark when it finally stops raining and her serene smile comes back. I vow at that moment that I must try to fill little Werner's absence until either she settles or he returns. That night I also remind Hans that he must try to help more with Mama and Lotte. It's hard this responsibility of being the "man" in the family but I'm learning fast.

The weather deteriorates into an exceptionally severe winter and thousands of German children die of hypothermia. German labourers live on starvation rations. Papa must never know how hard it is for us to survive. He would be heartbroken fighting in a war he doesn't believe in knowing he was leaving his loved ones suffering. It is such a relief that Werner has been put into hospital where he has a chance to survive as not all children have this opportunity. Mama and the doctors certainly have made the right decision as he's just too young to be so ill and to be lacking in sustenance.

Rudolf returns in December on leave from fighting in this awful war. He's been in the eastern front in Russia and the weather conditions have been atrocious.

"At least Papa has a warmer climate in Belgium and I am young enough to endure the situation" is all he would say. I dread to think how bad it must be for him.

Although only on a short leave of absence, it doesn't take him long before he is back meeting his old friends in the youth movement who have not yet been "called up". By the time he has to return to Russia, he takes plenty of socialist leaflets with him to distribute amongst the troops. He can see the futility of this war but so many of these men are dying for our country and have no idea that our Government leaders have imperialistic views and are backed by financiers pursuing their own financial gain. Did these privileged men ever have any concern at how many men are dying because of their views?

The Christmas festivity of 1917 is the worst celebration period we've ever experienced. No Papa, no Rudolf and now no Werner and hardly any food and very little heat in the flat. This year, only my mandolin playing manages to cheer us up. We try playing games for Hans and Lotte but my poor sister is still devastated that Werner has not returned from hospital. If only I could earn more money to make their Christmas better. Mama keeps smiling and trying to keep busy but Werner's illness is pulling hard at her heart strings.

Papa marked with cross

Werner & Lotte

Rudolf – 1.8 m tall

CHAPTER 4

1918

Ernst's Story

We just can't bear celebrating the New Year – what is there to celebrate? I dread to think of the battle scenes which Rudolf is experiencing, that is if he is still alive. This time of year there is the extreme cold of the Russian climate, let alone seeing the slaughter on both sides of the battlefield. The morale on the front line must be getting so low now seeing the reality of trench warfare. The initial euphoria many of them have had has gone when they believed our government propaganda which was heralded from "the roof tops" during the beginning of it all.

And then there's poor Papa who I hope isn't on the front line due to his age but who knows where they will put these old men when the numbers in the firing line becomes too low. These cold conditions cannot be good for him let alone seeing the casualties which must destroy anyone's mind. I know that we aren't the only family feeling this way. So many people here are suffering from hunger, lack of clothing and misery with their loved ones either dead, seriously wounded or still away fighting.

The leaflets printed by the USPD party[8] Rudolf took back with him to the eastern front line in Russia has obviously proved a success as in January I receive a request from him asking me to send him a regular supply. Perhaps reading these leaflets are making the soldiers really wonder if they are just being used as cannon fodder and whether the cause is really worth fighting and dying for. If Rudolf is caught distributing these mutinous documents, I'm sure he will end

---

[8] Unabhängige Sozialdemokratische Partei – Independent Social Democratic Party (left wing socialists)

up in front of a firing squad. Oh I do hope he will be discreet – that word is not always in Rudolf's vocabulary though.

One cold wintry day in January 1918, as I hurry home from work I hear a newspaper boy shouting "massive strikes in Berlin". I grab a paper flicking the coin into the lad's hand. Glancing at the headlines I see that 400,000 Berlin workers had gone on strike and now more workers have followed in other cities. I'm exhilarated hearing this as we in Hamburg are not alone as I had feared. At long last people are standing up to be counted as they also seem to want a democratic Germany and peace without annexations of other countries. I know that I am still young and perhaps naïve but I have ideals and hopes for a better future.

Perhaps this is our chance to fight against imperialism or whatever people call it just as the working class have done in Russia three months previously. Will our class of people have a chance of bringing home a decent wage and to live in reasonable conditions? Is there hope that this wretched war will come to an end? It's only six months since the mutiny of the sailors of the German fleet at Kiel. This had not been successful and the result was many sailors were imprisoned and some even executed. I feel my spirits rise and rush home to read the rest of the article.

Mama greets me with a steaming hot drink to warm me up. She sees that I have brought home a newspaper so sits next to me to read the important news. I spread the paper on the table to make it easier for us both to read. Mama is always keen to keep up to date with events.

In an article it states approximately 250,000 people in Germany have died from hunger in 1917. I'm shocked to read this but having experienced much hardship ourselves, it only confirms my fears. Then I start to read the report I'd bought the paper to read. There is a report about the general strike my friends and I have taken part in. Apparently there are estimates of between one to four million in many cities who took to the streets on 27th January 1918 in protest. On 28th January, 20,000 workmen in our Hamburg shipyards join in. They're demanding immediate peace without being occupied, release of political leaders, an increase in the potato ration, improved wages in order to feed their families, better treatment of the workforce by the foremen as at present we suffer from military discipline in the factories and shorter hours as we are all so exhausted. It also mentions that we have also been campaigning for the end of the black market in food.

Mama then quietly says to me "I'm amazed that this is all being reported so that ordinary people can see the situation many of us are in." I nod in agreement and continue reading the article. The result of this protest is that the dockyards have been placed under military rule and the strike collapsed. A state of siege has now been declared around the country and our leaders who organised the strikes have been arrested and court-martialled. One hundred and fifty have been imprisoned and 50,000 have been drafted into the army and sent to the front.

"What a terrible situation these men are in. If they refuse to fight, they will be shot" I say to Mama aghast at reading the last bit.

I put down the newspaper totally stunned. Mama squeezes my hand, sighs and gets up to start preparing a meal from so little ingredients in the kitchen cupboard. As I am just a youngster I hadn't realised what is happening to so many protesters. All we wanted was to end this unnecessary slaughter which is happening on the war front and for those left at home to have food, clothing and fuel to survive the ravages of the winter. What has happened to our nation and the hope of free thought! My mind is in turmoil as I realise I must be careful not to be arrested as an agitator otherwise I will not be able to support Mama and my siblings.

I might be nearing the age of only seventeen, but I have had to grow up quickly taking on responsibilities as the "temporary head" of the family. Papa has always encouraged us to take care of our womenfolk and younger members of our family. This task is so hard due to the war in Europe and Russia and the resulting naval blockade against us in the North Sea which means that crucial supplies of food have stopped. Despite our domestic difficulties, very discreetly over the next two months I manage to find time to get more varied leaflets to send to Rudolf.

In March a letter arrives from him which is quite unusual. Rudolf has never been the best at writing trivia to his family. Mama shakily opens the letter. Her facial expression relaxes having read the contents which is brief and matter of fact in its detail.

"He has been injured, but not seriously" she tells us. I can see how relieved she is at reading this. "His right ear drum is badly damaged and he is classed unfit to fight any more or at least for some time."

I didn't think hearing about an injury would be such good news for us but that is exactly how all of us are feeling. Thank goodness he will now be unable to take part in any future battles or at least for a time so I will see him again and share our bedroom together once again. Oh how wonderful. But what caused the injury? Was he in the middle of some horrific fighting and will there be any psychological problems having seen his friends die beside him? All sorts of images start flashing through my mind. I desperately want to go to his bedside.

Eventually he writes telling me briefly about his condition but there was no hint of any distress mentally. Apparently the pain he felt had been acute when there was an extremely loud explosions and there is the possibility that his hearing could be damaged for life but that is nothing compared with so many of his friends. What a relief that this is his only injury[9].

Arriving home one day from work I open the front door and it feels as though there's a wonderfully light atmosphere in our home. Everyone is smiling again as they did during the "old days". My heart seems to be missing a beat with excitement.

"Whatever's happened?" I ask.

"Our Rudolf is being released from hospital soon" answers Mama still clutching a letter she's obviously received today.

"Oh how wonderful – Oh I can hardly believe it." I want to behave the same as Hans and Lotte who are jumping about in excitement but I'm supposed to be the male in charge and that reaction would be childish.

He will be home soon and then during our time in the basement flat late in the evenings we can speak honestly to each other about

---

[9] But in hindsight it was an injury which would plague him for the rest of his life

the world situation. I love Hans, my younger brother and he seems to be fairly interested in politics having joined the youth movement last year but he hasn't the same spark as my older sibling.

"There's some more good news" said Mama. She was smiling from ear to ear as I arrive home the next day. "Werner has been discharged from hospital and has now been transferred to Cuxhaven to recuperate. Oh I'm so pleased to know he's improving and we'll have him home soon."

I give Mama a hug as I know how much she's missing the hugs from Papa. She's tried so hard to care for us and although I'm trying to be "the man" of the family, it's not the same. She deserves to hear such good news and I have to say I've missed young Werner being around and I know Lotte has felt lost without him. Fancy sending him to Cuxhaven though as that makes visiting almost impossible for us. When I ask Mama why they are doing this she explains that the authorities are going to give Werner extra food which he desperately needs and also medication to help him recover and gain strength. What a relief that he's been given this opportunity. I wonder if he'll miss us as we will him.

And then the day arrives when Rudolf walks through the front door entrance and stands in front of us as large as life watching us eating our meagre meal in the kitchen. I can hardly recognise him. When he left us in early summer 1917, he was still very young looking and I have to reluctantly admit he showed some naivety of his future life being so eager to see the big wide world. When he came home on leave in December he'd matured but the person now standing in front of us is a very tall strong looking man whose features show that he had definitely seen the world; although he still had a bandage wrapped round his head and covering his right ear.

His demeanour not only oozes with confidence and even leadership, but there is something else there which I cannot quite grasp. Perhaps it's the knowledge that perhaps someone of his age should not have, but it seems that war does that to people. I'm not sure which of us manages to get to Rudolf first, to give him the hug we feared we'd never be able to give him.

Rudolf's story

At long last I am home amongst my family and away from the battlefield. The pain in my right ear is horrendous. I'm not complaining though as I am so relieved that this is the only medical problem I have. The sights I have seen, the fear, the cries of pain of people who could not be helped, the cold, the mud and water everywhere underfoot is something humans should not have to endure. Fighting in the east means we also have the freezing temperatures snow and frozen mutilated bodies. It was a living hell and for what reason? Some of the people I have been with on the train back from the battlefield are hardly human any more with their wounds and their shattered minds. How are these people going to survive when they return home? How are the families, especially the working class families with little income, going to cope when their loved ones return in such a condition? Even worse what about the families who will never have their men folk return at all?

In a way I feel guilty that I have just this one medical problem and the advantage of so much love from my family to help me recover. No more will I have to hear sounds of ammunition firing or bombs exploding. My mind jolts back to the present when I study my family's drawn faces and their emaciated bodies. What sort of meals are they eating? Where is Werner? Why has no-one kept me informed of their plight?

Mama starts to explain about what has been happening at home whilst Papa and I have been away. She tries to paint a picture that all is well but after a few direct questions from me, the truth unfolds. I can feel myself getting angry now as we had all been encouraged to believe that we are fighting for our Fatherland and our folks back home would be all right. This isn't acceptable that our country has been brought to this level. I can see that I must pull myself together and take charge. Poor Ernst and Mama have been trying to look after the family to the best of their ability but they look exhausted. There is certainly something I can do immediately which will not affect my recovery and will help everyone.

"Look I know that you haven't been able to go to Cuxhaven to see young Werner, so first thing in the morning, I will go over and report back on how he's getting on." I see that I have said the right things. There is such relief on their faces and I am pleased that I can do something useful.

That night Ernst and I sit in our kitchen in the basement, and we speak honestly to each other in our family's absence. We exchange information on both our experiences since we last met and it makes me realise that we have both grown up. It's time for us to be proactive as we can no longer accept the treatment to the less fortunate people in our city.

"We must contribute to see if we can improve their working conditions and their lives. It is ridiculous that so many people should suffer whilst the few live a life of luxury. I am aware that their young offspring have also been sent to war and many will not be coming home but for those who do, they will not be coming back to lack of food, clothing etc and if they are badly wounded they will have decent medical help. It is also ridiculous that we should have been led into this war in the first place by the few whose personalities exhibit greed, imperialism and then there's businesses making a fortune out of this conflict.

Silence falls as we both are deep in our own thoughts and then "I'm sorry to speak like this especially when I've only just come home but it is about time that I start to learn how I can contribute towards changing this situation. When I think back to my conversations with our grandfather and the struggles he had all his life, it is not surprising that I want to continue to improve the standard of living for the poor".

I know people think I am too young but I see so little improvement for the financially lower end of society. I was indeed very fortunate to learn about our family history as Opa lived until I was thirteen years old. My siblings were really too young to understand the difficult life he had. From his childhood when our great grandparents were married in 1832 they could only just survive in life just after serfdom had been abolished. Our grandfather saw his parents struggle and then when he became a basket weaver, he married our grandmother. Unfortunately she died three years before I was born but at least I spent many hours listening to Opa. I am proud of him and I hope I can devote my life to improving the existence for others.

After I finish speaking to Ernst, he quietly studies my face and then tells me that he will do whatever is needed to support me in my quest. We grab each other hands and grip them tightly in our pact.

"I'm so glad you're back at home with us" he adds with a grin.

The next day I set off for Cuxhaven. When I arrive at the convalescent home, I'm surprised and concerned to find that Werner is no longer there. He had had an accident and is now at the hospital. I hurry off to the hospital and am shocked to find that without even trying to contact us they have operated on young Werner's leg. There he is this poor pathetic looking scrap of a youngster in hospital looking very lost. He is only two years old, without our family knowing anything about his plight, and no doubt wondering why he is left in such a place without Mama being there with him. According to the nurse, he has put on quite a lot of weight since living in Cuxhaven but I can see that he needs his family.

My cynical hard face melts looking at Werner's lovely open expression. He looks quizzically at me thinking I must be someone special in his life. Of course he will not remember me as I've spent so long away from him so I tell him who I am and it's not long before the love of two brothers albeit sixteen years age difference makes us both thrilled to be in each other's company. I spend a few hours chatting and playing with him managing to make him laugh with me messing about doing silly antics. His leg is heavily bandaged, but he's being very brave and doesn't complain. Poor Mama will have yet more worry to contend with when I tell her the news. I hear that she found it hard enough to part with him originally when he had to go into hospital.

I find a doctor and am assured that Werner will be allowed home in a couple of weeks. I tell my young brother that I will make sure that I will come to collect him home and with that give him a cuddle and quickly leave him. I dare not turn around to wave goodbye as I can feel his sad eyes following me as I make my way to the door. Leaving my very young sibling alone to cope all by himself is just too much for me to bear. The poor lad has not had the same secure upbringing I've had with both my parents being around for me plus my Oma.

Finally that day arrives and we're all so pleased when I manage to bring him home to Gertigstrasse. He looks shyly around the flat and then at everyone. Mama as expected fusses over him like a clucking hen and Lotte seems to be by his side at every possible moment, fetching and carrying for him and making him laugh so he soon settles back into the hub of our family. It is lovely hearing the laughter after all the sorrow. We have not had enough of the happiness which used to resonate in our flat.

Our pleasure improves even more when on 7th March 1918 Papa opens the front door of our flat and stands there beaming. Even though it will be for a short period, we are at long last all together. He gently opens the small bedroom door and looks over to where Werner is in bed, then smiles, coming out shutting the door quietly behind him.

"Upon my word, he's grown" remarks Papa. Mama came over and gives Papa a hug.

"He's over two years old now" confirms Mama. In an understatement so as not to worry Papa she continues "He's really had problems with his health not being very strong, but hopefully now things will improve for him."

She changes the subject looking at my father "But I'm more worried about you" she says studying his face. I have to admit that Papa really looks quite old now. Sending someone of his age to war is not right. It must be harder to experience the same misery as the rest of us there. He looks as though he cannot take any further bad experiences.

Later, when I have a chance to speak to him alone, he tells me the good news that he is not going to be sent back to the front any more. In April he is to be sent to the island of Silt. I sigh with relief.

The next day, Werner hobbles out from his bedroom into the lounge. Papa had gone downstairs to his empty shop.

"Who was that man in the uniform" Werner asks me. I can't help smiling at him. The poor boy doesn't even know his father. I wonder how many other children do not or come to that will never know their fathers.

My ear does not improve much. In the end I have to visit the army doctor in Hamburg. They decide that I will be of little use at the front as my ear is so badly damaged that further explosions will make my ear drum bleed again. I'm discharged from the army and told that I must take up useful war work and as I am qualified in metal work, I should go and work in the docks. Ships are badly needed so employment is not difficult to find. I manage to secure a job at Blohm and Voss and take this opportunity to join the German Metal Workers Union[10]. With my wages, life slightly improves for the family and that makes me feel good.

However, reports start to circulate between my friends who have just returned injured from the front. According to them, during the beginning of August, on one day alone 16,000 of our men had been taken prisoner. After that other military disasters follow for our "glorious" German Army. At least the battle is over with the Soviet Union as Russia is now known. A peace agreement has been signed with them.

"If our government do not agree to an armistice soon with the west, we will have to organise with other workers some kind of revolution to defeat this regime. Then at long last, if we succeed, our citizens will be able to live in a true democratic country and a socially just society. It's unbelievable being such a cultured nation and yet here we are living to fight wars and to provide wealth and prosperity to just one echelon of society. Something will have to be done."

Some friends of ours including Hans Hagen are sitting with us in our basement kitchen and I can't help myself taking this opportunity of putting forward my concerns. There is a consensus of approval with my comments and the others add very similar statements to mine. I'd joined the USPD along with Ernst when I had returned from the war and now I'm the cashier for Uhlenhorst and Winterhude. As it has a membership of two hundred it keeps me busy in my spare time but that doesn't stop me from taking part in several strikes.

---

[10] DMV – Deutscher Metallarbeiter-Verband

Finally we hear rumours that an armistice is being sought to prevent defeat in the "field" and avert any possibility of a similar revolution as had occurred in Russia. Does this mean that at last we might have a true democracy? What we hadn't realised until later is that President Wilson has insisted that Kaiser Wilhelm must abdicate and the military leaders have to be replaced prior to the armistice. The Kaiser obviously does not want to stand down and so a press campaign is launched aiming at bringing about the Kaiser's abdication. On my way home on 25th October the newspapers are full of details concerning these aims. Is this our chance?

We then hear that the Kaiser being surprised at the press campaign on 25th October 1918 to bring about his abdication he leaves his armies to return to Berlin to ensure that his son will not succeed him. Hindenburg as well finally loses control of the situation which is rapidly changing. A few days later instead of engaging against the British Fleet for one last battle, our German High Seas Fleet mutinies instead seizing the ships. This is our opportunity. We hear from our "brothers" at Kiel that they have set up a Council to represent the sailors. Support for the council is given by the dock workers and garrison troops in Kiel join them in solidarity forming a joint sailors', soldiers' and workers' council. During the first few days of November they start an armed uprising and take over the docks and then the city.

I volunteer my services to assist Hamburg citizens to do the same thing. I help organise the dock workers in the formation of the Council and can't help feeling exhilarated that I can put to good use my organisational and vocal skills towards an "uprising". Two days after Kiel, we also mutiny against the old government leadership. The working class women of Hamburg brave everything to fight against the hunger being suffered by those left behind whilst their men folk go to the battlefield. These brave women also protest against the war itself by taking part in meetings, demonstrations and strikes in the new war factories. At last, with all this anger at the way we have been abused, so many people are risking everything to change Germany forever.

At Blohm and Voss where I am working, 17,000 workers during our lunch break call an immediate strike. The workers pour out of the factories, joining the Vulkan shipyard workers as we make our way to the Trade Union House. Jan Appel tells me the problems they had at the Vulcan shipyard. The workers had held a secret meeting when they'd heard about Kiel. As the shipyard is under military discipline they were aware that they would not be allowed to strike. A delegation of seventeen workers then went to the union headquarters insisting to the union that there should be a declaration of a general strike in support of Kiel and for our own rights.

Unfortunately some reluctant leaders of the SPD and the ADGB[11] disagreed with the general strike and so there followed a pretty angry session with these leaders. Thank goodness the Vulcan employees refused to stay in work as they decided to join us in our march to the trade union house only to find that these so called leaders have disappeared. Other workers seize warships, taking possession of the port and the central railway station. Here we persuade many soldiers not to embark on the trains. These men are waiting for transport as they are due to return to the front at the end of their leave. Many then join us demonstrators.

Together with the soldiers and workers we march to Altona. All is going well until we have a skirmish with members of a right wing militia just at the boundary to Altona but it is only a minor incident. Some friends and I join others and storm the infantry barracks in Hamburg managing to obtain the weapons from the arsenal. The barracks surrenders without too many problems which is a great relief as if we intend to fight for our freedom, we desperately need more weapons. We have so many aims and must put everything we can into this fight for change. We want our political prisoners released; have freedom of the press and of speech and the abolition of censorship of mail. Many of the army soldiers risk everything by joining us as they want to be treated decently by their superiors as well as wanting personal freedom whilst off duty.

In Altona a Soldiers Council is formed and negotiations start with the local military command. They agree to our demands and

---

[11] ADGB – Allgemeiner Deutscher Gewerkschaftsbund (Confederation of German Trade Unions in Germany 1919-1933)

we take possession of the local military command offices. All the military and naval prisoners in Hamburg and Altona are released by 7th November. With machine guns we have military posts holding strategically important positions and I am informed that 18,000 soldiers are now under orders of the Soldiers Council.

To my amazement I hear that Kurt Eisner, leader of the local Independent Socialists, seeing the collapse of the old order simply walks into Munich on 8th November and declares Bavaria a Republic. He then administers the area with a coalition government along with the majority socialist party. We just can't believe what is happening. Has our own country's revolution started and is this the opportunity for a real socialist Country where we will no longer be ruled by the rich and their businesses?

Karl Liebkneckt and Rosa Luxenburg who are socialist leaders attempt an uprising in Berlin on 8th November with strikes and demonstrations. Due to pressure from other cities Berlin surrenders on 9th November. In his speech from the Reichstag balcony Social Democrat Philipp Scheidemann announces the departure of the Kaiser. I hear that the Kaiser hadn't agreed to his abdication but after the speech he has no alternative but accedes to the situation. Chancellor Prince Max von Baden officially announces the abdication and on 10th November Kaiser Wilhelm leaves Germany for Holland after handing over power to Friedrich Ebert. On 11th November, Germany signs the Armistice and we are now the Weimar Republic.

We have peace with other countries at last, and the Kaiser has gone. However all the generals and German general staff remain and they have the backing of the big industrialists (such as Krupps and Thyssen) who are partly responsible for the whole tragedy of the war in the first place. I know that they will not give up their aims for a "greater" Germany and to regain colonies.

Now we have a new fight to bring changes to this country. If we don't try to initiate this now, the future for our beloved homeland looks bleak as attempts will be made to defeat us and once again the working class will be the tools of the rich for a "greater" Germany. There are so many people behind us so this might be our chance of a socialist country.

At this point the workers and soldiers council becomes the real government in Hamburg. Unemployment is a serious problem having 70,000 totally unemployed in Hamburg alone and those only managing to find part time work numbers over 100,000. Before the revolution there were "intentions" of setting up a labour office but as nothing had materialised by November and due to resistance we have from the old establishment in trying to set it up, there are vast demonstrations of the unemployed. Military field kitchens are set up to supply food at very low prices to the jobless and these are run by people in these dire straits. Also there are strikes and disputes between the workers and the factory owners as at long last the imbalance of wealth and conditions start to be redressed. It's a busy time for me but I'm determined to help my colleagues.

The newly formed Council proposed to reutilise the material stockpiled in the shipyards which were intended for the construction of submarines. The new aims are to use it now for the construction of rolling stock for the railways.

Another problem which affects so many people is housing. Here again there's hope on the horizon of a scheme with the state buying all building construction materials to prevent land speculation for potential development. Our country at long last looks as though it might prosper again with the work force knowing that their future looks more hopeful. We will also need support from the countries who have defeated us but will they be scared of this new non capitalist country with ideas which might spread to their own countries?

For us though at last sense is beginning to emerge with "recognising that production is the basis of social life" seeking to "fundamentally transform the role of the working class in production, putting the factories under its control both socially and technically"[12] Unfortunately making good use of the capabilities and knowledge of our people fails as the new Berlin government seems to be getting caught up with compromise.

Piecemeal work for the shipyard workers has all but been eliminated despite the owners trying to reverse this improvement for all involved.

---

[12] Quote from Heinrich Laufenberg: The Hamburg Revolution

I don't really understand the intrigue and complications which are taking place all with the intentions of trying to transform our economy and to provide fairness in Germany. I accept that my age and experience hinders this knowledge but I am hopeful that life will change for the better. I put everything I can into helping so that this change can materialise but I can see the worried faces of our leaders as reality of the difficulties which are arising brings so many new policies to a grinding halt.

This German uprising is so different from the Russian revolution or even the French revolution. We cannot compare ourselves with any other country being in such a hopeless situation having been defeated in a major war. It only compounds our problems especially with rich and powerful men in our country having always gained their wealth from the working class poor. They are ceaselessly trying to destroy all our efforts.

Oh such hope we had in the beginning but it starts to dissipate when our dreams start to go wrong. I can see that we have not been very well organised but I am far too young to interfere and I know little about such things. My friends and I all struggle to accept all of this but accept we must so to my most abject disappointment, all our effort filters away. Power is relinquished as we start negotiating in order to make it possible for our government to become legal. This allows the people who were originally in authority to regain military control thereby stopping the legal process. We had come so close to our goal of a new way of governing. Will there ever be another chance like this one again?

Will there ever be any hope for the ordinary citizen to live decently? Friedrich Ebert makes every effort and promises the German people peace, freedom, law and order along with food supplies but can he carry out this promise? He says that until a newly elected Constituent Assembly is formed, he will work with the USPD. This sounds a good compromise and as I know he wants to avoid the extreme left wing ideas of a future Germany, he decrees an eight hour working day, guaranteed work for demobilized soldiers, improved sickness and unemployment benefits.

However there is a catch to all these ideas as in order to prevent a true socialist Germany happening, he makes an agreement with the army. This makes me suspicious as there are still the original generals in the army from before the war. This fundamental mistake means that it will be impossible to solve our original need which includes the elimination of the abject poverty. The original generals have always been "hand in glove" with the big industrialists who have no intention of increasing the welfare of the less fortunate. The generals put in a condition that the officer corps should remain and they have always had a free hand in the "security" of the state to combat socialism. My friends and I have grave misgivings over this agreement with the army and feel we cannot trust Ebert.

Unfortunately as a result of these peace offerings, our plan for the rest of Germany is now weakened. We in Hamburg have been far more proactive with the working class being involved in the governing of our city whereas the imperial government of Germany itself operates in coalition with the wealthy and it is now evident that we cannot continue in this change without the rest of Germany.

To my disgust the socialist right wing reverse their progressiveness towards the old way of governing. The army arrives to "resolve" the situation in the docks and storms the area with troops, but incredibly ordinary civilians and disenchanted soldiers come to the dockyard to help us strikers as I think they also mistrust the agreement which has been made. The army retreats, but we have to accept that we have lost the momentum although we have made our point. Now is the time to go home before anyone else gets hurt.

I speak to my friend Hans Hagen who has joined Ernst and me along with some other friends in our flat.

"I am worried Hans. I am not convinced that these same generals are going to accept the change in the style of government. I know what these officers are like having been in the army. They still consider themselves part of the imperial army and as such that is more important than any other government institution. I have a nasty feeling that despite the support of so many people we are beginning to lose."

I look at Ernst. I can see he also feels that our cause is lost. We were so close but when there are such well-established systems in place to deter the lesser mortals in society from having any rights, how can we defeat the establishment. I decide to battle on with my ranting and ravings. Ernst understands my frustration and totally agrees with my politics so he sits quietly listening as I continue.

"These higher echelons of the army always come from the aristocracy and they are backed by their highly nationalist political supporters. In turn they have connections with industrial management circles which are a strong political force behind everything which happens here in Germany. With such an establishment, what hope is there? They will never accept the new situation".

The trouble is that I am speaking to the converted and we seem to be powerless at the moment. The only thing we can do is talk over the same grievances.

"I have to agree with you" Ernst sighs. "This government is not strong enough to fight against the old system. We have done so much in the last few weeks but there is still malnutrition, hypothermia and disease and yet the generals are intent on keeping the old system regardless of the fact that we are a new republic. I don't think that the army will ever really accept the new republic."

At this tirade of rhetoric the room falls into silence. If we are all being honest, our situation does not look good. Edgar breaks the silence and speaks for all of us.

"I have a feeling that there is going to be great danger ahead. I think that the generals have every intention of punishing the leaders of this new government of Ebert and restoring us workers to our "proper place".

I look at Ernst who looks very worried now.

"Ernst, I think that we had better keep this to ourselves for the moment and not share our worries with our parents. Poor Papa and Mama have been through a lot these last few years. They need a period when they can live a more normal life"

I can see Ernst agrees with me, but there is another situation arising with the newly formed politically right wing paramilitary unit called the Freikorps[13]. They are armed and dangerous; a threatening menace within our war ravaged country. I have seen these types of

---

[13] The forerunners of the S.A. and S.S.

men in various army divisions when fighting in the war. They are inherently brutal and intent on causing trouble. I know that my time of fighting is not over but this time it will be in a civil war. I am so frightened that if we do not stop this threat we will be unable to prevent another world war.

Despite these worries, I just put everything aside in order to have a joyful Christmas. Our family is almost united once again. Papa is still in Silt but at least we have all survived these last few years and yes gained a new brother. Something good did come out of the war! Ernst and I bring our mandolins out and for the first time I have the pleasure of seeing our little Werner enjoying our singing and playing. He is so shy seeing us altogether but his little face finally lights up hearing our laughter during this festive period. He seems a little stronger now and I hope that as more of us are earning money, the food situation will improve and with better nutrition make him healthier. Also I'm sure that Papa will be home soon and then Mama will be at her happiest.

Rudolf – possibly March 1918

CHAPTER 5

1919

Rudolf's Story

When I look at our family and then to my friends who are suffering emotionally as well as financially even more than us, I want to do something positive to improve our "lot". Not only have our leaders taken us to war but we are now in a far worse state than before it all started. Overall food supplies are down to less than half and in some areas to one third of pre-war levels. The ordinary working class prior to 1914 struggled as the cost and availability of our food was pretty meagre, but this information shows how serious the situation has become. So many people want change but once again I'm so disappointed at the way things seem to be turning out.

News spreads fast amongst us when on 6th January 1919, in the centre of Berlin a mass demonstration is arranged but it seems the political leaders are unprepared for the event and consequences of their action. From what I can make out, they're late in arriving for the event as they're still deciding their next move. It's unbelievable but as the day is very cold and rainy and the meeting has not been organised very well so many went home.

However a small armed minority consisting of 200,000 people decide to continue with the protest but to counter it, the newly formed Freikorps suddenly appear. Many battles follow but the Freikorps take over control, murdering any political protestors they manage to capture instead of handing them over to the police for a fair trial.

The leaders Karl Liebnecht and Rosa Luxemburg are tracked down and brutally assassinated. What a violent nation we are to annihilate opposition in this way. I can see such a serious situation arising. A general strike is called but martial law is declared. The

Freikorps are let loose in the city resulting in 1200 men being killed. Several days later, the city of Berlin succumbs to the right wing militia and local trade unions are banned. What a terrible loss we've suffered of good and honest men and women.

In the middle of all this strife Germany votes for a new constituent assembly. Ebert wins the election as leader of the majority socialists known as the SPD, but as the independent socialists called the USDP do not get so many votes, he makes a coalition agreement with other parties. And so the Weimar Republic is formed. Either Ebert is weak or he cannot see the dangers facing us. Whatever is his reason for not destroying the right wing extremists I will never know. Instead he succumbs to their wishes by not providing enough reforms and improvements to help the working class. The new Weimar constitution is drawn up but the conclusion seems to be that very little needs to be changed in the system which was inaugurated by Chancellor Bismark in 1870! In fact the only alteration to me seems to be the strengthening of the old system both politically and administratively.

As far as I can see the President, although elected by the people, is invested with almost all the powers of the deposed Kaiser Wilhelm. He is the commander-in-chief of the armies and as such appoints and dismisses officers so why he doesn't dismiss the generals and officers who do not accept the republic, I really do not know. These men are a threat to our democracy and seem to be able to embark on dismantling the hopes of so many reformers and there seems so little we can do to counteract their violence. He can also now appoint and dismiss the Chancellor and assume dictatorial powers in an emergency. How can our leaders make such a serious mistake as that? This could mean that someone extremely powerful and possibly evil could legally take over this country and make it a dictatorship. Surely this has to be altered as this decision is extremely dangerous in the wrong hands[14].

The Freikorps are now a force to be reckoned with. They consist of highly paid ex-army officers who are politically right wing

---

[14] As we were soon to find out with Adolf Hitler

extremists and number in the tens of thousands. These men travel the country dissipating peaceful strikes, unflinching in their violence of shooting protestors and assassinating our men who are standing up for their rights. Thousands of people are being imprisoned after being arrested by the militia and to add fuel to the situation the employers then black list many who are involved in any of the strikes.

In Hamburg we are totally shocked to hear the news of the killing of Karl Liebnecht and Rosa Luxemburg. I join a large gathering of protestors outside the union headquarters. Among the mass of people are Jan Appel, Ernst Thälmann and many more committed men. During that evening we march at night on Barenfeld Barracks, Altona so that we can arm the population against the vicious evil militia. Our aims are hindered en-route when we become involved in a gun fight. This had never been our intention but we manage to occupy the building and obtain weapons to arm 4000 of the demonstrators so that we can protect ourselves against these Freikorps.

Once again the Freikorps are employed to dissipate our gathering. It's hard to explain the sheer violence which these Freikorps inflict on the ordinary citizen and protestor.

The heavy war machine guns and similar weaponry on display by these thugs threaten citizens and makes our beloved Germany look like a war zone. Why isn't the rest of Europe interested in the weaponry being used here to destroy any hope of a socialist democracy in Germany? We've only just lost the war and with all of this unrest, stability in Europe looks impossible. Why is the world looking the other way?

My family are really becoming worried as these troops seem to have no compassion but a determination to destroy civil rights. We seem to be going backwards in our society rather than forwards. It's hard to study the faces of these people as their helmets cover more of the face than the old war ones[15] but if anyone has the courage to look for a few seconds and hopefully not be attacked, these helmets hide cruel faces and steely cold eyes. The Freikorps carry their weapons

---

[15] Future SS helmets

with menace. Why haven't our "victors" seen this danger and try to take the power from the army? Surely we all want a stable Europe now. I am becoming extremely concerned for the future of Germany.

The Soldiers Council has been spreading rumours about us planning a *putsch*[16] which then gives them an excuse to start arrests including the leader of the shipyard workers who is accused of calling for armed resistance and the occupation of the trade union offices.

Despite the presiding judge in Hamburg not authorising the leader's arrest, legality is being ignored; the leader is detained and sent to Berlin.

A non-progressive socialist is elected president of the Council and he allows the increase of volunteer unscrupulous units who have weapons albeit illicit ones. These units are becoming more dangerous by the weeks. We seem to have totally lost the momentum changing our society to a socialist one but I will not turn my back for our just cause. In fact I feel more inclined to fight harder as I am fearful of the consequences if we cannot stop these people ruining our ideals.

During all this strife and worry, Papa is finally released from the army on 20th March 1919. We want to give him a wonderful celebration when he arrives home, but I am well aware that all is not well with him. The war has affected all who have taken part in it. Few of us will talk about the terrible things we have seen or what we had to do to survive. Too many of our friends have lost their lives after having been in horrendous situations. No man should ever experience this. We don't want our loved ones to know anything about our time at war, but the mental strain affects us in different ways. Papa being an elderly man by comparison has suffered emotionally. I therefore persuade my family to keep the celebration low key. It all works out perfectly, and Papa is so pleased to have just the seven of us around the table having our meal. In actual fact, this is our very first occasion where we are together as a family of seven.

The following day, Papa goes down to our old shop to start to sort things out. My poor father still cannot get over the fact that

---

[16] A plotted revolt or attempt to overthrow a government especially one that depends upon suddenness and speed

Mama sold all the shoes in exchange for food whilst he was away. He still doesn't realise how near our family was to starvation. Typically Mama wouldn't have told him so as not to worry him. After deliberating for a while Papa decides to open a cigar and tobacco shop, but he still carries on repairing and making shoes to order when he is asked by his old customers.

Reading one of the national newspapers it's horrible to know that in Bavaria there were 557 executions after the Freikorps put that rebellion down. The violence is extraordinary.

In June 1919, the Versailles Treaty is signed. There has been very little chance of any negotiations and it seems that our "victors" decided on rearranging borders so that we lose territory, pay war reparations, disarm our weapons and our army. The reparations are huge and with the chaos, poverty and internal military dangers for the majority of the population, things do not look good. I really am surprised that Europe is not at all concerned the situation we are in. I know our leaders are responsible for so many people dying, but surely most people can see how unstable our country is at present and that unless we have some help destroying the system which led to the violence of the Great War, further problems will arise later.

There is so much resentment within the army and the German armament industry, that rumours start circulating (originating from the right wing), that the German army was never defeated on the battle field. It seems incredible to me that here we are a newly formed republic and yet knowing the attitude of the generals within the army, new officers in charge are not appointed sympathetic to the republic and who accept that we as a nation are defeated. Instead anger follows from the generals of our German armed forces when they are instructed to reduce their size to some 100,000 men and officers. In order to comply with the new Versailles Treaty, manipulation of soldier numbers is arranged by making just the N.C.O.s and officers consist of the regular army.

To our horror, they feel quite justified in keeping the rest of the men trained in the various paramilitary Freikorps in military readiness as well as the Black Reichswehr soldiers. General staff are renamed Truppenamt so in actual fact there are far more than

100,000 retained for action. Part of this deceit is because they want to keep the Freikorps who have proved very useful to them to stop us trying to achieve our aims of a socialist country.

To make this possible the military have taken the equipment used in the last war and are now using them in our own streets against ordinary German people. Of course rich industrialists want to protect themselves from their obsession of a threat from the east which is the communist Soviet Union.

I realise that I have become hardened through my life during the war but I am still disgusted that Germany is such a dangerous place to live now. All we want is democracy and freedom. Ernst is absolutely distraught seeing how violent and frightening it has become now. It is happening outside in our own streets and our own homes where women and children want to live in safety. People are scared to walk outside now but the thought of us remaining pawns of the rich still make many of us want to stand up against this violence. I know this makes us sound as though we are extremists, but this is not the case.

We are ordinary people many of whom are battle scarred from conscription into a slaughter against men on the opposite side of the battle field being sent to their deaths by their leaders. Yet the marches and demonstrations in Great Britain of their working class have not been met with heavy machine guns and slaughter so why is Germany in this situation?

With the combination of Germany losing the war and my continuing activites in strikes and disputes, I lose my job at Blohm & Voss. Mind you I am certainly not alone. Due to the losing of control of a "socialist revolution", we have found that some trade unions are beginning to work closely with other organisations and against the workers. Some of us are being expelled from some unions and then fired by our employers not being members of unions. This is an extremely serious situation as there is mass unemployment and starvation prevalent here.

Some factories though are still secretively rearming. We cannot seem to overcome this as the generals from the army are from the aristocracy and big industrialists. They are still incensed that an armistice has been signed and a republic formed. Not only is their status threatened but their income from manufacturing armaments and the workforce are frightened of unemployment and starvation so they're not likely to inform authorities. If they did have the courage, the Freikorps are around to silence them. However I manage to return to my old firm Maihak which is located in Semperstrasse. As it is a precision engineering works with a large lathe operating facility, it is ideal for me. Maihak has many trade union members working there so this gives me ample opportunity to continue being an active member. I know that this does not please my employers, but they also know that I work hard and am a good engineer.

As recreation, I have joined a socialist's hikers group. It's a popular past time for many people who want to be away from the dangers of the city and to be able to talk openly about the political situation. It is already getting dangerous for us to speak in small groups in the built up areas of Hamburg as we feel that we are being watched. Oh the freedom of being with friends out in the fresh air and with a bit of luck in the sunshine. We can then talk of serious matters without fear but we can laugh, sing and enjoy the pleasure of being with people of like minds. As for the refreshing chance of being in the company of lovely young ladies it's at these moments that I realise how much I have missed these last few years!

It takes me away for a short time from other major problems. There are food shortages still for most of us who are working class. How can we exist on such poor quality of meat rations? Even people not politically motivated are disgruntled and angry at the situation we are all in. There had been mass demonstrations in April when the unemployed became desperate and started rioting and looting. Now in June there's fighting between the working class citizens and the Freikorps.

Somehow we manage to disarm the troops and they are paraded through the city. A state of martial law is declared followed by more troops being sent from Berlin. These units are inexperienced and small in number so it doesn't take much effort for them to be defeated and sent back to Berlin. The reinforcements though are stronger and resolute and we have to admit defeat and this means that the city has been placed under martial law until December.

Ernst has been really nagging me to do something about my right ear as I'm in constant pain and cannot hear well. There's no point denying that the army doctors had been correct in their diagnosis. With all the action I have been involved in since leaving the military forces the expected improvement never materialises. I now admit defeat during July and August and go into hospital for an operation. It is the only way to rid myself of this acute pain and hopefully then to continue with my resistance work. I'm sure the doctors operating on me are just trying to cure my pain, not realising my real intentions.

When I am finally sent home from hospital, I am given the position of group leader of the 1st District in Winterhude working for the independent socialist democratic party (USPD) and then this gets extended to include Uhlenhorst and Winterhude districts. When I arrived back from the war, I had been a co-founder of the youth movement affiliated to this party. Ernst I knew I could rely on being one of my first members. I had the feeling that belonging to the political organisation would be useful at a later stage if the economic situation became worse and the military threat from the Freikorps made our lives impossible. We are in very dangerous times – times which no-one has ever experienced before.

CHAPTER 6

1920 & 1921

Rudolf's story

My heart goes out to the families and to the wounded soldiers who have been mutilated during the war. Ebert had promised to put things right, but it is pitiful seeing our brave men sitting on the pavements minus arms, legs and or are blind and begging. I know how these men have suffered during the 1914-1918 war and now they are suffering in silence again. Why do they feel that these men can now be ignored as they no longer have any use to the "fatherland".

Hans Hagen looks very agitated as I walk into our meeting place so I immediately ask what is wrong. Spring has arrived and I have been feeling a little less negative as the thought of better weather means less heating fuel to find and the relaxing of our bodies as we stop to shiver and the bones of the more elderly will stop aching. Yet now I'm alert to Hans' behaviour.

"A right wing civil servant called Dr Wolfgang Kapp seeing an opportunity to seize power over the government decided to put a plan into action. He went to see the 12,000 Freikorps men stationed in Berlin who were going to be dissolved by our socialist Chancellor. Kapp was looking to them for support in him seizing power and making a dictatorship."

I'm totally alert now as this Kapp *putsch* is probably the army's long expected open revolt to the disarmament and reduction of troops agreed and signed in the Treaty of Versailles. This has proved all my fears correct with this attempt of a military takeover. Why has our country been left in such an unstable situation? I concentrate myself to listen to every detail I'm given. I ask Hans to continue.

"As the Freikorps had nothing to lose they came marching into Berlin with their heavy machine guns and weaponry. The government had to retreat to Dresden but before escaping, they managed to proclaim a general strike against the coup. The Kapp government declared military law and instituted the death penalty against strikers but I gather Kapp has no loyal troops available to implement this."

Situations like this though can change so quickly. As Hans has very little more to add to this awful news, I thank him for their information and immediately leave to discover what the latest information is and what will be expected for us to do in Hamburg. It's like a pendulum swinging so who knows how our country will end up and who will eventually govern.

Thank goodness Dr Kapp is hopeless and after four days of the strike, his new government is dissolved, along with this particular division of the Freikorps. I sigh with relief at this piece of news as it could have ended up disastrously.

I hear that as Kapp is about to escape a man called Adolf Hitler arrives on the scene. Hitler offers to co-ordinate the amalgamation of the Berlin coup with his own in Bavaria. Dr Kapp refuses and Adolf Hitler returns to Bavaria angry and disappointed. Who is this Adolf Hitler anyway that he thinks he is so powerful?

When the Berlin coup collapses many of these Freikorps who lost their jobs now seem to be joining the Stahlhelm which is another dangerous paramilitary group formed in December 1918.

As I expect, all of this danger activates the left wing stronghold of the Ruhr into an uprising against the Kapp *putsch*. After Kapp had been defeated, the victorious 50,000 men of the left wing army of the Ruhr refuse to dissolve. President Ebert and Premier Bauer who are still in Dresden, use the Freikorps to brutally destroy the left wing army. What sort of people would use Freikorps who had been part of the coup to overthrow the democratic government? It's frightening to realise how the tide will turn and who is on whose side. The Freikorps then go on to "pacify" Saxony and Thüringen.

In Harburg, Hamburg we are ready for action and as we are armed we manage to defeat the Berthold Division of the Freikorps. Some of the workers here in Hamburg, including myself have formed into a group willing to take up arms for the protection of our newly formed democracy, albeit a very weak one to fight against this right wing militia. Someone has to stand up to these brutal Freikorps and the threat of dictatorship against the working class people of Germany. We have hopes for some rights to a decent life. Once again we fail but not because of our efforts but because the different political groups representing us have not "jelled" together to overcome the threat. I despair that we cannot co-ordinate ourselves properly so that we work together for the same just cause.

On a personal level, the pain in Ernst's back is giving me cause for concern as it has been a problem for him shortly after he started work. I finally persuade him to ask the doctor if he has any other suggestions other than pain killers to help him. To our relief, the doctor recommends that he must take a complete rest so the doctor arranges for Ernst to stay and receive some treatment in the Black Forest.

I miss having him around but when he returns from his convalescence I can see how his health has improved. He even bought a little pottery cow for Werner[17].

Ernst's story

I feel so much better after my rest and physiotherapy in the Black Forest and can now earn my living without so much pain. I have finished my apprenticeship. Papa has come home so my personal life feels complete. My only concern is the fear and uncertainty for the future of our country so it's time I start taking a more active part in politics, as well as trying to improve our working conditions. I know that my fellow workers feel in equal measures both surprised and reassured by my actions as I enable changes through consultations with the management. Before I realise what has happened I have been chosen as shop steward. Both Rudolf and I are trade union members. I could never be as assertive as Rudolf as we approach problems differently. My policy is by quiet negotiations, but the end

---

[17] Werner has treasured this gift all his life and it still is kept in his bedroom.

result is usually the same. In actual fact Rudolf and I are the perfect "couple" with both having the same principles but having different ways of putting them into practise. We are becoming a good team.

One evening I'm home before Rudolf, but that isn't too surprising. I start washing and changing for our family meal, when a really dejected Rudolf walks into the kitchen.

"Whatever is the matter?" I ask.

"I've been sacked" replies Rudolf. "I knew the time would come as I just cannot keep quiet when there is an injustice which needs correcting."

I feign surprise at this statement which makes Rudolf laugh and then he becomes serious again.

"This time I was just called into the office and told that they were not prepared to have someone in their employment liked myself who is always causing trouble. They hadn't liked that I had taken part in that sympathy strike for the dock workers. You know that employers are really determined to remove anyone from their employment if they are militant".

"There are no laws to protect us Rudolf. We all knew this when we started fighting for workers' rights. Where are you going to find another job as I'm sure your reputation will follow you everywhere you go now?"

"Don't worry, I'll find somewhere. I'm a good hard worker and I know that I have a reputation of producing excellent quality work and always on time".

As I fear though the firm has made sure that his name is black listed in Hamburg. There are so many people desperate for jobs so they don't need people like him. A better description of many employers' requirements is "slave labour".

Poor Rudolf tries time and time again, but it's obvious that he has no hope. He has been blacklisted so he packs his belongs and heads the Ruhrgebeit (Duisburg District) saying his farewells to the family. Mama is upset, but she knows that he is doing the right thing. Shortly after he had left we receive a letter from him letting us know that he has found employment in the Ruhr at Beselino Metalhütten.

My life changes after Rudolf left. My soul mate is no longer here for our evening chats. After a while I hear about our group setting up top class cultural and artistic activities in our area. I love music and the arts so this might be the chance I've been hoping for with enjoying some decent recreation in the company of people with the same political and social opinions. The right wing militia stay away from this place and I can feel relaxed and happy here. I hate all the violence taking place in the streets and the threats against people who just want to improve their lives.

I take my mandolin with me and am rewarded with many an evening spent playing and singing with other mandolin players. Some people have guitars and this adds more depth to our sound. I have noticed for some time a lovely young lady called Anna Ketelhorn and cannot help becoming quite attracted to her. She sings many solo pieces as well as playing the guitar beautifully. What a wonderful sound she produces. I could listen to her for hours. She's such a talented person and although confident with regard to music, when she is not occupied with this, she is almost shy but very serene. I just have this feeling that Anna is a genuine person who I can trust.

I feel that I really want to know her but would she want to know me? I am not the gregarious, self-assured one in our family. Rudolf always seems to have the power to attract the opposite sex, but shyness always gets in my way. One day I decide that I will have to try and develop the friendship which we already have. I take the plunge and invite her round to my place to practise a duet together. I tell her how lovely it will be to perform this duet with her singing and playing the guitar and me playing the mandolin. I hold my breath and wait for her reply. To my astonishment, she smiles with pleasure at the suggestion and this is the start of our relationship. Oh what a lucky person I am to have such a wonderful caring and thoughtful girlfriend. Mama and Papa take an instant liking to her and I think they are also pleased that I have found someone who makes me so happy.

From here, my life changes for the better. We both still love going to the cultural activities and musical events and listening and talking to people of like minds. Many hours are spent talking about the current events taking place in our ravaged country and luckily

Anna feels the same. But then we have time to ourselves and that is precious for me as at last I have found the love of my life. Oh such sheer joy in the midst of so many worldly problems.

Yesterday evening we went to see a cabaret company which puts on performances with left wing leanings. They usually are clever plays so that the workers in the area can attend and hopefully learn at the same time. On the stage one particular evening is a complete scene entitled "Capitol" which depicts a strong and bare-chested worker giving a piggy back to a pot-bellied capitalist and his millions. The capitalist has a top hat and holds strings leading to his marionettes which are the police, judges and teachers. He has them jumping up and reciting capitalist texts. It causes much hilarity and I hope the result will be that our fellow workers will go home and think about what it all means and perhaps join us to try and change the situation we're in. Certainly the play has been well received.

The big industrialists are continuing to make arrangements to re-arm our country for the next war. It's so obvious that this is their intention. They want to make money; the threat of unemployment in these factories keeps many workers on their side and the army have not accepted defeat.

The Chief of Staff, General Hans von Seeckt is contravening the Treaty of Versailles by conducting foreign business and extending armament production abroad. Krupp is a major player in this aim of an imperial Germany but is only one of the many industrialists who have the same idea. Submarines are constructed in Spain, tanks and guns in Sweden, while Holland, Denmark and Switzerland provide the rest of the armaments needed by the Reichswehr. I have found out though that not only Junkers are being built in Russia but a poison gas factory has been constructed for chemical weapons. Krupp has a firm there which produces heavy artillery especially Howitzers. Krupp's business seems to be everywhere without a thought of the consequences of their actions.

I am horrified to think that Russia is helping Germany re-arm but I can only think that whilst the German army has an interest in producing weapons and munitions which cannot be controlled by the Treaty of Versailles, the Russians are thinking of something else.

Perhaps they want to learn from German industrial technology and are keen on getting an armament industry of their own and perhaps taking it over at some point. This may be an opportunity for them to learn to defend their nation should there be any future threat. Who knows the real reason? Whatever their policy is, I know that we want a true socialist Germany in our own right and not be beholden to any other country. We will not be copying other less perfect ideals in socialism as our situation is different and we have experienced a reasonable education and freedom of thought. The Soviets have never had any form of democracy and only the rich have benefited from learning and culture.

Added to the military fear which dominates most of our lives, there is also a financial crisis looming up like a dark cloud. I knew that our government has been keeping our internal economic situation artificially unstable so that it would become difficult to repay the reparations which were made at the Treaty of Versailles. Inflation is gradually increasing making it hard for us to survive but is there a reason for the inflation – something to do with the country's debt? I'm no financier but I am suspicious. After the war, our country had an internal debt of some 144,000 million marks. Foreigners are refusing to invest in our country so the trade deficit is catastrophic. In spite of all these problems, the victors gave us an invoice of 132 billion marks in reparations, of which two billions are due in 1921. It is hopeless to even consider these demands.

In March 1921, I'm jolted out of my personal happiness when one day I catch Mama off guard whilst sitting in the downstairs kitchen taking a rest from all the hand washing she is doing. She looks so worried that I ask her what is wrong.

"Whatever happens, don't tell Papa" she replies looking quite concerned that her facial expressions are betraying her fears. I nod in consent and wait although I can feel myself tensing up. She's silent for a minute, takes a deep breath and starts talking.

"As you will probably guess, I'm anxious about Rudolf. You know that the Freikorps entered the Ruhr to destroy the left wing army after the Kapp *putsch*? Well Rudolf, as you know went immediately after this event and I thought that he would be safe."

"That was a terrible and violent period for the people there. I gather about 1000 people were killed. What's happened now Mama?"

"Well I hadn't really followed it through but the Friekorps and the Reichswehr occupying the Ruhr means our country has violated the terms of the Versailles Treaty which has now given the French a reason to invade. I've just heard that Duisburg has been occupied by the French and Belgian troops".

I went cold with fear. My first thoughts are for Rudolf. Where, oh where is he?

"Have you heard from Rudolf Mama?"

Mama shook her head and looks forlornly down at the floor as she tries to hide her grief. I give her a hug and say

"I'm sure he'll be all right Mama – you know Rudolf. He gets himself into all these scrapes and yet always comes home eventually. You are right though, we mustn't tell Papa until we have to."

Time continues with no news and then to our family's great relief, Rudolf walks casually through the front door entrance one day. We try to ask him about the French invasion but he just shrugs and changes the subject. He just doesn't want to talk about his experiences but he is home thank goodness. He has no job, but he is safe. Max the dog goes absolutely mad with pleasure and jumped up at him and then ran round the room like a mad thing. Our Max is such a lovely animal who although is only a sandy coloured mongrel, has Labrador characteristics. Papa loves taking him for walks in the Stadtpark and the time walking gives him peace of mind.

It is so wonderful to have Rudolf back in our fold. We have our old basement together, but now we have to include Hans. Hans has lived with me down in that basement ever since Rudolf had left as Lotte is now a young lady and sharing bedrooms is out of the question. We just have to squeeze in and make our basement home for the three of us. We save our serious talks for when Hans has gone out as he does not have as strong views as us and he is not so involved politically at present. His time might come in the future but until then we have to be careful not to invite our friends back when he is around.

Rudolf finally chats to me about his life in the Ruhr. He certainly had gained a lot of experiences in this fight against the right wing politicians and the Freikorps. He also told me about how he and other people in the workforce had fought against the AAV and the right wing Christlichen Trade Union[18].

"The problems in the Ruhr are very similar to ours – we have the heavy industry and the docks and they have the coal and the factories. The poverty and conditions in both Hamburg and the Ruhr are the same along with the antagonistic paramilitaries. The Stahlhelm have swastikas on their helmets so they must be affiliated to this new Nazi Party and Adolf Hitler."

He pauses for a moment in deep reflection. "I'm really getting quite concerned about this man who seems to be a dangerous psychopath as far as I can see but people get caught up with his ideas and the backing of his cronies. As for the Nazi Party, do you know that it means the National Socialist Workers' Party? Anyone who wouldn't know how right winged they were, would be fooled into thinking that they were socialists and believed in the rights of the ordinary working man. How wrong can that thought be! I'm also concerned that during the Kapp *Putsch* I hear that in Dortmund swastikas were painted on the shop windows of the Jews."

This really shocked me as such hatred against another race or religion is usually connivance by unpleasant trouble makers and the start of a policy to target and blame others for everyone's woes. I stated my concerns to Rudolf.

"Yes I know Ernst. The situation is definitely deteriorating and is masking what is really going on. These thugs even attack people on the streets who look like they are Jewish. I really don't like how things are turning so nasty. If we would only have succeeded in the 1918 attempted revolution, things would be so different by now."

To our relief, after a long spell of unemployment Rudolf finally finds work at the Speditions factory at the shipping company Hapag as a skilled metal worker. At least he will be earning some money again.

Since he has been back, he hasn't wasted much time in contacting his old friends and making some new ones. He has

---

[18] Right-wing trade union

become friends with Ernst Thälmann[19] and Edgar André[20] who I knew were political leaders of the left. This is probably where Rudolf met Edgar André way back in 1918 as Edgar was Chairman of the unemployed dock workers in the port. Also he knew Fiete Schulze[21]. Rudolf seems even more determined not to take a back seat in the future of our country. He would not be my brother if he accepted the current situation. I am proud to be his brother as he isn't prepared to be bullied into accepting the deteriorating state of affairs but I cannot help but worry what will happen to him – he is becoming more outspoken. The particular circle of friends he now spends all his time seeing will, I know, be trying to stop our country self-destructing. There are too many people in high positions who were never replaced after the war and who seem to be trying to start another world war, never having accepted defeat in 1918.

---

[19] Ernst Thälman – arrested 1933, held in solitary confinement for 11 years and then shot in Buchenwald Concentration Camp 18th August 1944. International Brigade Battalion named in his honour

[20] Edgar André – arrested 1933 and beheaded on 4th November 1936. International Brigade Battalion named in his honour

[21] Fiete Schulz – on 06.06.1935 beheaded with an axe

CHAPTER 7

1922 – 1924

Ernst's Story

"We must never give up our fight" remarks my brother again. It's so difficult for him not to keep reminding me and I know that he is not just pushing me to do more. It's a way for him to try to come to terms with the ceaseless disputes and the frustration of never ending injustices. He never talks to anyone else like this as he is always showing self-control and good judgement but at times he needs to let off steam to someone he can trust so I sit down and listen to him.

"Now that these Freikorps seem to be disbanding, the men are just transferring their loyalties to the Stahlhelm[22] so they are our future threat. Did you know that between 1919 and 1922 there have been 376 *prominent* politicians assassinated but it has been estimated that about 35,600 people have been murdered?"

I'm horrified at hearing this information. I knew that there had been many people slaughtered for their beliefs, but so many leading politicians let alone the thousands of ordinary citizens meeting their end in such a way makes me shudder. The aim of the Freikorps, the Stahlhelm and other such organisations is to fight left wing socialists and encourage the nation to return to a monarchy with imperialist ideas. We do not want this to happen at any cost

During this time a campaign is going on which is known as the "white terror". These are terror attacks and assassinations in Hamburg led by right wing organisations such as the Stahlhelm. In 1922 a new law comes into effect to punish the assailants but to my

---

[22] A rival right wing paramilitary army to the Freikorps. It was set up in Dec 1918 to hide troop numbers with the "disbanding of the army after the Treaty of Versailles.

disgust, the German judiciary have right wing tendencies so there are only harsh punishments given to any left wing person who fights against this tyranny. No death penalty seems to be given to any right wing extremist but to people who have left wing tendencies are metered out severe punishment even though the majority of the terrorism and violence is by right wing groups.

"Perhaps we should start organising some form of protection for our leaders otherwise we won't have any left". Rudolf remarks to me one day. It's certainly something Rudolf could arrange with his abilities.

Finally the last of our siblings is about to step out into the big wide world when after Easter Werner starts school. It is a momentous day for Mama as well leaving the security of Mama's "apron strings". Mind you although he is over six years old, he still looks such a weak child due to all the poverty and malnutrition we've suffered. His face is thin and gaunt and his legs spindly and of course he has a limp because of his knee problems. Despite this, he never complains and although he is shy he has such determination to survive.

"He certainly is a Stender" I said to Lotte as she busily organises his clothes ready for the next day. We all feel really proud of his stoicism and he has Mama's lovely smile. Werner is always so pleased to see all his big brothers as we return from a day's work and Lotte is his special sister. We mustn't let him down as he needs some decent food and living conditions to strengthen him.

As I ponder about Werner, I realise that due to our financial plight, my parents have never had an official portrait photo of him. We shall have to put that right as all we have is a small picture taken of him whilst he was with a group of fellow children when recuperating on the island of Silt by the North Sea and another when he was a baby with Lotte. I went to talk to Mama about having one taken of him. I can see she is also keen on this idea but says

"I've also been thinking how nice it would be to have a picture taken of Werner. Things are never quite that straight forward though Ernst. It's the cost which is the problem" she answers.

"Rudolf and I wouldn't mind contributing a bit so perhaps we can get one done so we will have a record of him when he's still a youngster".

"That's really a lovely thought Ernst. Thank you for offering and yes I will accept your help. The next problem is that Werner is so shy so he will never pose properly. Werner's never seen photos being taken so he might not understand that he has to stand still for a little while."

"Max will make the difference if we take him too. He's always so much happier when he's around. He absolutely loves that dog and it'll also be nice to have a photo of the animal."

"Excellent idea Ernst" exclaims Mama. She hurriedly arranges for the man at the studio to take a photo of him so now we have a lovely photo of our little Werner. Studying the picture of him highlights how thin poor Werner is, but I'm determined this will change as soon as this terrible period in our history is over.

As expected the Reparation Commission reports in January 1923 that the Germans have deliberately defaulted over the agreed coal deliveries. This is another excuse for the French and Belgian troops to occupy the Ruhr and ensure that deliveries are made. The humiliation we have to endure with this happening to our country. Thank goodness Rudolf is no longer there.

The German government and the citizens are incensed at this invasion. The communist party immediately proclaim a general strike. There is passive resistance from the German population towards the French and Belgian invaders and the Freikorps conduct open sabotage and ambush foreign troops. This distracts from the rivalry which has been carrying on between the different Freikorps units. Until then they have been staging pitched battles in the streets against each other. Chaos spreads throughout Germany and our currency is rapidly collapsing.

"Now look at what has happened – we have a financial crisis to contend with on top of everything else" I say to Rudolf as we meet up that evening. "Germany is in really serious trouble now. In January the American dollar was worth 18,000 marks which is ridiculous and now things have got even worse. The only people who will benefit from this disaster are the landowners with mortgages who can now repay their loans, industrialists who have borrowed money can repay it with the inflated currency and our Government can pay off the war loans. What will happen to the ordinary person – total ruin?"

"Perhaps this is the exact scenario they have been intending in order to rid our country of its debt but it's a disaster for the rest of us" Rudolf answers deep in thought.

We all work as hard as we can and are grateful that we are still in employment. The trouble starts for us as soon as we receive our wages at the end of the week as we join the queues trying to purchase food before the value of the items has gone up beyond our reach due to the inflation. We walk home with thousands of marks but they are valueless by the time we can get to a shop. Max Brauer, Mayor of Altona directs that all city personnel be paid in part with gas meter tokens as these coins do not lose value from inflation.

The government who have been responsible for this political and economic ruin finally resign in August 1923 and the new coalition calls off the passive resistance and resumes reparation payments. The inflation reaches its peak in October 1923 when just one American dollar is worth four billion marks. For some time now, people have been literally starving and this situation makes it even worse. Women and children search for hours for lumps of coal as finding any leftover fuel for heating and cooking often means life or death. It is indescribable how bad existence is for us and our friends. People are paid millions and billions of marks and have to spend it on their way home in order to get bread. Poor Papa is in a hopeless situation as the money given to him one day for cigars or cigarettes becomes worthless overnight. Those who are lucky enough to have money before this started, have invested in property and goods and as a result do not lose everything. Life is intolerable and we really feel that we have no alternative but to take part in mass demonstrations.

One day I arrive home and find Rudolf in our bedroom holding a gun in his hand. He quickly looks up at me with a strange expression on his face.

"For goodness sake Rudolf, be careful"

"I will, I promise".

I have no idea what is going on in his mind and I know that there are times when it is inadvisable to ask. It certainly isn't suicide he's contemplating as it's not in his character.

But I do know that he has become leader of the Ordnerdienster[23] for the Barmbeck and Uhlenhorst district. I know only a little about this organisation. It is for protection of our leaders whom we have found to our cost have become targets for the right wing organisations. I shudder at the risks and danger Rudolf is now putting himself in but he seems fearless when in a military situation. Perhaps it's due to the battles he fought in the Great War. All I know is that I couldn't do this dangerous work. He says that he has been receiving military training which is just as well as I'm sure your mind set has to be completely different from normal.

A general strike and uprising throughout the whole of Germany has been planned. Rudolf disappears for three days as he and his friends fight against the overpowering superior force of the police and the Reich's army in the Hamburg rebellion. Then I hear that our city is the only one on strike as the whole thing has been called off. Why weren't we told that the strike had been cancelled? We have been left without support from others in our country leaving just us to protest at the dire straits our nation's population are in.

I'm beside myself with worry about Rudolf's safety as I know how much preparation and danger he has put himself into. Rudolf and his colleagues' storm the Humbold Police Station in Barmbek very early in the morning and having disarmed the police officers they manage to obtain weapons and ammunition. Hundreds of working men and women led by Ernst Thälmann fell trees then rip up pavements and make barricades out of tree trunks, stone and sand. Edgar André is also there and Fiete Schulze[24] leads the Schiffbek area. Meanwhile many hungry people loot grocery shops. Rudolf and his friends have to disperse eventually when they realise that the general uprising isn't going to happen. Ernst Thälmann has no alternative but goes into hiding for his own safety.

Later the police arrive at our home searching for arms but they

---

[23] Organisation for the protection of left wing leaders from right wing military groups

[24] Fiete Schulze fled to Russia in 1926 but returned to Hamburg in 1932, 16.04.1933 arrested and after long solitary confinement and torture, he was beheaded with an axe on 06.06.1935

cannot find any weapons. They have been hidden in the bottom of the cigar boxes in Papa's shop with the cigars on top but luckily nobody thinks to look there. More weapons are in the bottom of the cigar boxes of Mama's sister's cigar shop in Barmbek. Our family will always support Rudolf and help him as much as we can.

Even Carla Dunkel's father hides a number of arms. He is a good friend to our family and can always be relied upon to help. He even lets Rudolf keep a typewriter in his house which is used for preparing documentation and leaflets for distribution to the general public plus other resistance reports are typed there. Although we belong to different political parties, we are fighting the same evil. It's a shame that others don't follow this example!

All this uncertainty of our future makes me realise that I want to live with the love of my life and that there is no point in waiting as who knows what the outlook will be. With my parents blessing, Anna and I marry in 1923 and through all this misery surrounding us, we find happiness. I leave my home of twenty two years and move with Anna just next door to No 58 Gertigstrasse where some friends let us use a bedroom. Mama and Papa make the kitchen at No 56 available to us until we can eventually afford a place of our own.

It's February 1924 and feels so cold especially with so little fuel to heat our home. We are all suffering from lack of fuel due to the occupation of the Ruhr by the French who are now using the coal as reparation for lack of repayments. The people with little to start with are now living with little food and no heating. I sometimes wonder how much more any of us will be able to take. We are lucky compared to many as at least we have some money coming in to feed us even if we are so cold.

Anna and I arrive at Mama's to prepare what we can for our evening supper. Whilst we are busy organising ourselves, Mama wanders in looking very distraught so I help her to a seat and pull the other chair nearer to her so that I can sit next to her and hold her hand. Anna makes her a hot drink and then after a few sips Mama starts to talk.

"It's Rudolf – the police came a little while ago and arrested him."

"Whatever for" I ask with alarm.

"For his activities in the armed uprising last October and organising the O.D.[25] Oh Ernst – I hear so many people are being arrested – what will become of him?" Mama asks quietly, but really to herself.

I start making enquiries with friends of his and find that twenty three of his male colleagues and three women have also been arrested. The next day according to the local newspaper 1400 people in total have been detained. I can't help feeling anxious for Rudolf as he is a known "agitator" which is the way the imperialist inclined establishment see him.

It seems an eternity to us but in April he is fined 420 marks and released on bail. As we expect, his employers from the docks have no hesitation in dismissing him for taking part in the uprising. We are all so worried about him but we are grateful that the organisation he belongs to pay his fine. On 31st July the courts try to sentence him for taking part in the uprising and organising the O.D. in Barmbek and belonging to an illegal party but the police can find no evidence against him apart from visiting a banned meeting and belonging to an illegal party. Three hundred other people have also been sentenced – all connected with the event. He will have to be careful now as no doubt "his card" is now marked!

One day, Werner came rushing up to me in sheer panic. "Ernst, I've just seen some soldiers arrive in an open top lorry on the corner of Gertigstrasse and Geibelstrasse and they've put those horrible knife things on the top of the rifles".

I rush over to the lounge window where Werner had been sitting. Sure enough, I can see the bayonets on the rifles and the Reichswehr are walking down Geibelstrasse in an intimidating way. I rush downstairs and then casually walk to the corner of the street to see what is going on. Hopefully I'm not attracting attention to myself as I try sauntering over the road to look as though I'm heading towards Mühlenkamp. I can see that the Reichswehr seem to be scattering all the people who had been walking down the street as they try to get out of the soldiers' way. I look in a nearby shop for a few minutes and then return to the flat to speak to Werner.

---

[25] Ordnerdienster – organisation for the protection of left wing leaders from right wing military groups

"You must not go out today Werner. It is not safe. In fact, for the moment I think that you should only go out with one of us."

Werner looks really surprised by this and so I try to explain. "I'm sorry if I sound so strict, but it is just a dangerous time. It will get better" I add putting my arm round him. He looks so upset. "You must be patient as these times will end and then we can all be safe. These men are not very pleasant and you must make sure you do not antagonise them".

I try to be positive but I do not feel it. As for the Geibelstrasse, the road is renowned as having many residents living there with our views and is a target for unpleasant visits from paramilitary units.

Our friend Fritz Lux is also busy at this time building up the Rote Hilfe[26] in Hamburg. At long last we all seem to be more organised and there are many people with our beliefs and yet come from different backgrounds and are not destitute, are well educated and show leadership qualities. It makes us have faith in human nature that not all people are selfish and greedy but they believe in socialism and fair play.

Unfortunately this cannot be said for others. In 1924 General Morgan who is a member of the Allied Supervisory Commission wrote that "Germany is capable of reaching the maximum war production of 1918 within a year and correspondingly have its army on a war footing within the same period of time".

"What on earth are the victors of the Great War doing, knowing all of this and yet not preventing the escalation of arms and paramilitary units? Nothing has changed in the set-up of our country with the same generals and financial backers since the last war and now we almost have the same capabilities to fight again. There are still the same intentions of gaining a greater Germany and yet everyone is more worried about Bolshevism" Rudolf is really

---

[26] Rote Hilfe is a solidarity organisation founded by Wilhelm Pieck and Clara Zetkin aimed at supporting workers families in dire need during the turbulent early years of the Weimar Republic. In addition Rote Hilfe arranged legal support and legal defence for workers who were under indictment for their political activities or views. By mid 1929 the Rote Hilfe had helped nearly 16,000 arrested workers with a legal defence and supported legal rights of another 27,000.

exasperated at the lack of interest with this potential threat. "I reckon that Britain is more alarmed about the situation in Russia and less concerned with Germany's illegal acts".

"I think you are right. I have a nasty feeling that the rest of Europe is hoping that Germany will use the armaments against Russia to defeat the communists. Surely they must realise that Germany will have bigger aims than just heading to the east. They all seem so naïve and I don't know how we can make them understand the dangers" I reply.

Changing the subject Rudolf continues "I've been asked to expand my leadership for the Ordnerdienster to other districts. It will only be for another year. There are other plans afoot when eventually it will be disbanded with the initiation of a stronger unit I believe they'll call it the Rote Frontkämpferbund which will be shortened to RFB."

He's silent for a moment in deep thought. I have no idea what this RFB is but I'm sure he's about to tell me.

"You know my friends Ernst Thälmann and Edgar André?" he continues.

I nod.

"It'll take time for the RFB to be organised properly which is why in the meantime I have to extend my area of leadership of the O.D. but when they're ready I'm going to join this newly formed Rote Frontkämpferbund [RFB] with Ernst and Edgar as I can see that this is the only way that we will get anywhere."

He looks at me and sees I'm waiting for an explanation of this new political or military organisation.

"Ok I'll explain what it is. The RFB will be to protect the working class being attacked by both fascists and the police and no doubt at times we will be pro-active not reactive. We are going to have to be better organised now unless our government wakes up and sees what is actually happening".

"There's hardly any point is there in telling you that what you are about to do will be dangerous. I know that the RFB sounds your speciality but as your brother, I am begging you to be careful" I plead with Rudolf.

Rudolf's face relaxes into a smile at this note of caution. We're so close but so different.

"I appreciate your concerns Ernst but don't worry; I will try not to be rash in my actions. There are a lot of people wanting to stand up for their rights against these bullies and if that means fighting for it we will but many have not had any training. They need leadership and more to the point we must organise ourselves better and help protect our leaders."

In the meantime life in Germany starts to improve due to the Dawes Scheme. There has been dialogue for the withdrawal of the occupied forces in the Ruhr and there has been a renegotiation of the reparation payments. The initial payments will now be less than had been originally agreed and according to our ability to pay in order to help us with our country's recovery. We are now relying on American loans. Meanwhile the mark currency has stabilised thank goodness with the temporary currency of rentenmarks. The rentenmark is exchangeable for bonds in land and industrial plant and of course factories are busy with military rearmaments.

Finally on 30th August 1924 a new currency is introduced and all the old money in circulation is declared worthless. For people like us who have only been able to buy essential foods, many have lost everything including small savings. At least Papa still has goods in his shop so that will help. Poor Papa just stacks in the attic all the old money as it is now totally useless. The rich have been able to put all their money into valuables and property and as a result seem to have got richer. It's such an unfair world.

However with the economy improving now the continual large scale uprisings become rarer but political assassinations continue so Rudolf is kept busy with the OD and we move to our own small flat in Eilbeck.

Werner

By now I have been at school for over two years. I had started at Easter 1922 at 8 a.m. finishing between 12 noon and 2 p.m and then

I do my homework in the afternoons. I found school difficult in the beginning as I was often ill and my shyness has never helped me cope in crowds. I know though that if I am to make the most of my stay at this school in Barmbekerstrasse up until I leave in 1930, I will have to work hard as pupils only progress to the next class when they pass their exams. I certainly do not want to stay down with younger children. When I started school, there were about forty to fifty of us in one class but I have noticed that by the end of a child's allotted time at school, there are usually only fifteen in the top class. Many of the others have been left in the lower classes. It's a hard lesson but I'm determined to keep going up a class each year. The shame of being with younger children keeps me working hard.

Despite all my efforts I can't believe that my favourite teacher canes me for not writing very neatly and then the indignity of writing "lines" upset me so much. I'm not sure how this will help my lack of confidence with being so shy. I hate this particular teacher punishing me like this as I have always tried hard and want to please my teachers. I want to cry but boys don't do that so it is not good keeping on about it. I must just try harder in future.

Away from my lessons I've been looking forward to this autumn of 1924 as we are organising a special celebration for Mama and Papa as it will be their silver wedding anniversary. I have heard that our family used to have wonderful parties and family gatherings. Lotte keeps telling me that we can't have them nowadays as life is very difficult and we don't have much money but this autumn will be different.

One day Lotte tells Mama that she is taking me out for a walk to the Stadtpark. I can't help but look a little surprised as I am big enough to go out by myself now but she has a pent up look of excitement on her face and she tells me that I mustn't make a fuss to Mama. I'm so astonished when we walk into the same photographers who had taken a picture of me and Max. When we get inside, Lotte hands me my best clothes, which she takes out of her bag. It is a sailor's outfit and I love to dress up in these clothes as I only wear it on special occasions. She also has brought her best dress and we quickly change. Just as we came out of the changing room, my three brothers walk into the room, all in their Sunday best clothing.

"We're having a picture done for our parents as this is our anniversary gift to them" Ernst tells me. "But don't tell Mama and Papa what we're doing" he adds in mock sternness.

It's a very proud moment for me as I have never had a family picture taken with me in it. The last one taken of the family was just before I was born, then me with Max and finally there is that embarrassing one with me as a young child in a dress!

I'm bursting with excitement when we return home as I want to say what we've done but I can see the looks on my brother's faces so I take an alternative way of expressing my feelings by going to play with Max. This pleases Max no end and for me it releases my pent up excitement.

It has been worth keeping the secret as it's wonderful to see Mama and Papa's face when they open their gift from us on their anniversary. Mama smiles but strangely she has tears in her eyes. Why would she have tears when she's happy? When I asked her, she just laughs and gives me a hug.

"You have a lot to learn about women Werner" laughs Papa.

All that morning we work hard. Furniture, which includes the bed from the main bedroom, is dismantled and stored in the entrance hall outside the flat. Rudolf has been given the duty of providing the beer so he arranges for a large barrel of the drink to be installed in the hallway just inside our flat entrance.

I will never forget that day as all our relatives and friends came to our home. Rudolf even brought his new girlfriend who is called Käthe Mechaelsen. She lives in Semperstrasse, Winterhude with her parents. I think that she is very nice and she spends some time talking to me which is lovely as some of Rudolf's other girlfriends used to think it below them to speak to such a young brother. Let's hope that Rudolf keeps this girlfriend.

I can't believe it as even the street outside our flat is closed as musicians are in the street playing music for Mama and Papa. Rudolf, Ernst and Hans all play their mandolins and Ernst also plays some music on his violin. Ernst's lovely wife, Anna, produces her guitar and sings folk songs. It is so wonderful hearing them all play music together.

The flat is crowded with people. The main bedroom has been prepared for dancing and the lounge is full of chairs so that people can rest between dances plus take the opportunity to eat some of the wonderful food which Mama and Lotte have made. Early in the evening Papa scoops Mama up from her chair where she has been chatting with her sister and with both of them laughing like teenagers he pulls her into our main bedroom ready for the dancing to start. I didn't even think that parents can be so young and full of life as they dance their way through this wonderful evening. What energy they have and so much giggling between them. It is a day and night I shall remember forever. I don't think that I have seen so much happiness and laughter.

Life is certainly improving for us and I'm now looking forward to the next few years with more food and more celebrations and I've been told by many of the adults that the German economy is booming whatever that means!

1924 – Left to right Werner, Ernst, Lotte, Rudolf, Hans

1922 Werner with Max the dog

CHAPTER 8

1925 & 1926

Ernst's story

We are all so very proud of Rudolf's friend Ernst Thälmann who has become a candidate in 1925 for the German Presidency the election having been called due to the first President Ebert dying of appendicitis. I have my doubts that he will succeed but we are all hopeful as the election date in March arrives. Of course we all vote for him but unfortunately he fails to get elected with Field Marshal Paul von Hindenburg becoming President of Germany. Thälmann works so hard to support socialist ideals for our country at great sacrifice to him.

At long last Rudolf takes the plunge and marries Käthe. She is so good for him and her political beliefs are also left wing, being a shop steward where she works. I know that Käthe will be a great support to Rudolf which is good as he really does need someone who understands the total commitment he has to the improvement of ordinary people's lives.

Employment has now started to improve for the building trade due to investments given to our country, especially from America. It is decided to build more houses on land not far from us, in the eastern part of Winterhude. However, I know that Werner will be upset as this vast piece of land is at present being used as allotments. When he is well enough, Werner disappears over there for long periods of time with his friends to make wigwams with sticks and to play all sorts of games. Although it is lovely being on the outskirts of our city, we know that so many people desperately need housing. Rudolf and I have already experienced this difficulty so something has to be sacrificed.

"I hope the designs will be suitable" says Hans one evening deep in thought. "We have beautiful baroque style buildings for our flats which make the Winterhude area very impressive."

"I know Hans but unemployment is really bad and people need somewhere to live even if the designs are not be perfect" I reply. "Look at our family before Rudolf and I were married – we had to use two flats as they are so small and yet we often accommodated friends or family for weeks or months on end as they had housing problems. Remember when I was first married, having to sleep in a friend's flat and then using Mama's kitchen and toilet? That's hardly a perfect way to start married life. And anyway, I hear that these new places might have bathrooms".

"Hmmm. Now that does sound nice" Lotte mused who always feels it difficult being a young lady in a house full of men and no bathroom she can use. There follows quite a few playful pushes between Rudolf, Hans, Lotte and me. She laughs and adds "A toilet and wash basin is hardly luxury but I suppose we're lucky having an inside toilet". With that we all nod in agreement.

Sure enough, flat roofed flats in the style of Schumacher and Hoeger are built with brick facades, large windows and bath tubs. They do not look that attractive from the outside but when completed I decide to go and look inside them. The buildings cover a vast area, almost a small town in itself and in a completely modern design. They have lovely bright rooms and in the yards of most of the buildings, there are shared wash houses where the new inhabitants can do their laundry. What luxury for them. I have to admit though, that I still prefer the look of Gertigstrasse 56 and the buildings surrounding us.

Werner's story

I hadn't realised how different life can be when our finances become more lucrative and jobs for the adults seem easier to find. I am now feeling quite settled with this new life style having never experienced such a peaceful happy period. So many of my friends' fathers were either killed or maimed in the war and their lives are not as good as mine. It must be awful not having any man in your family able to bring a wage home in order to feed everyone.

Hans, my other brother, seems to be very keen on a girl called Carla Dünkel. I know that the Dünkel family are friends of our family so it all seems very positive but I wonder if she will marry Hans. Whatever is happening with all these young ladies around! Life has been so male dominated in our household apart from Mama and Lotte and now we have Anna, Käthe and possibly Carla. My sisters-in-law are so lovely and always spend time speaking to me.

However I should have known that this happiness will never last. Whilst playing a rough and tumble game in the school playground, I trip and fall over, my friend landing on top of my bad leg and I feel a searing pain ripping through my body. He rolls off me but the damage has been done. He rushes off to find a teacher to help me.

I try to bite back my tears as I arrive at the hospital to have an x-ray. Having had more food available to me lately, I have been feeling so much healthier so I thought my bones are getting stronger. When my parents arrive at the hospital they see my doctor in the ward so they speak to him first. Then Mama walks quickly over to my bedside trying hard to smile and to comfort me, but those wonderful eyes of hers show her real feelings.

"Werner, you've broken your leg just above your bad knee. They've decided to put a support alongside your leg and will cover it all with a plaster cast until the bone has mended. I'm afraid you'll be in bed for some time as they will be tying the bottom of your foot to some weights to stretch your leg while it's mending. It'll take a while but I'm sure it'll be all right in the end."

Oh no, that sounds painful and the thought of being in bed for such a long time sends my morale plummeting. I am determined though not to upset Mama any more than she is at present, so I give her a weak smile and say "I'll be all right Mama, don't worry"

She gives me a big hug and laughs back her tears.

The weeks that follow seem never ending for me and so painful with the weights pulling at my leg. The day has finally come when the weights are removed and they decide to remove the sticky bandages. Oh my, how that hurts. The sticky plaster rips all the hairs off my leg and it feels as though the skin is going to be torn off as well. This time, I cannot hold the tears back. The doctor finally tears off the last bit and I look at my spindly leg. I just have no strength and can hardly move my leg which they tell me is because I have muscle wastage.

They decide to take another x-ray where they discover that the bone has not mended correctly. The doctors decide to strap a leather support round my leg. My friends are pleased to see me but when they see me walking towards them in an awkward gait they decide that I shall now have the nick names of Beng and also Knick. It seems to be forever before I try to play football. It's hard but I will just have to accept that I will never really bend my leg properly ever again.

One day I hear the key in the door turning. I look down the corridor and see Rudolf and Käthe entering. Käthe sees that we are in the kitchen so she gently taps Rudolf on the shoulder and nods in our direction. Rudolf's eyes follow her gaze, smiles broadly at us and walks towards us.

"Käthe and I have an announcement to make" says a very smiley Rudolf.

"Hello Rudolf and Käthe, it's lovely to see you both. Would you like to have a cup of coffee?" says Mama gently chiding Rudolf's impatient behaviour.

"I'm sorry Mama," replied Rudolf looking sheepishly at her. Mama still reprimands all my brothers about manners if she feels they do not behave correctly, but it is always done nicely. He still can't stop himself though as he starts talking rapidly.

"It's just that we are both so excited. Käthe is pregnant and our baby is due in April". He draws in a large breath and smiles from ear to ear looking at each of us. "There I've told you".

"Well that was a very thoughtfully put-together statement Rudolf" laughs Käthe. She then looks anxiously at everyone and says "I hope that you are as happy as we are?"

The excitement is intense after this announcement. There's laughter, hugging and once again Mama's crying. Why does she do this when she is happy?

"Will this make me an uncle?" I ask looking from one adult to another.

Lotte laughs. "Yes Werner and I'll be an Auntie. Oh how wonderful" she adds in her quiet and serene way. As the years progress I've noticed how Lotte has become more like Ernst. She has never been as assertive and as sure of herself as Rudolf nor as self-assured and slightly selfish as Hans. She is sincere, loving and very supportive to us all. I wish a loving, caring person would walk into Lotte's life.

Early in December, Mama says to me "I think that it is about time that we should have a Christmas just as we used to have."

This is a novel idea to me as I have been brought up in difficult times. I don't know what this involves but I am really keen to experience it.

Regardless of some improvement to our finances the Christmas in 1925 will be an extra special one anyway as by then Käthe is getting quite large. By next Christmas, there will be a new member of the Stenders' playing amongst us. The whole family are so pleased for Rudolf and Käthe and seeing Rudolf being so proud that he will soon be a father is lovely for all of us to see.

Christmas Eve arrives and everyone in the family comes over to our place. First we sit down in the evening and eat a fantastic meal which I have been told is the great traditional Christmas dinner people used to eat in the good "old days". Fancy our family eating goose – what luxury. Where's Papa going? He quietly disappears out of the room. I wonder what he is up to. About fifteen minutes later, he comes back and asks us to join him in the upstairs flat. When we arrive, the lounge door which had been locked all day today as well as yesterday is opened by Papa with a flourish. A Christmas tree is in there; so that is why I've not been allowed in there yesterday. Now I know why Papa had slipped away upstairs as it was to light real candles on it. The candles are now burning brightly and underneath the tree presents have been neatly placed. I just can't believe that something as magical as this can happen. The excitement and loud chatter which follows when each of us open our Christmas presents just make the evening perfect.

In the back of my mind though I secretly hope for a musical finale but being so overwhelmed with all this happiness and lots of food, I dare not ask them. I shouldn't have worried as the mandolins are produced and we sing Christmas Carols and folk songs. Anna also plays her guitar. This continues until the early hours of Christmas Day and in the end I cannot keep my eyes open any more but oh what a marvellous happy time.

As the days quieten, I still feel the excitement burning inside me. I still can't believe how magical Christmas was and now I'm told there's more to come as it will soon be New Year's Eve. Mama has been busy making doughnuts and sausages and the men make a drink called punch. At midnight we fling open all the windows to the front of the apartment to see that the roads are crowded with people wearing fancy hats. Fireworks are ignited and it feels as though there is singing in every direction and in between the songs everyone is wishing a "Happy New Year".

Is this what life used to be like before the hard times? If so, I have missed out on so much but I will enjoy every moment now. Yes life is certainly good now.

On 16th April 1926 to everyone's delight, Rudolf and Käthe become proud parents of their son Rudi. As is the tradition in our family, the first born son takes the name Rudolf, the same as his father and Opa (my father). They decide to use the name Rudi though so as not to cause confusion. I am excited for the delighted parents, but close behind their love for Rudi is Mama and Lotte who just can't stop picking up this little bundle of pleasure. Käthe looks exhausted but happy and when I look at Rudolf, I swear that his chest has swollen with pride – a son, a new Stender. Our parents are now grandparents with a handsome grandson. Mama and Papa can't help wearing huge smiles on their faces and telling everyone who stops to talk that they are now Oma and Opa.

Life is so exciting now as one event follows another. My youngest brother Hans marries Carla and on 8th July 1926 and soon after they also become proud parents of a son whom they call Erich. And now our parents have two grandsons. What a big family we have become.

Ernst and Anna have lately been going into the countryside to a large house[27] within woodland in the Harburg area, which they had bought in conjunction with other people with the same political

---

[27] Heideruh is now used for conferences, courses by antifascists and left wing people. Hopefully one day a plaque will be displayed commemorating the bravery of its original owners who used it from the late 1920s as a place to discuss tactics fighting fascism.

beliefs as themselves. Because of the distance from their flat, Ernst takes Anna on his motor bike out to the country. The house is like a commune and is of wooden construction. There is a dormitory upstairs so they stay for weekends. It is a place of sanctuary for them to enjoy in freedom the company of people with like minds; they can talk without fear of spies, go hiking and just relax.

One day Hans and Rudolf decide to visit our parents at the same time and we all sit around the dining table having a cup of coffee. The conversation becomes quite deep and beyond my comprehension but I hear mention of someone called Bredel. Apparently he is an author and Hans works with him at the factory. It is a really weird conversation as Hans makes a remark about Bredel's latest article or book he has written about the uprising in 1923. Both he and Rudolf both agree that Bredel has written something incorrectly about this Hamburg uprising. I wonder what it is. Sometimes I can't help but feel frustrated at adult conversations!

Rudolf's story

It is wonderful to see my baby son start to develop into a little child. He has such curly blond hair and blue eyes and has a wonderful smile charming everybody in his presence. It's so easy to think your own child is very intelligent and I am no different from other fathers being pleased that he seems a bright little boy. Käthe is a good mother to him and so what more can I ask from life. I should be totally content with my family and not be so side-tracked with politics.

However, always in the background is the knowledge that our country is facing great dangers. We don't seem to be gaining enough ground to stop the frightening advance of the thugs who are employed to terrorise the population. Sometimes standing up for our rights is the reason for the assaults but at other times just being without others for protection encourages the violence against us. I can see in Käthe's eyes the look of concern she gives me when I kiss her and Rudi good-bye before I leave to meet my friends in the Red Front Brigade. She knows I have a gun to defend myself and that my instinct to fight for freedom is so strong, that it often overcomes the desire I have for happiness with my lovely family.

I am so lucky to have Käthe, Rudi and also my parents and siblings. Luckily, Käthe believes in the same cause. I wouldn't have pursued our relationship otherwise, as I need support in our marriage and her agreement for me to try and defeat the right wing in our country but equally I know it must be difficult for her. I do have pangs of guilt with the strain she must be going through, but I cannot accept the political situation which seems to worsen the violence against us.

The cold of February enters every nook and cranny of our home despite the fire burning in the kachelofen[28] which is just like the huge one at Mama and Papa's home. Sometimes we have so many warm clothes on that we must look a whole clothes size larger. I shiver and then try and concentrate on reading the newspaper.

"Listen to this Käthe. It says here that Germany has requested membership of the League of Nations."

Käthe wanders over behind me, puts a hand gently on my shoulder and reads the article. When we both finish she sits down in silence for a few minutes and then we start to discuss the arguments for and against this membership. What if the rest of the world considers that the present government is stable and safe enough to have entry within their fold? Do they not see what is happening in Germany? And yet perhaps within the League, there might be more influence to pull Germany into line with the rest of Europe. Brazil is not happy and obstructs the motion finally withdrawing their membership of the League of Nations.

★

I'm annoyed with myself as here I am sitting in a large cell within a prison along with some of my colleagues.

"We should have disappeared out of the way of the police" mumbles one of my colleagues as he paces up and down in our cell."

---

[28] Tiled or porcelain heater

I smile to myself. "Hans they arrived when we were in the thick of fighting the Reichsbanner[29] at the fire station. It's very difficult judging the timing. At least we didn't get caught with all the other skirmishes we have been doing against the Völkischen[30]".

"I know Rudolf. It's nobody's fault but it's frustrating that we have been sentenced to one year's imprisonment. What's going to happen whilst we're stuck in here not being able to stop these organisations from strengthening their positions?"

Some of my other comrades look at each other hearing this and I can feel an uncomfortable restlessness. I need to give confidence to my fellow inmates.

"I'm sure that others continue fighting our cause but as you say, being here in prison was not the intention when we set out that day. Our families, I'm sure, will be supported by our friends and there's the Rote Hilfe so we just have to hold our heads high whilst we are in this place. Just remember that we are not criminals but political prisoners. It's a great difference. Ernst Thälmann[31] is working really hard to try and claim our country's land back from the aristocracy but all we see is the Reichstag favouring the wealthy."

Next minute, we hear the cell door open and we're summoned to the Governor's office. He does not look very pleased so is this good news for us?

"You've just been sentenced for a year's imprisonment and now I have to issue orders for your release. An amnesty has been granted and you are free to go. Let this be a warning to you all so hopefully you will think twice before you behave in such a manner again".

I can see how angry he is but restrain from showing any emotion so as not to antagonise him.

As the main prison gates are slammed shut behind us, we walk in the direction of the nearest railway station. When we walk out of

---

[29] A paramilitary organisation connected with the SPD and possibly trained by the police

[30] A paramilitary organisation belonging to the Völkische Party which is a right winged anti-Semitic party.

[31] Member of the Reichstag and also my friend

sight of the prison buildings, we look at each other, burst into
laughter, slapping each other on the back in delight and I can see the
men starting to hop on and off the kerb and behave in a jubilant
manner as we make our way home. After a lot of joking I try to calm
the situation down as this is beginning to draw attention to our little
group and as such this can lead to either attacks or arrests.

"Well I think we'd better head for our homes and our wives but
we'll meet again next week. We must try and keep a low profile now
and over the next few days". They nod in agreement, clench their
fists in the salute of the RFB and head for their homes to very
surprised and hopefully pleased wives or girlfriends.

★

On 8th September 1926 I bought a newspaper which has headlines
stating that Germany had been finally accepted into the League of
Nations. Spain however has given notice to withdraw from the
League but this hasn't stopped our entry. Let's hope that the League
of Nations is aware of the true situation in this country.

Ernst Thälmann is chairman of the RFB and I am political leader
of the 6th RFB and also from last year, group leader at Hapag. Edgar
André becomes spokesman for the Hamburg jobless workers and
has stepped forward as co-founder and leader of the Wasserkante[32]
branch of the RFB. Edgar's partner Martha Berg also has leanings to
the left so we are an excellent team.

In October 1926 Ernst Thälmann arrives in Hamburg when the
Dockers come out on strike. This time the strike is in support and
empathy with the British miner's strike which started on 1st May
1926 and is still continuing. During this period with the British
miners not working, the owners of our dockyards seize this
opportunity in their greed to make big profits and provide an
alternative supply of coal. As a by-product this has made life difficult
for the British miners whilst out on strike for decent working
conditions and pay. If the British government are getting coal

---

[32] The name used by socialists as an area of Hamburg

elsewhere, why would they try to negotiate with the British miners? With Ernst's help, we are trying to stop strike breaking in solidarity with the British miners. I feel quite proud that so many of us are not selfish but want to help others. It's good that we are uniting our fight against the unfairness of conditions for the working class. If we can continue with this solidarity, hopefully we can overcome the tyrannical power of many wealthy businessmen.

Werner's story

I am really looking forward to this Sunday lunch as I've been told that the whole family is going to be here. Yet another Stender family occasion to enjoy. Mama and Lotte are rushing around and I am shooed out of the kitchen having been given the task of laying the table. That really is a challenge as there is going to be ten of us sitting round the table for the meal. Two babies have also to be accommodated which I shall thoroughly enjoy providing they don't cry too much! It's just so lovely having everyone together. I really adore Anna and Käthe but I have missed having Rudolf and Ernst at home with me.

During the meal, as usual, there's a lot of laughter and teasing with each other. As I feel shy with so many of us in our home, I keep quiet but smile a lot. I always feel warm inside me when we have these gatherings. After the meal has been cleared away, Rudolf and Ernst look at each other with twinkles in their eyes and then Ernst makes an announcement.

"Anna and I have something to tell you all. Anna's pregnant and we should be parents in March next year and yes, Mama and Papa, once again you will be grandparents." There were squeals of delight from Mama and Lotte and a roar of pleasure from the men. I know that our parents have been hoping for this day to come. Ernst and Anna have been married for three years now and we all are sure they will make wonderful parents. My new nephew or niece will surely be musical and have a loving personality just like his or her parents. Will Ernst and Anna break the mould and have a daughter?

Rudolf's story

For me, this Christmas ends up being even better than the previous year. We have our little son, plus Hans' son Erich and now a third is on the way. I don't think that I have ever seen my parents so happy. Mama is never more content than seeing all of us together and soon she will have three lovely little grandchildren to enjoy when Ernst's baby is born. Oh how I love our family. However, being the eldest sibling I'm only too aware of my responsibilities and there will be the situation one day when I will be the head of the family. I dread the awful thought of losing our parents as they are our centre and rock. I will never be as good as Mama and Papa but I will do the best I can. My resistance work might interfere with my duty to our family. I think the only way I can cope with this knowledge is to support and spend as much time as I can with them now as who knows what the future holds. I only hope that my aims do not destroy this happiness as it is too precious.

CHAPTER 9

1927 – 1929

Werner's story

After the New Year I overhear Ernst talking to Mama. I feel guilty listening to the conversation as I know that it is impolite to do such a thing, but as Ernst sounds so worried I can't help but prick my ears in the direction of the chat. I'd missed Ernst's initial few sentences but after a minute or two Mama makes a comment to him showing her concerns that she has noticed how tired Anna looks especially compared to how Käthe was during her pregnancy.

"Anna and I haven't wanted to worry you and Papa but I think that you ought to know that they've discovered that Anna has a serious heart problem. It's only since she's been going to the doctors with her pregnancy check-ups that it has been noticed. She's been complaining of feeling so tired and has to rest far more than normal. Mama, if I'd have known, I certainly wouldn't have risked her health with this pregnancy. We've always wanted a family but she's too precious for me to lose her."

I knew that at this point Mama must have been hugging Ernst as I can hear him quietly crying. I decide to creep away as this is not the time to be discovered listening to the conversation. What is to become of my lovely sister-in-law who is always so loving and thoughtful?

Nothing further is said about Anna's health, but I notice that Mama often pops over to their place carrying food that she has made for them. Anna's family live out in the countryside so Mama is determined to help her in every way she can.

On 11th March 1927, to our great relief, little Gretel is born. I have had no idea when she was due to arrive so I'm outside playing in the cul-de-sac part of the Geibelstrasse which leads down to the canal. One of our neighbours comes over to me and tells me that I am now an uncle. I rush home to hear the news that Anna is very

93

weak but the doctors think that with care, she'll recover quite well. It is at this point that Mama tells me that Anna will need a lot of help probably for the rest of her life as she has a weak heart. I try to show shock and surprise as I don't want her to know that I already know this. I make my mind up there and then that I will be Gretel's big brother (although really her uncle) and support her as she grows up. She won't be as lucky as me and have lots of brothers and a sister, but I'm sure I'll be nearly as good as a real brother.

Apart from becoming the proud father of little Gretel last year, Ernst has joined the Hamburg men and women's choir. He occasionally plays his mandolin and Anna plays her guitar but his other relaxation from the stresses in life is his singing. Whenever possible, Anna tries to accompany him once Gretel is able to be left with us. It's lovely seeing both their relaxed faces when they return after an evening of singing and music. When Ernst goes alone to the choir I understand that afterwards he rushes home to help Anna with Gretel. Mind you when he comes with Gretel to our home he has found that he has to get into the queue as we all want to help. Gretel is adorable and as soon as she hears music playing or anyone singing, she wriggles with pleasure and smiles broadly. Yes I really do think she will be a musician like her parents.

School is really hard for me with all the time I have taken off with my various ailments and injuries, but somehow or other, I still manage to progress up through the classes. The number of pupils in my class is decreasing now as when they fail their exams the students are being left behind. I don't want to fail and disappoint Mama and Papa. I know that they want me to have a decent job so that my living standards will be reasonable when I grow up.

Girls and boys are not allowed to be taught in the same class so once again, with a male orientated family I find mixing with girls socially a little strange. This wretched shyness is such a nuisance. Girls are on one side of the school building and we are on the other. Even at playtimes we are separated by having different playgrounds but it's nice for us boys because we manage to play lots of sport which is good. Even I join in as much as I can as long as I am careful. The fear of breaking my leg sometimes hinders me as I certainly don't want to end up back in hospital.

We have a geography teacher but all the other subjects are taught by our form teacher. This Geography teacher is very nationalistic as he tries to impress on us the danger of "yellow peril". I already have my own opinions on the subject and don't want his indoctrination. It is lucky that I come from such a progressive family where for hours during the evening, I sit with my brothers and parents listening to them talk and at times disagreeing with each other about social and political issues.

To my delight, I have been accepted to take the option, with my parent's permission, of becoming a "free thinker" rather than taking religious instruction. This is all thanks to the Hamburg November 1919 revolution. As from 1st January 1919 it is possible to renounce religion at the age of fourteen years so when I start work I will not be expected to pay subsidies to the church.

As for now about two thirds of the class decide on religious education, but that is not for me. Our alternative lessons consist of practical life instruction on what is right and wrong and how to become a better citizen. The books we read impress me very much. They are about real people, the dangers of alcoholism, the difficulties for people with handicaps, the suffering of families through poverty and also the problems surrounding under-privileged children. I love the discussions we have during these classes and how we can improve life for other people. It is almost like our discussions at home! I think everyone in the class is surprised how knowledgeable I am already but being the shy one at home makes it easier to listen and form my own opinions. I wonder if my friends at school have family discussions like we do.

I also love it when my cousin Kurt Bittkau takes me out canoeing in the canals. Kurt is the son of Tante Meale who lives in Barmbek and she is Mama's sister. He belongs to the Winterhude Fichte Sports Club's Water Division. They have a number of self-built Canadian canoes and kayaks. This club does not have any right wing militants belonging to it so we can just expect to have a wonderful time. We are lucky having so many scenic canals in Hamburg. I've been told that we are second to Amsterdam in the number of bridges crossing canals, but unlike Amsterdam, the canals are not visible from the road except from the bridges. Although Hamburg is a busy city, the canals are so serene and relaxing and we can canoe all the way along them until we finally reach the massive lake in the centre of the city. The only interruption to the quietness is the canal bus. People often use this form of transport rather than buses to get into the city centre. We even use the canal round the back of our home for swimming when it's a hot day.

As Kurt and I enter the Alster, we have a clear view all the way down the lake to the bridge leading to the Inner Alster. There's a rowing and sailing club on the left hand side, but not for people with our income. On the right is a beautiful park where people stroll lazily along the footpath admiring the views. Yes Hamburg is certainly a beautiful city and I am very proud of it.

The canal bus at this point criss-crosses the lake taking passengers to their destinations and finally finishes up in the Inner Alster where at Jungferstieg there is a large platform for passengers to disembark. It is the centre of Hamburg where the Rathaus and the main shops start. Both Kurt and I love to watch life on and surrounding the lake as we canoe towards Jungferstieg. At this point we head for the locks near the Rathaus.

"Do you still feel able to go a bit further Werner" asks Kurt anxiously. He is forever watchful that I don't over tire myself.

"Yes I'm fine" as is my usual answer, although I know that this is not the case.

"O.K. so now we will go through the locks and head for the Elbe".

Oh it is so exciting going through the locks and finally we reach the Elbe. Kurt looks at me with some concern.

"I think that's enough now Werner as it's a long way home".

With some relief I am so pleased that he has made that decision and not me. I'm exhausted but don't want to admit it. We turn round and retrace our route. What a lovely day and how well I slept that night.[33]

Ernst

Little Gretel is growing so well now having left the baby stage and walking beautifully at fourteen months old. When I think back at

---

[33] Kurt contracted typhoid at a later date. It is generally accepted that he caught this illness from the water in the canal. This makes me realise how lucky many of us were not contracting the illness as we used to swim in this water.

how poorly Werner was at her age only through the lack of decent food and warmth and here is our precious little girl progressing so well. Rudi has also grown into a strong boy with those lovely curly locks of blond hair. I can't help thinking that both these youngsters have the wrong head of hair as Gretel's hair has only a slight wave to it. I'm smiling to myself at the thought when Rudolf walks in to our flat.

"What are you smiling about" he asks. "Is it that you've already heard the news?"

"I've heard nothing and anyway, I don't know if you'd like to know what I've been thinking" I answer as I smile at him "so let's hear your news".

"The social democrats have won handsomely in the General Election and the communists have increased their number of seats to fifty four. Edgar André has decided to become a delegate of the Hamburg Citizenry."[34]

"That's really good news" I reply.

"The bad news though is that for the first time the Nazis have managed to get twelve seats in the Reichstag. Is this the start of their rise in popularity?"

By May 1928, life in Germany starts to improve. I just hope that this will continue as a collapse in our economy might increase the Nazi Party's popularity and heaven forbid where that will lead us.

This is Werner's last summer before he starts work. It always has been a special occasion for the youngsters as the school arranges a hiking week for the pupil's last year. For a week during the summer holidays they walk in the countryside during the day and sleep on straw in barns at night. When Werner comes home he is bursting with excitement and hardly able to stop talking. We all laugh at this as Werner is usually a quiet shy boy probably because we are always so busy having discussions amongst ourselves forgetting that we have a youngster in our midst.

This last year though I have been noticing that he is maturing fast. Perhaps soon he will be joining in with our conversations. He

[34] He will remain in the Hamburg Parliament until 1933

is changing and I wonder if it has something to do with this brilliant scheme of a "free thinkers" class which has made him more attentive to our discussions. I really will have to encourage him now to discuss his thoughts. We expect him to bring home a wage soon so he is entitled to input his ideas and opinions.

"Have you seen Rudolf in these last few days?" I ask my parents. It's the first week of May and the weather is beginning to feel warmer but this joyful feeling of warmth is thwarted by lack of contact with Rudolf. It usually means he is "busy" with his activities.

"I haven't" answers an anxious Mama. "You know that he won't talk about what he is doing as he says that it is better we know nothing. Is there a particular reason why you are asking?"

"I am just wondering if he is involved in the annual workers rally in Berlin. I don't know if you have heard how badly things developed there when the police intervened in the march using excessive force." I don't really want to worry them but I know that Mama often puts two and two together so she must have been wondering herself. These May Day marches have been in existence since 1889 but lately there has been more opposition to them.

"I hear that the police began firing into the crowds and have killed 33 people and injured hundreds including many bystanders. The reason why I'm asking is that apparently the RFB are supposed to have been involved but I don't know how much to believe and not having seen Rudolf, I'm worried."

Papa picks up a newspaper he has just bought. "There's an article about the event in this paper. Apparently Hans Litten[35] the lawyer

---

[35] Hans Litten filed an indictment against the Berlin Police President for 33 counts of incitement to commit murder. He lost the case but his objective was to warn about the growing fascism in Germany. He worked to put Nazi terror on display in the hopes it would awaken the public to the threat facing them. Litten later in 1930 subpoenaed Adolf Hitler to appear as a witness to a trial and cross examined him for three hours. Hitler never forgave him and arrested him on the night of the Reichstag fire. Litten spent the rest of his life in Concentration Camps enduring torture and interrogations. After 5 years he was sent to Dachau where he was treated even worse and placed in solitary confinement. He committed suicide on 5th February 1938.

who is connected with the Rote Hilfe[36] had been at the demonstration and had observed the brutal actions of the police. When he went to one man's aid and began writing down names of the people who were injured and also the names of the eye witnesses, he had also been beaten by a policeman even though he had identified himself as a lawyer.

"Let's have a look Papa" I ask him and start reading the article.

"It says that Berlin's Police Superintendent has declared a State of Emergency in the workers districts of Wedding and Neukölln." I gasp at the next section "13,000 police went round brandishing firearms. Well that in itself is a provocative act before taking anything else into account".

Papa nods and I can see how worried he is wondering where Rudolf is. I continue reading.

"Workers have been charged with severe breach of the peace."

"Oh please let Rudolf be safe" Mama mumbles to herself rocking backwards and forwards gently.

Rudolf arrives home a few days later but says nothing. Shortly afterwards the authorities make this demonstration the excuse to make the RFB illegal.

Rudolf's story

1927 was a year when I have to admit feeling so very tired and this continues this year. I don't think that up to now I have ever really thought about my health as I am too busy trying to make our country safer, but now I am beginning to struggle. My work colleagues have also noticed my deterioration and I suppose a few sleepless nights

---

[36] Rote Hilfe is a solidarity organisation founded by Wilhelm Pieck and Clara Zetkin aimed at supporting workers families in dire need during the turbulent early years of the Weimar Republic. In addition Rote Hilfe arranged legal support and legal defence for workers who were under indictment for their political activities or views. By mid-1929 the Rote Hilfe had helped nearly 16,000 arrested workers with a legal defence and supported legal rights of another 27,000.

with Rudi do not help. Käthe tries to get me to relax more and just enjoy family life, but in her heart, she knows that this will never happen. Justice and fairness for all the population of Germany is something I have to achieve with the help of my friends. It's now nearly nine years since we have been trying to improve the life style of the working class and it's been nothing but one long battle.

One evening after work, there's a knock on our door. It is some of my Union colleagues so I ask them in. Käthe is sitting in her chair, having just rocked Rudi off to sleep in her arms as he had been crying with teething pains.

"Rudolf, we have all been worrying about your health lately. You look so exhausted and it isn't with just having a young child in your home. You've taken on too much these last few years and we feel that you need to have a complete rest away from everything. We have made arrangements for you to go to the Caucasus for convalescence for a while" said one of my colleagues.

"I can't do that". I'm astounded at the suggestion. "First of all I can't leave my family and if I did, how will they exist without my income? Then there is our aim for a decent life for the working class without the fear of violence and threats from thugs. We can't stop resisting their intentions otherwise our country will be doomed."

"I know all of this. With regard to your family, I am sure that Käthe would prefer you being well and better able to support them emotionally and physically. We will help her as much as we can. As to our campaigns, what good will you be if you are too exhausted to lead us when the situation worsens again? The strike in the dockyard is over and at the moment we are going through a reasonably good period of our country's existence, albeit because our country is rearming but we all know things will deteriorate again. We will then need you to lead us so please take up this offer and go for a complete rest for a while."

My friend's face breaks into a smile. "And anyway, we really need someone to report back to us on the progress of the new Soviet Union. It's been such a short while since the revolution and it will be helpful to know what is happening over there."

I look at Käthe. She is holding back tears, but she nods in agreement.

"You need to go away for a complete convalescence Rudolf for our sakes as well as everyone else. You are always thinking of other people and never yourself. We need you but not as an exhausted husband and father."

I know that they were all right in what they say but the thought of convalescence doesn't come naturally to me. I am always on the move, never resting and yes I agree with them, never thinking of myself or come to that my poor family. I spend a couple of days thinking it over and finally decide to take this opportunity. I go into work as normal but when I tell my boss where I am going and why, as expected I was duly sacked.

"They've been waiting for this opportunity" I sheepishly tell to Käthe when I arrive home that evening.

A few days later, I leave my family with feelings of guilt in my heart as deep down I'm looking forward to this experience and yet I feel selfish leaving them behind. Half of me wants to change my mind but my restlessness deep with within me makes me kiss my farewells to Käthe and Rudi as I climb aboard the train which will eventually take me to the Caucasus area of the Soviet Union which is an area for people to recuperate from illnesses. Käthe moves back to her parent's place with Rudi as the cost of the rent without any income makes it impossible for her to stay in our old flat. At least she will not be alone.

I can feel my mood lifting along with the feelings of guilt as I look out of the railway carriage window to the landscape before me. As I disembark and settle into my temporary home I just feel pleasure. What a wonderful beautiful land and the people are so friendly and welcoming. For the first time in my life I have no choice but to just relax. The huge sanatorium where I am staying is three storeys high and against my natural instinct I am told to let everything go and regain my sanity and general health. Sitting in wicker basket chairs outside in the warm weather is something I have never done before.

It takes me some time before I can really unwind, but my fellow patients are the same as me, tense and jumpy when we arrive and then very gradually we start to enjoy the peaceful surroundings, knowing that someone isn't going to come round the corner at any moment with a weapon aimed at us. Many fellow residents are struggling to recover from the stresses and strains of the world war and then on arrival home having to cope with trying to get jobs and returning back to normal life. A part of a generation of disturbed, disillusioned and exhausted men are here with me and if I am being honest I have the same problems as them.

I finally feel alive again. My fellow patients notice a spring in my step and we start to gain a superb rapport with each other. I know that my time will be over soon in this wonderful country and I need to return to my homeland. I can't help feeling excited at the thought of seeing my lovely family again and the wonderful city of Hamburg. Will Rudi recognise me and how much will he have grown?

But before I return I have a job to do. My friends in Hamburg have also arranged that I should be their delegate at a R.F.B. conference in the U.S.S.R. Käthe doesn't know this. Some things are best left unsaid.

On arrival at the Haupbahnhof Station, I can't believe my eyes. All my family are waiting for me which I have hoped for, but I can't believe that all my friends and colleagues are there as well to welcome me home. There are so many people wanting to greet me, pat me on the back, and give manly hugs followed by lots of fun and laughter that I feel overwhelmed. They give me a few minutes to hug and kiss my family but after a short while, my family, all laughing, stand back and let the occasion take over. What a wonderful surprise. Even a brass band is playing working class songs and tunes. After a chaotic few minutes, we all rally in a formation to march all the way to Uhlenhorst/Winterhude which to the uninitiated is about an hour's walk away. On arrival at our destination I am given a chair to stand on and I give a short speech. Eventually I make my way home with my family feeling so refreshed and brimming with enthusiasm for the work I will continue to defeat these fascists from threatening ordinary people in their struggle to exist.

After a week of visiting one firm after the other for employment I decide to speak to Käthe at our new home which she has found for us.

"I'm sorry Käthe, I just cannot find a job. It's so frustrating not being able to work in the profession of dreher or on any part of engineering work. I know that I am being black listed and that this time no-one will employ me. I have friends though who will help me as I will now be needed to work for longer hours in the RFB now that I am political leader of the whole of Barmbek. Did you know that there are 450,000 residents here in Barmbek so it's a massive area?"

Käthe nods patiently. I am just so grateful that I have such a wonderful caring wife. She has to put up with such a lot. I know that I am not the easiest of husbands.

"Please be careful Rudolf. Remember you have a family. I know that you have a purpose in life but don't forget us."

"You know that I love you both and want to protect you. I will try not to let you down" is all that I can say.

I find odd jobs to do but word soon gets to the employer about my history and then I'm back out on the street again.

For the purposes of looking innocent, I am now technically employed in the Trade and Economic Department at Derutra which is a Soviet Union/German Trade Organisation. First I'm given the job as a messenger and then as a trade leader. My wages are not in the German currency but in dollars and I earn approximately sixty of them a month.

Life gets even more hectic as I take on leadership of a larger district of Uhlenhorst-Winterhude. Lectures to members of the RFB is an important part of my responsibility on subjects such as capitalism, socialism and answering any queries and thankfully I now have the energy to take all of this on. Where will this eventually lead I keep asking myself but deep down I know.

Our safe little bubble of financial security burst on 7th September 1929 when huge losses occur on the New York Stock Exchange. This hits our country almost immediately as the Americans who had invested so much money in Germany began to call in their short term loans and no further loans were issued. Obviously the end result of all this will be mass unemployment.

Dark clouds are looming over our country and I shiver at the thought of what might happen now.

I'm so busy worrying about Germany's future that sometimes I need Mama to remind me of family affairs and this time I'm amazed at the news that my baby brother, Werner, will have his fourteenth birthday on 21st December. Where has time gone as it seems only a short time ago we were all worrying about my little brother. Now it will be his last Christmas before he leaves school and starts work in the adult world. It seems so strange to think of him as a school leaver but as Ernst has said, he's grown up so much this last year and we must encourage him to express his thoughts as he is the future along with his friends.

There is something else worrying me though at present as there is to be a referendum on 22nd December and this could change the future of Germany. Alfred Hugenberg is leading a right wing contingent of the DNVP[37], the Pan-German League, the Stahlhelm and the Nazi party who are attempting to introduce a law against the so called "enslavement" of the German people. This law by these German nationalists aims to renounce the Treaty of Versailles and make it a criminal offence for German officials to co-operate in the collection of reparations.

This will be disastrous for our country especially when there are renegotiations afoot with the Young Plan[38]. I hate the way that this has given free publicity for the Nazis party and Adolf Hitler has now become a household name. He has access to free propaganda and publicity from the chain of newspapers controlled by Alfred Hugenberg and through him Hitler is able to meet businessmen and industrialists. Some of them, including Thyssens begin supporting the Nazis financially. The Fascist Party start accusing France, the Marxists, Freemasons, Jesuits and the Jews for ruining our "fatherland".

I must try to make my feelings known in some public place to make people think before they vote and what will happen if the referendum goes in favour of this new proposed law.

Christmas is approaching and the shops are beginning to get busy even though so many people are losing their jobs. I'm amazed that so few people are cautious with their money. Have they all

[37] German National People's Party

[38] Agreement between Germany, America, Britain and French expanding loan programme and lowering reparation payments from Treaty of Versailles

forgotten the unemployment queues or is it that it is better to enjoy now before poverty hits them again.

At the Karstadt in Hamburgerstrasse, Barmbek, there is often dancing on the roof garden and people are packed liked sardines in a tin in the toy department determined to see all the new toys, even if they can't afford to buy anything. It might be the only time many children will see train sets all laid out in a superb working display, all the trains rushing along to never ending destinations around the track. The children's huge eyes wide open in wonder at sights they will never see at home.

It seems the ideal place and time to arrange a so called "spontaneous" speech to the public about the dangers of the rise of Nazism and this referendum proposal. My aim is not to frighten the children but to speak to their parents. The children will probably carry on watching the trains. At one of our Red Front meetings, I had organised for some of my group to join me in the shop should there be any physical interruption to my speech.

I arrive at 17.00 in the Karstadt Store and sure enough the toy department is heaving with people looking with fascination at these expensive toys. I know that the majority of people are working class so it is time to put my plan into action. My friends, who are wearing wind jackets, surround the table as I climb on it to gain maximum height.

I know I am a good orator and with all the practice lately, I speak in a loud and clear voice and am gratified that quite a few people stop to listen to me. I start to explain the situation with the intentions of the right wing with the referendum and then amongst other things I warn them of the fascists who are working class. At the end of the speech, I mention that I am in the Red Front Brigade at which point my friends chant "Red Front, Red Front". By now some employees of the Karstadt lean over trying to pull me off the table, but my colleagues push and use their elbows to stop them. Two of the staff then shout at me telling me to leave. We finally sing "The Internationale".

As I jump down from the table two members of staff grab me and despite the furore of my supporters the staff march me towards the lift. It's surprising how many people put their feet out in the hope of trying to trip the employees up so that I can escape. My friends try to rescue me and a scrabble ensues. I manage to get away and start to run down the stairs whilst my friends continue to hinder the two employees. I hear yells of "skin that one" from staff as I run. Another employee catches me when I reach the second floor and he yanks one of my arms backwards. At this point I have no alternative but to stop and am forced to sit on the stairs.

Finally they push me into the office on the first floor and I know that there is now no alternative but to go through the procedures of arrest and punishment. A large man in the office threatens to assault me but I remain calm. There is a glass partition separating us from the rest of the office but everyone must hear his shouting. As a result of his intimidation the demonstrators outside become angrier. The large man demands that I instruct my colleagues to leave. I oblige as I have done all that I had intended to do with my speech.

I turn to my supporters and without a flicker of nerves I say clearly to them "friends go home. It is all finished" and to the Karstadt staff's relief, my friends leave the building. They then charge me with disturbing the peace and causing mischief and then I'm allowed to leave. At least no charges are being made about any assault. Hopefully this little episode might make some people aware of the dangers of fascism. I know that there will be a fine and a possible prison sentence but that will not be until possibly March next year.

What a year we have gone through with the "Bloody May" incident in Berlin and the resultant banning of the Red Front Brigade.

It's good news with regard to the referendum though as only 14.9% of the population voted which is lucky as we have a policy that 50% need to vote before a referendum is accepted. It is indeed fortunate that so few voted as 94.5% of the people who did vote were in favour of the proposal.

Now I will be able to relax and enjoy my Christmas with my family before the court case which will probably involve a custodial sentence. I have a nasty feeling that this festive period will be special for us as it probably is the end of a relatively peaceful period in Germany. What will happen by this time next year? Ernst and I have serious work to do but I hope our family will not suffer with our decision.

Rudolf in RFB uniform

Rudolf

Anna, Gretel & Ernst

The Social Democrat poster was made in 1928 in Berlin and translates as "Mothers – did you give birth to your children for this? Give your signature against another war and building battleships.

Poster from the book "Anschläge – Deutsche Plakate als Dokumente der Zeit 1900-1960"

Rudolf, Käthe & Hans

Rudi

CHAPTER 10

1930

Werner's story

Christmas and the New Year has long since passed and I'm beginning to feel nervous as my life is about to change forever by moving into the adult working world. I had been hoping to work in the printing business but Mama and Papa have been advising me not to venture in that profession due to the insecurities surrounding that trade. Will I get a job at all with so many people becoming unemployed? In Altona 4.3% of the population are already on some sort of unemployment benefit. I try to keep positive though and visit the employment agency. Mama anxiously asks me how I got on.

"I've got no idea Mama. I had to do lots of written tests and then I was given manual tasks to do in different subjects which might be useful in the electrical and engineering industries. The employment agency has told me that they will let me know which career I should follow".

"Well as soon as we hear, we'll try and help you find a suitable job so don't worry" Mama reassures me.

In the meantime I carry on working hard at school hoping my exam results will help me find employment. We finally hear from the employment agency and with help from my parents, I'm extremely lucky to be offered a job as an apprentice coach trimmer for Daimler-Benz and to add to my good fortune, I do not have to travel far to the factory. When I consider the rapidly rising unemployment, I am so grateful to know that I have an apprenticeship which hopefully will lead to good prospects if I work hard. There will be a small amount I can contribute to the housekeeping coffers so life for me is fairly positive which is unlike many others I know.

Easter is approaching with all the promise of warmer weather so my life feels quite positive at the moment. The end of term is approaching and my school life is coming to a close but before I leave, our "free thinkers" class is to have a special celebration in a local public hall. I have really been looking forward to this event even though only about one third of the school year pupils have taken these lessons whilst the other two thirds are soon to be confirmed at Church.

The special weekend arrives and I can't stop feeling the pride which is bursting trying to escape knowing that all my family are at the event. We celebrate the day with music, poetry and speeches.

I try to enjoy the extra two days Easter holidays but I feel so nervous knowing that I am about to become a wage earner. The night before my working life starts I sleep fitfully. In the morning I gulp through my breakfast, give Mama a peck on the cheek and head for the huge factory of Daimler-Benz which is only a few minutes' walk from my home. Although we are in the same building as the car production, our area of work is in a separate section. As Papa says the money will be very low for many years but Daimler-Benz is a good firm and it's marvellous that I am able to go to trade school in Wandsbek one day a week to learn my new career.

The upholstery in these cars is always made with good quality leather and I'm only too aware of the skill needed to make such good quality upholstery. Sometimes my mind wanders to the type of people who will be sitting on these superb leather seats. What is their lifestyle? What are their homes and clothes like? Then being a realist with all their money and home comforts I wonder if they are as lucky as me having such a lovely family?

Now I have more freedom to do things that I want to do. My parents have always been very fair but quite strict with discipline. It's nice to see that they seem to have relaxed a little so I have more time in the evenings and weekends to make new friends. I join a free youth organisation which is perfect for me as during the summer we spend many happy hours hiking through the countryside at weekends. When we stop to rest and eat, we usually start singing, accompanied by guitarists. Despite knowing that we are all probably going to experience the misery of this depression, pleasure can always be found by meeting so many people during our hikes and without spending much if any, money. It's also a great way to form strong friendships and as our political beliefs seem the same as each other, we have many discussions on current events.

Many people who have joined this free youth organisation come from Lichtwarkschule which is one of the top schools near the Stadtpark. There are a good number of progressive teachers in that school[39]. Carl Heinz Rebstock used to attend before becoming an apprentice carpenter and is one of my friends.

Fritz Winzer is the leader of our group within our organisation and above him is Rudolf Lindau[40]. Someone whose company I especially enjoy chatting and laughing with each other is Walter Beyer. He is a year older than me but somehow our friendship has blossomed the moment we met. He has such life in him and a wonderful sense of humour. His political beliefs are the same as mine and I can completely trust him in everything we say to each other. He, like me, is the youngest of five children but there the similarity of our family background ends. Walter's father died in 1915 fighting for our "fatherland" in the Great War, so he never knew him. When his mother died of tuberculosis Walter was still young and so the authorities agreed that he could move in with an uncle. Yet despite all this personal tragedy, he is such a cheerful person. I can't help but be drawn to him. He has also been fortunate to get an apprenticeship in his trade as a coppersmith and also attends trade school but we don't attend the same lessons.

Werner Etter[41] has become my closest friend although he is two years older than me. He makes orthopaedic artificial limbs which is a special skill which is still in great demand due to the casualties of the Great War. As the months pass our friendship becomes stronger

---

[39] When the Nazis came into power, this school was closed down. However not all pupils who attended had a left wing attitude as Chancellor Schmidt was educated there!

[40] Arrested 26.10.1933 at his fiancée's home and then Rudolf beheaded 10th January 1934

[41] Werner Etter beheaded Brandenburg 19th February 1945

and is helped of course by our same socialist views. He's much quieter than the others, very sensitive and yet there is no hesitation in his beliefs that if need be, we must be involved in defeating the rising tide of right wing extremists.

Georg Kehnscherper who is a few months older than me works as an apprentice in an office to the Russian and German Trade Organisation called "Derutra" which is where Rudolf "works". Helmuth Rohwer is a book printer, Siegfried Volkmann, an apprentice copper smelter. All these people amongst many others make up members of our group. Let us hope that we all manage to continue with our various careers. I know I keep saying this but it seems such a tragedy seeing the unemployment figures increasing dramatically. The mood in the city is becoming quite despondent with so many adults desperately looking for work to feed their families. To have a job at all seems a miracle, let alone getting an apprenticeship.

That is why I am so pleased that Rudolf is now being paid a salary at Derutra. When he was sentenced for his illegal speech, he was expelled from the DMV (German Metal Workers Union) and that means he has no possibility of further employment in his trade.

Leaving the cobbled streets behind us for a short while is a wonderful way to forget the poverty in this area. For many of us teenagers we choose to cheer ourselves up by meeting in the Stadtpark to enjoy many different ball games. We are all great believers in complete equality of the sexes and these games are a way to forget the worldly problems and have fun without spending money.

At the end of the summer, my easy walk to work ends. The Daimler-Benz site is relocated to a completely different area which is more suitable for car production. It does not suit me though as it means a long hard cycle ride in all types of weather. The new factory premises are now past Dulsberg to Wandsbek which is about forty-five minutes cycling distance. My boss who lives near me uses the tram and arrives looking far more presentable and smart as I often look very dishevelled in the bad weather. My journey though costs me nothing and that is very important with my low wages.

At long last my dream for Lotte finally becomes a reality when she finds someone really nice. I can see that they love each other but unfortunately his name is Hans. Will this cause confusion with my brother Hans and silly jokes at the misunderstandings! For me, it is worthwhile to see my special sister happy and on 26th December 1930 Lotte becomes Frau Wiemann. I'm so pleased the year is ending on such a high note for us.

Rudolf's story

Life for me never runs smoothly let alone normally. I cannot accept how our country is developing so I must suffer the consequences of my actions. On the afternoon of 23rd January, I make a statement about the disruption I caused along with my speech in the department store on 22nd December last year. I try to make it sound as though the event had not been planned but was a spur of the moment idea, the speech being a rather harmless exercise.

With a sigh of relief I hear on 25th February that no charges of physical violence will be made as nothing can be proved. Since the witnesses do not wish to press charges against me I know that my sentence might not be as bad as I had first feared even though the judge will know my past history of arrests.

On 12th March I am fined 400 Reich Marks for participation in a forbidden party, that is the RFB and for taking part in an inappropriate meeting. The judge dismisses the court after telling me that I have to go to prison for a month for committing "rough mischief" in the toy department along with several unknown accomplices and proclaiming "down with the fascists, down with traitors who have betrayed the working class".

I know that in truth I am lucky that the judge does not sentence me more harshly. Perhaps he is unable to give me a harsher sentence – who knows. Perhaps the courts are aware of my other activities and just want to sentence me for something however minor. Käthe is quiet and seems deep in thought. I have to say that I cannot really blame her reaction. She worries, I know, about our country's future with fascism becoming stronger. I wonder though how much strain I am putting her through being aware that I will not stop fighting against the threat of a fascist tyranny taking over.

My sentence will start on 2nd May but I will have to start paying the fine of twelve Reich Marks a month as from 24th March.

In the spring, the coalition Government collapses. The unemployment situation is seriously increasing so the benefit system is being put under strain. President Hindenberg then appoints the catholic centre leader Heinrich Brüning as chancellor but for now I have to cast my mind away from politics as I kiss Käthe and Rudi goodbye and make my way to the prison.

It's my second experience of prison life and I have this feeling that it won't be the last time. I'm marched to my cell which I find is already occupied by a youth. I soon find out that I am the only political prisoner or at least I have still not met any other political prisoner here. It is an eye opener, meeting people who are dishonest or a more polite way of putting it they have made an "incorrect judgement". Whatever I have been doing these last years, it has always been because of my honest belief in making Germany a safer and fairer place to live for its people. Some of the people here in prison with me just do not seem to understand the difference but I should in reality expect the clientele here to be dishonest; after all, it is a prison.

Regardless of this I must make use of my time here in a positive way. I have nothing to organise other than just getting through each day. In a way it's cathartic as I work for eight hours demolishing an old prison and read for two to three hours before going to sleep. The books in the prison are not to my taste though as I would rather read social history, political books or autobiographies. I still haven't found one book about the working class movement. Reading is quite difficult with my bad eye sight so I'll have to write and ask Käthe to bring my spectacles when she visits next. I'm pleased that she hopes to see me on our visiting day which is on Sundays. I must remember to apply for a visitors permit though.

The food is terrible and I hate eating the dry bread. Hopefully Käthe will bring 5 RMarks with her so that I can buy sausage and butter to go with the bread. If she is not permitted to visit, I will do

more demolition work, eat at noon and not eat the bread during the
evening as dry bread makes my stomach feel uncomfortable.

I wonder how my Opa survived when he was arrested several
times during the mid-1800s and what he would have thought of his
grandson ending up in prison fighting for social justice etc just like
him. He was only a basket weaver from Bornhöved, Schleswig
Holstein which is about 25 km south west of Kiel so to lose his
income must have left my father and his siblings with his mother in
dire straits. Now its over one hundred years later and we are still
fighting for better conditions for the working class.

Life becomes routine here but that is to change. On 12th May a
prison officer came into my cell before I had started my day's work.

"I've been given instructions to arrange for your immediate
release and to return in three days. Your wife has contacted us to say
that there has been a fire at your flat and your home has been
destroyed. You need to go and help her clear what remains of your
personal items and to settle her and your son somewhere else."

I feel sick hearing this piece of news. My poor family have been
put in such danger. Are they all right and more to the point, are they
safe from harm now as I don't know what caused this fire. I leave the
prison at midday and hurry home. Sure enough our home has been
destroyed by fire and there standing in the middle of our blackened
lounge is Käthe, her tear stained face looking around in disbelief at what
has happened. She sees me in the doorway and I walk quickly over to
her and give her a gentle hug. She sobs quietly against my chest and all
I can do is hold her tightly against me rocking her gently to and fro.

Eventually she stops crying and I feel I can now ask her
questions, the first being if Rudi is safe.

"He's all right. He's upset that he can't come home, but he's at
my parents. Rudolf, someone must have set fire to our home. Rudi
and I had only been gone for an hour as I needed to go and buy some
food and when we came back, our home was in flames. One of the
neighbours said that she had heard some people in the flat but
thought it was us."

"I want you to continue staying with your parents Käthe. It's not
safe for you and Rudi to be alone any more. This might have been

just an accident, but it could also be a warning from our enemies. Promise me that you will keep yourselves safe whilst I am away."

She nods and tightly holds on to me. Things are now getting very unpleasant due to my anti-fascist beliefs. What have I done putting my family at risk? So many colleagues have received similar treatment and some have lost their lives through these wretched thugs. I help Käthe move what little of our home remains and make sure that she is safe and settled with her parents and as agreed, I return to prison on 15th May. This time I am not so accepting being locked up as I want to be home to protect my family. My parents have also promised to help Käthe in any way they can until I return home.

At long last 5th June arrives but the day seems never ending. I need to go to Käthe's parent's home and find my family to check that they are all right. Finally at 15.45 I leave prison and head for Semperstrasse. There waiting for me is my beautiful son full of smiles and my ever loving and supporting Käthe. She is such a special person but perhaps one day she will have to make a choice whether it is worth risking the life of our son for what we both believe in. I just hope it never comes to that decision as I do love them both.

By now there are three million people unemployed. Whenever is this going to stop?

Not only is our economy in ruins but as I suspected might happen, extreme views are strengthening and becoming radicalized. The Nazis party and Hitler's S A henchmen seem to be blossoming in a frightening way.

It is worrying seeing democracy slipping away from us. It seems that whenever any unpleasant laws or reforms are put forward by the Chancellor and the government refuses to vote in the law, Brüning just appeals to the President to use this Article 48 to overrule parliament. This decree should only be used when security and public order are seriously at threat but is now being misused.

For some reason Brüning fears inflation and budget deficits more than unemployment. He is not spending to stimulate the economy and create jobs but he wants to increase taxes, implement wage cuts and reduce spending on things such as assistance in benefits especially unemployment benefits as there are so many jobless people now. Needless to say Brüning is becoming exceedingly unpopular amongst the lower and middle classes as so many people are desperate for help. When his financial plan is rejected by the Reichstag he uses the Article 48 emergency decree to pass it. The social democrats try and succeed to suspend the decree in the Reichstag. The result is Brüning asks the President to dissolve the Reichstag. It's absolutely ridiculous as where has democracy gone?

Unemployment is now around three million and to my disgust the Nazi party receive 6.5 million votes at the next election in September 1930 which means that they now have 107 seats. Hitler's main policies are nationalism, anti-bolshevism, anti-Semitism and the survival of the fittest with complete disregard for the rights of the individual.

Hitler reappoints Röhm to lead the SA under his command as he needs them to get ready for civil war in Germany. Röhm accepts and I hear will take up his position in January next year but this gives us warning of the future threat of violence and the dissolution of democracy. We in the Red Front have little choice now but to prepare for military action to fight this horrendous threat to our civil liberty.

The Nazis are now more provocative in their actions, organising demonstrations and marches using men wearing their Stalhelm and S A uniforms. The Stalhelm have been banned and are starting to merge into the S A. They're antagonising many people by marching provocatively through our working class districts. To counteract this threat, we march in our Red Front uniforms in defiance of their actions. Some members join us from the Iron Front[42].

I feel more and more disturbed by the increase in the support of the fascists so our group decide that we really should not waste any more time but to complete arming ourselves against them. If they take over power, then our country is doomed and many people will die. Due to my knowledge of weapons from the Great War, they decide that I should take control of the armaments. There are still old weapons around from that period which were never surrendered

---

[42] Which is the military wing of the Social Democratic Party

up to the authorities so that is one source which I can use. Some are old machine guns and are heavy but this is trivia when compared to the other weapons we've managed to get from other contacts and include ones we have taken when we stormed barracks and police stations and since then they have been hidden for safety.

The old weapons though need work done to them but my colleague called Otto Borstelman is quite good at repairing them. I am always able to supply the ammunition from one of my sources. It's all a bit "Heath Robinson" but we need to be prepared as soon as possible to fight these Nazis.

This awful year is coming to an end and I hope 1931 will be the start of great improvements to all our lives. I am startled from my thoughts by a knock on my apartment door. I open the door and to my surprise Ernst is standing alone in the corridor. I invite him in and we chat for a while. He tries to be cheerful and sociable but I can see that there is something on his mind. He is obviously in need of a brotherly talk. Käthe knows Ernst almost as well as me, so she discreetly makes excuses and retreats to the kitchen.

As soon as Käthe shuts the door, Ernst pauses, takes a deep breath and starts talking seriously to me.

"Anna and I have been discussing the political situation and like you, we think that the Nazis are getting too strong. Something has to be done about this now but it really is no good me joining you in what you and your friends are doing. It isn't in me at all and you know that."

"We all have different specialities and skills Ernst. I am not proud that mine is military but our "fatherland" gave me these skills fighting in the Great War. I'm not frightened of taking part in demonstrations, giving speeches and lectures and, if need be, to defend myself or others but I agree with you, your character is so different from mine. Ernst you know how close we are as brothers and we have exactly the same political beliefs, but I know you will never find it easy to be a military man."

I study his face and ask him very quietly "I can see you've thought this through so what is your next step?"

"Well I think my skills might be useful with persuading people to help us and to extract information from those who are working in sensitive positions or are in firms who are helping the Nazis. I have many contacts through various organisations and groups I belong to".

"Ah, you mean you may be able to help with espionage or spying?" I exclaim with a smile.

"I don't like those words as it sounds sinister and disloyal to our country, but yes if that is what I have to do to defeat the Nazis, it'll be my part in their destruction".

"At the beginning of this conversation you mentioned Anna. Is she happy with what you want to do because if you are caught, the prognosis is not at all good for your survival?"

"I know it isn't" sighs Ernst "but there comes a point when our lives are not as important as the future of Germany – we must succeed in the downfall of the fascists in order to give the people of Germany the chance to live their lives in peace."

I shake Ernst's hand firmly and looking straight into his eyes added "to the bitter end or wherever this leads us. Ernst you know that we must keep each other informed as to what we're doing. This way we can help each other as much as possible. We know that we can trust each other with our lives but of course we must never give each other the names of our contacts should either of us be arrested or tortured".

"I know" replies Ernst and with that he leaves my flat.

Gretel, Erich and Mama at the Steilshoop Allotments, Hamburg
(Photo courtesy of Holger Witt, Gretel's son)

Ernst
(Photo courtesy of Holger Witt, Gretel's son)

CHAPTER 11

1931

Ernst's story

Although I have been an active member of the trade union movement and left wing organisations, this is the first time I've decided to do something so dangerous. I know that if I am caught, this will be considered high treason against the state. But what else can I do? Our country is heading rapidly towards a fascist dictatorship and another war. How can I let the country I love, along with its citizens be caught up with these ideals. Unemployment is rapidly increasing with the financial crisis making poverty and hunger rife and this will certainly lead to a politically unstable situation. To walk through the working class districts to observe how people are surviving would consequently make anyone with a conscience weep.

I am so grateful that I have so much love and support in my life with Anna. She is my soul mate and then there's our Gretel, our most treasured daughter. To think I nearly lost both of them during the pregnancy and Gretel's birth. I can feel myself fighting back tears as I think of the rest of my family who are so special to me but all this happiness will evaporate if we end up with the fascists in power.

It is essential that I have to be careful how I prepare for resistance work. Rudolf has his route to follow and it suits him perfectly, but my next step needs me to be very cautious. Do I try to organise this alone and recruit people who I can trust? Rudolf is one step ahead of me on this predicament as I discover he had been busy notifying people in the right places of my intentions. Two very committed antifascists make a point of contacting me very soon after my conversation with Rudolf.Wilhelm Bahnik[43] also known as "Martin" and Fritz Lux[44] are both pleased to hear that I have decided to take a serious role in the resistance. Wilhelm is about thirty-one years old with shiny black hair. He is medium sized in stature but very strongly built and his features are certainly not soft in appearance. He is a very determined character and I know through Rudolf, that he is the leader of the BB apparat[45] for the whole of Germany and is based, I think, in Berlin. He had received training from abroad for this role and previously had been in prison for treason. These "apparats" are the different antifascist resistance groups and the initials denote their speciality. Wilhelm used two pseudonyms of "Fritz" and "der Dicke"[46].

Fritz Lux is an acquaintance as he is a dockyard worker by trade and was involved with Rudolf in the October 1923 uprising in Hamburg. Being a great organizer and orator, he was elected in 1928 to become a member of the Hamburg parliament. He's thirty-nine years old and has enormous knowledge and experience which he is now putting to good use as a leader of the resistance in Hamburg. I believe he is also still in regular contact with Rudolf.

Both Wilhelm and Fritz seem very pleased that I am now prepared to help them in collating useful information which can be used against the fascists. With Rudolf's support I begin to feel more confident, but I know it is imperative to act with great caution in order not to be discovered. Rudolf tries to reassure me.

---

[43] Wilhelm Bahnik continued to work in the resistance in Germany and escaped in 1935 to Russia where his family were. In 1936 he became an Officer in the Edgar André Battalion of the XI International Brigade in Spain. He was wounded in 1938 and died later of these wounds.

[44] Fritz Lux was arrested 25th July 1933 and committed suicide on 6th November 1933 in Fuhlsbüttel Concentration Camp after many months of terrible torture. This is sometimes the only way of avoiding betraying the names of colleagues

[45] I believe that the BB apparat was the division who were reporting abroad on all the operations being carried out and relaying information discovered by the operatives

[46] Although Wilhelm Bahnik is said to have been "der Dicke" in the later trials, I note that also in the SAPMO archives in Berlin "Der Dicke" is Willy Goldberg

"You are the quiet non-gregarious member of our family Ernst which hopefully will mean that you will not be on anyone's list of "the ones to watch".

I ponder on the pseudonym to use so as not to be identified should anyone be arrested. My mind wanders to what Mama would think about the decision I have put at risk so much by joining the resistance. Then it comes to me in a blinding flash. I would use "August" as my name in memory of my mother "Augusta" who is the centre and strength in our family. "Gerd" is another name I think I'll use. I've been told that future contacts will also have cover names. It is essential that as few people as possible should know each other's real name. My great friend Rudi Dassau[47] agrees to act as my courier and starts using the names "Munki" and "Max". I can't stop smiling when Gretel calls Rudi "Munki" when he calls at our flat. A few more of my friends decide to work for the resistance, and although these people still come to my flat socially, all future contacts will be kept separate from my home life. Immediately stopping old friends from coming to visit will look suspicious. The transition from my previous life to this covert one will be difficult at first.

A lot of my new contacts had joined the group of antifascists in 1928 and 1929 when our country reached such a desperate situation economically and socially. They had made the decision, like me, that we can no longer be passive and accept our democracy being obliterated in favour of power being given to the extreme right wing which I fear would lead to a second world war. It's upsetting seeing the deteriorating situation of Germany with some families in a desperate state with no employment and little food.

Our banks start to collapse and many businesses are going bankrupt. In March Heinrich Bruning our chancellor instead of investing in building projects etc, decides to put up taxes and implement wage cuts. How on earth is that going to help any of those who are struggling?

---

[47] Robert Dassau otherwise known as Rudi Dassau escaped in Spring 1934 and is known to have been in Denmark working for the Resistance from 1935-1940. In April 1940 Germany invaded Denmark and the Gestapo found and arrested Rudi. He spent the rest of the war in prison and afterwards returned to Denmark.

Many of my new friends meet at the Hamburg "Arbeiter Theater" which is a branch of the Workers Theatre Federation of Germany. It is an excellent opportunity for us to talk without the authorities infiltrating our set up or attempting stopping us getting together to discuss future strategy.

Franz Jacob[48] who is one of our resistance leaders makes good use of the "Arbeiter Theatre" group. There are so many people like him who attend, that it "feeds" our enthusiasm and the hope that we can really do something to stop the fascists.

"I have a very useful contact for you" said Wilhelm Bahnik when we met one day at a prearranged meeting place.

"Fritz Lux introduced him to me as he had discovered that this individual can obtain useful information regarding China and Japan."

"What's this man's name" I ask Wilhelm.

"Wolfgang Koglin" he replies quietly. "I have been paying him for this information which he "liberates" from the firm Carlowitz. It helps him survive in this terrible financial climate and also helps "oil the water" so to speak."

"Ah, I've heard rumours about our country's connection with China and Japan" I answer deep in thought. "But I know that officially the Foreign Ministry has urged for a policy of neutrality in East Asia".

Wilhelm smiles cynically at my comment. "Do you honestly think that the industrialists are carrying out that policy? They're only interested in stockpiling raw materials and in particular militarily important materials such as tungsten and antimony which China can supply to this country in bulk. I'm sure I don't have to say what that means Ernst."

I nod. Without doubt our future work will be extremely dangerous as discovery of what we are doing will mean an unpleasant visit to the police headquarters and then… I shudder at the thought as imprisonment will mean leaving my family without support or protection from fascist extremists. Our actions will also be considered as High Treason against the State so punishment will be very harsh.

---

[48] Franz Jacob was beheaded on 18th September 1944 at Brandbenburg

"When can I meet this Koglin chap" I ask, showing as much confidence as I can muster.

"I have asked Fritz Lux to arrange a meeting for the three of you. As I say, Koglin has already been supplying information to us. We now need you to be his contact and develop a structure for collating relevant information which can be abstracted from other industries and businesses. Who knows what might be useful for us, but the more we know, the more we can use against our enemies.

A few days later, Fritz Lux and I arrive at the Alster Café on the corner of Esplanade and Lombardsbrucke in the centre of Hamburg. It is by the bridge separating the Inner and Outer Alster. This sturdily constructed building was probably built about the beginning of this century or the end of the last, with half the building being along one road and the other at a rectangle along the next street. The restaurant/café is on the ground floor along both roads and the large windows lets in plenty of light. It is an excellent place to meet a new contact as the café is so large and frequented by many people. We should not bring attention to ourselves.

Fritz's eyes scan the café which by now is full of customers but he does this whilst casually chatting to me. He must have practised this technique many times as he looks so convincing. He sees Wolfgang Koglin sitting at a table drinking a cup of coffee so we saunter through the bustling room meandering between the many tables. When we reach Wolfgang we stop and Fritz introduces me to him. Wolfgang gives a nod in acknowledgement but looks apprehensively at me. He asks me for the prearranged password which I give him. I soon discover that Wolfgang will indeed be a very useful contact and he agrees to supply either written or verbal reports every two to four weeks on developments taking place in China, including economic details and information about supplies going to and from China with, it seems the agreement of the ruling government of Chiang Kai-shek. Wolfgang also can supply us with activities of the communist rebellion movements.

When I eventually arrive home, I give Anna and Gretel their usual kiss and hug trying to act as my day has been "normal". Anna smiles sweetly in her usual welcoming but quiet manner.

"How was your day?" she asks.

"Oh, you know the usual" is my reply shrugging nonchalantly, but we both know that my life is now anything else but "usual".

"Your father has asked if you and Rudolf wouldn't mind going to see him this evening as he has something he wants to discuss with you".

I sigh deeply. I feel so exhausted that all I want is to stay at home with Anna and Gretel. Surely Papa can't have heard that Rudolf and I are involved in dangerous work. No they can't have that knowledge as our parents have no real idea of our private lives or if we are part of the resistance movement. They must know though that we would not be accepting the political situation and Rudolf has only just come out of prison for incitement against the state.

"All right, I'll go now via Rudolf's place so that we can go together. Hopefully I won't be long". I turn round and quickly pick up Gretel and throw her gently in the air, catching her carefully and then repeating the move. Gretel giggles and squeals in pleasure and there follows a gentle scolding by Anna for exciting Gretel too much just as she is getting her ready for bed.

We laugh at each other having made a pretend sorrowful face at such a scolding, give them both a peck on the cheek and leave for Rudolf's flat. When we finally arrive at Gertigstrasse 56 we let ourselves in, only to find Lotte sitting in the lounge with Mama and Papa.

"Ah thank you for coming at such short notice" says Mama with her usual welcoming smile.

"What's happened" asks Rudolf after greeting the three of them.

"Where's Werner" I ask anxiously. I always have a terrible fear that he'll fall over and break another bone even though he is almost an adult now.

"He's out this evening with his friends which is an ideal opportunity for us to discuss Werner's increasing commitment to fighting fascism" says Papa.

"I presume from what you are saying to us, that he has started to do more than just attend meetings?" I ask.

Papa nods and looks so worried and miserable. We have been so wrapped up with our lives that I've been oblivious to how our parents are feeling. I feel sorry for him and also guilty as he has himself been through so much in his lifetime and then seen Rudolf becoming more involved in resistance work. He would really be concerned if he had any idea as to the full extent I had now become involved. He really thinks that Rudolf is the only one in real danger. And now his much treasured youngest son seems destined to follow in our footsteps. Poor Papa.

"What has he said to you Papa?" Rudolf asks.

"He won't say much as he doesn't want to worry me, but I know that he goes to many meetings about the problems caused by right wing elements. I'm sure that he's beginning to do more than just sit and listen. I feel that I cannot talk to him about my concerns as I don't want to argue with him. I agree that these people must be stopped but Werner is only fifteen years old and too young to be so involved in situations which could lead to violence."

"Papa, he's old enough to go to work, so he's old enough to form his own opinions" replies Rudolf. "He's a sensible boy though and doesn't seem to mix with mindless louts. He's spent all his life listening to us discussing politics and life generally so he's aware of injustices and he has high principles. You should be proud of him."

"Yes but look where that can get you Rudolf" admonishes Papa. "So far you've been lucky at only having two short prison sentences and two fines. Many of your friends have fared far worse. I do approve of your dedication which hasn't prevented me from worrying, but you and Ernst are men now. I know that something must be done as our country is in great danger of the fascist ideals."

I can understand Papa's predicament. Rudolf is extremely proud that his baby brother has finally grown up and wants to join us in our resistance work. Papa on the other hand wants to keep his precious little Werner safe and sound from threats of these right wing thugs. I feel for Papa as Werner has been such a source of joy but also concern with all his health problems and he did "arrive" late in our parent's lives. I try to be conciliatory as I intervene.

"Look Papa, you are right to worry about Werner, but he has too much of the Stender blood in him not to want to do something to help our cause. To be truthful, how on earth are you going to stop him? Chain him to his bed when he gets home from work?"

At this thought, we can't help but laugh.

"Now this is only a suggestion" I continue. "Lotte is closest to Werner. Rather than hearing this from you or Mama, why don't we ask her to speak to him and say that we "the family" understand his keenness to take action against the fascists and that we are happy he wants to do this, but whilst he is quite young and has such a lot to learn, can he take a back seat in anything which would cause you concern?"

Mama and Papa look at each other to gauge each other's reaction. After a few minutes, Mama breaks the silence.

"I think Ernst is right Papa. If we forbid Werner to take part in any campaign, then we might find he will carry on regardless and perhaps make some mistakes with serious consequences. I would rather he felt he had our blessing provided that he takes a back seat from anything illegal."

Papa is quiet for a while. I can feel how unhappy he is, but equally Papa can see that he cannot really stop Werner as when he leaves the flat, he has no control over what he will do.

Finally he nods his agreement. Mama then turns to Lotte.

"Lotte are you prepared to talk to Werner for us?"

"Of course I am Mama. I'll stay on this evening until he returns and talk to him tonight."

An air of relief sweeps over all of us. We relax together for a short while having a quick drink and then Rudolf and I leave the flat and head towards our own homes.

"Well, well, our little Werner has finally grown up. What do you really think Ernst" asks Rudolf as we make our way back home by public transport.

"I think Lotte will do a good job and Werner will say all the right things to Lotte who will then put our parents' minds at rest. Werner will then go to his bedroom smiling to himself thinking that the problem has been resolved and knowing him he will continue investigating what he can do with his friends to help the youth wing of the resistance movement."

Rudolf laughs at this. "You know Ernst, I think you are right. He has more of you in him than me. I just cannot be quite so tactful. You never know, when he is older, he might join you in your group."

"Let's hope that by the time he is older, we will have stopped this frightening spiral of events and our country then is out of this Depression before it is too late" I reply.

Rudolf nods in agreement and is quiet for a few minutes. We are both deep in thought about our dear little Werner suddenly growing up in the real world.

"Changing the subject a bit Ernst, isn't it wonderful seeing our lovely sister married and to a man who simply adores her. She seems to have blossomed lately. I've always felt that she has been in the shadows with so many men around all wrapped up with their own lives and now she has a life of her own. I know our parents are really happy for her."

I smile thinking of our Lotte and reply "I shouldn't be surprised if she doesn't have children soon. You know what she's like with our two children and also Hans' Erich".

"Now that would just complete everything just perfectly wouldn't it – Lotte becoming a mother" answers Rudolf shaking my hand. We have just arrived at the point when we part and go our separate ways home. He turns away, lifting an arm waving it in farewell as he walks away. What would I do without this brother of mine? As I start to climb the stairs to our flat I can't help hoping that we will all survive these next few months.

Werner

As I close the door to my bedroom, thoughts are whirling around in my head. Papa and I have been having difficulties lately as I know he is not happy where I go in the evenings. Mama always tries to calm him down when he gets agitated and so life continues.

Now Lotte's "little chat" with me makes me think again about the consequences of my actions on my parent's health when my position in the youth movement is questioned. She has quite surprised me in her quiet but concerned feed-back. Fancy the Stenders having a family conference about me. Until now, I haven't fully understood the extent of how concerned our parents are about my activities. I have just assumed that as Rudolf and Ernst seem involved in some way protesting at the right wing movements, there would be no problems should I follow their example. It's no good just sitting at home moaning about the consequences of these fascist intentions. If we all do that, then Germany has no future. So why should it be problem that I want to help even if I am too young to vote? If we don't stand up for our rights and freedom, no-one will have the opportunity to vote when our time arrived.

Why is Papa stopping me from following Rudolf and Ernst's examples? I can't help feel exasperated and lie on the bed thinking things through. I can't stay angry for long with Papa as in truth I have the feeling that he is really struggling with life. He never talks about his experiences in the Great War and unlike Rudolf being so young, Papa would have felt the loss of lives and the horror of war perhaps more as it seems with age comes more experience of life. Perhaps he understands the consequences of the increased tensions in our country but cannot express his real thoughts. Perhaps I am being thoughtless not appreciating his thought processes but I have so much to do.

I sit up, deep in thought, but then I start to think more positively.

Now come on Werner, this is not like you. Mama and Papa have always treated you as their last special fledgling, so it's no wonder they're worried I reason with myself. I can feel my face muscles relaxing and I then smile to myself lying back on my bed, with my hands stretched behind my head. Well I can see their point of view to a certain extent but as I think of Lotte's words as she explained Rudolf and Ernst's comments, I feel proud they consider their little brother should show interest in politics and the future of our country. I'm sure they know that I would never in a million years only go to meetings and then come home. I will just have to be careful that Mama and Papa never find out. That way, we'll all be happy! I certainly will not tell them that I'm also going round apartments knocking on doors and selling the socialist youth newspapers.

One day I arrive home from work having cycled as quickly as I can but I still feel quite cold from the March winds whipping through my coat. I see Rudolf just stepping out onto the street from our flat having called to visit our parents. My face lights up with pleasure at seeing him as he has been so busy lately that we rarely see each other.

"Hello Rudolf. What a lovely surprise to see you. Are you Käthe and Rudi well?"

"Ah, my not so small brother" Rudolf's solemn face changes when he looks at me from head to toe. "I can't remember when you grew so tall" he says distractedly and then "I'm fine Werner but how are you with your poorly leg?"

"I'm cold despite the physical activity of cycling and can't wait for the summer to arrive." I scan his face and add "You look worried Rudolf. Has something happened?"

He glances to the left and right and then asks "Do you know Ernst Henning?"

"Of course I do. He is a left wing member of the Hamburg Parliament."

"Unfortunately he was shot dead earlier today. He was on a bus when a gang murdered him. I think that they thought he was my friend Edgar André who as you know is also a member of the Hamburg parliament. The Nazis hate Edgar so much for being an active member of the working class defence organisation. It's getting so dangerous now as they are trying hard to destroy us."

He pauses and quickly watches my face not sure if he should say something and then he continues "I have to carry a gun permanently now Werner as I am sure that I am on their "hit list" and I have to be prepared to defend myself."

I have to say that the news about Ernst Hemming totally shocks me. He hadn't been doing anything but sit on a bus and he had been murdered. Even if he had been mistakenly identified as Edgar André, this did not make things any better as our left wing politicians are representing the working class of Hamburg and have a right of free speech. This violent behaviour is proving to me that the Nazis intention is to remove our human rights. We must stay together.

Ernst Henning's body had lain at the funeral directors in Jarrestrasse. On the day of the funeral, our youth group decide to attend. For the march to Ohlsdorf Cemetery, his remains are laid in a coffin and placed on a horse drawn carriage and with Edgar André standing in front of the hearse and the march starts. We feel overwhelmed with pride that this man, who has been so brutally murdered, has so much support even with his death. There are hundreds if not a thousand or more who also feel the same way as many people line the streets in support of the entourage as we walked solemnly the 3 ½ miles to Ohlsdorf. We are far back in the parade but proud to be part of the solidarity of the working class so that these Nazis know our feelings.

When we finally arrive at Ohlsdorf, another thousand people or more have been waiting for us. It is very difficult to judge numbers and be totally accurate but there is no problem with the large numbers of mourners as Ohlsdorf is an amazing cemetery with lakes and parks. Many speeches are made before our comrade is placed in his last resting place.

Feeling this support amongst the mourners and also grief at losing another good man makes us even more determined that the communists and social democrats must never give in to the brown terror of the Nazis otherwise our country will be once again at war and democracy will be lost.

Rudi Lindau has persuaded our group to start practising marching. We try marching properly in unison in the countryside away from prying eyes but we cannot be compared to the adult organisations, many of whom are ex army soldiers from the Great War. My bad leg also makes me look quite comical hopping and hobbling along with the others who are fit. The purpose of all this marching is to develop a strategy of protest marching and demonstrating without inciting any violence, especially in the Hamburgerstrasse area.

During a busy shopping period when we aren't at work, many of us would loiter around the shopping area and then one of us blows a whistle and within a minute, we have formed a demonstration, marching along the street chanting slogans. After a short while, the whistle is blown again and we scatter, hopefully before the police arrive, mingling with the ordinary shoppers. If we're unlucky and we see the police running towards us, batons raised, we usually escape inside the surrounding buildings and up the stairs as most apartment blocks have their main doors open. It's very rare that the police will follow as they're never sure if it is a trap. There is also a possibility that they might enter an apartment where the residents are not very tolerant towards the police's attitude to the working class movement. They will only enter these buildings when they are in sufficient numbers to counteract such problems.

At long last summer is here and once again I can gather at weekends with my friends to go hiking and enjoy singing and chatting as we walk in the beautiful countryside. We had been hiking earlier, but nice warm weather makes the past time even more pleasurable.

Rudolf's story

I would love to speak to my family about my activities but this is totally out of the question. I sometimes see their furtive and worried glances in my direction but all I do is ignore these looks. If they ever find out my involvement in secret assignments and radio communication to other countries, they will realise my destiny of certain torture and death if caught.

It is known that I am leader at the Russian Trade Organisation and party spokesman for the Hamburger Volkszeitung which is a Hamburg newspaper. I am a target of the fascists and although I know I need to continue in my work, the fall-out of possible threats to my family seriously worry me. Should I distance myself from my beloved Käthe and Rudi to give them a chance of survival? This heart breaking decision might have to come before long.

Ernst

I've had to change my life style completely in order to make contacts with people outside my usual circle of friends and colleagues. It's important to meet individuals from strategic organisations and utility firms and I've found frequenting pubs is quite a good source of making contacts. Although it is a place for drinking, many people who are in trade unions and/or have socialist beliefs meet up at these places to discuss politics and their financial concerns. As so few have homes large enough to socialise, pubs are a good place to visit and "listen".

It's exhausting, but I'm feeling incredibly lucky finding people willing to co-operate by providing information for me. Perhaps there are more people around than I had initially thought who are not happy with the political situation or is it the rapidly increasing hunger and poverty driving so many to take these risks?

One example is a man called Herbert Böttner who works for the Ottensener Iron Works. He is also a member of the Reichs Banner (Iron Front) which is the paramilitary branch of the social democrats. He's agreed to supply me his firm's engineering designs and details of how the ship engines and boilers are manufactured. He's also given me mechanical engineering technical periodicals.

I asked Koglin to discover which new machinery manufactured here in Germany, is finally to be delivered as armaments. I also need to know which of this equipment is intended to be shipped or transported to China or Japan. The political situation in China is of great importance to us due to the covert support our government is happy to give to suppress the communist rebellion movement in the Chinese Provinces. I give him 30 Reich Marks each time for any updated information.

My friend "Munki" collects all this information from Koglin and delivers it to Benno Dohrn's home. Benno lives in the area of Hoheweide and works for the Roten Hilfe. He has been working as a Russian commercial representative since 1925. Benno then copies the documents and "Munki" then returns the originals to Koglin. Finally "Munki" then makes sure that I have the copies.

Regardless of all this espionage work, the right wing groups are increasing the number of their marches and demonstrate. At least with Rudolf and his friends in the Rote Front, they are preventing these organisations from taking control of our streets and I hope that the citizens of Hamburg will soon awake from their dreams and join us in our resistance.

Edgar André, who is a politician, is now heavily involved with Rudolf's activities. He is just seven years older than me and is active in the Seaman's and Harbour Workers International as an instructor and propagandist spending much of his time in Belgium and France.

Likewise Rudolf has been busy being a contact man for the Hamburger Volkzeitung[49]. Athough Rudolf never gives me details as he's often on secret party assignments. What a family we are. I know that my Grandfather although only a basket weaver in Bornhöved (Schleswig Holstein), had been arrested several times trying to improve the living conditions for the working class to have a fair wage and better working conditions. It seems that history is repeating itself!

Poor Anna and Gretel see me rarely now, but thank goodness Anna is such a caring wife and mother so that that I do not need to worry as Gretel is still a happy little girl. Thank goodness I have no difficulties marriage wise. Oh I mustn't let anyone down.

Funeral of Ernst Henning in March 1931. Photo taken in Jarrestrasse and Edgar André is marked with an "X". Photo taken from the book "Einschnitte" sechzig jahre Mitten Mang über das leben des Hamburger Kommunisten by Tetje Lotz.

[49] Hamburg Newspaper

CHAPTER 12

Werner during 1932

I feel so tired working hard all day and then the exhausting bike ride home but I perk up seeing Papa busily reading his newspaper.

"You'll never believe this" he said acknowledging me as I walked into the lounge. He continued. "You know this chap called Adolf Hitler? Well he's runner up to Hindenburg in the second presidential round of the election so now he's the second most important person in Germany. What on earth possessed the German electorate to vote for him?"

I have to say that this shook me as well. "Whatever it is, he seems to appeal to so many people. Perhaps a simple idea like providing soup kitchens for the poor has worked Papa. Statements which attract prejudices without any just foundations or proper thought are his answer. Why on earth couldn't Rudolf's friend Ernst Thälmann have won?"

"I know Werner." He is silent for a moment. Somehow I think he is wrestling with his conscience of what should be done to put things right in life and the other side of things of being a father.

"I also know in my heart that what you and your brothers are all saying to me is right but it seems that the voters are thinking only of their immediate needs and not looking at the consequences which could possibly mean another war. What you and your brothers are doing trying to stop the frightening deterioration of events is right, I know. Someone has to stand up against Hitler and his cronies but you also must understand that I can't stop worrying about you all though Werner."

He then looks very stern adding "And don't forget that you are to keep a low profile. It's bad enough knowing that Rudolf is so heavily involved in the resistance. I wonder what Ernst is doing now as he seems to have so little time for us."

I can see that his mind is starting to "digest" thoughts about Rudolf Ernst and myself so I decide to divert him away from this direction of conversation. I have never lied to our parents, merely economical with the truth and only then to stop them worrying. It has never been my intention to be deceitful. I revert to the original conversation.

"Hitler's clever schemes to show support to the working class has been the main problem. He seems to think that if he shows sympathy with the people who have lost everything and are on the bread line, they will be so grateful that they will vote for him."

"Unfortunately he seems to have judged that correctly" replies Papa. He had, thank goodness forgotten his train of thought about me.

After our meal, I make my excuses and escape to meet my friends. There is really very little time for this activity during the week as Papa always insists that I return home by 10 p.m. Sometimes I feel resentful at this curfew. Werner Etter and Walter never have the same restrictions as me. Guilt suddenly enfolds me as I am the one who is fortunate to have both parents alive still and who care and have time for my welfare. Indeed I am the lucky one and must never forget that.

As summer is still a long way off, occasionally we meet up in one of the little bars and have wonderful evenings just chatting and drinking a glass or sometimes two glasses of wine. Sometimes it's good just to enjoy each other's company, just socialising without the serious business of making plans how to publicise the evil intentions of the Nazi Party.

This particular evening I lose track of time so when I see the clock on the wall behind Fritz showing that it is already ten o'clock, I give my apologies to my friends and dash out of the bar into the street. Sometimes it's so difficult moving quickly with my gammy leg but the thought of Papa waiting up for me makes me hurry. Just as I turn into Gertigstrasse, I see the silhouetted outline of Papa starting to walk in my direction. He stops as he sees me approaching him. I blurt out my apologies, gasping for breath.

"I'm sorry Papa, I hadn't realised the time. We were having such an interesting conversation."

"Hmm" is Papa's reply as we walk back to our flat. I sigh with relief at this seeming to be the only admonishment I'm to receive this time. I must be more careful in future. It's so difficult treading the path of a teenager in these troubled times but I mustn't lose my parents' trust otherwise I would not be able to continue with my group.

The following evening the "tables are turned" as I stay home and they go out. Mama and Papa had arranged to go to see Tante Miele[50], Mama's sister. She also has a cigar shop but it is in Barmbek which is about thirty minutes walking distance from us. Mama has a spring in her step which is lovely to see as she adores her sister and its good for them to be together. Onkle August, her husband, makes wine at home so somehow I have the feeling that they won't be back early! Life is so hard for Mama that she looks forward to seeing her sister, brother-in-law, her niece Carla and nephew Kurt.

A few weeks later, I came home from work to find Papa again reading a newspaper. He glances over the top of the sheets of paper as I walk in and looks in my direction but is muttering away to himself. Mama is sitting in her chair busily mending some clothes and after greeting me, she looks at Papa and asks what is worrying him.

"I'm just so concerned at the deteriorating situation Gusta" he answers.

"As expected, the remaining foreign investors now fear political upheaval and are pulling out of Germany altogether. It's been bad enough that the Wall Street Crash has caused financial crisis in our country but now the few who still have money to invest are concerned about the threat of this man Hitler. The United States of America is putting self-protection measures into place by placing tariff barriers on their imported goods. As you know they have been our largest purchase of industrial exports. Many of our factories will suffer as a result of this."

I can see Mama looking really worried now. "If they withdraw their money, this will mean total collapse of our economy. How are people supposed to live and survive if there are no jobs?"

---

[50] Miele Bittkau

"This is just the perfect situation for Hitler and his mind games" I hear myself thinking out loud. I busily read the newspaper leaning against the back Papa's chair and glancing over his shoulders. "The trouble now will be the increase in propaganda and hatred against the racial minority."

Sure enough, the economy does start to collapse and to our disgust scores of the non-politically conscious unemployed decide to join the S.A., boosting the confidence of their leaders. The Nazis are becoming more provocative by organising demonstrations with the S.A., marching through working class districts. To our disgust, they march with the strong protection of our police. It's horrible and frightening seeing attacks against the working class and an increase in their hatred of the Jewish population. The Jewish population have done nothing wrong but the fascists need someone to blame for this crisis.

Everyday life is becoming more hazardous, even to walk along the street. One day some open trucks driven at break neck speed came hurtling along the streets, sirens wailing. Wedged tightly together in the back section of the vehicles are green jacketed black helmeted police. Closely following the lorries are open topped cars, also full of police carrying rifles.

"They're off to deal with the communists" a passer-by said to me. "These left wing bastards deserve everything they get" he adds. I shudder and walk on making no comment to him. It's never wise to say anything to a stranger.

Mama and Papa seem to have lost their ability to chat and laugh. I know that they worry about all of us and it has not helped when they read the evening papers about the political murders taking place. Different political factions make use of their supporters who are prepared to dress themselves in uniform and disrupt opposing party events and in the case of the far right parties, to terrorise the locals in their own neighbourhood. It has made our country a very unsafe place to live. The right wing S.A. and Stelhelm with their knives and guns hidden in their pockets, along with the Police and their rubber truncheons seriously threaten the working class districts. I often worry about my friends and family fearing for their safety.

Thank goodness Rudolf and his friends are able to fight against this threat. Rudolf has such incredible leadership qualities. I've noticed that he always discusses the situation with his supporters so that they understand what the dangers will be and as a result is respected by his followers. He is such a fantastic orator but perhaps totally believing in the cause of justice for everyone, regardless of financial or social status makes his speeches so eloquent. His support is massive. Thus when clashes ensue from these demonstrations of the Stalhelm and the S.A., his supporters in the Red Front arrive with total convictions to disperse these thugs. I wonder if the unemployed who have joined the S.A. really understand what they are demonstrating about. Are they just enjoying the fear they are instilling into the local population? History seems to keep repeating itself especially since the Great War with all these mass hysteria demonstrations which intimidates people who are honest, hardworking citizens.

This though is fuelled by the effect on every one of the rapid decline in living standards caused by the financial crisis. I meet up with my friends Walter Beyer and Werner Etter that evening and we start trying to fathom the outcome of world events encroaching on all of us. Both Walter and Werner agree with me that we could be on the edge of a very serious and dangerous situation.

"I've been to my Trade School today and had some really serious discussions with my fellow students. The trouble is that so many of them seem to listen to the propaganda which has been released saying that all the problems lie with the Bolsheviks, Jews and of course the signing of the Treaty of Versailles. The fascists are offering to rid this country of these trouble makers and also retracting from the Treaty. They promise to somehow provide employment and in the meantime run "soup kitchens" throughout the land. Surely people will not accept these bribes?"

"I know Walter" replied Werner Etter. "I think we have a very difficult task ahead of us. You've been handing around that left wing newspaper "Die Junge Garde" though. Have you?"

Walter nods. "But who will bother to read it when the fascists promise eutopia"

We enter the Stadtpark and breathe deeply leaving suburbia behind us and into the nearest thing to countryside that we can get here in the city suburbs. We have arranged to meet some others from our group to relax and play football.

"I think Fritz Winzer's sister, Herta wants to start coming next week to our youth movement" I tell the others before joining our group of friends.

"Gosh, time really is flying. Yes, she must be fifteen years old now. I've heard her talking the other day to Fritz about the political situation. I think she'll be a useful addition but she is young" remarks Werner Etter.

I laugh at this. "You know that my parents are very friendly with Herta and Fritz parents?" They both nod. "Well according to Mama and Papa who you know are social democrats as are the Winzers, there's been quite a lot of strife talking about the political situation between Herta and Fritz with their parents".

"I can imagine, but it is healthy having discussions between family members isn't it Werner" teases my friend Werner Etter who knows we Stenders are famous for our family discussions.

I laugh again. He knows me so well!

"And to think that since we've been busy within the group Fritz has moved on to more important work and now you are one of the leaders of the group. I suppose it won't be long before we too will move on to higher responsibilities" remarks Walter just as we arrive at the large grassed area where all our friends are waiting for us. The conversation ends as we have a "friendly" football match to play. If only I could run around as fast as the rest of them. They don't seem to mind me playing though with my disability and it is good to "let off steam".

On our way home we walk past the planetarium which was opened in 1930. It's a very impressive building with a huge dome and was built by Otto Menzel as a water tower in 1915. It's one of the largest planetariums in the world and is right on our doorstep so to speak so we are indeed very fortunate. The building has a small waterfall appearing at the base and the position of the building is absolutely perfect, overlooking a vast expanse of grassed area and all the way down to the lake. The whole structure of this area is quite outstanding and I think we are all proud of our Stadtpark. People come from the city to spend the whole day here with the recreational facilities, lakes, gardens, sports facilities and many cafes. I have to say that all generations love this area as there is something to suit everyone.

Most of the facilities are free which is just as well. It is awful seeing the poverty and hunger in our area. People are becoming desperate. In Altona by the summer one in three people are unemployed. Hunger demonstrations are common throughout Hamburg and food shops attacked and emptied. What on earth can I do to help all these people suffering the food shortages? So many of them have the indignity of having no job and yet they have been hard working and conscientious all their lives. It is appalling to see what is happening.

In view of the coming election and the consequences if the far right gain many seats in government, it is felt by our leaders that we should prepare for all eventualities. Our group has been invited to join others in a massive meeting in Luneberg. Our youth organisation will be gathering its members from all over Hamburg, Luneberg and Harburg. We had been having many meetings on the Lüneberger Heath with our youth group where thirty or forty people have been attending but now the situation is becoming extremely serious. I decide that it will be better if our small group of friends should keep together so we meet up a bit earlier at the end of Gertigstrasse. We are all excited and ready as it means a weekend trip away from home and with people with the same political opinions as ourselves. This is our chance not to be wary about the people we will be with. I have a backpack full of food and drink which I hope will last me for the duration of the trip.

We all make our way to the pick-up point where lorries are waiting for us. Laughter and a feeling of comradeship with being in the company of many others who believe in the same future now make our spirits rise. We manage to scramble on board one of the open lorries, rather pleased with ourselves that we have kept together. There follows a very bumpy ride over many cobbled streets and we are "thrown" to the left and right as the lorry progresses along the roads to Harburg. It is an impressive sight with all the lorries in convoy, each full to the brim with youngsters laughing and joking as we are jostled about with the bends and bumps in the road. It is a perfect day, there being no wind and this helps us in a challenge as we start to catch the voices of the singing in the lorry ahead of us and join in with their song. The passengers in the lorry behind us then hearing our song join in. So it continued until we reached Harburg. It must have been impressive watching this procession of singing youngsters.

Suddenly all the lorries start to break and our voices quieten down as our attention is drawn to this new situation. There is a barrier ahead of us which causes many of us great concern. Policemen are lined up across the road and because there are so many, they are several rows deep. A line of policemen walk along each side of the trucks and then they start thumping their hands against the sides of the vehicles ordering us to disembark. We just can't believe what is happening. The police confiscate our lorries. Our boisterous behaviour has changed to a very subdued state of mind, and we stand around for a while not really knowing what we should do next.

Being one the leaders of our group I have to make a decision.

"Do you want to be defeated by this small matter of no transport?" I ask. "Are we going to let the police and their backers win trying to stop us?"

"No" came the reply from the crowd who are standing around me.

"Right then, it seems we have no alternative but to walk, but this means that we'll be walking all night. Are you prepared to do this?"

"Yes" comes the reply from the displaced youth. The energy and enthusiasm is back with all of us as faces light up with determination not to be beaten.

"Well done Werner" they add which is followed by a lot of slapping my back with approval.

Well I have to say that we set out with great fervour and for once I am quite grateful that we had been practicing marching as it makes our walking in formation so much easier. Once again our vocal chords are in full volume with singing folk songs as we march. Luckily the weather is glorious but we soon suffer from shortages of water as we hadn't expected to be walking such distances. Seeing Walter jump into a pond at one point causes us great amusement but it is understandable why he has done this. To be truthful I would have loved to join him but I don't fancy walking then in wet clothes, or the other alternative is to jump into the water naked with a bevy of lovely girls watching me.

As the dark of night approaches our marching becomes more difficult and naturally tiredness sets in. However I cannot help but admire the girls as they seem to have more stamina and determination to succeed than us boys. We manage to find some local sympathisers who have smaller vans to help transport the exhausted, invalid and handicapped people who are in some difficulties. As we walk, we come across so many others who have also had their lorries confiscated. We've all arrived at the same conclusion that this meeting is too important to miss so we are all making our way there on foot.

We finally reach our destination of Luneberg and although absolutely exhausted, we are overawed at the size of the event. There must have been into the high hundreds if not a thousand youths listening to exhilarating lectures made by leading members of our organisation.

The speeches over, we know that we have an arduous journey home. We walk much slower this time and I suppose as I am so tired, I am not concentrating properly. A comrade gives me a friendly shove and next second I am on the ground. Lo and behold I break my wrist – at least it feels like it as the pain shoots up my arm. How can I have been so stupid as to let that happen? It isn't my friend's fault as he meant me no harm and I can see he feels devastated at his actions but what on earth am I going to say to Mama and Papa?

To my relief, as we walk round a bend, our lorries are parked by the side of the road waiting for us. The trucks which had been impounded along with the arrested drivers had all been released at dawn and the men had driven towards our meeting place.

I creep into our flat that evening looking and feeling extremely sheepish. As expected my parents are upset when they hear of the events over the weekend.

"How are we going to resolve this problem Gusta" Papa asks Mama. "You know we will have to report Werner's broken wrist to the police as all such accidents have to be reported to them along with an explanation as the actual occurrence of the incidence."

He then turns to me and says "The police know of our family's political opinions and will probably guess as to where you have been Werner."

My heart sinks as I know he is right.

In the end, as there doesn't seem to be any internal bleeding around the injury we decide that it is best that I go to the police on the Monday and explain to them that I have just fallen off my bike on the way to work. Luckily they accept this explanation and after a visit to the hospital, I am back in plaster.

My parents though decide that I should be "grounded" and that includes my evenings. Daimler-Benz where I work luckily still pays me my pittance of 3 RM per week but at least I still have money.

Walter Beyer came to see me after work on the Monday. I'm frustrated at my ban from socialising and as a result have been simmering quietly to myself all day. Mama comes in with a cool drink for us both, chatted for a while and then leaves us to ourselves.

"I can't believe I've been banned from going out" I moan to Walter. "I'm sixteen years old now and not a child and have been bringing a wage home for two years now."

"Oh Werner" answers Walter with some amusement. "It might seem severe, but your parents worry such a lot about you. They're only too aware that their two older sons might be putting themselves into danger and they can see you following in their footsteps. If you had broken your wrist in a normal situation, then that would have been different, and anyway, be appreciative that you have parents."

At that point, my frustration lifts. He is right and my parents although strict in one sense, are quite liberal and very loving in other ways. They have a lot of worries but despite this our family is the most important thing in their lives and they really do mean everything to me.

I'm not going to let a broken wrist prevent me from helping with publicising and warning people of the dangers of the fascists. As soon as my ban is lifted I'm back distributing leaflets and trying to encourage the people in our district not to vote for Hitler and the fascists in the next election due at the end of July. Mind you, this task is difficult for me with my broken wrist, but I am not going to let this painful annoyance stop me.

On a beautiful summer's evening, I arrange to meet Walter Beyer and Werner Etter in the Stadtpark with some of my other friends. With all the political worries at the moment, meeting my friends for a relaxing evening and watching them play football is something I really love. Werner Etter arrives at my parent's home to see if I am coming along to watch and knowing how much they like him, my parents relent but warn me not to try and play yet. As we walking along the street, we meet Walter Beyer who is his usual bouncy, cheerful self, but he has the look that he is dying to tell us something.

As soon as we have no-one near us to overhear our conversation he says "Although I had nothing to do with this, I must tell you what happened at work yesterday" he jabbers to us in an excited voice. "I was at "Birnbaum and Warendorf", Hammerbrook, my workplace yesterday, when as I walked towards the building, I noticed that there was a red flag flying on top of the building for the entire world to see. You can imagine how angry my employers were."

We both laugh at the visualisation of this scene and of the furious employers.

"Then my employer asked one of the elderly workers to go up on the roof and take the flag down. This poor chap is still suffering from war wounds which were inflicted on him in the Great War. Can you imagine how difficult it would have been for him to manage this? Courageously he refused their request risking the wrath of our employer and possibly getting the sack. They then asked me to take it down as I was the only apprentice there. I did remove it taking my time but whoever initially put the "red flag" up, managed to put another one there last night or very early this morning. I've no idea who it was but don't you think that was brave as they must be an employee to gain access to the building".

"It's lovely to hear of other people are intent to show solidarity against the fascists" said Werner Etter who had been beaming from ear to ear hearing Walter's news. I had to agree with them both.

We enter the Stadtpark and as it is such a lovely evening, a lot of the open spaces are filled by locals who were keen to enjoy their free time before dusk starts. Everyone seems intent to enjoy these pleasures which cost nothing.

We stop walking for a while to watch some people who are thoroughly enjoying themselves with folk dancing. Some are dancing, some playing their musical instruments and some singing to the tunes. At the end of each dance, everyone who had been sitting near them clapped furiously in approval. The performers turn to their audience and curtsied and bowed, all laughing with the sheer enjoyment of their activity. So much pleasure and no money spent.

We carry on walking through the open spaces and into an area laid out with exotic plants. It all looks quite established now since it had been designed a few years ago. Would the government be able to afford to maintain these plants as the depression deepens?

Mama and Papa love walking through these gardens. Only having a yard for drying washing and looking after their chickens, gives them no opportunity for growing flowers. They do have an allotment plot though. I remember them both marking their territory around the plot and then the horrendous hard work of digging up grass and the rough ground and finally improving the soil before they could grow vegetables. It is wonderful since it has been established as we sleep in the hut during odd weekends and it feels like we are living in the country. Happy times and now the growing of our food pays dividends in the hardship we are now suffering.

There are 6 million unemployed now. This has resulted in Hitler attracting the disaffected working class voters and with his party's impressive but frightening marches were the S.A.[51] or brown shirts as we call them. Many of these working class voters have decided to join the S.A. and now there is more violence spreading in the streets. We try hard to counteract this deterioration in lack of freedom and

---

[51] Sturm Abteilung – stormtroopers

democracy, but it is becoming more difficult as the days progress. This Adolf Hitler is becoming too powerful.

It is 16th July 1932. Rudolf came round this evening and chatted with Mama and Papa for a while. I have arranged to go and meet a friend and just before I walk out of the front door, I make my apologies to Rudolf for not staying. He looks up sharply at me when he hears that I am going to be out tomorrow as well.

"I want you to promise me that neither you nor any of your friends will be in the vicinity of Altona tomorrow Werner" he says in a surprisingly authoritative manner which he uses when he expects unquestionable compliance. This rather shakes me as he never speaks to me in this way.

Papa also picks up what has just occurred and interrupts by saying "I presume you are not going to tell us why Rudolf?" Rudolf hesitates, not sure what to say to Papa. "I know that the SA troops are intending to march tomorrow to aggravate the locals in the working class district" Papa continues and then he looks straight into Rudolf's gaze, grasping his hands and says "I beg you, please be careful."

Papa then turns to me. "Werner, even your brother is telling you and your friends to keep away tomorrow so I won't accept any evasive answers this time. I want you to promise me on your Mama's life, that you will not go near that area tomorrow".

When I look at him rather surprised, Papa adds "Yes, Werner, you might think you are hood-winking us with some of your answers lately, but we know that you are not being completely honest with us about your activities."

This conversation between the three of us is so serious that I feel quite shaken. Rudolf has never behaved this way to me before so whatever is going to happen, might be very dangerous. I nod compliance and promise faithfully that I will stay away and will also make sure that my friends do the same.

By the Sunday evening, I realise that Rudolf had been wise in warning us about avoiding the Altona District[52]. I wonder if he had

---

[52] That day was to become known as Bloody Sunday

been there? I track him down to check that he is ok but he will not speak of the event.

Violence is increasing and anarchy seems to be descending on our country. To our horror the Reichstag is prematurely dissolved by Papen who takes over as the Reichskomissar prior to the Election and he purged the administration and the police of so called trouble makers[53].

Werner Etter calls round to see me. Mama has always made sure that all my friends are welcome. Our home is an "open house" for all friends and family so sometimes it can get quite busy! On this particular occasion though, Werner's our only guest.

"I've just heard from one of my Social Democrat friends who live in Kiel. Apparently in the Trade Union Hall there on the night of 26th July, the social democrat party members had waited all night for word of the executive's policy regarding von Papen's declaration of dictatorship. They had been hoping for calls of a general strike to fight for socialism. The alternative was to do nothing making it even easier for the reactionary forces of the right to consolidate their position. Well guess what? After waiting all night, the Social Democrats were forced to go home at dawn as no call for action was given."

I just feel so frustrated at hearing this piece of news.

"Why on earth don't the Social Democrats trust us? Why can't they see that our country is in great peril if we do not unite our forces? If we work together for a general strike, then there will be hope for the future of Germany."

"I know, I know, but we're so young and who will listen to us?" my best friend replies.

He is right of course. "Let's hope that people will listen to my brothers and their generation. Somehow I fear not as it seems so often that people have a tendency to think of their own immediate needs and not of the consequences of their actions. Why can't people think what will happen if we do nothing?"

The final blow comes on 31st July 1932 when the Nazis score their greatest success in a free election and they emerge as the largest

---

[53] Thus preparing the smooth takeover of power in 1933 by the Nazis

political party in the Reichstag but thank goodness do not have an overall majority. I just hope that the other parties start working closer together to stand up to Hitler's Party. We all feel very concerned so I am busy organising leaflet distribution amongst the working class warning them of the dangers of fascism and many from the left try to hinder the S A marches.

Winter is setting in and life is becoming ever more difficult for people to survive without work and no money. Somehow some form of heating has to be found otherwise not only will they starve, but they will also freeze to death.

Walter and I both attend a Trade School one day a week as we are apprentices and we are very keen to gain qualifications in our particular field of trade. Our earnings are minute but with a bit of luck these will improve once qualified. That is, if we still have a job as the depression is deepening each month. Oh the poverty and the look of hopelessness on so many people's faces. Surely this won't continue for much longer. I'll just have to work and study as hard as I can.

It is worrying seeing the infiltration of teachers in education who have far right tendencies. There is a teacher in our trade school who gives lessons of his version of what is happening in the world. It seems he expects us to be too young to have our own political views and is therefore providing us with the fascist version. Most of my classmates belong to the Hitler Youth and as a result applaud his opinions. Converting the young people has been essential in the Nazi psyche but I try to counteract this by spending a lot of time trying to discuss issues with fellow students.

"I take no notice of this teacher Werner. The talks you arrange at our youth group with our leaders I find far more informative. I spend the periods for refreshments at the trade school as an excellent time for airing my views to my class mates."

His enthusiasm brings out an involuntary smile from me but I try to temper his eagerness with advice.

"It's fantastic what you are doing Walter, but please take care as your fellow students could report you to the authorities as being a trouble maker"

Although he's completely trustworthy in being discreet about our activities, he's inclined to speak when he tries to convert people to our political way of thinking. Mind you, I am no better than Walter in what I am doing, but I feel that as one of the leaders of our group, I should warn him.

My warning goes unheeded though as a fellow left wing student asks him to help make use of a prime opportunity when fellow students will be in the open space near the entrance to the trade school. Walter readily agrees to help so during their refreshment break, Walter and two other students rush outside while another student stays behind to observe the reaction of the headmaster when the speeches start. Any telephone call to the police will need to be reported to the speaker so that he will have time to disappear before they arrive.

"Several other classes were involved in this too" relates Walter to me one evening.

"I couldn't believe my eyes as Hermann Wolter[54], started speaking by the entrance gate. We asked the people to move forward and to listen. Hermann Wolter spoke loud and clear about the Nazis believing that they are the superior race but their behaviour would destroy our republic. He then pointed to all the students saying that the Nazis want them as cannon fodder for the next war. He carried on speaking along these lines for some time" Walter adds. "There followed much discussion with the students who are in the Hitler Youth but then he and the organisers dispersed before the police arrived".

I can see that the experience obviously impressed Walter and he is pleased that he was part of this event. I have to say that I would have been proud as well if I had been able to have helped Hermann Wolter. What an experience. Later we hear the school authority suspect that Walter has been one of the organisers but he does not receive any punishment.

---

[54] A leader of our youth organisation, Hermann Wolter fought in the illegal group "Rote Marinesturm" in 1933 against the Nazis Party. He was arrested, charged and convicted with treason and released in 1943. He was re-arrested in 1944 and escaped, continuing his work "underground" in Bremen until the end of the war. He became a senator after the war until 1958.

Mind you, I am also unable to stand aloof from the teachers and students rhetoric concerning the present political situation. The day that I attend the school is different from Walter but my friends and I have been having many discussions with out teachers. As a result a fellow student gives me the shocking news that he is a member of the SS.

"Listen to me Stender" he snarls his face up close to mine. "If you do not change your present political outlook, you'll have to take the consequences and that will not be very pleasant".

Whatever he means, I'm totally shocked. Does this mean the end of free expression in schools? It only strengthens my resolve to carry on the fight. I won't be bullied and threatened[55].

The SS[56] had been formed in 1925 to provide personal protection for Adolf Hitler. In 1929 Heinrich Himmler had become their leader and its members had been selected according to the Nazi ideology of racial purity rather than the S.A. which did not have the same entrance qualifications. The SA seems to recruit from anywhere, including the unemployed. Initially the officer candidates for the SS had to prove German ancestry back to 1750 and have no Jewish blood. They feel they are the elite force and for us, the SS are a force to fear.

From just bodyguard status, they now have a membership of 52,000. Before 1929 the SS wore the same brown uniform as the SA with the adaption of a black tie and black cap with a skull and crossbones symbol on it. Himmler had extended the black colour to include breeches, boots and belts and armband edges. They are in the process of disentangling themselves from the SA although still officially a sub organisation of the SA and answerable to the SA chief of staff. They now seem to consider themselves elite from the SA and are dressed in an all-black uniform. I have to say they send shivers down my back when I see them marching.

Having said all this, the SA can also send a chill through my body when they march and sing "Die Fahne Hoch" by Horst Wessel. The words roughly translate to:

[55] I'm to meet this person again at a later date!
[56] Or the official name Schutz Staffel

Up with the flag! Close the ranks!
The SA marches at a quiet, steady pace.
Comrades, shot by the Red Front and reactionaries-
Their spirit marches within our ranks!
Clear the streets – for the brown shirt battalions!
Clear the streets – for the Stormtroops!
Millions already look to the swastika – full of hope.
For the daybreak of freedom and bread is upon us!
The signal sounds – for one "last charge"!
We stand ready for the struggle.
Soon, Hitler's flag will wave over all the streets:
The days of slavery will be short-lived!
Why can't people see the danger?

Autumn is just around the corner. Although not cold, the evenings have drawn in. This means that the terribly cold weather and the struggle to keep warm is approaching. What deterioration will there be this winter, both financially and politically?

I shrug my shoulders and try to think positive thoughts. Once again I am on my way to the Stadtpark to meet my friends. We try to get to the pagoda area above the Kaskades before everyone else arrives. It is firework night and something not to be missed. We'd decided on this meeting point as it gives us the best view of the evening.

As usual Walter arrives before me and is hovering, trying to retain as much area as possible for his friends. Much to his relief, he sees us approaching from all directions.

"Thank goodness you've all arrived. I wasn't sure how I was going to keep this place as everyone else seems to want to stand here. We've all got the same idea!"

"Never fear, the gang is here" teases Georg. "What a perfect evening it seems to be developing in to. There is no wind so the fireworks should look their best."

"Look, the barge is already in place" said Herta pointing her finger towards the lake. The Stadtpark lake, which is called the Stadtparksee, is connected to the canals which eventually lead to the

Alster so it's not unusual to see passenger boats entering the area. The barge is positioned in the middle of the lake and at the opposite end to us is the civic centre (Stadthalle) building which has pride of place overlooking the lake. In between the building and the Stadtparksee is a large area laid out with tables and chairs. It seems as though all these chairs are being used and we can hear the orchestra playing to the customers. The sound of laughter and chatter drifts over the water towards us when the music stops.

"Just look at all those lucky people who are able to relax and have fun." Herta makes this remark with envy in her voice.

"Yes and look how much it's costing them to have the same view of the fireworks as us" I console her.

"I know, but just for once, wouldn't it be fun to sit around one of those tables with all our friends and enjoy the music. Have any of you been inside? I understand that there's a domed ceiling with pillars supporting the surrounding ceiling and beautifully laid tables and an exclusive waiter service".

I can see Herta beginning to day dream wistfully but Werner Etter tries to bring her back to earth.

"So I understand Herta, but visiting there would probably be at least a month's wage if not more" he reasons with her. This bit of information works as she looks a bit embarrassed.

"Oh I know that I'm being totally unrealistic – I don't want to be in the restaurant knowing that there's such poverty around and people like us watching the extravagance and thoughtlessness of the people dining there. I just couldn't do it."

"I know you couldn't my "kleines mädchen". I often call Herta this as a friendly family tease. I am very fond of Herta and so proud that at such a young age, she is prepared to stand her ground for her beliefs. I laugh and give her a friendly hug. "It is frustrating though seeing how some people live on the backs of the working class. It's up to us to change it."

I glance to my left and see people sitting outside enjoying themselves on the patio of the Park Café. I know that excess behaviour of spending is offensive in this climate, but that does not stop people enjoying themselves if they can keep within a reasonable financial budget. I'm not a party pooper. We're all entitled to happiness and joy.

I glance down from the pagoda to the Kaskade below. I simply love water and to see it gushing down the brickwork to the two semi-circle steps and into the lake is a wonderful sight. I suppose from the Civic Centre it must look very impressive with the Planetarium in the background. Even in the Park Café, a side view of this waterfall is worth seeing. The Kaskade was only built five years ago so we still like to stop and watch the never ending flow of water.

We waited in anticipation along with many hundred other spectators for dusk to fall and the fireworks to start. We are not disappointed. What a wonderful evening. I need these interludes of relaxation as its hard work studying for my apprenticeship and also helping with our organisation, warning people of the terror of fascism.

I've been asked by my leaders to organise an event so that they can come and speak to people who live in our district. I manage to book the hall which is attached to "Wucherpfennig" which is one of our local pubs frequented by the working class. The best way to attract an audience for these speakers is to arrange for the theatre group Die Nieter to perform. They're really a popular left wing theatre group which is run by Gerhard Hinze[57] He's excellent at acting and his group have a way of play acting situations to make it easier for some people to understand what is happening in Germany. The room is large enough for several hundred people to attend, so it's an excellent venue.

I organised our youth group to distribute leaflets which we had made and these are pushed through the doors of the people we know might be interested in coming. The actual day arrives and all the dignitaries from our organisation walk into the hall.

"Well done Werner, you've managed to get the local neighbourhood here I see" says one of the leaders. I'm good at organising and can't help but feel pleasure at the praise I receive.

---

[57] After the war, he became known in America and Great Britain as the film star and actor Gerard Heinz.

They'd walked in seeing a long queue at the entrance door where tickets are being sold and the hall is rapidly filling up with hundreds of people. It is at this point that I start to panic. Give me the job of organising an event, then they can guarantee on total efficiency from me, but the next bit I'm hopeless at performing. I know that they will expect me to stand on the podium and speak to the audience before the play starts.

After this there will be other speakers. How on earth am I going to give a speech? It is just not in me. When it comes to helping anyone with their problems, I am expert at sitting, listening and helping to resolve any emotional, girlfriend/boyfriend problems and in particular help with our group in energising and bonding them into a worthwhile group. But as for my shyness – that's so difficult to conquer!

Why can't I be like Rudolf or even Ernst come to that? Ernst is the more reserved of the two and yet even he is a great orator. My legs start shaking and I know I'm not thinking straight. Helmuth Heine who has been watching me and understands my difficulties jumps up on to the podium and successfully addresses the audience. Thank goodness that evening is over! Shyness is a terrible thing. At least the evening is a success.

As winter starts to bite, my thoughts turn to Christmas. Will this be our last one together as a family? I have an ominous feeling that it will be as the fascists are now becoming too strong. What will happen to our family as we continue to try and stop this threat? I'm going to have to remember every minute of our time together!

CHAPTER 13

Rudolf during 1932

It's getting so difficult finding the time to spend visiting my family at Mama and Papa's place. It feels as though I am being split in two between the love for my family and the commitment I'm giving fighting against fascism. What can I do about it though as my colleagues say my leadership qualities and oratory abilities are desperately needed with the resistance movement?

Unfortunately due to the increased hostilities of the right wing, my knowledge of weaponry is needed more than before in order to defend ourselves against the S.A. and S.S. Sometimes I wonder at what point we have come to accept our fate of military action to counteract these people. Many of us are war veterans so perhaps our reactions are different from others. Whatever it is, the situation is set and there's no going back. I couldn't live with myself if I let Hamburg citizens down leaving the fascists totally dominating our land.

Today is different though and I have a lovely afternoon today with my family who I love dearly. We do not have much materially, but we all still have employment to pay the rent and provide food on the table. Then there's the music – oh how I love the music in our family and the joy and relaxation we all get from this special time together. Ernst knows how to get me in full singing voice as he starts humming Johann Strauss' Radetzki March. Before long we're all singing the tune and clapping at the expected places. At the end of the piece of music we're all laughing at our antics. Oh it's good to "let off steam" occasionally and just enjoy ourselves.

Lotte put a finger to her mouth to quieten us and then we could hear a knock at the door. A comrade is asking for me. Apparently a demonstration is becoming uncontrollable and I am needed to talk to the demonstrators to calm the situation down. Without any hesitation I give apologies to my family and leave with my comrade.

This economic depression just seems to make German politics more radicalised. The middle class who are also suffering financially are not following the true reasons for our plight and are joining the Nazis party. Do they not realise the consequences of their selfish actions? Even the unemployed are joining the SA in scores so there are now between 300,000 and 400,000 of them pounding the streets inflicting their terror on others. Whatever is going on in their minds, it is not constructive thought and this is bringing Germany to a dangerous abyss. A friend has told me that the Nazi students union at the universities is making surprising headway with support. Universities are usually the breeding grounds for left wing parties. Any government elections seem a pretext for street battles and yet so many people still seem adamant that fascist leadership is the answer to all our problems. We mobilise and arm ourselves for our own protection against organisations such as the Stahlhelm, the S.S. and the S.A. Death and brutality during demonstrations is increasing. These thugs are even targeting social democrats as well as their usual enemies of trade unionist and communist members in their homes, in the streets or anywhere they think they will not be caught.

At least with my friends in the Rote Front, we are keeping these organisations from taking total control of our streets and I hope that the citizens of Hamburg will soon stop dreaming and join us in our resistance movement. It is obvious now that power is no longer within the Reichstag due to over a hundred Nazis (under the leadership of Göring) being elected to this noble institution. They regularly disrupt proceedings with rowdy vulgar behaviour and this attitude flows into the streets and houses of the cities. Where has our democracy gone?

Thank goodness we have people prepared to be leaders and risk their lives because they have a conscience. Edgar André has been heavily involved with us. He is just five years older than me and a politician. He is active in the Seaman's and Harbour Workers International as an instructor and helps with publicity but now spends much of his time continuing campaigning in Belgium and France.

I have to say that I am more disturbed about the SS formation as their uniforms and behaviour are far more threatening than the S.A.

Their discipline is better and they wear the Stahlhelm type metal helmets rather than the more comical peaked caps of the S.A. However the S.A. seems to have become over confident lately. I hear that the Berlin S.A. rebelled against Hitler's leadership when he didn't want to seize power after the election. Is Hitler seriously not trying to seize power but only wants to use democratic means? Somehow I think he is biding his time. He is very clever and knows how to "work" the public especially with his rallying slogan of "Freedom and Bread". It is exactly the words that the starving wants to hear.

In June, Chancellor Franz von Papen lifts the ban about civilians wearing uniforms so now the S.A. and S.S. can legally march in their uniforms.

My thoughts flick back to my family. I cannot help feeling proud of Ernst and Werner. I'm an old war soldier, having experienced the horrors of the Great War. I know how bad it can get being in a battlefield and seeing my close friends being blown to pieces next to me. I'm desperate that this does not happen again as the next time with the sophistication of weaponry and now a lot more aircraft, the next war will not be in a far off land. There will be aeroplanes flying over Hamburg, shelling our homes and killing our women and children. I know the effects of war but Ernst and Werner have only read about it. Very few of us who were actually fighting will ever break our silence. Those horrors will go to our graves.

Now that Ernst is involved in a more subtle way than me in counteracting the threat against our country, his expertise and contacts, might mean we stand a better chance. I really mustn't say "now that Ernst" as he has been supportive for many years, but his activities are putting his life at great risk but if he is effective, he could help change the situation for the better. People such as Ernst are like shadows in a crowd and I know he is but one of many. He is risking his future when he has so much to lose with such a lovely wife and daughter.

Then there's young Werner who used to be such a reserved weak child and now he's organising his local youth group to distribute leaflets and informing as many people as possible of the dangers of fascism. I worry sometimes should he and his friends stop the marches of the S.A. Werner looks the typical Aryan, perfect for Hitler's superior race, tall, blond haired, fair skinned with blue eyes. I can't help smiling thinking that he is not one whom Hitler will have as a follower!

Even Hans does what he can at the factory where he works but I must not expect the same commitment from him. We are not all the same. Finally there is our dear Lotte who is not involved in resistance work, but is always there for us. She's always ready to help care for Rudi or Gretel, supports us whenever she can and keeps Mama and Papa from worrying too much. She's a wonderful sister. Hans, her husband dotes on Lotte and will always help the family, but Lotte's situation is difficult. Hans toes the line and I suspect actually believes the fascists. This is the easiest way to survive and although Hans knows we do not agree with him, I am sure he has no intentions of informing on us. Not everyone is strong enough to risk everything and we respect and love him for not interfering with our present way of life.

The provocative marching into the working class districts is increasing. They're looking for trouble and take every opportunity of beating up any poor soul who happens to be in the area alone and does not give these characters sufficient "respect". They think nothing of leaving their marching formation to brutally attack someone who does not give the Nazi salute. Many of these unfortunate people are not part of any organisation, but just happen to be innocently walking along the street at the wrong time.

People are becoming desperate through poverty and hunger. Hunger demonstrations are common with food shops attacked and emptied. We've had to arm ourselves against the terror of Nazism. These arms are from the stores of the armed forces, police etc. and filtered away by people who sympathise with our cause. It is important to have "sleeping comrades who help us by providing transport, hiding weapons or providing financial help. I am lucky having trustworthy friends including Carla Stender's father. Also Stemler, a quiet person living in Little Geibelstrasse hides some weapons and Müller, a dentist friend a few doors along who has transport. People like them are invaluable.

My responsibilities increase taking control of the Red Front Brigade for the areas of Stadtteil, Barmbek, Uhlenhorst and Winterhude. When we are in uniform, we greet each other with a salute of quickly lifting the lower part of our arm in a clenched fist movement. Far less elaborate than the Hitler salutes but I feel far more respectful.

Life continues in its precarious way but today I'm really enjoying the warmth of the July sun beating down on me. I'm walking to one of my meetings of the Red Front, when a contact from Altona stops me in the street.

"I've just heard that the Nazis are intending to march through our district next Sunday and they'll have police protection. Can you believe that the police are not only letting these people march through a working class district, but will protect them from any residents who live there who want to object. What on earth can we do Rudolf" he asks me. "It's nothing but provocation against us. Is there any way that your organisation can help?"

I am just as angry as my friend. Why are they marching through an area where they have very little support if it isn't to antagonise the local population and possibly cause injury?

"Look Helmut, we'll do all in our power to defend the locals. I'll pass this information on to my leaders and I'm sure we'll have orders to try and prevent these fascists from entering your District. No doubt they'll have already heard of this threat to the stability of Altona and none of us wants the locals being threatened in this way. Try to inform as many trade union leaders as you can so that they also know what is being planned."

Helmut sighs in relief at my reassurance. I'm not so sure though if these people can be stopped from marching as I know that the Nazis have every intention of causing trouble. Why else would they be marching in an area where they are not wanted? Without any doubt it is meant to intimidate the population.

Sure enough I discover that I'm not the only one in our organisation who has been told about Sunday. The following day, we organise our response to this threat. I don't usually like to inform other people about our future intentions, but when I hear that

Werner might be intending to go there with his friends, I bend the rules and warn him not to go. I just couldn't bear the thought that they might get caught up in this dangerous situation. I'd never forgive myself.

The next parliamentary elections are on 31st July. Are the Nazis hoping to prove something by this Altona march? There are rumours that there will be many thousands of uniformed storm troopers and yet neither the Altona Police Chief Otto Eggerstedt or his deputy or any senior police officer for that matter, intends to be in Altona on that day despite the threat of danger to the local population.

On Sunday 7th July, the S.A. starts to congregate at 12.30 between the Altona railway station and Altona Town Hall. There aren't a few thousand as I expect, but seven thousands of them, intent on terrorising the local population. This time we will have to take drastic action to stop them. This intimidation from them is now getting out of hand. What are they intending to do apart from demonstrate their power? Many of us position ourselves in the flats which overlook the main streets. Others manage to climb onto the roof tops with the rest on the pavements and we now wait.

At 15.00 the seven thousand uniformed S.A. start marching towards Ottensen and Bahrenfelt. By 16.30 the procession reaches Altona Altstadt [Old Town] going through Grosse Bergstrasse and then they turn into Grosse Johannistrasse towards Schauenburgerstrasse. Their intentions are clear by heading straight into the built up working class area by the intersection at the east side of Marienstrasse and the west of Schaunbergerstrasse. As the marching continues with their troops singing offensive songs, the atmosphere becomes ugly and threatening. I hate their singing of "Die Fahne Hoch" and then "Siegreich Wollen Wir – Durfen es nicht sagen" which means "victoriously we shall march against – but we are not allowed to say"[58]. They then start their latest favourite bloodthirsty tune "When the Jews and Bolsheviks blood drips from our knives, things go twice as good". A cannot help a shudder enter through my body. The SA are intent on blaming the Jewish population for all the

[58] Which means France

nation's problems and yet they have done nothing wrong and as for the Bolsheviks, they mean anyone who opposes them, not as in the true sense of the word. I can see that this time the S.A. are intent on a far worse scenario than on previous occasions.

Then at 17.00 the expected violence starts when members of the 1st and 2nd Division of the S.A. push into the crowd who are standing by the roadside. The S.A. then make a sortie into Grosse Johannistrasse towards Münzmarkt where they grab local people and beat them viciously, kicking them hard as they fall to the ground.

This is too much for us to watch. These thugs have to be stopped. Seven thousands of them who are out to cause trouble in an area where they are not wanted. The S.A. troops return to marching along the street, ready for their next sortie. Shots ring out from the marching S.A. formation and return of fire comes from the tenement buildings overlooking the streets. The police seem to have no intention of protecting the community and so others will have to do this. Two S.A. men fall, fatally wounded.

At this point, the police force the Nazi marchers towards the station where they must have called for more reinforcement as more police arrive. Why hadn't the police stopped the march in the first place? The Nazis having completed antagonising the district decide to leave, their job done.

The police then force all the local residents to shut their windows. To our horror, the police then start shooting at suspected snipers. This is appalling behaviour from the police who have protected the SA and now they are turning on the inhabitants. Orders are given for all of us to withdraw from the buildings so as not to cause any problems to the local population. Considering the residents from Altona are the ones who had been endangered by the seven thousand S.A. and S.S. marchers, why are the police deciding to take their revenge on the locals? We have only been in Altona to stop these SA & SS brutes. At 17.40 the homes in the Johannistrasse and Schauenburgerstrasse area of Altona are searched and the police arrest about ninety people. At 18.45 there is more shooting.

We regroup and started building barricades in the roads as the police are using armoured cars. They attack us with rifles, pistols, hand grenades and tear gas. We retaliate and as a result many of the armoured cars are ablaze. The riot continues until after midnight before we finally withdraw. By the end of the day, there were about sixteen dead and at least fifty people had been seriously injured[59].

It seems as though the S.A. have won the day again. On 20th July 1932 the imperial government under Franz von Papen use this incident as the reason for discharging the Prussian government.

The "Bloody Sunday" incident in Altona as it has become known has made me realise how dangerous the situation has become. Seven thousand S.A. and S.S. men had been intent on trouble and violence that day and their numbers are rapidly increasing.

Our organisation has once again been banned, but that will not stop us fighting fascism and now that the general election on 31st July is over, this means Adolf Hitler has become the second most important politician in Germany having the largest party in the Reichstag, but thankfully with the coalition, not the overall leader. Thank goodness they are not in the government but now I really do feel that it will only be a matter of time. We are rapidly reaching the point when we shall lose our freedom and democracy.

Who else is going to counteract Hitler's militias? We are indeed fortunate that we have some very brave men who will try their best. I'm also really pleased that Fiete Schulze has returned to help us with our resistance. He was brilliant with my comrades in the October 1923 uprising. Now I must organise a greater defence against these fascist thugs.

It is breaking my heart to see thousands of children dying of malnutrition and hunger related diseases. This is not because of lack of food but because of the unemployment, millions of people had no financial means to purchase food. We manage to help where we can by breaking into some wealthy stores and redistributing some of

---

[59] After the seizure of power by the Nazis, four defendants were Tried at a Nazi Special Court and on 1st August 1933, were sentenced to death and beheaded with a hand held axe. The four were Bruno Tesch who was only 20 years old, Walter Möller [who spoke to the students at the trade school], Karl Wolff, and August Lütgens. These were the first executions in the Third Reich. The remaining twelve other defendants received long prison sentences.

the food, but it is never enough to really solve the problem of so many starving children.

Ernst came round to my flat one evening and we sit down with a glass of beer each to relax but also to catch up with each other's lives.

"Summer is over and even greater danger seems on the horizon" said Ernst. He is really looking quite tired lately but I do understand how difficult it is for him working, being with his family as much as possible and now the strain of the resistance work. I can guess what is on his mind.

"Are you meaning the S.A. taking over the taverns?" I ask.

Ernst nods. "These taverns have always been the venue for the working class to have meetings whether it is for trade union business or the left wing political meeting place."

"I know. Even way back as far as 1890 it was recognised that it is the only place where our working class can meet and discuss common problems. These SA are trying to break the tavern culture. I've seen the swastika flags outside the pub in Allee in Altstadt and it seems that small traders who are active in the Nazi Party are frequenting the pub now. It's now become the headquarters for the S.A."

"But that used to be a communist party meeting place" answers a horrified Ernst.

"Yes but now it is the SA base of operations for activities around the area. This is the start of pushing out any people who are trying to organise any protests against them. It will end with us having difficulties finding meeting places, but we're not going to let them win". I changed the subject slightly. "I obviously don't want to know details, but how are you getting along with your new work?"

We both know what I am talking about but Rudi is still awake and I have to be careful even though he is still so young.

"Very exhausting but I hope things are beginning to fall into place" answers Ernst with a weary smile. "However I must tell you that I have heard that some of our leading industrialists including Dr Hjalmar Schacht, Kurt von Schröder, Fritz Thyssen, Alfred Krupp, Siemens and Robert Bosch have written to President Hindenberg and have put pressure on him to include the Nazi party in the Government."

"God help us if he heeds this letter" I mumble quietly.

Ernst nods in agreement. With millions of unemployed, poverty and hunger everywhere, the ruling classes and big business are frightened of a social revolution. Also the general army staff still wants to bring about their old aims having been rearming Germany to regain their old colonies for a 'greater' Germany."

It is a worrying time. On 6th December the Reichstag reassembles and elects Goering as its president. Thank goodness that although the Nazi party is the majority party, it has insufficient numbers and is still excluded from the presidential government. But how much longer can we hope that this continues?

Frustratingly I have no alternative but to leave the trade union organisation as I'm too well known everywhere with my activities. I have taken over as district leader for the 2nd group of the RFB in Barmbek.

What a year it's been. Mind you it's been marvellous how Carla's family has been helping me. Carla's father has been hiding some of our weapons and letting his premises be used for preparing literature to go into the factories. Hilde Dünkel whilst working at the Gross Einkampf Gesellschaft has also been helping us but unfortunately lost her job as a result. The big problem for that family is Carla's brother who has different political views to the rest of the family. This year he joined the National Socialist factory organisation. This could be a potential threat to the safety of that family as such people are encouraged to betray their relatives if they have different views to the Nazis. I've warned the Dünkels to be careful and as a result Carla's father has banned his son from entering his home[60].

---

[60] Carla's brother I believe became an SS concentration camp guard during Hitler's reign.

CHAPTER 14

Ernst during 1932

Oh how I hate these winter months with the bitterly cold easterly winds howling across our beautiful city. Food is short and we have to be careful not to waste fuel for heating. Its worrying leaving Anna and Gretel each morning when I go to work as I know that Anna tries so hard not to use too much fuel in the kachelofen[61]. I keep telling her to keep herself warm. She just smiles sweetly at me and says that she and Gretel are warm enough and an extra layer of clothes makes all the difference.

My clothes are becoming more threadbare as we are not able to afford replacements now. Both Anna and Käthe[62] are brilliant in dismantling old outfits and restyling several items to make one item of clothing wearable. It's a shame that Rudolf and I haven't had children of the same gender as we could help each other more when our little ones grow out of their clothes.

Today has felt particularly cold as sleet has been beating down in a diagonal direction on to the cobbled streets. Sleet seems to penetrate through all the clothing more than when it snows. Pavements are so slippery with the dreadful old shoes I'm wearing. The factory where I work is never warm with draughts howling through the cracked and broken windows. It's a problem knowing how to counteract the cold blasts. There is the safety issue with working on a lathe with layers of clothes and gloves.

We all feel intimidated not to complain for fear of losing our jobs and with unemployment reaching horrendous levels, there's just too much of a risk chancing our luck at protesting. The positive point

---

[61] A porcelain or tiled heater from floor to ceiling which contains burning wood or if we are very lucky – coal.

[62] Rudolf's wife

to sleet is that the temperature must be getting slightly warmer, even though with the dampness and wind chill, it feels cold.

As I climb the stairs to our flat, I can smell some food wafting under our door. Anna has been making soup out of the few scraps of food we have left over. How wonderful that smells after such a dreadful day.

As usual, as I open the door Gretel stops being Anna's little helper and she rushes over to me to give me a hug. I laugh as she suddenly releases me from her grip.

"Oh Papa, you're absolutely soaking wet. Let me take your coat off".

"You're sounding just like your Mama" I mock at her. Seeing my little girl who is not yet five years old, trying to reach up in order to take my coat off and hang it over the back of a chair really amuses me. Somehow she manages it with Anna's help and places the chair near the kachelofen so that the coat can dry ready for me to wear the next day.

"And what is wrong with that?" asks Anna standing back to watch Gretel. The coat duly deposited near some heat, all three of us embrace each other and we can't stop laughing. How lucky I am to have such a lovely family.

The next day is Sunday and I have promised to take Anna and Gretel to lunch at Mama and Papa's place in Gertigstrasse. Before this though, I have a meeting with Fritz Lux. I look out of the window and to my relief, the sleet has stopped. The coat was still slightly damp from yesterday, but it is better than nothing.

"I won't be very long Anna. I'll be back in an hour, I promise."

Fritz Lux and Wilhelm Bahnik are already sitting in the local café waiting for me. They'd already drunk a cup of coffee each. Fritz glances up and smiles at me as I open the door to enter and then he turns to the waitress and asks for another three cups of coffee.

I take off my still slightly damp coat and hang it up on the coat stand which is by the entrance door. Fritz observes me closely whilst I am doing this.

"Is that the only coat you have Ernst?" he asks. I nod.

"It looks still damp from the sleet we had yesterday". I nod again.

"It's the sign of the times we're living in. I have a family to feed and clothe and also the rent to pay. You must know how difficult that is."

"I'm not criticising you Ernst, but only showing concern. I know you put your family first in providing for them. There is a problem though as this can affect how well you perform for our organisation."

"How can that be? I give everything I can to help you" I ask quite hurt now by this comment. Wilhelm and Fritz look at each other and then back at me.

"There is some really important work we want you to undertake now. You have proved to us that you can be relied upon and we feel that you are ready to take on new responsibilities" said Wilhelm.

"We need you to organise infiltration in the transport services, chemical factories, utility services and telecommunications. Furthermore we must find out which enterprises are manufacturing armaments" said Wilhelm in a hushed voice.

"These will all take time to do it properly without being discovered, but I will prepare a plan of action. Will I be in charge of a certain district?" I asked.

"Yes, you will be the Leader of the "U Apparat" which has these specific functions but the area of cover is for Hamburg. I want you to organise this into smaller areas, each with a person in charge reporting back to you." replied Wilhelm. "Fritz has overall responsibilities over the different Apparats in Hamburg and I am sure through speaking to Rudolf, you are only too aware that he is a man you can trust."

Wilhelm had been closely watching my reaction. All our lives were dependent on each other and any doubts of a contact had to be recognised immediately. He had nothing to fear though as I had thought long and hard before making this commitment to the Resistance Movement. I nodded and shook his hand.

"Welcome to our dark and dangerous world" he said earnestly.

"And this brings me back to the question of your clothes" added Fritz.

I was so surprised by this remark and again queried why this should be a problem.

"Look Ernst, you are a very intelligent and reliable man but to achieve the aims we have for you, turning up to meet people in distinguished positions in their business looking like you do at present will not bring about the desired outcome. We know that your finances are very tight so we have some money with us and we want you to go and get some suitable attire so that there will be no problems when you approach the appropriate businessman we want to recruit into our Organisation."

I knew that Fritz was right. I was suffering from hurt pride at realising that I am not suitably dressed for my future assignments. Finally I give way to accepting the reality of my financial situation.

I humbly take the money and promise to improve my personal appearance at any future meetings. These clothes would be kept closely safeguarded in my bedroom wardrobe out of the way of prying eyes and only would be used at a time when I needed to impress a new contact. Any use of these clothes at other times would raise some eyebrows with people wondering where I suddenly had obtained some spare money and then they would be asking questions as to why I needed them in my station in life.

When I got home, I spoke to Anna about the money I had been given. I felt guilty that I couldn't give it to her to spend on herself and Gretel as they were also in desperate need of new clothing.

"Don't worry about us Ernst. Your friends are right. How on earth do you think you will be able to approach people who have certain positions in life and expect them to join you in the Resistance if you look like a ragamuffin?"

"I know, I know, but I just don't want you to feel that I'm neglecting you."

She gave me her lovely gentle smile, put her hands round my waist and kissed me on the lips. What could I say after that?"

Spring at long last was arriving and my body was beginning to stop aching with all the shivering from working in the cold and then cycling home. Never mind, I mustn't complain as at least I'm one of the lucky ones with a job. I just cannot understand why people voted for Adolf Hitler in the Presidential elections of March and April. Can't they see that he's only offering employment to the population by preparing this country for war? Soup kitchens is another way of bribing people – where do they think Hitler is getting the money from to provide all these facilities – from the big businesses who want to make money out of rearmaments. It's all so frustrating that the voters only seem to think of themselves and their immediate needs and not what is behind these promises.

Anna has been a great help. She's offered to put leaflets through letterboxes and little Gretel has been keen to help her Mother.

"Are you sure that you want to do this?" I asked her one evening. "Are you up to all that walking with your poorly heart? If you are seen by the fascists, I dread to think what will happen".

"I'm fine and you know how Gretel loves doing jobs like this to help us. Anyway, this seems to be about the only way that we can get information into the homes of our Hamburg citizens. I just hope that they read the leaflet as the situation in our country is becoming extremely dangerous".

I nod in agreement. "So many people just say to me "Oh don't worry Ernst, Hitler will not be around for long. All these cheering and supporting of the fascists marches is just a way that people are protesting over their living conditions, their starvation, their unemployment. As soon as Hitler gets into power, people will realise how he's just full of words and no substance. Let him "hang himself" so to speak"". I'd mimicked this is such a way that Anna must have heard the same phrases and behaviour. "It's just so hard trying to get them to understand that it won't end up like that" I add.

"I know" agreed Anna. "Once in power and with all his S.A. and S.S. supporters, our democracy and freedom will end, but what else can we do to change people's way of thinking?"

One evening during the summer, Anna, Gretel and I were walking home after we'd all been busy distributing leaflets, when we saw Werner walking along the pavement with his best friend Werner Etter. I couldn't believe seeing him with a plaster covering his arm.

"What on earth have you done this time Werner? I thought your bone problems had improved" asked Anna.

"Don't you start" laughed Werner. "I've just had a lecture from our parents".

"His feet are too big for him and now he's grown so tall, it was all too much for his body" added Werner Etter who was all too ready to add to the teasing.

After this continued for a while, Werner explained about his weekend at Luneburg and the very impressive speeches they'd listened to. Werner and his friends might still be young, but they're developing very quickly into a useful group who will be able to support us in our Organisation. I'm really very proud of them and they've formed such a good friendship. I'll have to speak to Werner when we're alone together and tell him that if he needs any advice, then he can come and see me at any time.

The atmosphere is becoming so tense in our neighbourhood. We had a big banner across the outside of our flat supporting our cause against Hitler, but the other night it had disappeared. This is very worrying as who had removed it? We've also had to tell Gretel not to go near the windows if she hears gunfire at night. My precious family must be kept safe from all of this.

Many other people have put banners outside their flats, especially when they know that the Nazis are going to march through a District. Look what happened in Altona when the S.A. and S.S. marched through their District in July with all that violence. Thank goodness Rudolf has not been injured or arrested.

Bruno Stöck is very busy lately. He'd become a cashier collecting and distributing literature and also selling a left wing newspaper, the Hamburg Volkzeitung in his office at Bortelmannsweg in the Hamm District.

There's a young lady called Mary Schmidt whom I'm beginning to think might be useful within our Organisation. She's twenty three years old, attractive, intelligent and seems very committed to our cause. She goes to the Workers Theatre Group along with many other people who are showing interest in fighting fascism. She told me the other day that she had managed to buy a typewriter from Heinrich Fuchs for 40 RM. Now that is useful information as I might be able to persuade her to do some illegal typing for me.

I'm also rather pleased to hear that Herbert Wöhrlin who is an attorney and does quite a lot of travelling to and from Moscow is very supportive towards us. We desperately need outlets to other countries so that any information we receive about the fascists can be relayed abroad. Herbert stays at Gustav Kljukow's place when he's in Moscow so that is also an excellent contact.

Bernard Kotzer has been helping us by providing Herbert with information about the armaments being made in Hamburg. Our resistance group is really beginning to fall into place.

In the meantime the U Apparat is forming into a functional unit. This is such a massive task and puts both myself and my family at great risk.

There are now three leaders in my U-Apparat. Schmidt will be in charge of Area One which is the old quarter of Hamburg, the New City and St Pauli, Christel is in charge of Area Two which is the City Centre, Sternschanze, Eimsbüttel and Eppendorf and finally Alfred Karpinski is in charge of Areas Three and Four. This is by far the largest part being Winterhude, Uhlenhorst, Barmbek-Central, Barmbek North, Barmbek South, Barmbek-Dulsberg, Hamm, Hammerbrook, Rotherburgsort and St Georg. We have to prepare for an uprising and part of this will involve taking over the utilities etc.

In addition we have to find out what is being produced in various factories. I'm astonished how so many firms are already looking ahead by manufacturing equipment ready for a future war or military aggression. Why are so many other countries turning a blind eye to this knowledge? I sometimes wonder at the lack of correct media coverage to the general public in ours and other countries. It is almost as though people are manipulated with the information the media and governments want voters to hear so that the real threats to our peace are ignored. Will things ever change?

As I walk home one evening, I reflect on a meeting we'd held at the Arbeiter Theaterbundes[63]. The people who attended have been told to prepare for illegal activities. I wonder if they realise how dangerous this work will be if we are caught. Because of the

---

[63] Workers Theatre Federation of which Die Nieter is connected to this federation

possibility of capture we will all have to think carefully before making a decision to do this work.

I approach Mary Schmidt if she will consider working for me, but she reminds me that she is already committed doing other work for our organisation. I'm not going to give up asking though as I think she has the ideal character for subversive espionage. This sounds terrible using such words as I know it conjures up all sorts of thoughts of betrayal, but I know we are working for the good of society and for ultimate peace and it is the present system which is being disloyal to our country.

Herbert Wöhrlin has a new contact from the Soviet Union who uses the name "Konrad". We give Konrad details of staffing and in particular the production and shipment of war material taking place, at the shipyards of Blohm and Voss, Heidenreich and Harbeck and Kampnagel Menk and Hambrook. Konrad is also enquiring about which of these firms manufactures also transport war material to Eastern Asia (Manchuria) or other areas. In 1931 Manchuria was annexed by Japan. This incident created a demand for military assistance which the big manufacturers were only too eager to supply.

Antonia Kröger who lives in Altona and works at the local Italian Consulate is reporting back to us about to the Italian Resistance. The spectrum of our investigations is widespread and varied. The people I've mentioned are but a few of the people working for me now.

I glance up from a deep conversation with my colleagues to see Gerhard Heinze and his acting friends preparing another political play. It is so good to watch this theatre group and to congregate here without bringing too much attention to ourselves as it is known officially as a cultural club.

Where has the time gone? The dreaded cold is starting to filter through my thread bare clothes as winter rapidly approaches again. It is lovely wearing the decent clothing which I put on for my work connected to the organisation, but it will not be worn for normal daily duties.

Fritz Lux has left for Denmark. The Central Committee for the whole of Germany has decided that he needs even more training in preparation should our organisation be outlawed soon. This is a real concern for us and for the future of democracy. Just as Fritz leaves, I am invited to party headquarters and I am asked to take over Fritz's position. What can I say? I really do not want the extra responsibilities and risk, but this is not the time to start quibbling about our individual needs in life. What will 1933 have in store for all of us I wonder?

Unemployment is reaching record numbers and the population is becoming desperate. I can see this ending either with what I hope will be a socialist uprising or the fascists will persuade the majority that they have all the answers. Our family is working so hard for improved legal rights for the working class, along with resulting living and working conditions, making life tolerable. Somehow I fear that we might be losing the battle.

17 – Herderstrasse at the junction of Humboldstrasse
The banner says "Hamburg has no place for fascists – Hamburg remains red!"

The banner on the top floor balcony says
"Hamburg has no place for Fascists!"

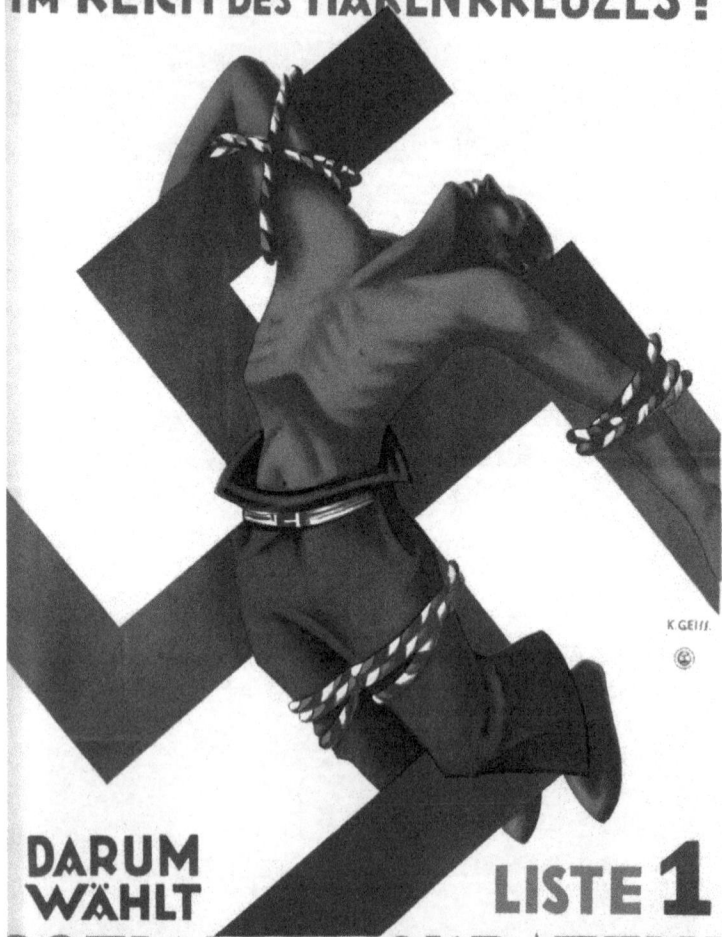

*Poster made in 1932 prior to the elections. Translation is The Workers living
under the Swastika. Therefore vote Social Democrat
Poster from the book "Anschläge – Deutsche Plakate als Dokumente der Zeit
1900-1960"*

CHAPTER 15

Werner during 1933

The best part of the winter is over and now there's the long hard struggle until the Spring arrives. Christmas had really been special this year and our parents were totally relaxed, joining in with the laughing, chatting and of course the music… ! Lately Mama and Papa's faces have started to look really strained but over the festivities, things were different. I hadn't said anything to Rudolf and Ernst prior to Christmas, but it seems we have been on the same wave length as all of us have made a special effort to make the occasion memorable. I have this foreboding that this might be our last Christmas together. I dread to think what is going to happen.

We hide our fears from the younger generation and of course from Mama and Papa. Rudi, Gretel and Erich had the most wonderful magical time, even though the presents weren't very expensive. Opa did his usual trick of banning us from the first floor lounge just before Christmas Eve. After our meal, we all left the basement flat, braced the cold wind in the Gertigstrasse and climbed the stairs into the main entrance of the flats. We entered our main accommodation and to a lot of "oooohs" and "aaaahs" from the youngsters. The room is covered in a soft light from candles lit on the Christmas tree. When I make a comment, really to myself, that it seems a long time ago when I first experienced this, I'm duly put in my place as my elder siblings laugh and comment that it feels like yesterday! I submit to their age superiority and join in with their laughter. Yes, it certainly will be a special Christmas to remember.

I pull up the collar of my coat trying to stop thinking about our happy time together and come back to our present situation. Now it is 1933 and I fear for all our futures, especially Rudolf. I have had to grow up very quickly recently. Hitler has displayed his strength organising a huge rally of S.A. in the Sportpalast in Berlin. He's a clever orator, I will give him that, and apparently he spoke for hours. There are six million unemployed people now who are desperate for work. I've been told that's about 26% of the population. Although food is available, being made redundant has meant that they cannot afford food. Children are starving to death and yet Hitler is managing to manipulate these situations to his advantage. I can see great danger ahead as so many people are "clutching at straws" getting caught up in the feeling that Germany will be all powerful again soon if they back him. "All powerful" though is a terrifying prospect for me as in the end it will be tyranny, dictatorship and death for so many of us.

Hindenburg weakens making Adolf Hitler the Chancellor on 30th January. To our horror we watch massive torchlight processions making their way to the Rathaus Markt in Hamburg and I gather that similar marches are taking place all over the country. In Berlin the SA and the Stalhelm march for hours on end carrying lit torches. We all waited in various homes all over the city of Hamburg waiting for the call to defend freedom and democracy by any means. This call never came and at this point, democracy is ending. Now what will be Hitler's next move I wonder?

One of my friends, who has a head for heights, managed to climb the factory chimney stack on the corner of Weidestrasse and Osterbekstrasse. He bravely puts a red flag on top showing defiance to Hitler. Thank goodness he wasn't caught.

Although February is cold and the snow showers blanket Hamburg in white, we still enjoy occasional frivolity visiting the Stadtpark. One or two of us have sledges and so we take advantage of some slopes to have some fun. There are times when we still like to be immature! However this particular day I am anxious to get back home as I know that my brothers will be there.

"I have to leave you Walter. It's been great fun but Käthe, Ernst and Anna are coming around this afternoon to see my parents. Lotte will be there as well, but Hans Wiemann has to go and help his father".

I didn't mention Rudolf as I'm not sure if he will be able to come. His life is becoming very precarious. He could be arrested at any time and I fear is in great danger. To see him at our home for even a short while would be marvellous. Sure enough, my family are together squeezed into the small flat and Mama has as expected produced the wonderful coffee but with the financial hardships the cakes she used to provide are no longer available. Only very plain ones have been made. Rudi and Gretel though happily play on the floor in the lounge trying to keep clear of so many pairs of legs – a perfect scene. They all greet me when I walk in and after a little while, the time I love the best begins – the family discussion starts and I listen for a while. Rudolf becomes more forceful in his speech and voices begin to rise. I don't mind including myself in the conversation now that I am bringing in albeit a small wage and considered a fully-fledged adult member of the family.

"Surely our Allies in Britain will intervene and help us stop the threat of such an extreme Government?" I ask.

Rudolf laughs with some derision. "No – they have a fear of the U.S.S.R. becoming all too powerful. Don't forget that this upstart Hitler had in his book 'Mein Kampfe' that the future for the Reich is in The East. The people who are in government in Britain and also their allies want Germany to invade the U.S.S.R."

At this point Oma intervenes and reminds everyone here that children are present.

"Perhaps someone could take Rudi and Gretel out for a walk?" she enquires hopefully looking in the direction of Lotte and Käthe.

"Come my little one" said Anna getting up and holding out her hand. "Let's see if we can go and play somewhere else". Gretel looks a little disappointed but stands up.

"The boy should not be listening" remarks Rudolf looking at his son Rudi.

Käthe interrupts Rudolf saying quietly "Please don't be so blunt."

"I say it for his protection and our safety. Children can inadvertently betray their parents. These are hard and dangerous times Käthe. We have to be careful" replied Rudolf.

"Ok, Ok, but please talk to him gently" said Käthe. I cannot help but notice that there seems to be some tension between Rudi's parents. I have recently been aware of this barrier recently and that hurts me as I love them both.

Lotte turns to both the children "Come on Rudi and Gretel, let's take a walk down to the Stadtpark and see if we can find a friend of yours to play with. There's loads of snow out there and I have the most wonderful toboggan which is Uncle Werner's so you can use it to slide down some slopes"

The two children happily skip over to Lotte. She is without doubt their favourite aunt who gives lots of love and cuddles. After a few little affectionate comments given by all the adults, they put on their coats, gloves, hats and scarves and rush out of the front door, down the stairs, through the main front door and out into the street.

"But the U.S.S.R. is not intending to take over Europe and anyway our socialism will not be the same as theirs. We are a more democratic nation and believe in the rights and welfare of each Citizen or at least we were" I persist. I'm really enjoying myself now, as at long last I can say my beliefs and join in with the adults.

"Ah, but if Germany becomes socialist, then greed from "big business" firms and their financiers will no longer flourish and the poor will expect more of a say in their lives. They will have expectations of a decent chance to improve themselves, for freedom of thought, assistance for the less fortunate and a more caring state. The British poor would then see that there is hope for them, which would threaten the "big businesses" over in Britain" said Ernst.

"But with socialism, the economy will flourish without the few benefiting. Surely that is a better outcome" I ask.

"Why would the British government help us achieve the annihilation of the fascism threat and help us form a socialist state?" said Rudolf.

"Surely the British government and their allies wouldn't be so short sighted and just think of the power of the rich and give power to Hitler and his henchmen" I argue back. Perhaps I am being inexperienced and are my brothers being realistic.

"The British and Soviet Union governments and their secret services are being informed of the situation here and yet they are choosing to ignore it. Why? The German government is re-arming and getting ready for war. The British are hoping that our country will march to the east. Don't forget that the rich and powerful men here have a lot to lose. This is why so many of them back certain politicians in order to get the politics they need to survive." said Ernst

"Look at the backing which Hitler gets from Dr Hjalmar Schacht, Kurt von Schröder, Fritz Thyssen, Alfred Krupp, Siemens and Robert Bosch. Most of them are connected with the arms industry. They want war and for Germany to re-arm." said Rudolf

"If there is a God may he help us and the rest of the world" mumbles Opa.

"Help is not coming for us. Believe me, they know that Germany is re-arming and yet what is anybody doing about it? These governments know that there are so many citizens trying to stop our present right wing government and for our pains, we are being murdered in the streets by our own countrymen who are fascists. Leading members of the socialist parties are just being mown down by extremists and yet what is the rest of the world doing about it?" Rudolf continues. "No they are more concerned about the rise of the working class who just want a decent wage, a decent life and food on their table. Whatever happens though, we must not give up the fight. We have our set our course against the fascists and we will have to fight, no matter the risks to ourselves. The cause is greater than the individual. All democratic parties and races should stand together and fight for democracy. We should not get involved in petty squabbles about different beliefs. Jews, social democrats, communists must all fight together to rid this world of fascism."

"You may be right Rudolf, but you are also correct that we must not let these doubts about the lack of support from abroad stop us. We must carry on." is my last comment.

Rudolf looks at each and every one of us and says "The time is near when things might get worse for all of us. The one thing that we can all be proud of is the strength and conviction of all of us around this table in our fight against fascism."

"May God help this family" said Oma agreeing with our father's earlier comment.

I know that Rudolf and Ernst are extremely close and I have the feeling that they also work together in the resistance, but I have no idea what they were doing. When they said that the British and

Russian governments and their allies know about the intentions of our country, how do they know? I wonder if they are sending in people from Britain or elsewhere to spy on our government or do Rudolf and Ernst know something about information being sent from us to them. Do they have anything to do with this? Is this why they are so confident in what they were saying? The last thing that they will do is to tell us. That would be a danger to all of us. I am so proud of their bravery and a little envious of their closeness. I am the little one who still has a lot to learn.

Horror and dismay strikes the hearts of nearly all the population on 28th February. We awoke in the morning to discover that at 21.25 the previous night the Reichstag had been destroyed by fire. Who has done this? What is the reasoning behind this tragedy?

We soon discover that an unemployed bricklayer who had recently arrived in Germany has been arrested. His name is Marinus Van der Lubbe and it is said that he is a communist. Of course the Nazis make great use of this information by saying that the communists are plotting against the German government. As a result our new Chancellor gets his way and persuades Paul von Hindenburg to pass an emergency decree to prevent an uprising by the communist party. Igniting the Reichstag according to Hitler is supposed to be a signal to the communists for a revolution. If it is a signal, then none of us had heard of this through the grapevine. My friends and I feel that a fascist dictatorship is underway.

This is the opportunity they have been waiting for. The Nazis can now start to flex their muscles and our country is at a turning point. It is too late for the left wing parties to successfully fight the Nazis. We've spent too long with in-fighting amongst ourselves. This is probably the beginning of the end of our democracy.

Many of my friends are on the same wave length as me as they all turn up at my home so that we can discuss the new situation. We feel that to meet in a café is no longer safe.

"Whoever caused the Reichstag to go up in flames might not even be politically motivated" said Harry.

"I know that they're saying a communist did it, but I hear that he's also an arsonist" adds Siegfried.

"Surely if it had been a plot, it's more likely to be a fascist one as Hitler's managed to get an emergency decree out of it", I add.

"Yes and because of that, all civil liberties have been suspended, all the communist delegates arrested along with mass arrests of other communists" remarks Werner Etter.

Silence reigns for a few minutes with each of us deep in our own thoughts. The silence is broken when I speak.

"It is a dangerous time ahead so for the moment, I think we ought to wait for orders as to our actions. We mustn't make silly mistakes now." I tell them. With that there was a consensus of agreement.

Hitler persuades Hindenburg to call a general election. With the communist party banned and our delegates arrested, there seems no hope. The social democrats finally awake to the dangers but it's all too late. The Reichstag Fire Decree not only suspends civil liberties in Germany, but the Nazis ban publications not considered "friendly" to the Nazi cause. How can we warn the population without getting arrested ourselves?

We continue to distribute illegal leaflets as best we can but we have to be so careful. We are beginning to realise that there are many people ready to report our activities. We also need to organise ourselves better as I realise that this new phase of our resistance against the fascists is extremely dangerous.

Outside the polling stations the Nazis as usual show their power, hovering menacingly as people arrive to vote. Despite all our efforts, to my family and friend's dismay, on 5th March, the Nazi Party and Hitler gain power. Fear for the future spreads throughout our community.

I'm summoned to a meeting at Maschen in the nature reserve in Horst, along with two other members of the local youth organisation. This will be our last meeting. The weather has turned exceptionally kind so we could sit on the grass and heather even though it is still March. When we arrive I see a crowd of eager faces looking around ready to do what is needed. We sit within our own groups according to the districts we are from. This is to ensure that our leaders can come and join us to privately discuss our future aims.

Gone are the days of general knowledge. Too much information concerning other groups will bring danger to all. Hitler, we know is trying to pass the Enabling Act in Parliament and once through, he can pass laws by decree without the involvement of the Reichstag. Hence tightening of the dictatorship will increase and our lives will be at risk. At times an involuntary nervous shudder vibrates through my body. I'm only seventeen years old and have committed myself to a dangerous future.

Before they come round to see us individually, we are given a talk by Walter Knut[64], the leader of greater Hamburg. He speaks to us about the organisation's plans that there will be contact to the central organisation and the importance to continue to produce leaflets. Security and precautions are essential for our survival.

I'm part of the Winterhude/Uhlenhorst districts and when the leaders arrive at our little group of three, they chat to us about what they hope and also expect from the Winterhude youth group. At the end of our session, Walter Knut appoints Hans Scharzmeyer, who is three years older than me to be the political leader, Werner Etter to be in charge of propaganda and finally I am to be the organisation leader. We come away from the meeting in silence. In a way, we had all been rather shaken by the experience as the seriousness of our mission starts to hit home. Our leaders thought that we are the best for being in charge of our district so we must not let them down.

What a responsibility has been put on our shoulders in organising our youth group into a safer unit. If any of us are caught, the less we all know about each other, the chance of betraying our friends under torture will lessen. I split our group into smaller ones of five people in each with a leader who will report to me. I make Erwin Wagenknecht a group leader and he later manages to form another group in Barmbekerstrasse with Siegfried Volkmann in charge. Making smaller groups hopefully will avoid mass arrests. It

---

[64] Walter Knut was born in 1912 and died in the dreaded 999 Division in 1942. Many people who had been political opponents of the Nazi regime were put in this unit to be used as "cannon fodder" or for the clearing of mines by walking potentially dangerous territory in front of the Army. The people in this unit were not expected to survive.

is quite rewarding that my analysis of people's characters and their thought patterns is really paying off now that we need more recruits. It is not that I feel the need to boast. We all have different skills and this is mine. I might be the quiet one, but my observations of people is turning out to be accurate and very useful.

We also need someone trustworthy to become our treasurer. Herta Winzer will be ideal for this position. Despite her tender age of sixteen, she accepts this task without giving it a second thought. What a brave girl.

As expected, the Enabling Act is approved on 23rd March 1933 and will come into force on 27th March. Our lives are now turned upside down. Thousands of members of the social democrat party and also the communist party are arrested and we hear that the majority are being sent to Germany's first concentration camp at Dachau. This is opened on 22nd March, a day before the Enabling Act is passed. How can any opposition delegates oppose this Bill at the Reichstag if they have been arrested? We hear that these concentration camps are called "re-education centres" but the SS who run the places call them concentration camps.

The Nazi papers are full of pictures of concentration camp inmates, unshaven, ill clothed with the worst possible appearance. We're horrified to see how badly opponents to fascism are treated but I wonder if the Nazis are oblivious to this as they are so convinced they are right and do not seem ashamed the citizens of our realm end up looking like this. Are they trying to convince the nation that these people are criminals and Jews who have been destroying our Fatherland?

We try to put our fears behind us and to reinforce our comradeship in these difficult times. Our youth group had been out all day having a lovely long hike in the country. The weather has been glorious and it is our only chance to get together without being observed as political opponents of the Nazis. Just for our differing beliefs we could be arrested. Whilst walking in the open countryside we can talk freely and there is a lot to discuss with the events rapidly deteriorating.

As we start to walk along Hamburgerstrasse, Karl Heinz points to a poster which had been stuck on a wall. We all wander over to see if it is important for us.. Karl Heinz starts to read out loud as there are some of us who are not able to see the writing properly with so many encircling the notice[65].

"For our Defence! On 30th January 1933 Adolf Hitler, the leader of the German Freedom Movement… " At this phraseology there are quiet derisions of laughter.

We have learnt not to gain attention from any passers-by as it is now so dangerous to have opposing opinions to Hitler.

"I'll continue" said Karl Heinz. *"Adolf Hitler, the Leader of the German Freedom Movement was appointed Chancellor of the German Reich and on 5th March, the German people showed their allegiance to him and his liberating work. The national revolution, the old system has been struck into rubble and Marxism crushed to the ground. Germany is now approaching a new ascendance. This is a grandiose German fight for Freedom."*

"A fight for freedom?" remark Werner Etter in a very sarcastic voice.

"Shush" is the unanimous response. We are now alert and wondering what is to come next.

Karl Heinz continues. *"The international world of Jews has accepted this with hate and fury. They see their power in Germany ending and they are now unable to make Germany a Soviet-Jewish criminal colony. The Zionist Leader Theordor Herzi declared in 1897 at the Jewish Congress in Basel (excerpts taken from the 7th meeting)*

"As soon as a non-Jewish state dares to take action against us Jews, we must be able to prepare war against them and world opinion will be with us, the whole press will be with us with a few exceptions. The whole press of the world is in our hands!!"

After this great planning, the press of the world have expressed their hatred of Germany accusing the Germans of the worst crimes.

A Jewish Lie – "In Germany Jews are tortured to death"

A Jewish Lie – "Jews eyes are burnt out, hands chopped off, ears and noses cut off and even corpses carved up".

A Jewish Lie – "Jewish women are killed in indescribable ways and Jewish girls are raped in front of their parents".

---

[65] In italics translated from poster in the book *"Anschläge – Deutsche Plakate als Dokumente der Zeit 1900-1960"*

The Jews spread the same lies in the last war. They want to incite the world against Germany. They have asked the people of the world to boycott German goods and by doing that, they want to increase the misery of unemployment in Germany. They want to run German export. German people and Comrades! German womenfolk, your companions! The guilty ones towards these crimes particularly the German Jews mean hatred against us and they want to start agitation and for Germany to be boycotted."

"Oh my goodness, I can see which way this is going. I don't like the sound of it one little bit. The Nazis are making the Jews the cause of all Germany's problems" remarks Walter in horror.

Another "shush" is unanimously uttered. Karl Heinz continues.

"They are calling on their Jewish race who live abroad to fight against the German people by announcing lies and slander. Therefore the decision of the German Freedom Movement, the Reich's leadership is to defend ourselves against these criminal agitators and their hatred.

It has been decided that on Saturday 1st April at 10.00 a.m. all Jewish shops, department stores, chancelleries etc should be boycotted. Therefore we call upon all German women and men to refuse to buy from Jewish businesses and department stores! Do not go to Jewish attorneys! Avoid Jewish physicians. This will show the Jews that it is unacceptable to dishonour the German race. Whoever acts against this request proves that they are supporting the enemies of Germany.

Praise the venerable Field Marshall from the last war and realm, President Paul von Hindenburg!

Praise the leader of the Chancellor of our realm – Adolf Hitler!

Praise the German people and the holy German Fatherland!

Signed on behalf of the Central Committee for the defence against the Jewish cruelty and boycott everything against their race.

Streicher" Karl Heinz finally finishes speaking but this time there is absolute silence for at least a minute.

"I think that before we say anything else, we must go back to my flat" I announce quietly and then in a loud voice "After our lovely day in the countryside, I'm so thirsty as I am sure we all are, so would you all like to come back to my place for a drink before you all go home? I think my place is the closest".

I see my friend's startled expressions and shock after hearing this proclamation, but thankfully they all pick up my warning not to say anything until we are safe from listening bystanders. Since we first started looking at the notice, quite a few other people have gathered around us. We move away leaving the others to read the news.

As we walk into the flat, Mama looks up from repairing some of my clothes.

"Hello everyone, did you have a nice day? The weather has been kind to you". Her voice trails into silence as she studies our faces. She puts down her sewing and quietly asks. "What's wrong?"

We tell her about this proclamation and I can see by her expression that she is now very worried. Mama, like us, knows so many Jews and is a frequent customer in their shops. Some of them are good friends of ours.

"Oh my goodness, what will happen to these people? The Nazis are obviously making them targets along with the communists and social democrats "agitators" for all the trouble our country is in. Are the Stenders on their list I wonder?"

What can I say to Mama? Three of her sons are trying to stop the fascists. When will the Nazis discover this? Will ignoring this order bring attention to our resistance movement and endanger everyone connected with us? It is a terrible thing to say, but it looks as though we will have to abandon our friends who have Jewish shops. We all feel dreadful about this as they are innocent. I have several Jewish friends; one of them is called Goldzier[66]. A number of Jews take part in our groups but I think we might have to help them leave the country soon as it is becoming dangerous for them to stay. Rebelling against this order will put our organisation at risk as we cannot afford for anyone to be detained for whatever reason.

After my friends left, Mama came and sat next to me. "Werner I am worried as I am not sure if you realise what could happen if you or your friends are arrested. You know Papa is so worried about Rudolf's activities and to know that you youngsters are seemingly following his footsteps would devastate him. For once I agree with

---

[66] After the war, he turned up at my parent's place asking after me. He was dressed in an American Air Force uniform having escaped the country after his imprisonment in the youth prison in 1934/35.

him. Werner, we will do what we can to help our Jewish friends but discretely so I am pleading with you not to do anything rash."

"I will be careful – really I will Mama".

Sure enough, on 1ˢᵗ April, the SA men loiter outside the shops of the Jews intimidating anyone who dares to think of entering the buildings. My heart bleeds for them as this means the end of their shops, therefore no income so what will happen to them? Life is hard enough now with poverty and hunger but how are they going to survive? And yet so many of the population are ready to listen to this Nazi propaganda. It seems an easy way to blame someone else for the problems of the country. A few people brave the menacing threat of the SA and enter the shops, but they are badly beaten by these thugs.

A great number of the population look to the Nazis to resolve the terrible crisis we are in. They are offering a better life if the left wing citizens are imprisoned along with the Jews, blaming these people for all the misfortunes the people are experiencing.

On 7ᵗʰ April laws come into effect barring Jews from holding any Civil Service position, University and State title or status.

On 26ᵗʰ April the Geheime Staatpolizei or the Secret State Police are formed and is known to everyone as the Gestapo. None of us have come across them yet but I have a feeling that we will in the future as they carry out arrests and interrogations of political suspects. Göring has been put in charge of them so this does not bode well for any of us.

Carla surprises us all one evening by calling round to see us. Hans and Carla are not as close to me as my other siblings but it is still good to see them. However the look on Carla's face alerts me that all is not well.

"The Gestapo turned up at our place and have taken Hans." She starts crying and Mama puts her arm around her to comfort her. None of us speak about our "work" so she has no idea how serious this situation can be. We do not know if this is to do with the fact that he is a brother of our Rudolf and hope that a bit of "persuasion" might make Hans talk or has Hans been quietly involved in some way with the resistance?

I know that Hans works with Willi Bredel[67]. Whatever the problem, we must all support Carla whilst Hans is being "questioned".

By the end of April, 18,000 communists, 12,000 social democrats have been arrested. The newspapers supporting these parties have been outlawed so the German states (i.e. the Nazis) have sole access to official propaganda. This has now been welded into a powerful machine supporting and encouraging aggression. We try as hard as we can to distribute leaflets warning of this aggression but we are beginning to feel like small fish in a huge ocean of evil.

Rudolf is now living back with us. Although I love my brother so much and am pleased to see more of him, I do feel sad as I also love his wife Käthe. I know how much they think of each other, but poor Käthe has been living in terror as their home is always being searched by the Gestapo and they have frequently been questioned. It's no place for Rudi to live a normal childhood but it is hard to watch their marriage deteriorating. Rudolf is such an important part of our resistance movement and this has meant a huge sacrifice for Rudolf's family. Even I can see that it is near impossible for their marriage to continue when Rudolf constantly puts his life at risk and this obviously threatens Käthe and Rudi's lives as well.

Very early on the morning of 1st May, Rudolf came to my room to speak to me. Sitting on my bed he chats for a while about mundane matters. This is not his usual subject matter as his mind is usually totally connected with the current crisis. Finally he starts to speak seriously to me.

"Werner, I think I should tell you this just in case I should never return. You will then need to speak to Mama and Papa and tell them what has been planned for today and you must tell them how much I love them."

I'm now terrified for my brother. He's everything to me but I know how completely dedicated he is to fighting fascism regardless of his own welfare.

---

[67] Willi Bredel was a German writer. In 1923 he participated in the Hamburg Uprising (as did Rudolf), was arrested and sentenced to two years imprisonment. In 1933 he was arrested and sent to Fuhlsbüttel Concentration Camp and released in 1934.

"Werner, we've arranged a short demonstration as it is Labour Day (1ˢᵗ May) as you know. We have decided to go ahead with this even though it is dangerous for us but it is to prove that the fight for freedom loving people is not over. We will be armed so if the Storm Troopers arrive too soon, we are prepared to fight them to our last man. As you know the Storm Troopers are armed so it is our only way to protect ourselves."

The thought of Rudolf being harmed is an emotional feeling so very hard to describe. He's everything to me but I have to accept his decision as he would not be true to himself if he sat back and did nothing. I smile bravely at him and tell him that I will be thinking of him all the time until he comes home. He puts a hand on my shoulder, looking straight into my eyes and said "You know Werner, I'm so proud seeing how much you've grown into a true socialist and a caring son to our parents." I gulp back my tears.

Luckily for everyone concerned Rudolf's demonstration is successful. The SA and SS along with the police, arrive too late as the freedom fighters disperse in time. This gives us all great encouragement, as lately we have all felt despondent knowing that more and more indiscriminate arrests are taking place. News begins to seep through to us of the first murders of prisoners who apparently were "trying to escape".

That evening Ernst, Anna and Gretel call round to see us. I think it is to check if Rudolf is all right. I am sure that Ernst and Rudolf discuss a lot with each other and give each other support. Our parents are oblivious of the May Day events and are just happy we are all together. We all sit down together and chat generally to each other and then Ernst starts talking to us about an event which happened that day.

"I am very proud of the local women folk in Eimsbüttel" said Ernst

"And what's wrong with the women of Winterhude?" asks Mama in a mock hurt voice. We all laugh.

"Nothing Mama, but you know that the red flag is forbidden? Well the working class women in Eimsbüttel decided to hang out their red feather-bedding out of their windows in order for them to be "ventilated". This happened today being Labour Day. Apparently the Nazis are boiling with rage, but as nothing can be proven, they cannot arrest the women. What a clever and brave move these women took."

"Well I take back my comment. Why didn't we think of that?" replies Mama.

"Sometimes it doesn't have to be aggressive resistance to show the national socialists and I think that it was a brilliant idea" Anna agrees with Mama. We all murmur conformity to that.

When I arrive home from work the next day, my parents are sitting at the kitchen table looking extremely upset. My stomach churns over. I'm almost too frightened to ask them what is wrong with my three brothers in danger. I give Mama a hug and then sit down next to her and wait for the news.

"It's Rudolf" Mama manages to say. Now I'm really worried. I hold her hand which is nearest to me. I glance over at Papa. He's as white as a sheet and unable to speak. I wait for a few minutes and then Mama takes a deep breath and starts talking.

"I expect you have noticed that Rudolf has been on edge lately and I have suspected that he might be in trouble. He never speaks to us about his activities and I don't know how much you know Werner."

At this I cannot help looking a bit sheepish showing a bit of guilt. Rudolf never really says much but I do know that he is in the military wing of the resistance and our family name seems to be known in so many of the different places I attend in connection with my resistance work. I also know that Edgar André had been in charge before Rudolf and now he has been arrested; who knows what his fate will be.

"Mama continues. "Well this morning Rudolf behaved in a very restless way as he has these last few weeks and he kept glancing towards the door which was slightly ajar. You know the one which leads to Papa's shop. The bell above the shop door rang and next minute Papa was talking to some men who are asking for Rudolf. Papa answers in quite a raised voice so that we can hear and he starts prevaricating to delay these men. Rudolf jumped up listening and next minute I watch him run out through the open back door, over the fences and disappear into one of our neighbour's home and I presume straight through their place and out onto the streets."

Mama stops speaking for a moment. I stroke my other hand over our clenched hands. She takes a deep breath and continues.

"It was the Gestapo coming for Rudolf". She looks up at me with pitiful eyes and then she looks over at Papa.

"If it hadn't have been for your father stalling them, who knows what would have happened."

"Mama it sounds as though Rudolf has got away and he has so many contacts, that he has probably already arranged an escape route. You'll hear from him soon I'm sure, but I think we must presume that he won't be able to come home any more."

"I know Werner, but as long as he is safe, then that won't matter" answers Mama. Papa nods his head in agreement.

We sit in silence for a few more minutes, and then Mama in her usual stoic way, stands up and prepares some tea for us. She is the rock of our family. Her mother I understand was just the same despite the difficult situation she had in her life so perhaps it is in their genes to be so strong.

The following day, we hear even more bad news. All trade unions have now been banned. This took place the day after Labour Day[68]. The leaders of the trade unions have been arrested and sent to the concentration camps. Without the opposition of the arrested leaders the fascists have put all the old unions under the control of the Nazi party and have changed the name of the "trade union" to the labour front. How much worse is this all going to get I wonder.

All anti-fascists movements have been re-organised to work "underground" for we cannot abandon our fight as it will mean the ultimate destruction of Germany. We realise that an uprising against Hitler at this time is no longer a reality. However we all think that it is our duty for our country to carry on our work against the Nazis. Our main task is to consolidate and strengthen the illegal resistance groups by printing leaflets, papers etc so that people are informed

---

[68] 1st May

about the true events and that Hitler's policy will eventually lead to a new world war.

In her capacity of treasurer our young recruit Herta Winzer takes it all within her stride when she meets our leaders Walter Knut and also Helmut Prosche[69] who is responsible for financing our organisation in Hamburg.

Our problem is that we have no printer and I do not know what to do about it. One evening Ernst arrives to see our parents, so I decide to ask him when we are alone together if he can suggest a solution. We are so desperate to do something positive such as warning the local population about Hitler will mean war and the end to all of our freedom.

It seems that Rudolf or Ernst always have a solution to any such problems. Ernst tells me to type the articles on stencil paper with the ribbon of the typewriter not being used. This way holes are made in the paper instead of the letter being pressed onto the ribbon where a piece of paper is on the roller. He gives me instructions to go to the chemist and buy a particular assortment of chemical compounds which we have to mix together. This has to become thicker like a soft wax substance about an inch thick and the size of the paper. Once the paper is out of the typewriter, the backing sheet is destroyed and the stencil paper is pressed gently but firmly right face down on the wax type of compound so that the wax shows through the stencil. By brushing ink on the hardened wax type substance, it is then possible to place a clean sheet of paper gently on the "printer". The trouble is that this is very labour intensive and only a few can be printed but it is better than nothing. We have been promised a printer at a later date but initially we will have to manage like this.

Hans Schwarzmeyer composes the contents of the leaflets warning people of the dangerous times to come. He then types it out using the typewriter Werner Etter and I had bought. Werner and I then print it out in Werner's home when his Mother goes out.

---

[69] Helmut Prosche later went to Denmark and then to Spain where he was killed in the Spanish Civil War.

Werner Etter has also written some excellent articles, although the whole system is very primitive, we have at least started.

We all help to deliver them to houses around the Winterhude and Uhlenhorst area. I let the group leaders know the allotted streets for each of them so that they push the leaflets through the correct letter boxes. It is then up to the leaders to organise their groups. I am just anxious to ensure that there is no overlapping of deliveries. We also put adhesive leaflets on walls as well as painting slogans directly on suitable brickwork in the area.

One piece of good news for us has made Mama smile again. We've heard that Rudolf has managed to avoid being captured and is now in hiding. We understand that he initially went to my brother Hans's parents-in-law. Rudolf had some time ago helped Carla's sister and now her parents returned the favour. Since then he's been moving from place to place so that the Gestapo will not catch up with him. But at least, so far, he is safe.

I know a lot of the leaders of the Hamburg resistance not only because of my position in the youth organisation, but because of Rudolf and Ernst. The Stender name I should imagine is beginning to be mentioned too many times at the Gestapo headquarters. Ernst and I will have to be careful. Poor Papa keeps getting questioned as to where Rudolf has gone. Thank goodness Papa has no idea, apart from him being reasonably safe.

On 10th May life again takes a turn for the worse. To our horror, books which had been written by political opponents of the Nazis and other novels and non-fiction books which have not been approved by the state, (which includes Jewish books) have to be burnt. By this action so many books of our earlier culture in Germany will be destroyed forever. What a terrible crime as this is our heritage being obliterated for our future generations.

We all try to keep calm, not to bring attention to ourselves but Herta arrives one evening at my home looking quite distressed. I instinctively think of her brother whom I know has been very active within the resistance movement.

"Werner, the Gestapo came to my flat a short while ago. They're looking again for Fritz but thank goodness he is in hiding. I told the

Gestapo that I hadn't seen him for weeks. I don't know if they believe me. I'm so frightened for him."

She is near to tears so I give her a comforting hug and try to reassure her that Fritz will find a way of escaping. She then hesitates before saying "Is there any way that Rudolf could help him get out of the country?"

She looks at me earnestly, pleading with her eyes. I'm distraught feeling so helpless and I feel for her family's situation. Fritz had been an excellent youth leader and has been totally dedicated to the defeat of the Nazis. Oh I wish I could help them.

"Even Rudolf is in trouble and has had to go into hiding. Despite his contacts in so many places and being a leader within the organisation, he is finding it difficult to escape out of the country."

Poor Herta's face is crestfallen. "I hope you haven't minded me asking. He means everything to me and I just want to help him get to safety."

I really feel that I am letting the Winzer family down but what can I do?

"We'll just have to hope that his own friends will be able to help him" is my rather weak response.[70]

As the warmth of summer finally arrives, the first few political prisoners are released from "preventative" detention. These are the first people who had been arrested in March and April. We are shocked to see these brave men and women walking along the roads looking like frightened animals. They avoid being stopped by any of us and we now have confirmed the fate of anyone who is arrested.

We discover the truth from people who have experienced the gruesome torture of the Gestapo. Ernst had been quiet for a few days but his silence breaks by telling me that a wife of a very good friend of his received by parcel post; an urn containing the ashes of her

---

[70] Fritz worked with Rudi Lindau within the resistance movement. In December 1933 Fritz was arrested and imprisoned in Fuhlsbüttel Concentration Camp until 1939. He was later sent to Sachsenhausen Concentration Camp where he was eventually liberated in 1945.

arrested husband. I feel numb when we hear this. His friend had been arrested and this is the result. Werner, Hans[71] and I decide to ask each member of our youth group if they are prepared to carry on, knowing what to expect if we are arrested. Only a few people decide to pull out and nobody condemns them for it.

We now start using cover names so that in the event of arrest and torture, hopefully the most we might reveal under torture are pseudonyms and the next meeting place. I decide to use "Kuhl". No arrangements are made of any future dates beyond the next one. In some instances a colleague has been forced to reveal details of a meeting and the Gestapo have then put the prisoner there as a trap. I've heard that sometimes when the approaching, unsuspecting resistance fighter is seen by the exhausted and terrified captive the prisoner tries in some way to warn the person before the Gestapo realise who the contact is. Often it will involve throwing themselves under a tram or car so that no further punishment can be mitred out by the Gestapo. It takes courage to do such a thing but at least the rest of the group are saved.

About a month after Hans' arrest, he is released and like all the others before him, he is a changed man. His "questioning" has been extremely physical and whether it was to find the whereabouts of Rudolf or if Hans had been involved in any resistance work, I shall never know. It is never good to know too much.

We are all on edge seeing the country deteriorate. By June, more than half of the communist district leaders in similar positions of authority as Rudolf are in "detention" and hundreds of Nazi opponents have been killed.

On 14 July a law is passed excluding east European Jewish immigrants from German Citizenship. It really is time for the Jewish population to consider leaving our country while they can as this hatred towards them feels very menacing. I know that Papa has been asked by some of our Jewish friends to get Rudolf to help them escape. I do not know if Papa is passing on these requests to Rudolf when we know how precarious Rudolf's situation is.

---

[71] Hans Schwarzmeyer

That same day, a Law is passed making it illegal to form any new new political parties. The Nazi grip is tightening.

Life is becoming so frightening now. However my friends and I are determined to carry on as the right of freedom and democracy for Germany is far more important that our individual lives. I never thought that this conclusion would be on my agenda at the tender age of seventeen and a half years but these are not normal times.

Sometimes though it is so nice to let off steam and do "normal" activities for youths of our age. We love going out for the day and enjoying hiking in the countryside. Visiting the Landhaus, Borgweg[72] in the Stadtpark or the Milchschänke further along that road always is an enjoyable event. They both have beer gardens so we have wonderful evenings listening to the music and drinking beer or wine. I love the shape of the Milchschänke building which is probably one of the last original buildings left when the new Winterhude district was built. It is constructed in the old north German farm style with lovely warm reddish brown bricks and the roof sloping down to the first floor.

Why is life so cruel at the moment not allowing me to have a happy carefree youth? I suppose if I didn't have a conscience, then yes, I could have this but could I then live with myself? Deep down I know the answer to that one.

I am not the only one in my family whose life is not "normal". One day I wait rather nervously in the Stadtpark having arranged a meeting with a comrade. Whilst keeping a close eye open for anything suspicious happening, Ernst walks past me. I notice him approaching but his gait is not his usual one. I realise then that he is about to do exactly the same as me and meet an arranged contact. Neither of us acknowledges each other for fear our activities will be noticed by the Gestapo should they be in the vicinity. We are both obviously gainfully employed in our own resistance work.

Later when Ernst came to see our parents, we chat away about everyday things to try and keep a certain degree of normality in our household. This act helps detract any concerns our Mama and Papa

---

[72] Borweg becomes Hindenburgstrasse at a later date

may have with regard to possible risks we might be taking. I had been talking about Walter Beyer and some of his antics on the football pitch. Ernst then makes a remark about Walter's sisters in a very general way. This takes me aback as I do not really know them and I certainly did not know that he had any contact with them.. Ernst then quickly changes the subject when he sees my surprised look as he'd obviously said too much. Are any of Walter's sisters involved with Ernst I wonder?

Early one evening, just as I'm having my evening meal with Mama and Papa, I hear the key in the door. To our surprise it is Rudolf who is dressed in a dock worker's uniform. He is alone and I can see that he has no intention of staying. Mama and Papa both stand up to welcome him as he approaches us. They hug each other tightly for a while before Rudolf starts to speak.

"I'm sorry to have put you through so much worry. You have been such good parents to me and I have given you nothing but anxiety. I've been told that I cannot stay in Germany to carry on the fight. I have to leave now to join a ship which will take me away from here. I promise that I'll find some way to let you know that I am safe."

At that point he turns round to me and gives me a hug.

"Werner, look after our parents won't you. I know that I can trust you to do this for me."

I nod in confirmation and without further conversation he turns and walks out of our flat and our lives.

Winter is drawing in and the chilling winds from the east have started to blow. Lately Mama has been cooking a dish which I love called Eintopfgericht which is a meal cooked in one pot. When I say to Mama how I enjoy the dish she says "I have to admit that I also like it but it is this Goebbels idea of Winterhilfswerks for the unemployed. We have to cook this dish on a Sunday. I don't know if you have noticed but someone knocks on our door collecting money which is the difference between the usual price of a meal and this one. The money is supposed to be going to the unemployed and needy which I do agree with, but is it going instead to the Nazis to rearm?"

"The trouble is Mama that when I say this to other people, I just get told how cynical I am. At least this collection is not forever. We can stop cooking Eintopfgericht for the Nazis in March next year but then we can continue to enjoy it ourselves."

"Yes but that could be five or six months of us paying for more armaments to be used in another war" Mama replies in dismay.

I cannot dispute that point as in October 1933 I hear that orders have been given for 1000 war planes to be built and also military barracks. To add to our concerns our country withdraws from the Geneva Disarmament Conference when France refuses to accept Hitler's plan of the French disarming to our official level or alternatively our country to rearm to the level of the French. Isn't it obvious to the rest of the world what Hitler is trying to do?

On 30th November, Anna and Gretel visit us unexpectedly. Both of them look distraught and my heart sinks. Something must have happened to Ernst. Anna sits next to Mama and holds her hand.

My sister-in-law tries desperately to compose herself. She takes a deep breath and starts to explain.

"Mama, Papa, the Gestapo have just been to our flat and they have arrested Ernst." There is a gasp of horror from both our parents.

"Oh no" moans Papa to himself. Mama has taken a sharp intake of breath.

"What happened?" asks Mama quietly.

Anna starts to explain how they had been just about to eat their evening meal when there was a loud banging on the door.

"Ernst went and opened it, but he was pushed back hard by some brutish SA men. He lost his balance and fell backwards and sat on the floor and was ordered to stand up. Behind the SA stood two Gestapo men who were sneering at Ernst's surprise and apprehension. Some of the SA started pulling open cupboard doors and the drawers searching through everything. By "searching", I mean knocking furniture over, books etc being opened then thrown in any direction. It was terrifying. Poor Gretel just clung to me in total fear."

At this point, she pulls Gretel towards her and sits her on her lap, giving her a lovely cuddle and then continues. "The Gestapo weren't interested in asking Ernst anything. All they said was "at last a Stender has fallen into our hands."

I shudder at this point.

"The Gestapo then told Ernst that he is to be taken to the Gestapo Headquarters and before I had any opportunity of wishing him well, he was grabbed and almost dragged out of the flat."

"Oh no" mutters Papa again.

I feel that I have to say something as everyone is silent.

"Look Anna, I'm sure that we will be able to arrange a rescue for him. I know so many people so don't worry, we'll save him."

At this point, Anna turns round to me and smiles gently.

"Werner, that is a lovely thought, but you must understand that nobody escapes from arrest. If you and your friends try to stage any rescue attempt it is doomed to fail and then they will have two Stenders. How do you think Ernst would feel if he found out that you had also been arrested trying to free him?"

"Anna's right Werner" adds Mama. "You must promise us that neither you nor anyone else will attempt such a thing."

"I just want to help" I mutter quietly. Anna squeezes my hand. "Little Gretel needs her big brother now more than ever". I am always called this as Gretel and I are so close. I reluctantly nod in agreement.

How much do the Gestapo know of Ernst's activities? I do not know anything really but I know Rudolf does. I'm sure to a certain extent, they help each other.

Each day seems endless as we cannot stop worrying about Ernst. The story of the urn containing the ashes of his colleague sticks in my mind. My two heroes of brothers are both at risk of losing their lives and I can do nothing for either of them. For a while we hear nothing about Ernst's welfare.

Then on 15ᵗʰ December Käthe is taken in for questioning. No doubt they're trying to find out where Rudolf is. Poor Käthe, she really does not deserve this treatment. None of us do come to that, but Käthe although supportive and in agreement with Rudolf's actions, has taken no actual part in the resistance movement to my knowledge. Lately she's showing signs of total exhaustion with the

Gestapo keep visiting her and now she's in Kolafu (Fuhlsbüttel). What will they do to her? All she ever did was support her husband.

Papa keeps taking to his bed. It is all too much for him and Mama keeps a smile on her face trying to show the world that all is fine. What strength of character she is proving to have.

Life is becoming unbearable with the worry about my brothers. I should have faith in Rudolf though when he eluded arrest and showed that he has determination to survive. To our amazement after weeks without any news, he writes to us from Russia using two different names. One is Otto and the other is Carl but at least he seems to be settling into his new country. Although Käthe and Rudolf have separated, they still communicate with each other and there seems to be no bitterness between them.

He tells us that he is busy working in engineering and he needs us to send some technical books to the U.S.S.R. I know the Soviet Union is working hard to modernise but they are lacking in information of modern technology. I miss him a lot but at least he is safe. I hope he settles into his new life and perhaps when Hitler is defeated, we will be together again.

As the year ends, we have no Rudolf, Ernst or Käthe here to enjoy a family Christmas. We had been right in that Christmas 1932 was a special Christmas being all together.

Here in our changed country, there are 209,000 SS men in existence and even worse 150,000 political prisoners in the concentration camps, one of whom is my brother Ernst.

CHAPTER 16

Ernst during 1933

The New Year has come and gone having spent as much time as possible celebrating the occasion with our family. I think that we all have the feeling that life might never be the same again so it has been so important to be together. No-one can take happy memories from us. But now the winter has closed in and is trying its best to bring down all our spirits. The vicious easterly wind is blasting icy cold tentacles over the flat lands along the north of Germany and it seems as though it polarises over our beloved Hamburg. Perhaps this is just in my imagination because of my mood at the moment. If only I could have enough money to provide clothing and warmth for Anna, Gretel and also my parents.

My thoughts wander back to the current political situation. I must really concentrate on co-ordinating the resistance movement in my unit so that we will be ready for the revolution to take place. It must happen before the ever increasing threat of Hitler and his party taking power and Germany losing democracy to the tyrant. The seemingly lack of concern by the social democrats towards the welfare and conditions of the working class melts into insignificance compared to the frightening thought of fascism taking hold in our country. I have two engagements that I have to attend on 9th and 10th January. Anna understands that my resistance work is dangerous now, but she just smiles encouragingly and carries on with her daily life. What would I do without her?

As I arrive at the first meeting, my spirits raise seeing fellow socialist believers arriving in the room. We are not provocateurs and anarchists as is often stated in the newspapers. We are normal upright citizens who have been forced into this position due to the threat of a right wing dictatorship looming in the very near future. Even when innocently walking in the streets, being in a shop or meeting friends can be hazardous. Without warning, the SA can appear and if they feel that they are not in the presence of like-minded people, they threaten, physically attack us or even worse. What sort of life is this?

It is disheartening when so many citizens seem to be enamoured by the pull of false promises of a better future. Hitler seems to produce speeches and events which look brilliant to some easily influenced public, but why don't they really listen to the contents of his speeches and analyse them properly?

Unemployment is now six million and people are starving and desperate. Hunger demonstrations are common and food shops attacked and emptied. Some of the young social democrats are prepared to work together with us to defeat this tyrant but there is very little cohesion with many of the older social democrats towards other main stream parties. It is frustrating that some of them are not thinking very deeply and instead they seem willing to ignore the dangers. If only they realised that they are being enticed into the spiders' web. This will be Germany's downfall if we don't watch out.

I am not alone though. Throughout Germany, other "free thinking" people are also worried about our country's future. Unfortunately we are not the majority of the population but we are strong with our beliefs. This network of people has joined our resistance organisation in the hope that we can become effective. We have to be a trustworthy unit otherwise we will all fail together and who knows what will happen to us then. We've all been given tasks and my mind is now churning over what I have to do next within my group. It is wonderful listening to others who are experts in different fields of operation and it helps me to form my own unit within the group. I know that we must never talk too freely but with Rudolf, I make an exception. We are bonded together in blood and we totally trust each other.

As Rudolf is a leader of a 'military wing', it helps to be aware of some of their plans and he knows to a certain extent our aims as without co-operation, the coup which is being planned to stop Hitler can never effectively take place. Also many of our leaders are interconnected. It is true that our set-up is not as safe and secure as we would like but we did not expect this dangerous situation to develop. Initially we thought that fascism would never progress and ruin our country so we had no inexperience in covert operations.

After the Great War, our leaders were unaware that the future would be violence and loss of freedom. They thought that the only way to attract attention to this political situation was to make themselves high profile with their speeches and warnings. By doing this, have we now left ourselves vulnerable? Since our enemies have become so powerful, they will know who to target and eliminate. I see so many people here who could be such a target.

Fritz Lux who has been listening intently at one of our lectures, stands up, looks around the room studying our eager faces.

"Welcome fellow citizens. Thank you for giving up your time to attend to this meeting. I am pleased to see the quality and high standard of people willing to take on the important tasks ahead of us. The citizens of Hamburg, along with the rest of our country deserve to live in a truly democratic Germany. Comrades, it is such good news that we are all prepared to risk our lives to stop fascism. If we are honest, we must come to the conclusion, seeing the current situation, that we can only destroy the threat of dictatorship by an armed rebellion. It is upsetting for us to have to take this action, but the violence and arrests of many of our comrades gives us no alternative. We have to co-ordinate with the 'military wing' of our organisation."

At this point Paul Tasteson agrees with him saying "the Red Front Brigade should also be involved in any discussions."

I smile to myself as in spite of the family connection with Rudolf who is one of the leaders of this brigade, we all have knowledge of the heroic work that the RFB have been doing over the years. Of course they will have a role to play whilst we will be busy ensuring that as many workers as possible support the campaign. If we plan this carefully, hopefully we will succeed. We look back at Fritz for him to continue.

"Our colleague here" holding his hand in my direction will have an important role to play as his group needs to discover where the vital enterprises are and where the war material is being manufactured. At the start of the uprising we will need the Hamburg gas services to be

switched off and the city to be without electricity. To call a general
strike will help us and then we should take control of certain factories
along with the Post Office, radio and telephone communications and
transport. Hamburg must still function but under socialist control
until free democratic elections can take place. We all know that there
will be serious risks of retaliation which could involve the opposition
releasing poisonous gas so contact will have to be made with
employees of the relevant laboratories to prevent this happening."

"Another group" Fritz points in the direction of another
colleague "will be infiltrating the police with the intention of
dividing police loyalties. We also need to find out if there are any
high ranking policemen having extra marital affairs, or drink
problems or any other weak points which we can exploit."

Fritz then looks at us generally, holds out both arms to us and
continues "It's a massive task which I am handing over to you all,
but I know I have a good team of people here who will endeavour
to succeed in saving Germany from annihilation. We must fight these
fascists and then we will be able to give freedom back to the masses."

We all look at each other, shocked with the knowledge and full
realisation of our task, but I know that the situation is getting so
serious that we are teetering on the edge of either anarchy or
totalitarian dictatorship under Adolf Hitler. We have to do something
as drastic as this for our future as well as for our children. Ordinary
freethinking citizens as well as our leaders are being persecuted,
beaten and killed for having socialist thoughts.

"I know what I am asking you to do is dangerous work, but I
have chosen all of you very carefully as I feel that you are capable
and trustworthy citizens of Hamburg. If we plan this carefully,
hopefully we will succeed" finishes Fritz Lux.

After this morale boosting but thought provoking meeting with
Fritz Lux I know my efforts must increase. I must not be foolish and
decide to speak to someone until I have been recommended a person
or after I have been quietly listening to conversations. It is really quite
a precarious situation as should my views come to the attention of
any right wing workers they would instantly report my activities.
After assessing the situation, I discreetly 'spread myself' into a wider

contact circle of people discussing views with various factory workers who I think might be useful to us. I feel that I have no spare time at all as I'm so busy. I have many useful contacts but I can see that I am just scratching the surface.

Transportation of military material is an important task to discover as we must fully understand the extent of rearmament within our country. All the information I can gather is given to Henry Meyer who is delivering the details to the relevant person.

Karl Rattai is a leader of the political/military section and his courier is L.… She is the fiancée of Rudi Lindau who is known to our family so if Rudi trusts her she must be all right. Werner knows Rudi[73] as he was involved with the youth marches into the countryside last year which Werner attended. I couldn't help but smile when Werner explained his difficulties of learning to march due to his bad leg. I can picture the scene of Werner hopping and skipping trying to keep up with the rest. As for these connections with so many of our leaders, it is a problem as we all have known each other in happier times. I hope our enemies are unaware of the connections. We are reorganising so that in future this should not happen, but before the 1930s we had no idea that familiarity would jeopardise our safety. I just hope that we all survive without arrests otherwise the end result could mean a collapse of our leadership. None of us know how strong we will be if we are "questioned by the Gestapo.

Franz Jacob is another leader of the group and connected with the Arbeitertheaterbundes (Workers Theatre Federation) which has been an excellent 'breeding ground' for new recruits. He only lives in Jarrestadt which is short distance from Gertigstrasse. Franz and I have had yet another discussion about Mary Schmidt. She's an attractive young lady, very intelligent and is totally committed to our cause. She would be quite an asset to our group if only she would agree to join me.

"I have a meeting at Bezirk, Hamburg with the Workers Theatre Federation on 30th January so this might be an excellent opportunity

---

[73]　Rudi Lindau

to approach Mary again. I agree with you Ernst that she would be ideal material for us – exactly what we're looking for. After I've given my speech and if she attends the meeting, I will speak with her to see whether she is prepared to help us."

All this becomes insignificant when on to our horror that very day the president of the Weimar republic, Field Marshall Hindenburg announces that he has asked Adolf Hitler to become his chancellor. Hitler has just a third of the seats at the Reichstag so what on earth has possessed the president to ask such a man to take on so crucial a position? On the night that the man with the silly moustache but very dangerous ambitions becomes our chancellor, the SA and Stalhelm march in torchlight processions to the centre of their cities. Anna and I are in absolute despair at the scene taking place in Hamburg. The singing, marching and the torches bring an indescribable feeling of dread. The scene seems almost from a film about the Roman Empire over a thousand years ago. How are we going to stop this evil power from manifesting itself from this nightmare scenario into unstoppable reality?

Ernst Thälmann tries to organise the SPD and the KPD joining together for a general strike in order to topple Hitler. Once again, the two political parties do not work together. It seems that SPD leadership are still hoping that they can peacefully remove the Nazis from power and live in a dream world that Hitler will not succeed in his attempt to destroy our democracy.

Hitler's next move is predictable now that he has control of the state communications including the radio and press. He wants another election but this time Göring calls a meeting of important industrialist and I hear that he has told them that the next general election could be the last in Germany for a long time. The NSDAP will need considerable amounts of money to ensure this victory[74].

Göring, who is Minister of Interior, then sacks senior police officers and replaces them with Nazi supporters[75]. They've recruited 50,000 members of the SA to work as auxiliaries. We need Rudolf

---

[74] He is given three million Reich Marks by these industrialists
[75] Who become the Gestapo

and his friends more than ever now. Who else will protect the population against these thugs?

My friend Franz Jacob, true to his word speaks to Mary Schmidt after his speech at the Workers Theatre Federation. Instead of refusing to help due to other commitments within the organisation, she says she'll let him know her answer in the next few days. Perhaps like the rest of us, she fully understands the danger our country is now in.

On 4th February it is announced that a decree is to be put forward in parliament to protect the German people by giving Hitler the power to ban political meetings and newspapers of rival parties. We all feel frightened for the future.

In desperation, on 7th February a meeting takes place at Sporthaus Ziegenhals, Konis Wusterhausen near Berlin where opposing political leaders discuss the violent overthrow of Hitler and his government before total military control is established. We all wait and hope that the plans we have been preparing will be put to good use.

Göring then raids the headquarters of the KPD in Berlin which he explains is to uncover a plot being made to overthrow the government. Leaders of the KPD are arrested but no evidence is found. How did he find out about the plan? However, he then announced that he had discovered a communist plot to poison the German milk supplies. Of course propaganda like that will not help our cause at all. Why would anyone in their right mind try to poison the milk and kill a whole population? These rumours provide more fear to the populace but we cannot disprove these claims as we have no 'right to reply'.

When I met Fritz Lux one day, he introduces me to Alfred Barthel[76], also known as "Emil". He has arrived from Berlin.

"I would like you to assist "Emil" as much as you can Ernst. I am handing over the 'reins' to him as I fear that I will not be able to continue in Hamburg for much longer. Emil is extremely anxious that we concentrate on infiltrating major local industries."

---

[76] According to Berlin Archives, Alfred Barthel later uses the pseudonym "Benno" during 1938/39 when he was part of the AM Apparat in Paris

I shake hands with "Emil". Fritz has been a good friend and colleague and I'll miss him but he has a very high profile due to his position as a member of the Hamburg Parliament. It's better to let other people do the secretive work. This will then lessen our exposure to the Nazis. I assure Alfred or rather "Emil" that I will help him as much as I can.

"I presume that you are interested in the utilities such as the gas, electricity, water, transport utilities, the harbour and our local area generally?" I ask him.

"Emil" nods and waits for me to talk now that Fritz has left us. We spend quite some time together whilst I update him with all the information I know. I take "Emil" to various places of strategic importance.

"Emil" attends many of my meetings where he takes the opportunity to encourage comrades to infiltrate the important industries. He makes it clear that decisions have to be taken as to who will be responsible for the sabotage in each factory or industry, both in Hamburg and the surrounding area. This takeover will have to be controlled properly so that although nothing will operate for our enemies, it can easily be reinstated for us. The essential utilities will have to function in order to prevent chaos.

I assure him that the district of Altona, the railway management and railway workshops in Banksstrasse in the Rothenburg area, the gas, water and electricity, Hamburg port and the shipyards should all keep functioning when the time comes.

The workers have started to protect themselves against frequent attacks from the Nazis, by filtering away weapons stolen from the stores of both the army and police. We are very grateful to sympathisers who are employed within these bases. Being a non-violent person, it hurts me to admit that it is impossible to *discuss* different views with a Nazi as all we ever receive in reply is physical abuse. Unfortunately I have to admit that we have no alternative but to defend ourselves. I am not a military man and the use of guns is abhorrent to me, but I can do my part at least by helping with the infiltration of organisations.

Oh how I hate all of this. All I have ever wanted is a democratic socialist government. Will this ever be achieved? Why is it that other powerful countries cannot see the danger evolving here and help us to remove this evil?

One evening Rudolf arrives at our flat and after a while Anna discretely busies herself with Gretel in the bedroom so that I can talk with him.

"They've decided not to go ahead with an uprising Ernst. After a long debate, the overall majority thought that it would just end up a blood bath for the nation. At present there are just too many military supporters of the Nazi party. Just look what happened on 30th January after Hitler became chancellor. The numbers of his 'troops' and supporters marching was prohibitive which makes an attempted coup totally impossible. I often wonder you know – have we missed our moment?"

Rudolf looks so downhearted. He's given up so much of his life fighting for the rights of the downtrodden workers and yet has anything been achieved? My involvement is relatively recent. I took it on when I could see no other way of defeating Hitler and now what will happen to Germany? I try to put a brave face on things but realising his chance of gaining power, Hitler insists on another general election.

"I think that we will just have to continue with both your military and my intelligence work and hope that the people who have become infatuated with fascism will finally wake up before it's too late when Hitler has total control. If there is a chink in his armour and people see the reality of the situation, then we must act but until that time, we cannot do anything but let the public know that there is an alternative to fascism and to keep 'annoying' the Nazis."

I cannot really think of anything more positive to say at the moment and looking at my despondent brother, it is heart breaking. Do I really believe what I am saying? Now come on Ernst, pull yourself together. If we start giving up our fight, then this country will be doomed.

Rudolf smiles weakly at me. I know that his depressive thoughts will only be a blip in his usual positive proactive manner. Before long, he will be back organising his Red Front Brigade into action and giving morale boosting talks to different resistance groups. He usually puts me to shame.

A few days later, Franz Jacob gently pulls me aside to speak to me.

"Mary Schmidt has agreed that she will work with you Ernst. I'm sure that her contribution towards our cause will make a big difference. Because of the type of work we need her to do we've given her a test to see how she will operate under pressure or danger. We have to know if we can use her for sensitive work so we asked Käthe Brandt to help as she is an active member of our organisation and also works with Mary at Derutra".

I nod in agreement as I understand all the precautions we have to take now. I do know these people through Rudolf but I will never include him in any conversation. Franz continues.

"Käthe invited her to a comrade's home and then asked Mary to type out a list of people who need to be observed. When Mary was absorbed in the typing someone started to bang on the door and shouted that they are the police. Her reaction was excellent. It's a shame the poor girl had to experience that, but as I said, we need to observe her reactions in a crisis."

I am relieved that she 'passed' the test and answer "I feel quite comfortable with Mary as she has good reports from Stange or "Peter" as others know him. I know Hildegard Braun from Kiel has also worked with her so she has excellent references."

"Good. So I will leave it up to you to approach her to explain what you hope she can achieve. Are you happy to do this?" I nod in assent.

When I meet Mary in Wagnerstrasse, we talk for some time as I let her know what I would like her to do. She then tells me that she'd bought a typewriter last year from someone within our organisation. Typewriters are like gold dust to us as they are a means of preparing leaflets and also typing out documents when we have no facility for photocopying them. She explains to me that it is kept at her boyfriend's home. His name is Wilhelm Müller.

On hearing about Wilhelm, I'm a little concerned that he may be Mary's 'Achilles heel' as I have never heard of him within our circle and he has not been investigated. I ask her for more information about Wilhelm.

"I can understand your concerns Ernst. He has not been connected with any political organisation but he is in agreement with our aims so I feel that I can trust him. I initially had tentative political conversations with him in order to discover his thoughts and then whether he might be willing to help us fight fascism."

I study her face to try and read her thoughts. I'm not sure if his commitment is to Mary or our cause but Mary feels confident as to his reliability.

"Wilhelm has started calling me Maria so I think it is time for everyone to use this as my name. Apparently he thinks that it sounds nicer with the surname Müller." She smiles shyly.

"Oh so he has honourable intentions towards you then?" I ask laughing. It's so nice to be reminded that normal relationships are still developing despite the political situation. It's so easy to forget this at present. I decide to take the chance knowing Mary's (or should I say Maria's?) judgement is usually so accurate. I meet Wilhelm at the Arbeitertheaterbundes and discuss the possibility of him joining the organisation. I make it very clear to him the implications and dangers of the work involved.

Another 'cog' needed for us to function efficiently is someone willing to act as a central point for the collection and delivery of post. Jonny Stüwe has agreed to help us. Accepting 'the post house' position is just as dangerous as many other of our 'jobs' should the police discover his activities. As for the police, on 22nd February Göring united the SA, SS & Stahlhelm into one single police force so we are in a growing police state.

I stop mulling over these concerns when I arrive home. This little flat is my sanctuary and my time with Anna and Gretel is precious. Anna put down a newspaper when I arrived and her face had lit up from the worried expression she had previously shown. As usual Gretel rushes over to greet me and the ritual hugs to her and then Anna take place. It's so wonderful to be home with my family. After a few minutes of sheer joy, my thoughts return to Anna's expression whilst she was reading the paper. I've been so busy today that I haven't realised that anything significant might have happened. When I look at the front page I realise why she is so concerned.

"The Reichstag has been burnt down Ernst and they're blaming the communists for the arson attack." Anna put her hand gently on my shoulder as she stands behind me continuing to read the article. The KPD candidates for the next election have been arrested including Ernst Torgler, the KPD's leader in the Reichstag and also Ernst Thälmann. Göring has announced that the Nazi Party plans to exterminate German communists.

"I'm sure that I would have known if the communist party were responsible for the fire. That rhetoric is typical propaganda from the fascists. This will be a very good excuse for them to take action against citizens who are against their policy."

We are both silent for a few minutes, both deep in thought. "We must all take good care Anna as retaliations are bound to happen now".

We squeeze each other's hands and try not to look too concerned for Gretel's sake. She's a clever little girl though as I notice she has observed our reactions but as usual never asks questions. She realises that she is not allowed to have any knowledge of what we are doing. I remind her to keep away from the windows just in case someone should fire a gun at one of the panes of glass. I have no doubt that we are on a list of some of these SA people.

Civil liberties have been suspended and the communists have not been allowed to take part in government proceedings since the emergency Reichstag Fire Decree came into force. This decree is supposed to be for the protection of people and the state. In fact the communist party has been dissolved and hundreds of thousands of people have been disenfranchised. As a result there is absolutely no hope of defeating this man. Our country is in mortal danger.

During the election as has been the situation over many elections lately, there is intimidation outside the polling stations. The storm troopers terrorise the opposition making it a violent campaign. Left wing election meetings are broken up by SA and several candidates are murdered. Rudolf and his friends try to help protect us as best they can.

On 5th March as we predicted the Nazi Party gains power over the German population. They manage to get 43.9% of the total vote. Do the public really know what they have done by voting for him I wonder? I mustn't be so hard though as many people's candidates have been unable to stand for election; how can anyone vote for their choice.

On 6th March the communist and socialist party headquarters are occupied by the state police. The trade union headquarters and buildings of left wing publishing companies are also occupied. On 9th March all states previously not in agreement with the Nazis have 'loyal' state administrations installed to prevent any opposition. Four days later, Göebels sets up the Reich Propaganda Ministry. A week later an announcement proclaims the establishment of a concentration camp at Dachau.

Having given the Nazi party the right to govern, the citizens of Germany are about to lose their most precious commodity. When the newly elected Reichstag parliament meets on 21st March the government tries to make a new law which will destroy any hope for our democracy to continue in Germany. The social democratic members of parliament will be allowed to vote in two days' time, unlike the left wing opponents and I am pleased to hear that at long last social democrats seem to have woken up and are going to oppose this bill which is called the Enabling Act.

Things are happening so quick at the moment that it is hard to draw breath before something else occurs. What is the purpose of a racial hygiene department which is being set up by the Interior Ministry?

On 23rd March, Otto Wels[77], the SPD leader makes a dignified speech warning the assembled politicians and also Germany as a whole, of the purpose of this bill. I hear that he said "you can take our lives and our freedom but you cannot take our honour. We are defenceless but not honourless". That was very brave of him as his party was under a great deal of pressure from the SS & SA. All ninety six SPD members of parliament voted against the bill but unfortunately the communist party were prevented from voting as they had been banned.

---

[77] Otto Wels Chairman of the SPD left Germany in June 1933 and went into exile. In August he was deprived of citizenship. He died in Paris 1939.

"Munki"[78] and "Jenson"[79] met me after work. It's so good to have some people who I can trust in our resistance work and yet are also very good old friends of mine. It's not ideal for the organisation but sometimes I need this type of relationship. Of course Rudolf and I still discuss and resolve difficult problems or situations with each other, but apart from him, I have to work without talking to anyone. As we order three cups of coffee in the café I cannot help to notice how concerned "Jenson" looks.

"The Weimar Republic has just voted to remove democracy out of existence Ernst. The politicians have voted themselves out of politics, can you believe that? What is wrong with them? Mind you some social democrat party deputies were prevented from taking their seats in Parliament due to arrests and intimidation by the SA. As a result the social democrats were under represented in the final vote tally and with no left wing politicians being allowed to vote, it was a foregone conclusion really. I understand that Otto Wels intends to leave Germany and to be honest I don't blame him. He's bound to be arrested if he stays."

"I only hope our leaders will also leave here" looking seriously at Gustav. "Your fate along with others is very uncertain now. Many of our leaders are well known to the fascists as they have been prominent members of society including members of Hamburg or Berlin parliaments. You will all be the first targets who will be arrested or worse" I answer grimly.

"I know Ernst, but I shall stay 'underground' so to speak for as long as I can and then I shall also have to leave if it puts the safety of others at risk" he answers.

Rudi can see he needs to assure Gustav that we shall continue.

---

[78] Munki" is Robert or Rudi Dassau – remembered by Gretel even in her old age

[79] "Jenson" as mentioned in the Berlin Archives is Gustav Gundelach, a friend of the Stender family. He worked with both Rudolf and Ernst and will be mentioned again later in the book and in the follow-up book. He was a Member of the Hamburg Parliament from 1924-1933 and then went into hiding but still working in the resistance. Later he continued his resistance work but in different countries, finally returning to Hamburg after the war, again becoming a member of parliament

"At least we have organised ourselves a little better now with people who are less likely to be known to the Nazis, but we must all be careful."

On 27th March, one of our worst fears happens when thousands of social democrats and communist members are arrested and concentration camps open.

Gleichschaltung[80] is introduced. I know that the elected deputies have been put en mass into "protective custody" and sent to concentration camps. Many of my friends and colleagues no longer seem to be in the city of Hamburg. They've just disappeared off the face of the earth.

On 28th March the first open attacks start by the SA against Jewish businesses. As I walk through our city streets, it's awful seeing the Star of David being painted on the shop windows owned by Jewish families and warning notices not to enter as from 1st April. SA troops stand outside ensuring that no-one opposes this ban. What will happen to all these people? So many of them fought in the Great War for our 'Fatherland' and now they are the victims of this new dictatorship. I hear that so far 235,000 Jews have departed from our country, including the professional and intellectual strata of society. As a result of this anti-Semitic policy our scientific knowledge has been diminished. Jews have also been expelled wholesale from all liberal professions such as medicine, law, journalism, fine arts, radio, cinema, music and the civil service. Universities have suffered with both professors and students abandoning these places of learning. Our nation has always been very cultured but with this proclamation, our society will change out of all recognition. Jewish finances have also been confiscated. Where will all this end?

On 26th April a new form of secret police is formed. They're called the Geheime Staatspolizei but the name has been shortened to the Gestapo. Göring is their new leader so this does not bode well for the future. I have a foreboding feeling that we will be hearing a lot about this new police force. They will certainly not be allies of ours. That is definite.

---

[80] Gleichschaltung is the forcible removal of all known opponents to the Nazis

Fear permeates everywhere in Germany – in the streets, in the workplace, even in the home. That is unless you are a believer in the Nazi regime or have no opinions about life, 'sticking your head in the sand' so to speak. By the end of April, the Nazis have arrested 18,000 communists, 12,000 SPD members and many others. We mustn't give in to this terror and aggression; otherwise we will all be lost.

As for my little 'band' of men and women I feel proud to be working with them. Maria is as reliable as I thought she would be. She's working from Hammerbrookstrasse and uses her initiative. She has secret meetings in the streets, does clerical work and also goes to various homes and carries out missions as I ask. I'm really pleased as she is totally committed to our cause. As time progresses, I will give her more responsibilities and prepare her for a higher position. She might have to take over from me if I get arrested and I know the risk of arrest is high.

Fritz Lux seems on a mission of giving me as many contacts as possible. Perhaps he realises how much danger he could be in. He introduces me to Benno Dohrn who also has been involved with the Rote Hilfe since 1925 and is still active within that brilliant organisation. He lives in the same flat with Alfred Barthel. Benno is very useful as he prepares photographic work for us concerning manufacturing industries. This he passes on to my friend "Munki" who then gives it to me. Our organisation is really becoming like a well-oiled machine. I often go to Benno's home for copies to be made of documents and plans. Benno works at Derutra, the Russian Trade Organisation where Rudolf had worked once.

I wonder how many people know about Hitler's policy with regard to East Asia I ponder to myself walking home from work. Before the Nazis rise to power, the Foreign Ministry under the Weimar Government had urged for a policy of neutrality in Eastern Asia. As a result it had discouraged German industries from involving themselves directly with the Chinese government. Import and export firms also tried to keep neutral. Now that the Nazis have a war economic policy, there has been a decision to import and stock pile raw materials, particularly militarily important resources such as tungsten and antimony. China can supply these materials in bulk.

Wolfgang Koglin has been supplying me with this information and on general trading relations between China and Japan. In particular he has told me about the firm Carlowitz where he works, as they have been providing China with armaments which have been made from the raw materials they have sent to Germany. He also has representatives in China who have kept him informed about Germany's involvement in weaponry supplied to the east. I have also been paying him for reports he has made to me about other firms involved in research and design relating to re-arming Germany plus details of the weaponry and machinery sent to China. He has even been supplying me with details of the designs of buildings which will contain naval arsenal storage in Germany. It is very dangerous work he is doing for us.

As China is run by a right wing dictatorship it suits both countries to work together. This Asian country is unbelievably large and a potential threat to the western democracy so we need to know about China's railway network and intended new building projects. In addition it is useful to gain information about the so called 'rebel' movement which is gaining strength in China so I meet Wolfgang at regular intervals where he gives me both written and verbal reports. It is even useful to know about the general economic situation in that country.

The world population in general seems to be in an unstable plight and I wonder which country will start the implosion. Our country seems intent on 'feeding' extremists with weaponry. Herbert Wöhrlin is taking note of suspicious transportation of individual shipping companies in connection with the Gran Chaco conflict[81]. Until Konrad 'disappeared', Herbert had been providing him with the information. "Peter" or Stange is anxious to know from Herbert

---

[81] The Gran Chaco conflict took place between Bolivia and Paraguay from 1932 to 1935. Briefly, it originates from the outcome of the war of the Pacific 1879-84 when Chile defeated Bolivia and annexed that country's entire coastal region. As a result Bolivia tried to gain access to the sea through the Rio de la Plata system to the Atlantic coast. The Bolivians also thought there were large oil reserves there. They were trained by German advisers including General Rohm who became the SA leader. This conflict was one of the largest and bloodiest in the history of South America.

Wöhrlin about the war material being transported to South America and which German private shipping companies are supplying weaponry in that direction. Luckily Herbert is able to tell him about the armaments being shipped from Hamburg via Antwerp and Rotterdam to La Plata and Paraguay.

More people are disappearing and it's difficult to know if they are in hiding or have been arrested. Bruno Stök is one who I know has been arrested. He'd been working for us at the port of Hamburg so this is a major blow. My friend Franz Jacob has also been arrested. Wilhelm Bahnik is in hiding[82].

What is going to happen to Rudolf? He is in an extremely dangerous situation, constantly evading arrest. I don't think that they have proof yet of his activities but with this new Gestapo, it's only a matter of time before someone is 'persuaded' to confess and give names of the organisation they work for. The trouble is that my brother puts the love of his country before his own safety. I can feel tears welling up inside me so decide at this point not to continue my thoughts. In truth I have committed myself to the cause as well and it seems Werner is following in our footsteps. Our poor parents seem to have brought into the world three revolutionaries who would have been just ordinary citizens had it not been for fascism.

Actually I am being unfair as Hans, my other brother must have been involved in some resistance work as he was arrested a couple of weeks ago and we are all anxiously waiting to hear if he is all right. What has he been up to I wonder or is it the connection with Rudolf which is his downfall? Carla, Hans' wife has a brother who has right wing tendencies. Has he said anything which could cause Hans' arrest? The thought that he might be suffering from torture is something no-one is speaking about.

As I ponder on the fate of all of us, the person who is worrying me the most catches up with me as I turn into Gertigstrasse. Obviously we both have decided at the same time to visit our parents

---

[82] Wilhelm Bahnik became an Officer XI International Brigade, Edgar André Division in the Spanish Civil War. He was wounded in 1938 and died of his wounds.

to try and cheer them up. I know how worried they are about Hans.

"Have you heard anything about how Hans is?" asked Rudolf.

"No I've heard nothing at all. It feels as though the noose is tightening around our family Rudolf."

"I'm probably going to add to the problems. We're going to take a risk and be involved in a May Day demonstration even though this event is banned. If the S.A. turns up, then we will fight to the end."

"Does this mean that you have every hope that the SA will come and fight you as you wait for them?" I ask with some concern.

"Now Ernst you really are getting cynical!" He smiles and slaps me affectionately on my back.

"No. It'll be our usual pattern of demonstration with the sudden appearance of a marching formation and then "melting" away in the crowds hopefully before they arrive but we will not run away if they do appear. We are not cowards".

"That I know – you have proved that time and time again Rudolf. I'm only too aware though that you will have to go into hiding soon as I'm sure you must be on the Gestapo's list of people to arrest."

"Yes I agree. When that time comes, and I know it will be soon, I have one or two places already prepared for the occasion. Hopefully I will try to see you if it is safe. If I have to go into hiding it'll then be over to you and young Werner to support our parents Ernst. I won't leave Hamburg though as I want to continue fighting these bastards until we win."

Just as we arrive at No 56 I return the pat on his back and open the heavy door leading to the flight of steps and up to our parents flat. After a few minutes as is the usual custom, Mama starts to make a cup of coffee and life feels normal and wonderful for a while. If only normality could be a reality again.

On 2nd May, SA troops break into and occupy all left wing trade union offices, arrest their leaders and officials and send most of them to concentration camps. Just four days later the Deutsche Arbeitsfront[83] is introduced to replace the unions. Both employers

---

[83] German Workers Front was introduced to replace the unions. It was a right wing organisation.

and employees are forced to join. This union is not intended to help the down trodden employees but to advance employers unreasonable demands due to the increase in war production.

One evening Papa came to see us looking very upset. Sure enough Rudolf had had to go into hiding and only escaped from Papa's home by the 'skin of his teeth'. So life will never be the same for us. Hans is still in prison or rather Fuhlsbüttel Concentration Camp which is called locally Kolafu. I try to speak positively to Papa, but I feel cold with dread.

"Look Ernst you are going to have to let me help more" lectures Anna after Papa had gone. Your parents I know need more support and encouragement with Rudolf and Hans lives being at risk. They don't know about your situation and also Werner seems to be involved in some resistance work now. Both of you have enough to cope with plus having a full day's work to do. You'll collapse with exhaustion if you don't delegate the 'caring' bit to me."

I know Anna's right. "Anna you are not well with your heart condition and then there's our beloved Gretel to look after" I reply anxiously. All I get for a reply is a scornful face in reprimand which is very rarely seen from the love of my life. I hold up my hands in defeat.

"All right – I surrender and thank you Anna."

"We work better as a team. Isn't that so?" she adds smiling at me.

The next evening Gretel came rushing up to greet me as usual but she suddenly burst into tears.

"Why are books being burnt in the streets Papa? I've seen wonderful books being thrown onto huge bonfires."

What can I say to a child brought up to love books?

"It's not something we want to happen at all Gretel, but we are being told that certain books are not suitable for the people in our country to read and as a result we are not allowed to keep them at home any more. It is not advisable to refuse this demand."

"But they are famous books as well as others Papa. Why are they suddenly not good for us to read?"

Anna takes Gretel by the hand and sits her down next to her.

"I know its hard Gretel, but we have people in charge of us who have made this decision. We mustn't say anything against the burning as we cannot risk bringing attention to ourselves. One day I hope that all this will change and we will all be able to buy copies of these books again. In the meantime we must say nothing. Do you promise to keep quiet?"

Anna wipes Gretel's tears away and Gretel nods accepting the situation. She is such a good and understanding little girl acting so much older than she is. I hope she will not suffer psychologically from all of this when she grows up. She seems to keep all her thoughts to herself but I worry about her.

As for the burning of so called 'un-German' books, it is a sacrilege taking such action. Our country is cultured so removing books of different thoughts, leaving us with propaganda material is very upsetting. How can our younger generation think about our past and our future if they do not have true facts laid out in writing for them to study?

"I tell you what Gretel. How about us going to our cottage at Heide for the weekend? Hopefully some of our friends will be there and we can have lovely walks in the countryside together. I think I'll invite Werner to come this weekend as I know he also loves the place and I know how you love your Uncle Werner."

That was enough to totally cheer Gretel up. Also "Munki" will be there and I know that Gretel likes Rudi Dassau. At this she jumps up and down with joy clapping her hands together and then she skips round the room singing. By then Anna and I both are laughing at her antics. Anna knows though that this weekend has not been decided upon the spur of the moment. Our little communal chalet in Seppensen was bought a few years ago by our anti-fascist friends and ourselves so that we can get together to discuss future resistance plans[84]. No-one can complain about us retreating to this cottage as it is in glorious countryside and we can go for walks, play music and sing. We keep our real purpose to ourselves but at least our children for a change have happiness and freedom to play together. After some very involved discussions between my comrades, at the end of a rewarding day we totally relax singing and playing instruments. In

---

[84] Heideruh is now being used for anti-fascist/left wing meetings and conferences, a photo of Ernst has been displayed there.

the end, we collapse on our beds in the large upstairs attic which is used as a communal dormitory.

We all find it very upsetting though when we think of the many people who bought "Heide" with us who have now been arrested and have an uncertain future. I mustn't dwell too much on this though as it'll affect my work. This weekend will not only be relaxing with friends and family but will also involve strategy for regrouping.

When I arrive home one evening, Anna begins to tell me the news about Hans, my brother.

"He's been released at long last. Mama told me today when I went to see her. Apparently Carla came to see her to give her the news. She didn't stay long as she was anxious to get home again but Hans has suffered quite badly through the 'questioning'. Carla has told Mama that she thinks it better if she and Hans are left alone for a while as she doesn't think contact with us will help Hans' situation. He needs peace and quiet to recover."

"It sounds to me as though Hans wants to keep himself clean from any connections with us in order for him to survive" I retort. I instantly regret my recriminations.

No that is unkind of me to even think that. I can't possibly imagine what Hans has been through.

"We don't know the reason for his arrest, whether it was because of Rudolf's activities or if Hans was involved in some other resistance group. I know he worked at the same factory as Willie Bredel. We must respect their wishes and try and calm our parents. If they knew how involved I am with the intelligence resistance movement, poor Papa would fall to pieces. Young Werner is also not idle but they have no idea what he's up to."

"Your poor parents, Ernst, must be suffering. I'll keep visiting them as often as I can. What a family they've produced". She half smiles at me and went on with preparing our meal.

Early the next day, as it is Sunday morning, I knew that I would have a short amount of time free so I arrange to take Gretel to meet Rudolf. Gretel has missed seeing her Uncle since he's been in hiding. I've warned Gretel that she will get a lovely surprise this morning, but she mustn't show any excitement which would bring attention to us. She looks up at me innocently, smiles and holds my hand as we walk to our meeting place. I saunter slowly along the path, when, from nowhere it seems, Rudolf starts walking next to Gretel. He holds her other hand and squeezes it gently. I can feel Gretel wanting to jump up and down but with great restraint she carries on walking happily between us. Oh what joy to be together even for a short while. We arrive at a child's play area so that Gretel can go and play, leaving us time to chat long and hard about our futures.

As we left Rudolf, I hand him a photo I had taken of his son Rudi, with our parents. Rudi looks very happy in the photo as he is with his beloved grandparents at their own allotment. The building behind them is their wooden hut which is where we have all slept in our childhood during the weekends having the most precious relaxing time. Being in the big outdoors on our own plot of land is heaven after living in our flats. It may have no running water or toilet, but it is a place of happiness and poor Rudi needs that so much now. Käthe is the most wonderful mother to Rudi despite the problems surrounding us; she still makes certain that our parents have all the access to their grandson Rudi. Rudolf looks at the photo and I can see how pleased and moved he is at having such a valuable picture. He puts it in his jacket pocket and I know he will always treasure it.

As June arrives, more than half of the communist district leaders are now in detention and hundreds of Nazis opponents have been killed. The Christian trade unions have now received the same treatment as the left winged trade unionists.

On 22nd June, the social democratic party is dissolved as the fascists' state that it is a subversive party and they confiscate all the SPD property. Finally on 5th July all political parties other than the Nazi party are banned. 'Sitting on a fence' has not done anything to stop Hitler from gaining power and now they have been expended as Hitler no longer has any use for them. I wonder if they now understand what they have done.

On 14th July the Government decrees that Germany is a 'one party state' and that forming any other party is judged to be a treasonable act punishable by imprisonment. There is further discrimination against the Jews and all political parties and their newspapers have been totally outlawed; that is apart from the Nazi party and their propaganda machine. In other words we have total dictatorship. What has the world to say about this decree? Will there be any condemnation?

Also a sterilisation law for the prevention of hereditary diseases is made legal. Is the Nazi party now trying to produce only perfect Germans? Will this make us a pure Arian race?

Some days it feels so hopeless but if we don't continue to fight then we will all be lost. Even though so many of us have been arrested, the intelligence we have accumulated within my group has been amazing.

"We are getting better at acquiring knowledge and I am pleased that I have managed to recruit people who are not connected to my past life. This will make it difficult for the Gestapo if I am arrested and hopefully I can keep this knowledge from them. Maria Müller is a great asset and totally dedicated to fight fascism so I am sure if I can keep her name out of the fascist's awareness, then there is hope."

"Munki" and I are once again in deep conversation about our tactics.

"Now come on Ernst, nothing has happened yet" "Munki" reminds me.

"I know but look around us Rudi. One after another of our old colleagues are being arrested. How long will it be before they connect us to our comrades? I know that the ones detained have been more in the public eye prior to Hitler gaining power but we cannot guarantee that any of them will not buckle under torture. I can't blame any one to give names under such situations."

Rudi has to agree with that comment. And now we hear really bad news. I can't tell you how upset I'm feeling when on 25th July my friend Fritz Lux was arrested. I hadn't seen him since May so I don't know really if he's been in detention since May or July. Whatever the date, my stomach is churning in fear for his safety. He's such an honourable man and has also played such a large role in setting up our group. Will he survive and how much will he be able to withhold from the Gestapo?

Herbert Wöhrlin who is two years older than Rudolf, works very hard for us and it helps that he does a lot of travelling in other countries so we can make use of his ability to travel without bringing attention to himself. I hope that when he visits friendly countries they can use the intelligence we have against Hitler. Herbert's given us details of the staffing and war production within major Hamburg firms and in particular the shipyards of Blohm and Voss, Heidenreich and Harbeck, Kampnagel Menk and Hambrook. He works as an attorney for Carlowitz and Co.

"Herbert, with your contacts, is it possible for you to get other leaflets from abroad? It's all very well trying to print some ourselves, but we just can't do enough and in safety."

"Yes of course. I know someone who will provide the leaflets and there's someone else who travels on the steamer "Wiedau" which regularly sails to England. Leave it with me Ernst."

Sure enough Julius Grönwald who is a steward on the ship, starts to bring the Baseler Rundschau and other leaflets and magazines plus very important letters. At long last we are able to send letters to various contacts and Julius posts them upon arrival in England.

To our whole family's relief, I manage to get Rudolf a false passport in the name of Otto Kammers. It's been such a worrying time with the Gestapo looking everywhere for him. They've been pestering all of us, constantly searching our homes and also his old friends' places saying that Rudolf is wanted for treachery and high treason against the German state. It seems as though the net is closing in on Rudolf's entire group so it's only a matter of time before he'll be caught if he stays here. I don't expect him to survive if this happens as the Gestapo have been very keen to arrest him. He's been so reluctant to leave Hamburg but I hear that he now has been given orders to escape.

The day arrives when Rudolf is due to leave. We provide him with a uniform of a dock worker and after a very quick farewell to our parents, my contacts smuggle him into Hamburg docks. My friends manage to hide him in a container on board a Russian ship without the customs discovering him. To the relief of our family and his friends who have not been arrested yet, he leaves Hamburg on

2nd August 1933 destined for Odessa. Let's hope that he will be able to write to us to let us know that he is safe.

Shudders down my back express my real thoughts when I hear that on 24th August the old guards at Fuhlsbüttel Concentration Camp have been replaced by SS troops. This really does not bode well for any of us ending up there. Any fragments of decency will have gone the moment the last normal guard walks out of that concentration camp. These SS guards are unemployed SS volunteers and they apparently get a remuneration of two Marks pocket money with food and lodging provided free for them. There are two hundred and forty of them with Sturmführer Dusenshön in charge. I've heard of this man as he has been a national socialist for a long time and is militarily trained and 'exact' in his duty.

Now all prisoners are treated under a new protective custody law after a speech made in Kolafu by Max Lahts on 4th September. The gist of this speech explains the new regime and one of my contacts relates it back to me.

There are now three groups of prisoners.

The first group are people who behave themselves and are imprisoned in a community hall with other prisoners. They will be allowed to receive post once a month and they are also allowed to write once a month. They can smoke outside in the recreational area in their free time but will always be strictly observed.

The second group includes everyone who does not behave themselves and has committed a crime against the state. These people will received no privileges whatsoever and are not allowed to receive or write any letters home.

The third type of prisoner is someone with a bad record and not trustworthy and who opposes the ordinary person and the German state. These people will be kept in solitary confinement and will receive no privileges whatsoever. On top of this, they will only receive three days of warm meals during the week. The especially "dangerous" ones will be put in dark cells.

These rules are in place according to Max Lahts "for the protection of the German people and the German state as long as we have these enemies". It doesn't take much guessing to think which treatment our friends and colleagues are getting. I hope that they can survive this and also the torture by the Gestapo.

In September 1933 the Reich's Chamber of Culture has appointed Dr Göbbels as the new minister of propaganda and henceforth all manuscripts have to be submitted to the ministry before being published. Most independent thinking writers have already emigrated abroad. They cannot bring themselves to write untruths. Millions of copies of the book "Mein Kampf" are sold and Hitler is now a millionaire. How appalling to think that this man can become rich on writing such rubbish with incitement to hatred.

All the books available for the education of our youngsters are being rewritten in the Nazi spirit plus the school and university curricular have been changed overnight. Indoctrination of the youth of tomorrow is in full swing and without their parents being able to speak the truth due to fear of arrest, a whole generation will now grow up being fascists.

Young people start to be conscripted in order that autobahns can be built. Are these roads to be used for transportation of troops and the mobilisation of armaments? Young girls are sent to work on the land. Unemployment is rapidly decreasing and Blohm and Voss are in full swing working day and night building war ships and planes.

Is this an unstoppable machine? We're informing the neighbouring democratic countries concerning the dangerous developments in Germany but are they just 'burying their heads in the sand'? Are they just sitting back hoping for Hitler to attack in the east as he wrote in his book Mein Kampf? He's spoken for some time of Germany's need for additional living space in the east[85]. Are they considering communism more dangerous than fascism? If this is the case, are they hoping that Hitler will destroy Russia, therefore resolving the so-called threat of that country and then expecting him not to invade the democratic countries which surround Germany? How wrong can they be! In our newspapers the rhetoric being written is that we have to rearm because our country is encircled by enemy states which will destroy our 'Fatherland'.

---

[85] Lebensraum

Maria's been brilliant managing to get state secret plans and designs of armaments and also details of the aircraft industry. Somehow she's discovering about innovations or inventions in our area which might be relevant to help allies willing to fight fascism. She knows that she has a completely free hand as to how she infiltrates the firms. I'm so pleased that she is part of our set up but she must be protected from being discovered should our circle start to be 'rounded up'.

Wilhelm, her companion, has become extremely concerned that a typewriter we use is still kept at his parent's home. I can understand why he worries as there are so many house searches now and if this typewriter is found his parents' safety is threatened. However, this typewriter is still needed so I will ask "Munki" to go and remove it and take it to Herbert Wöhrlin's place.

When 'Peter'[86] is arrested, I really have no choice but to take on his responsibilities. We're being arrested in quite quick succession now so that there is very little time to regroup and also recruit new members. Thank goodness for Maria. I shall have to make sure that she has enough details to carry on should I be arrested.

Germany has withdrawn from the Disarmament Conference on 14th October 1933 and has left the League of Nations. We are now in a war economy footing. Is anyone out there listening to the beat of war drums?

Alfred Barthel or 'Emil' leaves his lodgings with Benno Dohrn and in the autumn goes into hiding. He will be a big loss as he is the main link to Berlin but I can quite understand his actions as it is only a matter of time before he will be arrested. Wilhelm Bahnik then takes over from 'Emil' and supplies information to Ewald Jahnen[87] from Berlin (known as der Lange) about the knowledge he has gained concerning armaments and in particular modern German naval weapons. He has contact with Wolfgang Koglin and Wilhelm Bahnik when he met them in Berlin.

With all the intimidation and also the removal of all opposition,

[86] Stange

[87] Ewald Jahnen is mentioned at later Trials as 'deceased' according to the Gestapo. Unfortunately I have no further information.

on 17th November the Nazi party has now won 92% of the votes cast. It seems our country is doomed.

We are all trying to fill more and more gaps in our organisation. I'm beginning to feel that the Gestapo are getting the better of us. Even the SA does not need to inflict violence so much on the population as the web of control seeps through everything. I know in my heart of hearts that my time for arrest will come. I can't go into hiding and escape though. Anna with her weak heart and my gorgeous little girl need me. I'm just going to have to take a risk that I might not be discovered.

Some really marvellous news has arrived and has completely lifted our spirits. My parents have received a letter from "Otto" to say that he is well. He's even managed to send us some food. Of course he will never put his real name to any letters as Rudolf knows that all post for our parents will be intercepted. Oh thank goodness he is safe.

But now our own situation is rapidly deteriorating. Karl Rattai, also known as "Albert" and leader of the organisation is arrested along with his plump dark haired Courier L…[88] who was employed as a

---

[88] In Ursel Hochmuth's book *Nieman und nichts wird vergessen* Rudi Lindau, who was L…'s fiancé was arrested in their home on 26th October 1933 and 10th January 1934, Rudi was executed (beheaded) for his activities against fascism. The records of the trials of Ernst and his friends are kept in the Berlin Archives. Within these records, L… had made a statement at some point for one of the trials which took place in November 1934, a year after their arrest. She gave details of people involved in this resistance group and the organisational set-up; it was stated that after giving this information she had fled abroad.

According to Astrid Louven who has written an article in *the stolperstein-hamburg* website, L… produced or was aware of illegal leaflets being printed in the back room of Lammers grocer's shop. Someone reported Kurt's activities in 1935 and so he was arrested.

In Denmark she lived with Willi Adam, an informer for the Gestapo.

L… was later sent to Kolafu, sentenced to imprisonment after her trial on 26.06.42 but later suffered the same fate as many other Jews by being sent to Auschwitz where she perished.

I recommend anyone who understands German, to read page 70 of *Skandinavische Erfahrungen erwünscht?: Nachexil und Remigration* by Michael F Scholz

secretary. L… being Rattai's courier knows quite a lot about our organisation. I just hope that she withstands any interrogation.

There are rumours flying around that Fritz Lux has committed suicide in Kolafu. Does this mean that his treatment had been so harsh that he felt that he could no longer withstand the "questioning"? As I collapse in my chair totally exhausted there's a loud banging on our front door.

"Open up immediately – it's the police" a voice yells.

It's finally happening to me. I glance over at Anna and Gretel's terrified faces and can only say "sorry" to them followed by "I love you both".

The 30th November 1933 shall remain a memory for the rest of my life. How can human beings be so cruel to others? Sitting outside listening to other people being tortured breaks the soul. The door is thrown open and a poor pathetic limp and disfigured human being is pulled along between two sneering SS guards. Whatever happens, I mustn't reveal Maria's name and the others who hopefully will carry on the fight. Maria is our future hope. I must only divulge the least I can without incriminating others.

And now it is my turn as they look in my direction…

My parents with young Rudi at my parent's allotment and weekend hut.

CHAPTER 17

Rudolf during 1933

The violence of the SA and other right wing followers is escalating to unfathomable proportions and no-one in authority is standing up to them. It feels that our RFB is the only group of men who are prepared to do this when the SA organise fascist meetings in our working class strongholds. These meetings are always protected by men of the SA who are hoping to provoke violence. I am sure they have been formed to take the political fight to our streets.

From the late 1920s we have helped so many people in dire straits due to unemployment and resulting poverty and starvation by preventing a lot of the people being evicted to live on the streets. Why is it that the government is spending money on rearmaments instead of improving the welfare system? Now violence and intimidation on the streets is an everyday occurrence so we must try to counteract and protect the citizens.

Something also has to be done to stop the SA from taking over of the working class district pubs in Hamburg. It obviously is intended to be antagonistic act and it also prevents us from meeting and speaking freely in safe places. We have always valued these hostelries as our homes are small and in winter we struggle to heat them properly. Now we feel threatened. Sometimes the Nazis use gangs of SA who drive slowly past our taverns and fire shots through the glass windows then drive off at break neck speed. I know 'two wrongs do not make a right' as people say but we have to fight these thugs. For other people living in a peaceful democratic country, it must be extremely hard to comprehend the violence, fear and intimidation we are suffering so we have to accept that the RFB's behaviour could easily be misinterpreted in the newspapers.

We are going to have to fight back to stop the violence the SA keep inflicting on us. I have to say that I'm grateful for my military training which the German state gave me during the Great War. This can be put to good use now that we have contacts of people who have infiltrated military establishments and can obtain all sorts of useful equipment and weaponry. I can see that I'm going to have to train my volunteers militarily in order to protect our citizens against the SA otherwise the fascists will gain full brutish power over all of us.

Hitler's henchmen then marched by torchlight through Hamburg, singing their bloodthirsty songs through our streets to celebrate Hitler's appointment as chancellor. Oh how I can feel my blood curdles in disgust and also dread. We must show the people of Hamburg that we haven't given up.

Göring has been made Prussian Minister of the Interior which gives Hitler has state control of communications and the media. Göring is also responsible for the security in Berlin and elsewhere and has started to alter the establishment of the police authority by dismissing twenty-two out of the thirty-two senior officers. Thousands of ordinary policemen have been removed and replaced by members of the SA[89]. I hear that he has issued orders to the new police force must show no mercy to enemies of the state and to use firearms against them if necessary. Of the 50,000 auxiliary police drafted in by Göring, 10,000 are Stalhelm men and the rest are SA men so there is no possibility that that the police can be trusted. Violence towards opposition is obviously the intention which means that we will have to risk our lives to protect and stop these people from succeeding.

My friend Ernst Thälman wants the SPD and KPD to organise a general strike to topple Hitler. The central committee of the KPD meet at Konigs Wusterhausen near Berlin but it is considered too late to take such action as it would cause a blood bath. The power of the fascists is now too strong. I fear we are losing this battle. I wonder if the answer is to wait to see if the citizens of Germany will wake up and reverse Hitler's power. I have a nasty feeling though that it will be too late as our country will be under military rule by then.

---

[89] Göring later dismissed these SA police when they had 'performed' their dirty duties

"Rudolf I've just heard that the Reichstag in Berlin has been badly damaged by fire."

"What!" This is horrendous news to hear. I rush out to get a newspaper to find out what has happened. Sure enough the billboard poster by the newspaper stand confirms the dreadful information. I purchase a newspaper and start reading.

At 21.25 on 27th February an alarm rang out as a fire had started in the session chamber of the Reichstag. The communists are blamed for this event as apparently it was started by Marinus Van de Lubbe, an unemployed bricklayer of unstable mind and an arsonist who just happens to be a communist. Without doubt Hitler will put this information to his advantage. I wonder if one of his men is behind it and using this Van de Lubbe as a scapegoat.

At the last election the fascists had not been able to change the constitution in order to govern in their own way. They had needed a two thirds majority but the Emergency Decree which came into effect the day after the fire, suspends all civil liberties. This fire has been perfect timing for them and they disqualify eighty one elected communists from sitting in the Reichstag. The KPD party has been outlawed but not officially banned but I am sure that this will be on the agenda soon. The Nazi party forbids all publications not considered 'friendly' to the Nazi cause. Why would any political opponent intentionally set fire to the Reichstag when it is obvious that Hitler would manipulate this situation to his advantage giving him these emergency powers? I can only think that either his party is responsible or that Van de Lubbe did it without any political backing being of unstable mind.

The fascists start mass arrests of communists including communist parliamentary candidates. One of these people is my friend Ernst Thälmann[90], being arrested on 3rd March. We've been through so much together and now I have to fight without him. I have grave doubts that he will be treated decently but I must put this to one side. It is no good worrying about something you cannot prevent. We must concentrate on our campaign to defeat fascism. Ernst Thälmann would certainly not want me to give up.

---

[90] Ernst Thälmann was executed on 18th August 1944 after being tortured and receiving eleven years of imprisonment.

Another set of elections is due on 5th March but with so many of the opposition leaders having been arrested or in fear of arrest, the situation does not look good. The voting population will feel reluctant to vote for the arrested candidates. Violence by the SA troops during this campaign period is horrendous. Paul von Hindenburg can still remove Hitler from his position of chancellor and that would bring us back from the brink of disaster but I have no doubt in my mind that Hindenburg is too weak to carry out such an action. As for the poor electorate having to make a decision in the polling booth, the intense bullying outside the polling stations is the final 'straw'. The fear and propaganda leading up to the occasion leaves me expecting the worse.

I am right in my prediction. My heart sinks when looking at the evening papers I see that the fascists have succeeded to gain 43.9% of the vote and with the 8% of the German National People's Party have formed a coalition with them, making it a 51.9% majority. With heavy hearts my friends and I have to accept that on 23rd March 1933 the short-lived Weimar Republic has come to an end with the Enabling Act.

Another of my friends Edgar André[91] is arrested. He has worked so hard for the resistance movement. It is devastating news but we mustn't give up hope. Concentration camps are now in existence and are being filled with thousands of political prisoners. Jewish businesses are being attacked and the air is thick with fear. Violence is rife with the new police force along and other SA men all against anyone daring to show any dissent against them. It makes me very angry.

---

[91] Edgar André was held in custody for 3 ½ years during which time he was also badly tortured. When it was over, he could only walk on crutches and he had lost his hearing. The trial began on 4th May 1936 in Hamburg. The prosecution could not present sufficient evidence of his guilt. Nevertheless, the prosecutor asked for the death sentence. This was imposed on him on 10th July 1936 and he was beheaded on 4th November 1936 despite international protest. A few hours after the execution, 5000 Fuhlsbüttel prisoners went "on strike". In Spain from 1936-1939 both Ernst Thälmann and Edgar André had battalions named after them in the International Brigade.

To coincide with new laws coming into effect on 1st April, we feel that we have to do something to show our objections. We decide to show how angry we are at the loss of the pub Wucherpfennig as a meeting place. This pub like so many others has been taken over by the SA. We must try and stop any further advance by the SA into the working class district and show the citizens that we will not be bullied into submission. Ressard makes some explosives with the intention of throwing them into the main hall of the pub. I stand nearby at Löschplatz Osterbeckstrasse to watch the proceedings but for some unknown reason the bombs do not explode. Sometimes these explosives cannot be relied upon which is so frustrating but I think that we have to be satisfied with the panic reaction of the SA who were inside the building at the time.

Most of my time is taken up with trying to prevent the SA from eliminating all opposition to their regime. If they do succeed, our country will be a totalitarian dictatorship so we must at all costs prevent it from happening. Many of our leaders have been arrested but we must carry on. When this happens I become the organiser of the RFB for the whole of Wasserkante (Hamburg). Further armed attacks on SA pubs are carried out as well as 'hits' against the SA and police in the Barmbek, Uhlenhorst and Winterhude area. It's not pleasant but is necessary to be militant. Negotiations and discussions are not on the fascist agenda and I have the experience of this behaviour! We try to prevent evictions of people losing their homes and who are in desperate need of food.

There are times when I get quite concerned about discipline within our unit. One of my men seems to boast about his activity. He is responsible for making arrangements for the places where the bombs have to be supplied to. He keeps telling his relations what he is doing and in fact boasting that he is doing more. He is bringing danger to all of us. Life is becoming so perilous but there is no need to add to problems by loose talk. Another of my colleagues, Friedrich Grüpe has been arrested so yet again I shall probably be named as an associate. I have no animosity towards anyone who is forced to reveal names as it is so difficult keeping quiet when 'interrogated'. I am fortunate so far to have avoided being 'questioned'.

My old colleague Fiete Schulze[92] is arrested 16th April 1933. How many more will they arrest I wonder? Gustav Gundelach a close friend of mine and also member of the Hamburg Parliament has gone into hiding. How can we continue when our leadership comrades are being detained or even murdered? Ernst and his friends are able to obtain an amazing amount of information and in a way our RFB units distract the Gestapo and others from Ernst and his group so I must try to continue for as long as possible but the rope is tightening around our necks.

After the May Day demonstrations, I have to admit defeat and go into hiding. Leaving Hamburg is not an option so I will fight to my death or capture. I had been warned by Herr Holzfuss who lives in a flat above our parents' home that the Gestapo are trying to find me. It was decent of him to risk his life by warning me, especially as he works at the Gestapo offices. I was indeed very fortunate to manage to escape when they turned up at the shop but that was Papa delaying the men from entering our home.

I do not go there anymore. It hurts me not to see Käthe and Rudi even though our marriage is now fraught with problems. I am under no illusions that this has been caused by my activities fighting fascism. I have to keep away as the Gestapo regularly turn up there and make life so difficult for both of them. What have I done to them?

I don't think the Nazis are aware that I have a hut in an allotment garden at Steilshoop, Bramfeld, which we sleep in at weekends. It has always been such a wonderful opportunity to escape from our flats and enjoy the countryside around us and grow our own fresh food. My brother Hans also has a similar plot and his one is opposite

---

[92] Fiete Schulz lived in the next road to us at Geibelstrasse; after being imprisoned during a long solitary confinement and torture, Fiete Schulze was beheaded with an axe on 6th June 1935. This was despite international protests. During the night, the street signs in the square in front of the Court were painted over and out of solidarity to this leader, his colleagues named the square after him. His prosecutor demanded three death sentences; such was the hatred of this man. He said that Fiete Schulze's tongue is more dangerous than bullets.

to mine. Sleeping in the allotment "house" without any electricity, water, w.c. or heating can be a challenge on these cold nights, but I feel safer there and it will not put my family at risk. They don't deserve the danger I put them in.

I would like to see my son as I have not seen him for so long. Käthe has agreed to take him to a secret location as he's growing up so fast now and it's so difficult for me to see him in safety at the home of any of my family. Just before I leave the hut, I peek from behind the closed curtains to check if it's all clear. I see a lady struggling along the path with a bucket of water she'd just filled from the standpipe a few minutes away from here. The coast is clear so I leave the hut and close the door behind me.

These garden allotments are so wonderful and are lovingly tended by their owners so at various seasons there are trees in blossom or bearing fruit, there are raspberries, strawberries and vegetables in abundance. At the moment the blossom from the fruit trees brightens up the area. At about 100 metres from the hut, as I near the exit to this vast area, my heart sinks as a large group of SA thugs appear from around the corner of the path. In front of them are three or four plain clothed men with rather unpleasant mannerisms about them. These newly created secret state police are a completely different bunch of characters and we try to avoid them at all costs.

Do I run and hope to get away or try and bluff my way out of this situation? Then the man nearest to me starts to speak before I have had a chance to make a decision.

"Do you know where Rudolf Stender's plot of land is?" he asks.

I just can't believe it that they haven't asked who I am or to see my identity papers. I point them in the direction of my allotment and as they disappear down the path, I run in the opposite direction as fast as I can until I reach a street where there are people. So as not to draw attention to myself, I walk at a normal pace blending in a busy crowded street until I feel reasonably safe to relax.

My thoughts are in a state of turmoil as I just can't believe that these Gestapo agents didn't even think to ask for my identification papers. Who on earth will believe me that such an encounter has happened as it sounds as if it comes from a pretty poor spy thriller book[93]. If I hadn't decided to leave my hut at that particular time to see Rudi, then I would have been arrested. At this particular moment I have no doubt that they are angrily throwing the furniture around and seeing the food left on the table and my spare clothes on the bed. Perhaps they now realise who this person was who gave them directions to the Stender allotment. I'll have to be more careful now and use other hiding places.

A few days later I'm shocked to hear that Hans, my brother has been arrested. Surely they didn't think that he knows where I am? Although his allotment and weekend hut is opposite mine I wouldn't involve him in my activities. Has the Gestapo assumed differently or are they wreaking revenge? I feel enough guilt that Käthe and my parents are at risk so to hear about Hans is distressing knowing that I can do nothing to help him.

Being leader of the Wasserkante (Hamburg) RFB I can't give up the fight. I know that my fate will probably end up the same as our previous leaders who have been arrested. Others have escaped so we are beginning to get very thin on the ground. At the time when we were banned in 1929, there were 130,000 members but now former RFB members have been the first to be arrested and put into concentration camps.

Those of us who have decided to continue despite the risks are constantly trying to avoid capture; most of us are not living at home anymore; others are trying to escape the country. We still manage to persist in carrying out attacks on the national socialists including at their headquarters and during their intimidating marches through the working class districts. We will not give up but it seems all we can do now is to just make the lives of the Nazis as difficult as possible. They have really become too powerful.

I'm very grateful to the Dünkel family as once more I'm able to call on them for help. Way back in 1923 Johann Dünkel[94] helped our organisation and this has continued over the years. Now Johann is

---

[93] I confirm that this event did actually happen although if somebody else had written this paragraph, I would be the first one to say that it sounds implausible!

[94] Johann Dünkel was Hans Stender's father-in-law

determined to save me and I have started using his home as a safe house. The family have always been supportive with the exception of the son who has such right wing tendencies.

"He is no son of mine" mumbles Johann to me one day.

"It's not unusual to have someone in a family who is not the same as the rest. I do agree that he is the 'bad apple' of your family but I really do appreciate what you have done for me and the resistance group."

"I've given strict instructions that he must not enter our house under any circumstances Rudolf. If he had any idea that you were here, then the whole family is at risk and I will not give him the opportunity to gloat." Poor man, he finds it so hard to accept that he has brought such a person into the world but some people can be taken in by strong characters within their peer group. Did this happen to him? On the other hand, the rest of his family are believers in socialism.

One of his daughters keeps pestering me to tell her more about life in the Soviet Union. She seems fascinated to hear about the education system over there since the revolution.

"I know if you are ordered to leave here then you will try to escape to that country. I'm just wondering if I should follow and come to help the youngsters as I know they're desperate for teachers over there."

"Hanny it's a hard life over in that vast country. The conditions have not really improved for the lower class since the revolution. Food is in short supply, there are no luxuries and the hours of work are long. However I do admit that the little food available is more fairly distributed to everyone including the poor. Think very carefully before you make the decision even though you will be safer away from the threat of arrest from the Nazis."

"So if it's so bad in the Soviet Union, then why are your colleagues going there to live?" she asks me.

"I'm not going. I'm staying to fight until the end – either with a victory against the Nazis or to my death".

I try shrugging off her questioning. I want to continue over here. We're busy at the moment trying to decide who should escape. A family friend of ours, Fritz Winzer[95] is in desperate need to escape our country as the Gestapo are looking for him. I would like to help but there are so many others who are in greater need who must leave before I could put forward his case. Then my father has received pleas of help from Jewish friends who need to leave and know about my contacts.

In mid-July Egon Nickel[96] accompanies Fesler in order to meet me at a secret meeting place.

"I need you to provide information for me as to who within the RFB needs to leave the country first Rudolf".

To be honest, it does not take me long to think of people whose lives are in danger. I quickly prepare a list for him and reasons why they have to leave. They are Karl Bargstadt, Willy Fellendorf and Buby Evers, also known as Bramfeld.

"I will stay in my position as leader for as long as I am able to" I assure him.

"There is a problem as to how many the Soviet Union will accept as immigrants." He looks at the list. "Well Karl Bargstadt I can see should be high on the list for leaving"

"We must do something to help these people Egon. I know that a court has sentenced two of our comrades in the RFB to death. Willy Fellendorf has done similar work to Karl and Buby has been accidentally released from prison. He has been accused of attacks on two SA pubs as well as protecting the group connected with the Wucherpfennig pub bombing." I stop speaking knowing that I was involved with that bombing. I look for a response to my report.

Fesler had been quietly listening to this conversation. He's a member of the Emigrant Commission.

"We will consider these people so thank you for your input. In the meantime we have to instruct you to give up your position at once.

---

[95] In December 1933 Fritz Winzer (the brother of Hertha who is part of Werner's group) was eventually arrested and spent until 1945 at first in Fuhlsbüttel and then in Sachsenhausen Concentration Camp. He survived and was liberated at the end of the war in 1945 having been a prisoner for 11 ½ years.

[96] Egon Nickel was arrested in 1933 and died 28.03.41 in Sachsenhausen Concentration Camp

You need to be the first one to leave for the USSR. You are too well known by the SA and Gestapo in Hamburg for your long period of resistance work. There is without doubt a high certainty that you will receive the death sentence if you are caught; that is after you have been tortured. No-one can be certain if they will survive without confessing and you know too many fellow resistance fighters. You have been involved in numerous clashes with the SA, been involved in various bomb attacks and to top it all, the Gestapo are looking for you. The whole leadership of Hamburg has come to this decision so that is the end of the matter. Do not take this as a criticism Rudolf – far from it as you are without doubt a very brave and dedicated man. We feel that you are still capable to continue elsewhere so hopefully you will be able to put your talents to good use as soon as you leave this country."

I cannot help my expression as I am totally stunned. I had accepted my fate to fight to the end and now I am being given orders to leave. I hesitate for a few minutes, look away in disbelief and then after a few minutes think about their decision and reluctantly nod in agreement. I have always been disciplined in my outlook even though I do not blindly obey instructions. I have always thought through orders and adapted them as necessary in the 'field'. With reluctance I can understand the latest command. It is awful though to admit defeat and accept that I too will have to leave. It has never been on my agenda at all.

The following day I'm due to meet some colleagues at another secret meeting place. My friend is very jumpy and nervous but is obviously trying hard to look casual. Hopefully it's only me noticing his behaviour.

"Rudolf, they've arrested Egon Nickel and I understand that the Gestapo found your report from yesterday about who should leave and why along with a lot of other material not connected to you. Others in the leadership have also been arrested."

I look around, checking that we are not being watched. So the military organisation is totally collapsing. I've been dreading this moment.

"Ok, I'll report this to the secret intelligence section and they will get this information through to the higher strata" I reassure my friend. "With a bit of luck the Bezirksleitung[97] will have time to rearrange our organisation."

"I hear from our informer that the police authority in Altona intends to arrest the whole Bezirks leadership shortly" warns my friend.

A few days later I hear that the arrest are mainly with the secret intelligence section so has my message got through to the highest authority? I have no alternative but to inform the leadership for the whole of Germany as to the events in Hamburg. When I do not receive a reply, I send the information again but still nothing.

I meet up with my good friend Johann Dünkel. "Egon was right you know Rudolf. You must leave this country immediately. If you are caught, the Gestapo will ensure that you receive the death sentence and of course there will be the torture first… I'm going to get in touch with your brother Ernst to see if he can get you out via the docks".

Being a close family friend and my protector for the moment he tries to take control of the situation. After some time everything is arranged and on 1st August I have my false passport in the name of Otto Kammers and Johann provides me with the dock workers uniform. It is a very emotional and sad farewell which I make to the Dünkels. I take the opportunity to thank Johann.

"What's this you're giving me" he asks in genuine surprise.

"It's the only thing I have of value Johann. You have been such a wonderful support for me over the years and as a result risked your own life. I won't be able to take anything with me and it's just a thank you".

Johann at this point looks at my much treasured stamp collection. He knows how proud I am of the valuable album and I'm sure he'll look after it or if need be sell it. I have nothing else to give him.

A couple of my friends walk with me back to my parent's home. As we arrive, they split up and saunter into two strategic areas to keep watch for SA troops or the Gestapo should they appear in Gertigstrasse. I slip inside the flat to say a quick farewell to my parents, running up the few stairs taking two steps at a time and

---

[97] Resistance leadership of Hamburg

stopping in the hallway of the flats. I glance up at the spiral stairway leading to the other flats knowing that this is the last time I shall do this. I can't help a sad sigh escaping from my mouth as I turn back to the flat which has meant so much to me and all the inhabitants who have lived here since it was built.

As I quietly open the door and glance inside, I see my beloved parents. This is one of the hardest things I have to do as they are the most precious parents anyone can have. Will I ever see them again I wonder. Come to that, will I ever see my beloved Hamburg again? What about my son Rudi and my wife whose lives I have ruined? What has happened to humanity when an ordinary loving family has to sacrifice so much? After a few loving exchanges and embraces, I quickly leave the flat. Whatever happens, I mustn't be selfish and risk my family's lives with a long emotional goodbye. They know this and they try to keep positive for me.

The poignant ties have now been broken and now my task is to get on board the soviet ship. At least trading between Germany and the Soviet Union is still occurring but I have no idea for how much longer.

Thank goodness I had been employed in the dockyard at an earlier date so know where I am going and how to behave without attracting too much attention. My friends help me through the customs and up the plank of a soviet ship destined for Odessa. Another colleague is also escaping the country with me. Richter and I hide in a container trying to keep as quiet as we can. Finally on 2nd August 1933, the ship leaves Hamburg docks and heads for the long two hour journey along the River Elbe towards the estuary and safety. I'm longing to vacate the container and to watch the flat lands pass by as the steamer slowly edges towards the open sea. I shall probably never see this countryside again. It's so tempting for me to watch the land as we sail but it is still German territory so I shall just have to accept the situation and try to occupy my mind.

As the engine noise alters, I know that at long last we are out at sea. Richter and I are now free to join the ship's crew. We keep to our new names when we emerge introducing ourselves to those who have no idea who we are and then volunteer to help crew the ship.

It's the least we can do for those who did know about us and despite the risk agreed to hide us on board. I wonder if we will end up being a hindrance to the crew, not being sailors.

The weather is perfect as we leave the North Coast and we see the coastline of the Netherlands, Belgium and France glistening in the sun. The calm sea changes as we cross the Bay of Biscay and my stomach empties not having good sea legs. I have never had the opportunity of exploring Europe. I can only see the different countries from a distance but the absolute beauty of the Mediterranean cheers me up even though the blistering heat burns my very pale skin. Finally we sail through the Bosporus Strait and into the Black Sea. On 23rd August the port of Odessa looms up in the distance. I peer desperately out along the skyline of my new country. There are no hills or mountains surrounding Odessa and it reminds me of Hamburg especially when we get close to the shore and I can see the architecture of the buildings which look the same European style of my old home.

As we disembark, both Richter and I do not get the welcome we had hoped for. It seems either the Emigration Commission of Wasserkante (Hamburg) or our contacts in Berlin have not sent our particulars through so we are not expected. Perhaps my colleagues were right that it was crucial I left Hamburg immediately but this does not bode well for our reception here as the soviets are naturally very suspicious of anyone arriving unannounced. Spies have been trying to infiltrate into the Soviet Union for some time now and claiming to be German refugees. It cannot be helped that after being 'detained' we are given the arduous job of writing a letter to the German section of the Commintern, explaining why I have arrived here in Odessa without any notice. I hate sitting down with pen and ink – always did. I have always been a 'do-er' rather than an academic. In what seems to me an eternity, I carefully compose and write five pages explaining why it appears we have arrived unannounced. Perhaps it is already known that the military side of the resistance has been infiltrated so they will obviously be extra vigilant about our explanations.

On 23rd September I get a questionnaire to complete about myself in order to get identification papers allowing me to enter the

Soviet Union. I know that all this red tape has to be done, but it's so frustrating trying to prove who I am and also my trustworthiness. Who on earth am I going to put down as a guarantor of my character when so many of my colleagues have been arrested in Germany? Gustav Gundelach is I think still in Germany or perhaps he has also escaped and on his way to the USSR, but at least to my knowledge he hasn't yet been arrested. Oh there's also Max Magdalena who is in Moscow who will always support me. I think that I will also take the opportunity to write a bit more about what I have been doing when fighting the fascists in Hamburg. This might shorten this questioning period so that we can all move on.

After a few weeks in detention, I'm finally released having been issued with a soviet passport. Heckert of the I.K.K.I.[98] confirms that the information I have given is correct and Scheider Friedland confirms that from the information he has, I am an active and responsible person who has carried out the tasks given me and can be relied upon to see the assignment to the end. At long last, it looks as though I have been accepted so I've now got to go by train to Moscow.

In the short time I have before leaving, I'm keen to see Odessa. It is so like my home with the architecture and beautiful tree lined avenues with trams scuttling along the streets. It was once a wealthy tourist area situated by the Black Sea with a large sandy beach at Arkadia.

As I make my way to Odessa Golovna, which is the main station, I decide to take a slight detour as I really would love to see the Potemkin stairs. In the film Battleship Potemkin which was made in 1925, they showed these steps as the site of the 'workers uprising' by the crew of the Russian Battleship Potemkin in 1905. In actual fact this event happened nearby but after seeing this film, I'm just so pleased to see the magnificent steps and picture in my mind the scene from the film.

The main station is very impressive as I enter the building to buy my train ticket. Moscow is over a 1000 kilometres away so it will take

<hr>

[98] Executive Committee of the Commintern

one or two days for me to reach my destination. The country is so vast and beyond comprehension to fully understand these distances.

When I finally arrive in Moscow and I alight from the train, my body aches after sitting for so long. I report myself to the authorities and once again settle myself down for a long wait. I find all this sitting around so frustrating but I suppose I am just one of many people going through this process. Eventually I am ushered into an office where a man is busy working at his desk. He looks up as I enter.

"Welcome to Moscow Rudolf Rudolfovich." He studies my face and then continues to look his paperwork, reads for a few minutes and then adds "I see that you are an expert in explosives according to this list we have been given".

Our eyes meet and he again studies me hard for a few minutes at his last comment regarding explosives. My new name seems really unusual to hear but I will have to get used to it I suppose. Apparently the surname means 'son of Rudolf' (my father's name). I think very carefully before I reply to his two sentences.

"Thank you. I will do whatever work you require of me."

The man I'm speaking to just nods in approval and he explains that to start with I will be living in a hostel and will be given a job to do in an engineering factory. I'm a bit surprised being told that I'll be expected to do engineering after his initial comment, but I suppose they want to know my character before they make use of other "talents".

At long last I'm able to write to my family in Hamburg to let them know that I am safe. I have to use my false passport name of Otto. In my letter, I ask Ernst to send some technical books to help us with engineering problems as the standard of this type of manufacturing work needs improving due to the lack of investment during the Tsarist era. They are so far behind technically here and I can see possibilities on how to improve. It is almost like living in the dark ages but I shall do my best to help them modernise. As far as my family is concerned, as soon as I am able to purchase enough food, I will be able to send a parcel home to my parents. Food is still short for them so it'll be wonderful to help them especially after all the sacrifices they have made for me.

As expected, my brother Ernst does not fail me as almost by return, parcels of technical books arrive and I can put my knowledge to good use and the other employees can learn new skills.

Winter is beginning to arrive here and I cannot believe that it is so much colder than in Hamburg. I shall never again moan about the cold winter winds of my old country. I now realise that was almost balmy weather compared with the cold freezing conditions here in Moscow.

CHAPTER 18

Werner during 1934

What a sad and downbeat event Christmas and New Year was, mainly due to the lack of Rudolf, Ernst and Käthe's presence. Only Anna brought her guitar, so we could sing along with her but it seems a poignant moment instead of a joyous one and even she stops playing when her sadness becomes apparent to everyone. We're all missing them so much but with Anna's heart condition and her worries about Ernst the strain must be intense. I am sure she is wondering if he will survive the torture which he must be receiving. Yet she is so kind, never complains, carrying on with dignity, smiling to Mama, Papa and Gretel. I try to help her by going over to sit next to her and hold her hand when I see her deep in thought. At other times I put an arm round her shoulder. I can't help but feel sad about their situation.

Anna and I are very close. We both think a lot about our loved ones and although we're not the extrovert members of our family, we always want to help by supporting emotionally with problems many of us are experiencing. Mama, Lotte, Anna and I often say that we are magnets, attracting people to talk to us but none of us mind as we know how much this is needed these days. The problem though is we sometimes need support ourselves but perhaps we hide our needs too well. I will make sure that Anna will have my support and this will be my mission by calling regularly at her home, taking Gretel out for little treats thereby giving Anna a rest.

When Gretel either goes to bed or is playing by herself I spend time talking to my sister-in-law, to help alleviate her suffering wondering if Ernst will survive. She's been told by the Gestapo so many fearful outcomes concerning my brother that it is a wonder with her heart condition, that she is still alive. Is their intention to exacerbate her condition to bring on a heart attack in order to punish Ernst more? Do they want Ernst to worry so much about the strain Anna is going through that he will give away names and shorten the 'questioning'? Are they hoping that Anna might tell them something of Ernst's activities in order to save him from more torture? These men seem to get pleasure from the pain, misery and terror they inflict on their victims and relatives. The Gestapo had told Anna at one point that Ernst has been shot dead and then that he has been sent to Berlin and has been sentenced to death. Is any one of these tales correct? What has happened to my quiet natured brother?

Mama and Papa invite Gretel to stay with them for the day to give Anna a rest so I decide to call in to see her on my way home from work. She looks broken in spirit sitting there all alone with time to spare for her thoughts. She's sitting in her dilapidated old chair by the unlit kachelofen. She looks up to the ceiling as though she expects answers from somewhere, her face tear stained and so much older than her years. Then her body jerks to attention when she hears me speaking to her. She takes a handkerchief out of her pocket, quickly wipes her tears, blows her nose, making an excuse that it was caused by chopping onions.

"Whatever has happened Anna" I ask as I went over and knelt down in front of her, holding her hands firmly. Too many people have been in Kola-fu[99] and never returned so that my heart just will not stop beating loudly and I can't stop myself shivering with fear. It is cold in the room as Anna cannot afford to heat the flat but this is a involuntary nervous shaking which has taken over my body.

---

[99] Fulhsbüttel Concentration Camp. Kola-Fu is short for Konzentrationslager Fuhlsbüttel. The Nazi regime established this concentration camp mainly to persecute and oppress its political opponents and intimidate the population. Thousands of Hamburg residents were imprisoned during the 1930s until the end of the war. By the time Kola-Fu was liberated in May 1945, over 450 men and women died there. They perished as a result of maltreatment, were murdered or were driven to commit suicide. Later this place transferred prisoners to Buchenwald, Neuengamme, Ravensbrück or Sachsenhausen concentration camps. Within the walls of the concentration camp was a remand prison and ordinary prison.

"I'm sorry Werner. I try to be brave in front of Gretel and your parents but when I am alone, my feelings and worries cannot be suppressed."

"I've just come back from Kola-fu. The Gestapo 'invited' me there." I look in surprise hearing this but then she follows with "Who in their right mind would refuse the Gestapo as the end result can be worse?"

I nod and encourage her to continue.

"They took me into that dreadful place." She was quiet again for a few minutes while she collected her thoughts. I could see that her mind was struggling to accept the event and was in a reflective mood.

"Those walls surrounding the concentration camp seem to hold all the fear and agony of the inmates. "Help us, save us from our fate" they seem to say – oh those walls seem to say so much, I know not literally but they ooze with this mixture of despair, misery and warning."

I wonder if Anna has lost her sanity by saying this. She continues.

"It's bad enough when we have to stand outside to deliver clean clothes for Ernst and to wait to collect his dirty clothes which are covered in blood. How cruel can these people be making us women folk suffer or do you think it is done intentionally to make us confess knowledge of our husband's resistance work, so that the torture will top for them?"

She sits for a moment not saying anything else. I can see she's absolutely exhausted both mentally and physically but I can do nothing but be there for her. How can anyone do this to such a lovely caring wife and mother? I try to give her words of comfort but I know this does little to alleviate her distress. I've never seen her so distraught and decide the only thing I can do is hold on to her until she is ready to continue. She studies my face, uncertain whether to continue.

"You are so young Werner. Please be careful as you must not get caught by the Gestapo. Age seems immaterial to the way they treat people. I should say no more."

I plead for her to continue as I need to know about Ernst. After a few minutes of thought she continues again.

"I was marched into one of the buildings. I know that it is winter, but those corridors are icy cold. Some corridors are empty but I can hear piteous sounds coming from behind closed doors. First there are voices from the SS Officers or the Gestapo and then cries of agony from the prisoners. And then… " she stops speaking.

I keep quiet for a while almost too frightened to ask but then I ask her "and then?" She stares into the distance, deep in thought, and then looks at me.

"And then I recognise one of the sounds coming from inside the room. It was Ernst, I know it was. I then turned to the guard who had been closely watching my face and all he said was "Yes it is Ernst your husband. Do you have anything to tell me?" All I did was shake my head. We'd already had a conversation before he was arrested where we agreed that on no account would we try to help one another by admitting anything so all I did was to shake my head".

We are both quiet, but my imagination is in over drive. I want to do something to help him but I know I cannot – but I can help Anna.

"At least I know that today Ernst is alive and hadn't been executed as they'd told me earlier. I actually heard his voice Werner but how can human beings be so evil? What possesses one human being to hurt another in such a way? No other species of animal I know can be so cruel. I could hear the Gestapo or SS intermittently talking to him and then shouting abuse and finally the sounds of my poor Ernst being beaten and kicked."

She stops talking again, composes herself and starts again. "In other parts of the building there is a mixture of men in their Nazi uniform marching briskly along the corridors, the sound of their feet echoing as there is nothing to absorb the noise. Some of them carry limp figures with their feet scraping along the ground as unconscious prisoners are carried back to their cells, blood dripping from various parts of their bodies. Prison cell doors clank shut, and the sound of the huge keys being turned in the locks. It's a living hell in there Werner."

She starts sobbing again and this time she is not alone. Tears had been falling down my cheeks whilst she had been talking. My lovely quietly spoken brother who loves us all so much has lost everything and is now in such pain and fear, because of the devotion he has for his country. He's risked his life for the rights of ordinary citizens and for freedom and is now himself incarcerated in that dreadful place. I put my head on to her lap and hug her round her waist. She bends over and we stay interlocked in this position for some time.

Eventually we are shaken out of this comforting position by the sound of a key in the lock of the front door. I disengage myself from Anna and look round to see Papa standing there holding little Gretel's hand. Her horrified little face with her eyes as big as saucers looks at both of us and seeing us both so upset. Gretel let go of her Opa's hand and rushes over to her mother to try and comfort her. Anna manages to smile at little Gretel and gives her a hug. I stand up and walk over to Papa.

"Papa, I think it would be good if you let Gretel sleep in my bed tonight and I'll stay here with Anna. She's had a terrible experience and needs time to recover."

Papa had turned grey and looks as though he would collapse. I try to reassure him.

"Ernst he is still alive and all right". The first part I hope is truthful still but a white lie to the second is something we all have to adopt for our parent's sake. "I'm worried about Anna's heart giving out so I think a complete rest tonight will help calm her down."

Papa nods in approval and calls to Gretel. "Come my little one. Oma has forgotten to give you a cake she's made especially for you and she really is looking forward for you to stay the night. It'll be fun and as your Uncle Werner has just said, you can have his bed for the night."

Gretel studied each of our faces. I can't help thinking that she's older than her years as she knows that her Mama needs peace and quiet, but I can understand from her viewpoint she's already lost her Papa and wants to look after her Mama.

"Thank you Opa but I'm not leaving Mama tonight. I need to look after her. I promise that I will be good".

Papa studies both their faces and then looks at me.

"I'm all right Papa, really I am" Anna says to my father. Gretel and I shall look after each other" she adds giving her daughter a wonderful hug.

I reluctantly leave them but return early the next morning. As I had feared, Anna looks really unwell so I call the doctor. After a thorough examination the doctor admits Anna into hospital. Will this strain finish poor Anna? What of my beloved Ernst?

On 20th January, Käthe is released from 'questioning' and straight away goes to her parent's home to see Rudi. For several days we hear nothing from her. However her parents kindly reassure us not to worry as she just needs time to recover from her ordeal and to consider her present situation. Poor Käthe has really suffered as a consequence of being married to one of the Stenders. Rudolf's commitment for social reforms and justice and his fight against fascism has been over a longer period and Käthe understood his 'calling' but it must have been hard for her that Rudolf never really settled into a quiet family life. He always put his political beliefs first. As a consequence she and Rudi became a target for the Nazis but nobody expected she would be arrested by them. Käthe always knew Rudolf's beliefs before they married and if Rudolf gave up on them to become a loving husband and father spending his spare time always with them, then it wouldn't be Rudolf.

I know Rudolf loves Käthe and Rudi as he does us. He's always been fiercely protective of every one of us. Poor Käthe – she has always been there for Rudolf and her behaviour towards my parents and the rest of the family has been exemplary even though they separated a little while before he left Germany.

Eventually she calls round to see us and is greeted with love and concern for her welfare. She looks drawn and has the look of so many of those who have been released from Kola-fu. Mama produces the traditional cups of coffee. We chat generally for a while before Käthe pauses, takes a deep breath and says "I don't know how to tell you this, but I've decided that I can no longer carry on being married to Rudolf. I love him so much and this is so difficult for me to say to you. Rudolf has a mission in life and a cause to fight and I feel that Rudi and I are holding him back. I've spent weeks if not months churning my feelings over and over and I have finally decided that it will be better for both of us to go our separate ways."

Mama puts a comforting hand on Käthe's hands. Käthe lips quiver with emotion.

"I've had constant visits by the Gestapo who have made a habit of searching my premises and threatening me because they're trying to find Rudolf. They have been terrifying me and our son and now after my "questioning" and imprisonment in Kola-fu I've decided that little Rudi is the most important person for me to protect. I'm sorry if you feel I'm deserting Rudolf and letting you all down."

Mama was the first to reply.

"Dearest Käthe, you have always been very close in our hearts and we have seen that you have suffered due to being married to our first born. I know Rudolf loves you and Rudi very much but he has said to me on many occasions that he fears that he has expected too much from you. He has chosen to take a very dangerous and lonely path but he also has to be true to himself. If our country had managed to have peace and a socialist government after the Great War, then you would all be together now in perfect harmony and I would probably have more grandchildren" adds Mama with a smile.

"You must go ahead and arrange the divorce. Hopefully the Gestapo will then leave you and Rudi in peace. Anyway I don't know if we will ever see our Rudolf again. He cannot return to this country whilst the Nazis are in power so you have no hope of continuing a normal marriage. I hope though that we will all remain friends as I still will count you as my daughter-in-law even if you remarry. Have as happy a life as you can Käthe as you deserve it" added Mama.

At this point we all murmur in agreement with Mama's statement. What a wonderful counsellor Mama has always been. I hope that I can continue in her footsteps.

"Mama" replied Käthe "And that name I shall always call you, I thank you with all my heart". And then in tears turning to the rest of us she continues. "The Stenders are and will be my family despite having the need to split from Rudolf. Rudolf will always be in my heart and my soul whatever happens in the future and I thank you for the love and understanding you have given me. Of course Rudi would still like to visit you" she adds.

"As I hope you will do my dear Käthe" I pipe into the conversation. She nods and smiles. Her ordeal is over and I can see that she is relieved that we all understand and that we still love her."

Despite all this period of fear I have no intentions of discontinuing my resistance work. I'm quite pleased that I've managed to increase our membership and have been forming new groups. Our supplies of illegal material and leaflets have now improved as we are getting better organised. The people who have been forced to leave the country when they suspected that they were about to be arrested, arranged information leaflets to be smuggled into Germany via couriers. Most of it is coming from Denmark where there is a strong unit of resistance fighters who have had to leave Germany but are continuing to work hard to support us. Let us hope that the set-up in Denmark never gets infiltrated by the Nazis as this could lead to mass arrests here[100].

It has been difficult though trying to prepare myself for the finals of my four year apprenticeship. This involves theory and practical examinations as well as still attending the trade school. There are times when I wonder how I'll manage to fit everything in. It is unsurprising I am so thin even though I am quite tall. I'm grateful that my employers know that I am a conscientious worker and produce the best standards of my craft that I can. If I can only qualify and become a skilled worker, then my wages will improve. Then should I ever become unemployed, I might have a better chance of finding a new job. I wonder if I will succeed in finishing the apprenticeship or will it be my turn soon to be arrested?

I manage to persuade some of my colleagues in the factory at Daimler-Benz to receive a regular supply of newspapers from some of the trade unions which the government has banned. Not all my colleagues have the same political views as myself. I have to be wary of the man in charge of the tools and spares who always make us give the fascist salute each time we need some more spare parts or tools. He has threatened to report us if we don't acknowledge and return

---

[100] For the reader who understands German, an excellent explanation of the situation in Denmark is on page 70 of *Skandinavische Erfahrungen erwünscht? Nachexil und Remigration* by Michael F Scholz

the salute so we have to comply even though I grind my teeth with distaste at this action.

One day a Mercedes belonging to the Gestapo is sent in to our factory for repair. On inspection, we find horsewhips on the back seat which we have heard from ex-prisoners are used for 'interrogations'. The disgust I feel seeing these articles and the thought that they might have been used on my poor brother and other colleagues who have been arrested, makes me rally as many of my friends in the factory to see these articles. How strange that these horsewhips 'disappeared' by the time the car is collected!

Despite my disgust and hatred of guns I finally make the decision, along with my resistance comrades, that perhaps it is time that we should start thinking about obtaining some pistols to arm ourselves in order to avoid arrest. We now know too many people who have been detained and also the fate they have suffered.

At the beginning of 1934, there are three million S.A. in Germany so it doesn't take much imagination to think how many there are in Hamburg. It's disgusting seeing the SA march along the roads singing their songs and *all* the people in the road have to stand to attention and salute the Swastika flag. Anyone who is not prepared to do this is attacked and beaten up by the S.A. I often try to avoid having to acknowledge these people by dashing down a side road before they get too near me.

On 28th February Hitler decides to issue a warning to the S.A. that the "revolution is finished" and only people entitled to wear armbands are the "Reichswehr" which is the army. Why is he making this announcement? This decision does nothing but end up irritating the S.A. and tensions between the two organisations seem to be increasing. What is Hitler up to now I wonder? The SA are not the type of people you want to cross swords with. On 16th March Hitler announces an increase in the size of the army.

As for us, an uprising against Hitler at this time is no longer a reality. I feel that it is our duty to our beloved Germany to carry on our work against the Nazis. We must consolidate and strengthen our resistance groups and also print more leaflets warning people what is really happening due to Hitler's policies and that it will eventually lead to a new world war. Hans Schwarzmeyer composes and types the leaflets. The printing has improved since we obtained a printing machine. We are getting quite good at the production of pamphlets especially after Werner Etter and I had bought the typewriter. Werner is also pretty good at writing political statements.

Alfred Drögemüller[101], and myself have been busy printing the leaflets in Harry Schoning's loft. We have to be careful not to be seen when we stick leaflets on outside walls and paint slogans directly on to walls and brickwork. We would be arrested immediately at carrying out such action especially as the subject matter is warning people of fascism.

I just can't help pondering on our situation as in a normal democracy we would just be political opponents distributing information objecting to the present government. And yet, here we are listening just in case anyone is approaching in the fear that if we ever get discovered, we will automatically be arrested and sent to a concentration camp. We will then be 'questioned' to give the Gestapo the names of other people involved with us and who knows what will happen to us then.

Even if anyone not connected with our organisation is found with a leaflet in their possession or in their home, they end up in a concentration camp. My work colleagues are risking everything taking leaflets and trade union newspapers from me, but there are many free thinking individuals who want to know what is really happening in Germany. It is all such a dangerous situation but we are determined to spread the truth before it is too late. We might be young but everyone in our organisation cares about the future of our country.

Just as I turn down Geibelstrasse early one evening a lorry screeches to a stop and a great many Stormtroopers jump out of the vehicle. Behind me at the other end of the street, another lorry full of the troops turns into street and out jump more SA. SS troops join in with searching and stopping everyone who is in the street. I can feel my hands getting clammy and my heart is racing, but whatever

[101] He later escaped to Denmark and worked in the resistance movement there

happens I must not look nervous as this will draw attention to me. No doubt they are looking for arms and illegal literature and the Geibelstrasse is a well-known district for "rebellious" residents. Thank goodness we are now prepared for this type of regular event. The incriminating documents which will mean instant arrest are hidden in my shoes. Up until now we have never been asked to remove our shoes but will these troops wake up to where we hide them?

A Stormtrooper starts looking through my pockets whilst I have my hands up and another one stands behind me ready to hit me if there is a look from the man searching for evidence against me. I hold my breath and try to look as innocent as possible. I mustn't show fear or come to that, look too confident as they detest being mocked. The SA man sneers and studies my face hard for any reaction. I receive a rough shove from the Stormtrooper behind me and I scurry away as quickly as I can without drawing attention to myself. However I can feel sweat beginning to drip down my face and feel so grateful that this outside show of nerves hadn't happened earlier for them to notice. I've survived another street search, but how many more will there be before they catch up with me?

In spite of constant searches, we keep busy printing leaflets, putting them in letterboxes and some we leave in certain factories. Werner Etter and I also have another method of distribution. Because of my knee problems, I'm the lookout as he disappears up the staircases of apartment buildings and other high premises. Having reached to roof, with a huge fling of his arms, Werner throws the leaflets over the side and to our delight they flutter into the streets below. He is such a quick fellow that he manages to run down the stairs three or four steps at a time and then we disappear before the Stormtroopers arrive. I can always rely on dear Werner Etter and although he shrugs aside any congratulations, I know how brave a person he is.

Trying to convince the local people that Hitler's intention is to lead us to war and destruction is very difficult to achieve. In the first year of his power, Hitler has reduced unemployment by opening or expanding factories which are manufacturing armaments or related items. The resulting increase in the labourer's actual and financial well-being seems to blinker them from thinking about the items they are producing. I really find it hard to accept how so many people put themselves first before understand the consequences and dangers to our country and the world as a whole.

Sometimes I do not know which way to turn as my family also need my support. It is awful seeing Anna struggling to cope without Ernst. She flits in and out of hospital and Gretel frequently comes to stay with us. I try to make Gretel's life with us as enjoyable as possible. We have always been close but finding free time is very difficult as I'm working hard studying for my final apprenticeship qualification and I'm also busy organising my local resistance movement. Anna is unable to work and the State only gives her the barest minimum which Ernst will have to repay should he ever survive and be released. If only we could help her but our finances are not much better than hers. Papa does not earn very much from his cigar shop and my apprenticeship money is virtually nothing.

Ever resourceful, Anna decides to let a room to a stranger to increase their income. Gretel is the one to suffer here as she is always told to keep quiet so as not to annoy the lodger. I've noticed how introverted she is becoming worrying about both parents and having very little money for food, warmth and clothing. She knows she must not talk very much and upset the lodger as he could report the family to the authorities. She is becoming a mixed up child, and at one point Anna had to go to Gretel's school to explain why her little girl is so quiet. It seems there is a personality gulf developing between the children of families in fear of arrest and are very wary and the assertive behaviour of those who are profiting from Hitler's dictatorship. We can do very little to help Gretel with this problem apart from give her as much love as possible.

When I call round to see Werner Etter one evening after work, we chat about neutral subjects for a while so as not to worry his mother. He then says to me

"I'm sure Mutti does not want us disturbing her any more so come upstairs to my room." His Mutti then laughs and says "be off the pair of you and leave me in peace." When he shuts the bedroom door, he turns to me and whispers that he had been given a document which he wants me to see.

"If we're found with this document, I dread to think what will happen to us" he continues quietly as he hands it to me. He looks apologetic as he adds "I'm sorry as it is bound to upset you with Ernst having been taken to Gestapo headquarters and being in Kola-fu, but this is a very important document."

I glance at the papers. It must have been written about February time and I note that the circulation list is to go to all the important and influential people of Hamburg including the General Chief Prosecutors of Hamburg, the lawyers and also pastors.

Werner then tells me "It mentions in there that our comrade Fritz Lux has committed suicide, probably because he'd become too weak after being tortured for so long".

"I had heard rumours that Fritz is dead but not how" I answer. I am still stunned to hear this news as he had been a close friend of Rudolf and Ernst. He'd been arrested way back on 25th July 1933 by commander of the Special Forces who are now known as the Gestapo. Not only had Fritz been someone high up in the resistance movement, but he had been a member of parliament for Hamburg. He'd obviously been tortured from July to 6th November when he died, poor man. I glance down at the document Werner has given me and start to read the letter dated 7th February 1934[102].

The Hamburg Police Authority
7th February 1934
Hamburg 56
Neuerwall 88

To the Chief State Prosecutor Dr Drescher
Your respectful Mr Chief State Prosecutor!
The leaflet sent to me a few days ago, I return with thanks. In the meantime that same leaflet has been sent to me from a number of lawyers and pastors. From this, one can assume that the same leaflet has been sent to all lawyers and pastors in Hamburg
    Heil Hitler

---

[102] Document translated from original held in Hamburg University Archives

Dear German People and Comrades

The present situation in today's Germany prevents the German people being informed about the truth of what is happening in Germany. Therefore we are asking you to read this accurate document carefully as to events taking place here in Germany. In this report you can see since the national revolution how Germans are being treated, and their later trials.

Even the Christian churches are used to cover up this dreadful situation. We ask you to protest with us against these happenings occurring in our beloved country.

<u>*Events after an arrest*</u>

The K.z.b.V. (Commander for Special Duties) arrives at the home and takes the accused in a car which is waiting outside. They take the prisoner to the "Grossen Bleichen" (Cleansing) where they enter the building and are led to the first room and receive brutal treatment. In the room on the wall there are posters with the words "Please be quiet, please be friendly. There is order here" etc. The arrested person is hit and kicked and all this is before any questioning has started. The prisoner has to stand straight ahead facing the wall so that the he is unable to see and recognise any faces of the people who are attacking him. After all that they are led to a larger room and the same treatment continues along with initial questioning. In the room they are brutally assaulted by several young men but if all the treatment does not have the expected result, they are taken by the S.A. to yet another room which even the aggressors themselves call the torture room. The S.P.D. and K.P.D. prisoners enter different rooms and each room has the symbols of their own Party displayed on the walls. In the room of the K.P.D. is the picture of Lenin and the prisoner is asked who this person is and again he is brutally treated until they get the right reply which is "He is a Jew". In this room one man does the questioning and three to four men stand by ready with ox whips. This is a leather whip about 1 ½ meters in length covered by 2 mm of rubber and then again leather. The questioner rarely takes part in the brutal treatment. If this so called questioning is not successful, everyone attacks the prisoner and he is pulled over a table which is like a butchers table and they abuse him most dreadfully. Crying is usually impossible as a towel is tied over the mouth.

One of the main torturers is "Weber" and another is called Schlachter (Butcher). This brutal treatment is repeated three to four times until the prisoner becomes unconscious and then he is revived with a glass of water and even a cigarette. But after this the torture starts again. Identical treatment is used in the rooms of the Staatpolice (Gestapo) Headquarters in the Department of Commissar Kraus, Room 205. Kraus himself does not carry out this treatment but is fully aware of it.

In room 203, which is a room all the prisoners are frightened of entering, is used to 'finish up' the prisoners. This means either they confess, tortured to death or they are forced to commit suicide. The main torturers in this room are von Rönn, Deutschmann, and Wienecke.

After the torturer gets all the answers he requires, the prisoner is transferred to a cell and from there, finally transferred to a remand prison to sleep often in a room with other prisoners. They are put together in a room so that they can hear and understand unbelievable tales of horror.

The physician Dr Schädel who works in the military hospital then has the unenviable task of trying to heal the injured prisoners. He is not liked by the Nazi authorities as he puts down the correct cause of the injuries which have been done to the prisoners. A large number of people have been treated badly. After twenty weeks of "protective" custody there are injuries to the head, ears and in particular many prisoners have renal diseases/failure, all through being mishandled. These injuries still show on the bodies of the prisoners. In the dormitories which are allocated for sleeping, there is hardly any thought of sleep due to the whimpering and whining of the abused and injured prisoners, plus consequential nightmares making sleep impossible. I and nearly all of my colleagues are stunned about the results of the ox's whip. There are injuries from this torture where the prisoners are black from the neck to the knees from bruising and the whole body is covered in blood. From the prison dormitories, the prisoners go into the concentration camp. During the admission to the camp, twenty to forty men have to face the wall where they have to keep awake as the lists of the prisoners are taken. Nobody must move. One or more SS men walk behind them to ensure no movement. The prisoners must stay in this position for four to five hours. The smallest movement is answered immediately with abuse by being struck on the face and physically maltreated. It is encouraged for one prisoner to kick another. Also a very popular means of punishment is to hit the prisoner with the large cell keys.

At least half of the prisoners admitted had to slow run around the yard several times. The yard periphery is approximately 350 m and all this abuse can be seen by the prison guards who have houses surrounding the prison. The prison officials who live in these houses have already complained about this situation.

As he passes the prisoners, the Commander of the Camp, <u>Dusendschön</u> (who is protected by Gestapo) and other people, strike prisoners in the face. This has been done in my presence. He is accompanied by officials of the State Police (including Rönn and the Government Advisor Ellerhusen[103]) and their behaviour is also not passive as regulations would expect. Then the abuse takes place in the halls and cells. Here are some examples. Some of the worst wardens are the SS – people such as Zirbitz, König, the brothers Teutsch and Nussbeck.

At night one often cannot sleep because of the cries of the abused ones. It starts at night at 1 am and persists then until the morning at 4 a.m. The warden in charge of the solitary confinement strikes the prisoners at the slightest opportunity. A whole row of prisoners has lain in the basement for weeks wrapped in chains. Depending on the mood of the guards they bind the prisoners putting them on their stomachs on a heap of sand in a cell in Basement A. If they need to go to the toilet, no facilities are available so they just lay there and use the sand. Not having shaved, their full beards make them look wild. On the Kzb.V. Dr Elaku had his arm broken during his arrest. He had bundles of hair pulled out and Swastikas cut into his heels. The photographer took pictures of him but he could not be recognised after this treatment.

<u>The Commander of the Camp</u> – the dog Dusendschön was present watching all of this and often he and also participated in the abuse. He often tore the clothes off the prisoner and repeatedly injured them. He instigated this abuse.

<u>Guard Zirbitz</u> lambasted nearly all the prisoners of our hall one night when informing on a brother who was not normal. Many were sent into solitary confinement. Barbier made an attempt to commit suicide in the morning by cutting his wrists, opening his veins. Very often people committed suicide because of their treatment. The KPD Member of Parliament Lux took

---

[103] After the war Ellerhusen received 12 years 6 months Zuchthaus (harsh prison) for his behaviour in Fuhlsüttel. He also lost his Citizenship during this time.

*his own life after such a "hearing". The brother of the KPD delegate Reith
who had been previously arrested as a hostage for his volatile brother hung
himself. This was when he heard that he was going to be arrested again.*

*The Case of Sollnietz. Sollnietz is no longer in Fuhlsbüttel in Hall 81
in Block A. Sollnietz had been in solitary confinement and had been tortured.
In our hall he made several attempts to get himself shot. We reproached him
about endangering people. There were strict instructions not to go near the
windows behind the beds as the guards had orders to shoot immediately if a
person got near the window. In A2 Hall, four people had been shot by guards.
The result was one dead, and one or two severely wounded. Hearing this
Sollnietz made an attempt to try this. He tried several times to climb on to the
window sill but we prevented this. He tried the same thing in the toilet where
there was a window after the passageway.*

*Some days after his attempts to get himself shot, there was an inspection.
Among them was Senator Schröder from Lubeck who knew Sollnietz.
Sollnietz was an editor at one time for the newspaper in Lubeck. He spoke to
Sollnietz and on the same day Sollnietz was put into solitary confinement in
the cellars. The following night he was abused so that he had a lot of blood
around his head. The guard made it known to us that the Jew Sollnietz had
a headache that morning. Sollnietz then was told that he would not get food
for three days. He received only drink.*

*On the following day Mrs Sollneitz went to see the Commander of the
Camp Dusendschön, and an SS officer. She was approximately twenty six
years old and went, to complain about the treatment her husband had received
since the Gestapo had accepted the decision for his release. Dusendschön refused
to release Sollnietz, probably because he was not allowed to release him. Mrs
Sollnietz then went to the Ministry of the Interior in Berlin and obtained
permission for his release. When she appeared at the camp with the document,
she was told that her husband had hanged himself. An official told us that he
had written three farewell letters which should not be handed over to the relatives.*

*"The Jewish pig did right" was the opinion of the guards. There is no
doubt that the degradation of the treatment Sollnietz received was connected
with the visit from Senator Schröder.*

*On Monday 4ᵗʰ September all the prisoners were transferred to the old
women's prison which has now become a concentration camp. The guards
communicated to us that no prisoners were allowed to look through their*

windows as the guards had instructions to shoot everyone who tried to do so. Two were shot one with severe injuries and some received slight wounds at Station AIII.

On Saturday 9th September, when the prisoners expected to sleep they were separated into cells and then Koppenlriemen indiscriminately attacked them with clubs. During the second half of September whilst working outside the prison grounds digging, many prisoners started speaking to each other. They were struck in the faces by their supervisors. In addition they were put against the wall and had the usual orders to repeatedly stand "Up-down, up down etc". A junior lawyer Oppenheimer received several impacts to his face during one of these occasions and was given the remark "You Jewish lout, you are condemned. You want us to teach you a lesson?" Oppenheimer had supposedly spoken to one of the prisoners. As to the most popular method of the "educators in the SS uniform", this was to make the prisoners slowly run with a cart fully loaded. On this particular day, a Danish airplane was doing a short loop low over the area where they were working. (This example is appropriate as Hamburg Airfield is close by). The Government advisor Ellerhusen suggested using a rifle to start shooting immediately if they started dropping leaflets.

At the beginning of October there was a new prisoner who was a Jew and about fifty years old. A guard made the following remark to him. "Aha, there you are you old Jew sow. Around the free space march, march". When the Jew Blumenthal thought he had finished, the guard said "You are to keep running, you pig until you fall down." After the old Jew was completely exhausted, he was discharged. Later I discovered that in the Great War he had taken part and received honour medals. I was a witness of the procedure because I was busy with some work in the yard. <u>Government advisor Ellerhusen</u> regularly carried out such treatment.

During the ill treatment by the SS during the day– a man played an organ in order to cover the sound of the prisoners crying during their torment.

From this description, you can now see how the <u>real conditions</u> are in Germany, and this is only one report amongst hundreds of similar ones. Each true national thinking German man and each true German woman must be indignant and appalled over hearing such conditions in our Fatherland, which is one of the highest cultural countries. Can we say still that today?

Fellow citizen, this is a true report on how we treat our people when we send them to trial in our new national socialist Germany. Our country is or was *well known as a cultural country so please read this important document carefully.*

Therefore each German man and each German woman and each true Christian must ensure that Germany soon awakes from this bad dream.

I finish reading the document and lay it on my lap. There are tears in my eyes. I had been told similar stories but this is actual proof of the situation and includes names. We look at each other in silence for a while.

"Whoever wrote this report is extremely brave. He must have worked there and could not keep quiet any longer. I hope that they never catch him" remarks Werner.

"We must be very careful who we pass this on to. All I can say is thank goodness at least Rudolf has escaped, but I'm so worried for Ernst. I can't say anything to my family about this as they are clinging on to hope that Ernst is surviving".

Werner puts a hand on one of my shoulders, squeezing it gently showing me that he understands. I must "get a grip" on my feelings and carry on. We mustn't surrender to these people.

In April 1934, Himmler takes over control of the Gestapo from Goering. This does not bode well as I fear that Himmler is more evil and callous than Goering. How much worse can things get for anyone who wants a free and liberal country?

Easter time means with the improving weather that we can get out into the countryside again and enjoy our walks. We are off the Buchholz and hopefully I can form some more groups of five. I'm keen to persuade more politically aware youngsters that they should join us in the fight against fascism. I really love getting out and about in the company of like-minded people and not feeling intimidated or being overheard by an informer. For anyone watching us we look like an innocent party of young friends enjoying the fresh air after spending so much time living in the city.

Herta, my 'kleines mädchen'[104] being treasurer of our group is busy collecting as much money as possible to help pay for our expenses. She meets many of our leaders as her position requires these connections.

---

[104] German for 'young girl' as I fondly tease my good friend

Despite all our efforts to encourage and inform especially our own generation, of the dangers of fascism we do not have the propaganda machine working on our side. Hitler has made it clear in all of his speeches that whoever has the younger generation on their side the result will be that the future belongs to that political party. In typical manner, he's organised the young people to join the Hitler Youth. This proves to be very successful for Hitler and the parents who have left wing political beliefs soon learn that their views have to be kept from their children. The doctrine these youngsters receive from the leaders of the Hitler Youth encourage all of them to report their parents, family or friends who do not believe in fascism as they are enemies of the State. The motto of the Hitler Youth is 'we are born to die for Germany' and this many of them believe in to the extreme limits.

We have further discussions on how to counteract these ideals of the young fascists. We decide that we must not isolate ourselves from the mass of the German people so we join the movements affiliated to the Hitler Youth in order to infiltrate into their workings. Much to our disgust we have to sing Hitler Youth songs but by now we have all become good actors making everyone believe how loyal we are and faithful believers in "the new way". Carl Heinz and I join a football club associated to the Hitler Youth. For me it's difficult as playing football is not the best sport for my gammy leg but only when we have the chance of gaining their confidence in fun sport can we psychologically study each person and then at the appropriate time try to influence them to think again. Making a wrong move attempting to influence the wrong person could be disastrous so understanding our fellow youth is vital.

How can we counteract Hitler's success in his first years of power when he has been reducing unemployment albeit by rearming and preparing for war? There has been the forming of 'Strength Through Joy' organisation – the combination of all these policies is blinding the German people. But anyone who has doubts about the change of life style sees the resulting terror arrest and even death of many of our resistance fighters and this frightens us as well. At least now since the initial rise to power of Hitler, the ex-trade unions, social democrats and communists are at last starting to work together. A few individual liberals who are opposed to Hitler and are not active in resistance organisations are now especially helpful to provide "safe houses" and also for hiding places for materials, weapons etc.

Now that the weather is improving Mama and Papa decide to visit Papa's sister in Rendsburg. To be perfectly honest, I think my parents love the Gertigstrasse so much that they are reluctant to leave. Papa though is keen to see his sister and family so they decide to go now that life is getting very dangerous. Who knows what is going to be happen in the near future. I can see that I shall receive instructions from them before they leave. Sure enough, the duty falls to Mama to speak to me.

"Now Werner, I know that you are grown up and hate to be told what or what not to do, but I feel that I should at least plead with you to be careful whilst we are away." Mama says anxiously to me. "You tell us nothing about what you are doing. Despite us asking you not to take part in illegal activities, I somehow fear that you are ignoring this. We are going away for a few days but we want to come home to find that you have not been arrested."

I really do feel guilty at this point. My poor parents never say much about their concern for our safety, but with Rudolf having escaped the country and Ernst in Kola-fu, they are obviously suffering a lot of stress.

"Mama, I promise that I will try and be careful. You both need this rest away from Gertigstrasse, and Papa is so looking forward to seeing his sister so you must go and enjoy yourselves. I will keep the place looking tidy ready for when you return."

Mama does not really look that convinced and I'm sure has noted that I have not denied taking part in illegal work. She knows though that if they don't visit Rendsburg now, this might not be possible in the future.

It's glorious weather this weekend and we notice that although it is still early in the year, the huge pool in the Stadtpark is full of youngsters. This pool is more like the size of a lake and families sit and have picnics laid out ready for when the bathers come out of the water. The café by the edge is crowded with people taking the opportunity to relax in this fine weather. There is fun and laughter to be found all around the Stadtpark this weekend. At long last it feels that summer has finally arrived.

My apprenticeship is almost over. Will I qualify and finally be a coach trimmer by trade? I have been working and studying so hard to make sure I pass both the theory and practical exams. The net around our resistance group though seems to be tightening. One or two of our leaders have been arrested so I fear that it may only be a matter of time before we might suffer the same fate, unless we are very lucky.

Early in June 1934 Ernst Schacht, Walter Knut and others are also arrested. This shakes me as they are leading figures in our resistance for Hamburg. Shortly after, Helmut Prosche who is responsible for the financial side of Hamburg resistance is also arrested. So all our leaders are being rounded up and being 'questioned'. Do I try and escape or do I stay and sit it out hoping that the rest of us will not be named? If we all try to escape the country, our level of resistance in this area of Hamburg will be finished. I will never be able to return when the dust settles as we will have given ourselves away by disappearing. If we stay and bluff it out, our names might not be given to the Gestapo and we can therefore continue in our work. We're all very jittery but decide to keep a low profile and not take any risks. I do wonder if we are expecting too much of these men not to give anything away during any torture which they must be receiving at this very moment by the Gestapo?

Erwin Wagenknecht catches up with me as I walk along the street on my way home. Despite being twenty years old which is only two years older than me he looks grey this evening and so much older than his years.

"Whatever has happened Erwin?" I ask, although I suspect it will be far worse news than we have ever had before.

"I went to see Hans Schwarzmeyer just now and found his parents in a terrible state. Honestly Werner, I promise you that I hadn't gone to his home for any other reason than to see him as my friend."

I give him encouragement to continue but I know what he is about to say. He doesn't really have to continue. That awful feeling I had felt when Ernst had been arrested is beginning to manifest through my body.

"He's been arrested Werner – the Gestapo came to his home and took him away".

I try to carry on walking and act normally. I don't know if we are being watched so I mustn't show any reaction. My mind is racing trying to decide what to tell Erwin. I'm the organiser of our youth organisation so now I must show leadership qualities.

"Go home Erwin. Don't go and see anyone else of our group as the Gestapo might be watching us. You must not contact anyone until I give you instructions. Who knows what information the Gestapo have? Keep walking straight on as I turn right here and give me a cheerful pat on the back as we part. You must show no other reaction and then keep walking. We must not let anybody see our concern about what has happened".

He carries out my instructions and I hurry home. As I close the front door, my hands are shaking. Hans, Werner Etter and I are the three leaders in charge of our district Winterhude as well as Uhlenhorst. Now one of us has been arrested so what is my next step? I try so hard to act normally when I sit down with Mama and Papa for our evening meal. Papa as usual sits quietly, but Mama keeps the conversation flowing. I can see that she is looking anxiously at me. Perhaps I have that haunted restless look that Rudolf had before the Gestapo decided to come looking for him. Mama is very perceptive but knows that it is unsafe for all concerned to ask questions.

About a week later, Hans Schwarzmeyer and I were due to meet in the Stadtpark. Obviously I will not turn up, but I wonder if the Gestapo know about this meeting? Hans cannot have told them my name and address yet, otherwise they would be banging on my front door. Has he been forced to reveal this meeting though? No man can be expected to totally withstand the fear and pain of torture. We all know that it is likely that he will admit something.

The date and time of the meeting arrives and then is over and still nothing happens. Has Hans managed not to involve Werner

Etter and myself? Shadows under my eyes have appeared as I struggle trying to act normally but the nights are so long as fear breaks through in the darkness. The entire Winterhude and Uhlenhorst group of young resistance fighters have been warned to lie low and do nothing for a while. We avoid meeting each other, even in secret. Then the silence is broken when news comes that Hans Schwarzmeyer's parents have been arrested. Why have they been detained? They have nothing to do with the resistance. Could it be that the Gestapo are aware of the meeting we had arranged but they had no details about me? If that is the case the Gestapo will know that Hans' parents must have warned someone within the group of his arrest.

A few days later, news filters through that on 12th June 1934 Erwin has been arrested. Hans' parents must have told the Gestapo that they had told Erwin about Hans' arrest. Do I run or do I try to brazen it out? If I go, then there is no further chance of living in Hamburg any more and I will not see my family again. I'm only eighteen years old but how I wish that I have an older more mature brain to help me decide what to do. Surely this cannot be happening to us? I hardly sleep that night, but the 13th June arrives and nothing happens.

What is my next move? I can't speak to the two people who would be able to give me advice. Rudolf has escaped and Ernst is in prison, no doubt receiving terrible torture. I'm so exhausted with all this waiting. Mama keeps asking if I'm all right and all I can do is smile weakly and say "I'm fine – just tired Mama". And yet I can see I haven't convinced her or myself for that matter. I slink off to bed early, hoping that I might get a good night's rest for a change. As I lay in bed, I toss and turn restlessly but at long last sleep comes.

It seems only a matter of minutes before I'm startled awake by a loud banging on our front door. My bedroom is to the left but just by the entrance of the flat and I can hear the dreaded words being bellowed from the inside entrance foyer and our front door.

"Open up, it's the police. There's no point trying to escape Stender. The building is completely surrounded". And then my nightmare begins.

There follows another round of very loud banging on the door. I push the bedcovers away from me and sit on the bed with my legs dangling over the side. I can't help shaking from head to foot with fear. I can hear Papa making his way to the front door shuffling his slippered feet along the corridor between our bedrooms.

"I'm coming, I'm coming" he answers as he nearly arrives at the entrance. By the time I reach my bedroom door and open it I glance into my poor father's face and feeling very ashamed. He looks back at me in abject fear. Rudolf had to escape to save his life, Ernst has already taken by the Gestapo and to what fate I wonder and now it's my turn. Mama hurries from their bedroom and stands next to me. She squeezes my hand in support as the SS burst into the flat, followed by a couple of Gestapo agents.

"Well, well, what a lovely family gathering" snarls a Gestapo agent looking at the three of us.

The SS have already started searching the flat, pulling out drawers, scattering their contents and showing contempt for all my parent's belongings. One of the SS quickly searches me.

"You're required down at Gestapo Headquarters Stender" he says looking at me. I glance over at my parents. How sorry I feel that I have caused them so much pain. Papa looks shocked and upset but Mama tries not to show emotion as she doesn't want to give the Gestapo any satisfaction at our plight. I try to pull myself together. I must keep alert even though it is only just past 4 a.m.

"I'd like to freshen up if you don't mind" I asked the hard faced agent. He nods but also glances at one of the SS and with eye contact with each other, the SS officer yells at me.

"Quickly now and no messing around". He follows me as I walk towards the toilet. I then head towards the kitchen. The triangular sink is in the corner of the kitchen. It is the only sink in the flat so it is used for washing ourselves as well as being the kitchen sink. I turn on the tap and cupped my hands under the cold running water. I have to wake myself up and also give myself some time to gather my thoughts. I splash my face, shocking my system into life. I can hear the SS officer behind me. I'd better by careful and not dally too much. I mustn't give him any opportunity to mishandle me. I'm sure that time will come at Gestapo headquarters but my parents mustn't see their treatment towards me.

It is just getting light outside. Being June, daybreak is very early, but our flat is quite dark so all the lights are on. I wonder how many people in our apartment block have been disturbed by all the noise in our sanctuary of no 56? They're probably laying in their beds terrified that they will be the next to receive a visit from the Gestapo.

"You'd better get your clothes on ready to leave when our search is finished" said the other Gestapo agent. It's odd that they haven't told me why they're here and I haven't asked. It seems an unspoken subject. The SS man assigned to watch over me follows me into the bedroom and I quickly take my pyjamas off and put on my pants, shirt, trousers, socks and shoes. Delaying dressing will only antagonise my guard. My parents just stand together holding hands and trying not to upset anyone. I'm sure Mama knows a lot more than she ever says about my resistance work and also about Rudolf and Ernst, but I do not think Papa had realised that his youngest son has also been involved with illegal work.

The search of the flat comes to an end and as I know there is no incriminating evidence which could be found I can see the annoyance on both the SS and the Gestapo's faces. I had made sure that my parents could never be blamed for anything I have done. Our eyes meet briefly and in those few seconds I show my apologies to Mama and Papa and they show me their love and support. Those few seconds of eye contact with each other has so much meaning to the three of us. The SS men bundle me out of the flat into the foyer, out through the wooden and glass main door which leads from the internal steps to the apartments, down these short flight of steps, through the heavy main door and into the street. The SS have their guns and whips at the ready.

In the street an open topped Mercedes is waiting for me and I'm unceremoniously pushed into the car, followed smartly by some guards. The Gestapo sit in the front of the vehicle. Another similar Mercedes is also parked outside the flat but this one has no unfortunate passenger in it apart from SS guards. Both engines start and the vehicles are driven quickly down the road. It isn't cold, just slightly damp with the morning dew but it is fear that is causing me to shake from head to foot. My nightmare is about to begin.

At this point the questioning starts. I cannot absorb what they are asking me as I'm just so scared and still suffering from shock. I can hardly even remember who I am. Come on Werner, pull yourself together. If I betray anything through this fear, then my friends will suffer. It is a hard task though for a teenager in such dangerous situation.

We arrive outside Herta Winzer's home which is just round the corner from Gertigstrasse. She lives on the second floor at No 17 Geibelstrasse. Oh no, why did I ever ask her to take on the cashier and financial support of our group? She's so young and now will she cope with what is sure to come? The people in my car sit and wait with me whilst the others in the second car quickly get out. Other SS guards appear as if from nowhere and they surround the area.

After about thirty minutes, Herta, "meine kleines mädchen" being only sixteen years old, appears between two SS guards. She looks like a scared rabbit, her face as white as a sheet as she is put in the second car. Our next port of call is Harry Schoning's place. It is at his home that we have been printing leaflets so they must know quite a lot about our activities already. Printing these leaflets is a criminal offence, punishable with very severe sentences including being sent to a concentration camp. I try to slow down my breathing by taking deep gulps of breaths. Come on Werner, keep calm and collect your thoughts.

Both Herta and Harry have been put in the other car. So it seems that our group is finished – that is it – all our hard work over and now what is going to happen to us? What has happened to the others? Are they about to be arrested or will any of us betray our friends through torture?

The large building of Gestapo headquarters looms up before us. By now people are walking to work and I can see their furtive, fearful and yet sympathetic looks on their faces as they glance quickly in our direction and then away. I have never had any wish to walk past this building but here I am now about to discover what the inside is like.

The next few minutes become a blur as I am taken into the

"house of horrors". My name is checked, my date of birth and my address and then I'm taken down to the basement. I just cannot believe my eyes. In front of me are wooden boxes with little holes at the top. There's a table and chair on the other side of the room where an SS guard is sitting. He looks up when we walk in.

"Stender is here waiting to be questioned" says one of the guards reporting crisply to his associate, having just frog-marched me to this room.

The guard jumps to attention and then picks up a bunch of keys. I realise that I must ask for the use of a toilet as the thought of being locked up horrifies me, let alone not knowing if I could 'relieve' myself. I can feel the anger from my guards when they hear my request as I virtually get man handled down the corridor to a very basic toilet. Having finished, I step outside the door and receive the same treatment back to the room with boxes.

This time, one of the doors has been opened, revealing a tiny little wooden seat. I am turned around and shoved back into this little cupboard, being forced to sit down. I knew better than to argue. The door is banged shut and blackness envelopes me apart from a few shafts of light showing where a few air holes have been drilled. There's so little room to move as the box is about half a metre wide and slightly deeper. There's hardly a sound apart from smothered coughing and shuffling from people who are in a similar position to me. Occasionally a trembling voice is heard from within a box when a prisoner timidly knocks on their door and pleads for water or to go to the toilet. Are any of these people from my group? I cannot recognise their voices but I'm sure my voice is not my usual one being muffled with fear.

The darkness within this enclosed space and the terror I feel plays terrible tricks in my mind. That report about the torture at the Gestapo headquarters never mentioned this. Can I expect other unpleasant experiences not mentioned in that document? Sometimes I hear footsteps, a door opens and orders are barked at a prisoner to stand up straight. Having sat for hours in the blackness, this will surely be a very difficult thing to do. Then the footsteps of the detainee and their guard fade as they walk along the corridor to whatever fate awaits him or her. I can see that the SS guards seem to be taking pleasure at the whole experience.

What seems to be hours later, there's the sound of dragging steps and harsh words from the guards as the poor prisoner is returned. The fear and the waiting is torture in itself. Quiet sobbing is a sound I shall never forget as we all sit in our dark boxes awaiting our fate.

The lack of air doesn't help. I want to scream "let me out", but I know that the SS guard waiting outside our boxes is waiting for an opportunity to punish one of us. Where have my friends gone? Are they here as well?

Just as I am feeling at my lowest, the door just in front of me is unlocked. So my time has come to face the Gestapo. The light seems intense having been in this black hole for hours on end.

"Stender, stand to attention. You are wanted upstairs". Just as I suspected, to stand up properly is difficult now. I try not to delay and am marched upstairs to my fate. And so my questioning begins. The Gestapo certainly know their business of finding out information from the prisoners. What sort of person can possibly enjoy working as a Gestapo agent? Are they really human beings? Have they got a conscience at all? Do they go home to happy families? Do they think of us when they are in their nice comfortable homes playing with their children? Despite these thoughts, I keep my wits about me and retain the information they really want from me. When my questioning finishes, I'm given a pen and paper to write down my life story. I suppose that they are hoping to pick up something from this for my next interrogation so I must be careful.

The worst moments for me are the journey to and from being questioned when I hear helpless crying and screaming from fellow prisoners. I hope that they are not my friends who are making these noises. Our group has worked out a strategy should we be caught. There is no point in totally denying everything. We have been arrested because our names have been given to them under torture so denial would aggravate the Gestapo. Only the barest information should ever be revealed which would do the least harm to our organisation. I know that my name will be mentioned the most and I accepted this risk a long time ago. I am the group's organiser and have to take the consequences. How much will they discover from all of us I wonder?

I really begin to lose track of time. Being in my black hole and only being allowed out to go to the toilet and for questioning, leaves my mind totally unable to comprehend time.

Sitting in my black hell hole one day (or was it night?) I reflect on a piece of good news. The Gestapo have been to my place of work at Daimler-Benz to ask all the people I work with about my political leanings etc. but nobody has said anything revealing about me. This is simply amazing as I had supplied lots of people with leaflets and other information but nobody has admitted this and they have apparently said that they know nothing of any resistance activities. Whether it is because they are frightened of being implicated with me or because they want to help save me, I will never know.

More good news is that Alfred Drögemuller must have managed to escape. I refuse to show any reaction when I am told this information. This is excellent news as I'm sure that he'll continue to fight against fascism wherever he goes. The Gestapo are furious, but at least one of us is still free.

How many more times will I be "questioned"? I try to stand upright as the evil Gestapo man nonchalantly walks around me. Having your torturer going out of sight is very unnerving especially when he suddenly bangs a whip hard against the table making me jump. He smiles slowly at my reaction.

"Well Stender, I've finished with you *for the moment*" he emphasizes. I'm sending you to Fuhlsbüttel Concentration Camp and whilst in there you can decide if you would like to provide me with more information before I find it out from someone else which will make things worse for you."

I'm not quite sure at this point whether or not I am pleased, but I just keep quiet. Just keep motionless so as not antagonise them is something quickly learnt by anyone being confronted by Gestapo agents, the SS or SA guards. There is absolutely no information I will voluntarily give to these people. Only if someone reveals our organisation details will I ever say anything and then I shall trivialise everything but there is no point denying information they already know about. So far very little seems to be known apart from who we are and a little of our work so if we can keep to this level, the outcome might be good for our friends who are still free. Mind you, I still don't know the full extent of who else has been arrested.

To my greatest relief, I do not return to the basement and that dreadful box with a few air holes. For the first time in many days and only for a very brief moment the sun shines on my back and the day light hurts my eyes, not having been in natural light for days. Exhilaration of leaving this place of fear is dampened as I'm bundled into a prison van and ordered to sit in another dark compartment only large enough for one person. The door is bangs shut and locked and I sit in the stationary vehicle for ten or fifteen minutes. It's hot and stuffy and again air holes in the door are the only form of ventilation. I wonder if I shall have nightmares of these enclosed spaces if I eventually survive these next weeks, months or even years. I've never suffered from claustrophobia until now, but for anyone who prior to arrest finds being confined in small rooms as a difficult experience then our present situation must be sheer torture in itself.

The van rocks with the movement of more people being put in the vehicle, doors are shut and locked. I hear the sounds of people trying to get comfortable, clearing their throat etc., but no-one talks. We are too frightened. At long last the engine starts and we are on our way possibly Fuhlsbüttel Concentration Camp or Kola-fu as we know it. Being in the dark I find it difficult to balance not knowing if the vehicle is going to turn a corner, stop or take an unexpected direction or speed. It's all very disconcerting and if I had been privileged to have been given some food, I would have been travel sick by now. After a drive of about twenty to thirty minutes we arrive at our destination.

Almost immediately the rear door opens and then one of the compartments. The prisoner is ordered to get up and out of the vehicle. A few minutes later another is order to leave and finally it is my turn. Who else has been in this van with me? Were any of the others my friends? I'm searched again and my name and details taken and then taken down to the basement. Anna is right, the footsteps do echo as I'm marched along the corridors.

Suddenly we stop, the door is opened and I'm given a shove to enter. The cell is larger than the wooden box at Gestapo Headquarters. It's about one and a half metres by three or three and a half metres and joy of joys, there's a window, albeit too high to look out of but at least I can see the sky. The cell door keys rattle as they are turned in the lock, the footsteps melting away and I am left here in silence. I study my new home and shudder at the chill in the air. I have summer clothes on as it is June but the cell walls and the cement floor are perishing cold as we're in the basement. There is a bucket placed in the room for me to use presumably for a toilet so that will eventually make the room smell unpleasant too with my bodily fluids. Is that a bed on the floor?

I peer through the gloomy light and take a couple of steps over to it and bend down to touch it. It's just a straw mattress which feels damp being on the ground and it feels prickly with the straw's sharp edges poking through the sack cover but I don't really care how scratchy and damp it is as I feel a wave of exhaustion sweeping over me. I sink down on to the mattress and despite the unpleasant damp smell I lose consciousness not having slept properly for days.

This oblivion is shattered when suddenly there's a loud bang as the cell door bolt is pulled back and an SS guard stands in the entrance of the opened door. I raise my torso into a sitting position and start to stand but the guard starts yelling at me.

"Stender this is your first and only warning. When the door is opens, you must jump to attention and stand at the furthest part of the cell shouting out your name and prisoner number in a clear and distinct voice. Punishment will be given if these instructions are not carried out."

Hearing this warning I jump up from the disgusting mattress and stand at the furthest part of the cell from the door standing as best as I can to attention. I yell out my name and prisoner number and then wait in apprehension. I look into the face of my tormentor and see nothing but maliciousness and distain. I think better of continuing to look and drop my vision so as not to antagonise him. I have obviously done the right thing as he stands aside to let someone put a bowl of soup on the floor just by the entrance. Both men leave me in peace, the door bangs shut, the outside bolt is shot across the closed door and a key is turned in the lock.

The smell of tepid warm food makes me rush over to the bowl. I pick it up and start to spoon up the water soup into my mouth. It does not really taste of anything but I'm starving hungry so I don't care. Is that all we're given at midday – just a small bowl of water soup and nothing more to eat?

The meagre food helps my train of thoughts as it seems that this place is to be my home for a while. Perhaps it might be a good idea to try and keep track of time. I take the end of the spoon and scratch a short line on one of the walls and decide to do this every day. I have to start pulling myself together otherwise my sanity will become questionable. Why have I been put in isolation down in the basement? In that report about Kola-fu which Werner Etter had been given, it mentioned that some people were put in together but it seems that this is not my destiny. If I'm to be kept apart, then I must work hard to keep my brain active.

Solitary confinement plays terribly with the mind so I start the habit of pulling out three strands of hair to make my brain concentrate on plaiting the hair in a neat organised way. I keep my body fit by walking from one end of the cell to the other even though it is hardly big enough space to move in.

Days become weeks in my freezing cold damp cell. The little lines scratched on the wall and grouped in sevens, become a long line. I feel quite ill with such a bad cold which undoubtedly is due to living in such conditions. Food is virtually non existent and I have trouble keeping my trousers up due to losing so much weight. I receive a piece of dry bread both morning and night with occasionally a scraping of jam for a treat and at lunch is the water soup which sometimes contains potatoes. This is hardly sufficient food for any one.

The loneliness is interspersed with being "questioned" by the Gestapo. They really know how to weaken people mentally and physically. I'm not going to let them win though. I'm a Stender and have been brought up to be strong and to fight against these fascists. They will not get the better of me.

I dread the times though I am taken upstairs and the SS make me stand for ages with my nose and toes touching the wall. The guards are just waiting for the opportunity to punish me should I collapse with exhaustion. It is nothing unusual to collapse before questioning has even begun. I am sure that the fear of not knowing what they are going to do next plus suffering from exhaustion will stay on my mind forever. Usually I have two or three Gestapo agents questioning me and the SS are there to 'help' them. Each time more of my friends are arrested, I am summoned for more of this "questioning". When will it end?

As the organiser of our group, it is obvious that I have to take the blame and I feel no anger to anyone who mentions or holds me responsible for any actions they took. I know how terrifying the interviews can be and after all, my friends did undertake my instructions. There is no point in denying it but I just give as little information as possible.

The guards enjoy telling me that Mama and Lotte wait outside the front prison gates once a week and bring clean clothes for me. They have to wait until eventually the outer doors are opened and they are then given my soiled clothes, sometimes covered with blood. What must they be thinking? Oh if only I were allowed visitors.

As time continues I become more observant about my surroundings. The SA seem to be quite restless and nervous and the SS guards more confident. I wonder what is going on. It is bad enough being in this place but observing the nervous behaviour of the guards makes me very concerned[105]. I have found that learning body language is an important lesson in the art of survival. Hitler seems to revel in mind games and internal strife for any superior positions within his organisation. Is he thinking of encouraging competition between the S.A. and the S.S.? I have a nasty feeling that the end result could be frightening.

The S.S. is supposed to be just a subsidiary of the S.A. but they seem to be establishing themselves within their own right.

---

[105] The 'Night of the Long Knives' is approaching. Details of this are in Rudolf's chapter of 1934.

As I sit plaiting another three strands of my hair, I hear the cell door being opened. As usual I jump up and run to the furthest corner ready to give my name and number. As the door opens, I see three SS men standing there. My mind goes into overdrive as this is surely bad news. Then to my horror I recognise one of the SS men. He was the one I went to Trade College with and with whom I had many discussions about our different beliefs. He starts talking to me.

"Well look who we have here. So it is the same Werner Stender who has such high ideals and who thought he could persuade us all to change our political opinions. Now look where it has got you. Didn't I warn you that you would end your life here unless *you* changed *your* outlook?"

I decide it is better not to answer his taunts and then I hold my breath waiting for the expected ensuing violence. He turns, having given me a superior sneer and then all three leave the cell, banging the door shut behind them. My legs are shaking and I feel weak all over, so I crouch down on to my haunches in the corner of my cell totally oblivious of the cold floor and walls. He'd obviously seen my name on the prisoner list and thought that he'd pay me a visit. As the days and weeks continue, to my relief this particular guard never did ill treat me. Perhaps I had under-estimated him as beneath his cold exterior there must have been some kind of conscience.

As I think about this guard I hear footsteps approaching outside the cell. I jump up and stand back waiting for the door to open. It's lunch time and my stomach is aching for some decent food. The guard brings in the usual pathetically weak water soup but he has an envelope in his hand. He just throws it at me.

"I don't know why you have suddenly been allowed post. I shall have to check to make sure your privileges have been altered."

I wait until the door shuts and the footsteps fade into the distance. I then pounce on the envelope. My hands shake as I look at the handwriting on the envelope. It's Anna who has been able to write to me. How wonderful and brave that she should try writing a letter to me when Ernst is also under arrest and hopefully still alive somewhere. Will this letter tell me where he is I wonder?

As expected the letter has already been opened. Any lucky person able to receive post always has the contents checked and censored. There are two letters inside, one from Gretel and the other from Anna. I start reading little Gretel's letter which is neatly composed in her own childish handwriting. It must have taken her a long time to do but she must have some spare time as she is on school holidays.

I see the address on the top of the letter. How wonderful that Anna has taken Gretel to their retreat in the country. It seems a life time ago when Ernst and Anna had financially joined forces with their friends to collectively purchase the property[106] for their relaxation and also for them to have the opportunity to talk of future strategy against fascism. Now it is a sanctuary for Gretel before they return to their difficult life. It sounds as though Gretel has really enjoyed her time away and now they are home.

I wonder if Anna has explained to Gretel where her father and Uncle Werner have gone. Does she know that we are both in prison? She is such an intelligent little girl and has always understood that she must never talk about our lives just in case someone is listening. Poor Gretel must be scared having lost her father, Uncle Rudolf and now me.

I then pick up Anna's letter. She writes that they've been in the country house for four weeks and the change of air has helped them try to cope with their situation without Ernst. Oh and I see she mentions that she is still in contact with our parents. How lovely to know that I can rely on Anna to keep their morale high. I hug the letters close as though doing that will bring my family close to me. Oh how I miss them all. Nobody can appreciate the effect the mental torture of this concentration camp has on a person, not knowing what is to happen or if it is possible to survive to the next day.

I cannot help but feel low knowing that I have been implicated in so called crimes against the state. I love my country and am not a terrorist. During one of my 'questioning' sessions I find out that it hasn't been decided if my activities might come under the new law

---

[106] This cottage is now Heideruh and is currently used regularly for meetings and courses for people who are antifascists and have politically left wing tendencies. It is often advertised in the magazine Antifa. Ernst and his friends would be pleased that their dwelling is still appropriately used.

or not. With great pleasure they tell me that if they can prove that I was active on or after 1st May 1934, then I can receive the death penalty or life in a Zuchthaus[107], that is unless I provide them with further information which would help lessen the sentence. It's strange, but after the shock that my life might be about to end, I realise that they can't do anything worse to me apart from inflicting pain. I'm nearly nineteen years old and this might now be the end for me. I have to accept my fate as so many others have done.

Despite this knowledge being constantly on my mind my one pleasure is when I'm allowed on very rare occasions to be taken outside for exercise. We're told to keep about two metres apart from our fellow prisoners. I'm so desperate to talk to the others having been in solitary confinement for so long, but I dare not try to show any facial movements just in case it gives the guards an excuse to punish me. How white my arms and legs are, but it comes as a shock seeing the other prisoners' deathly white faces totally devoid of expression. Do I really look as terrible as they do?

As I walk round the exercise yard, I glance up at the walls of the concentration camp and prison. My mind flashes back to seemingly a life time ago, when I was at Anna's home. I remember now what she had said about those walls absorbing all of our fear and sorrow inside this place and screaming out to all who passed along outside in the freedom of fascist Germany. "Help us, save us from our fate". How right Anna had been. Her empathy is amazing. I wonder how she is. How are they all coping at home? Are my parents all right or are they being victimised by the Nazis for having three sons fighting fascism? What has happened to my wonderful brother Ernst? Is he still alive? Are they still torturing him? Is he here in this hell hole? The organisation was correct making Rudolf leave this country.

My thoughts return to the yard where I am walking. The guards seem to enjoy punishing us just for sport and today it is my turn. Perhaps it is my own fault to let my mind wander into distant places. My day dreams are unpleasantly interrupted when one of the guards taps my shoulder with his whip and I look him straight in the eyes. His expression is as though he is about to gorge himself on a meal.

---

[107] Extremely severe penal establishment

He points the whip to the wall and there I have to stand in the hot blazing sun with my nose and toes against the bricks. Oh that heat – because my skin is very fair I have never been able to take a lot of sun and now I am expected to stand out in it for hours under guard. I cannot remember when I collapse with exhaustion, but for once I am relieved to find that I have been returned to my cold damp cell. My whole body feels as though it is burning.

A few weeks later, two guards come to my cell and take me to a larger room where, to my absolute delight, there were about thirty to forty fellow prisoners. How wonderful being able to talk to like-minded people but within a very short time the conversations only reveal more of the terrible treatment given here by the SS. I do not need confirmation having seen the injuries on some of them. That document Werner Etter found is so accurate. I just hope that the recipients read and believe the contents but I honestly believe it is too late to prevent the spiralling down of man's inhumanity to man. I had not realised how many men there are in our country that seem to enjoy inflicting pain on others and they are being employed by the Nazi government to do this.

"Did I hear that you are Werner Stender?" one of the prisoners interrupts my thoughts.

"Yes but do I know you?" I ask cautiously

"No but are you the brother of Rudolf?"

I nod in confirmation of this fact.

"I know your brother well. I used to be a policeman until my arrest. Do you know if Rudolf managed to escape from Germany? If he has, I can then put on Rudolf's shoulders some of the blame for certain activities we did together."

"Yes, I've since had letters from him and he is safely out of the country" I assured him. Having experienced the methods of the Gestapo, I know how desperate people are to blame others who have escaped but I don't want to give him more details just in case he is a spy.

"I'm so pleased for him so now I am able to give his name" he answers.

I glance around the room at my fellow prisoners. Another man looks as though he has physically had a tough time but still has defiance on his face. What courage – but there again we're all trying hard to be like that.

"Do you like our exquisite food" he lisps seeing me look at him. Half his teeth are either broken or have fallen out. It is shocking to see this, but despite seeing the state that so many of my fellow prisoners are in I cannot help but feel elation. Oh it is a joy to talk to people and my heart is lifting. I laugh at this man's comment – yes I actually laugh – what joy.

"Try putting a little salt on the dry bread – it will make it tastier."

"Do you know I never really thought about it but thank you for the suggestion".

"You have a dreadful cold considering it's summer" said another observing me closely.

"It's not surprising as I've been locked up in a basement cell and it's freezing in there. You don't know how lovely it is here." That makes them laugh cynically at the thought that they are in a pleasant place.

Suddenly the door opens and everyone jumps as fast as possible trying to stand to attention in a line. A few SS guards are standing in the doorway. Unfortunately I am not as quick. I glance at my fellow prisoners faces and can see their frightened looks. One of the SS men holds a revolver at the ready and shouts to me "Raus". He continues to shout at me as I am chased up and down the corridor, being kicked like a helpless animal until I finally collapse. When I eventually become conscious I groan in pain and open my eyes. I'm encircled with the concerned faces of my new cell mates. How kind they all are in trying to help me recover. To have people caring and looking after my welfare is so precious after all that solitary confinement.

"They're always on the lookout for the slowest of us Werner. This treatment is normal for us so you'll have to learn to be quick" warns one of my new comrades.

One or two people who are imprisoned with us arrived after me so they fill me in with news from outside. Apparently on 2nd August, Adolf Hitler proclaimed himself Führer and Reichskanzler[108]. As a result the armed forces must now swear allegiance to him. Total power is now in the hands of just one man – how terrifying.

---

[108] Leader and Chancellor of Germany

A few days later, the door opens and my name is called. My spirit plummets as I approach the guards. Is this more questioning? No, for the moment I am not wanted by the Gestapo but for me it feels even worse as I'm thrown back into my old cell and solitary confinement. I sit on my old mattress and tears fall down my cheeks. Here I am once more cut off from the whole world and only able to hear the crying of fellow prisoners.

I will never understand why the SS take such pleasure in beating and torturing other human beings. Obviously my little treat of being with other prisoners has been another ploy by the Gestapo in the hope to break my resistance. For a little while it feels that they have succeeded but then the Stender fight resurfaces in my body. My will-power will override whatever they do to me. Then another thought occurs to me. Was that ex-policeman a stooge who had been put in the large cell to discover where Rudolf is now? Thank goodness I hadn't said where he is – something had stopped me from giving out that information.

Over the following weeks I start to feel confused. Lack of food, the interrogations, and the loneliness are all contributory factors. To counteract this, I try to think of many ways to try and occupy my mind such as mathematical problems. Exercising from the window to the cell door helps me keep fit and also warmer. I must not break down and let them win – remember I'm a Stender!

The old routine settles in again and questioning is very rare these days. Autumn arrives and then the onset of winter so my cell feels even colder than before. Will I be here forever? Just as I condition my mind into not seeing a solitary person again apart from the guard at "meal" times, I am called back for questioning. This time the Gestapo had come to Kola-fu.

A member of my group told the Gestapo that I had produced leaflets in a loft of someone's house and this had surprised them as previously they had not been aware of this fact. I had been so pleased that so little had been discovered and now this information has been revealed. What can I do as there is no point denying it? It only delays the inevitable as the Gestapo have their ways of finding out.

Finally the day arrives when I am told that I am to be transferred to the remand prison. At last hopefully this dreadful ordeal might be over. I leave the building and am marched over to a different part of the prison. I can't believe my luck as I depart from the grounds of Kola-fu. Will I be treated any better now I wonder?

As I enter the building, my name and number is taken again and I'm roughly pushed towards the stairs which are ascending and not descending to the basement. Hopefully my new cell might be a little warmer. On the first floor I'm taken along a corridor to my new prison cell. This time although I'm still in solitary confinement, I have been allocated a real bed which is off the floor. What luxury, so perhaps my flu-like cold will go at long last.

On 27th December 1934 one of the guards hands me a document. It is from the General State Prosecutor of the Hamburg Supreme Court of Justice. I am being charged that between 1933 and June 1934 I conspired to overthrow the constitution of Germany by highly treasonable activities. The deeds and aims of all of the people who are being accused of this crime (being my comrades in my group) point to preparation of High Treason, by forming an organisation trying to influence citizens of the realm. This has been done by producing and distributing papers and leaflets. Crime Paragraph 80, 24th April[109].

My hands start shaking at the realisation of the seriousness of this charge against me and my friends. So this is why I have been put in the remand prison. My body is being given time to recover ready for the trial. I know that the fascists never like the prisoners who are being presented for trial, to arrive looking bruised and broken. I slowly read the papers. This is my first opportunity to see who else has been arrested and when. As Werner Etter and I had agreed prior to arrest, we would accept most of the blame for the work which we carried out, but I have to say how relieved I am to see that the Gestapo haven't discovered as much about us as I feared. I look carefully at the details of their case against us as I can follow what happened with regard to our arrests.

Two days before I was arrested, Erwin Wagenknecht had been arrested. I suspected that this had been the order of events. Poor Erwin had been the one to warn us of Hans Schwarzmeyer's arrest

---

[109] Which is the new law which could mean a very severe punishment

and I cannot blame him for revealing our names. I know the Gestapo's persuasive questioning methods.

I knew that Herta[110] and Harry had been arrested at the same time as me, but I see that Werner Etter, George Kehnscherper, Helmut Rohwer were also arrested the same day as me. Elizabeth Ebarhardt, and Siegfried Volkmann, were arrested six days later, Karl-Heinz Rebstock was arrested on 26th June and finally Walter Beyer[111] on 10th July.

Now I have to wait until 17th January 1935 which is my trial date. In the meantime I will have to keep my sanity during my solitary confinement.

---

[110] Herta Winzer at the tender age of 16 years old, was sent initially to Kola-fu's basement (probably near me and later whilst on remand was on the top floor in a cell with two other people. The other two girls were criminals, imprisoned for burglary and prostitution. All the cells were full and Herta suffered during her four and a half months imprisonment there. She was then released on bail until her trial.

[111] Walter Beyer had received a telephone call whilst he was at work informing him that the Gestapo had called at his house. He knew that we had all been arrested. Finally he was arrested and sent to Kola-fu. He saw from a distance many of his friends. After a lot of questioning by the Gestapo, he was put in a large room with many other prisoners. This came as a relief after spending many mornings and afternoons standing to attention with his nose to the wall with SS guards behind making sure that nobody moved. One of Walter's sisters approached the authorities and asked for a temporary release. He was released on bail on 19th October 1934 prior to the trial but could not find employment. He was very grateful that he had finished his apprenticeship before his arrest.

CHAPTER 19

Ernst during 1934

If there is such a place as hell, then it must be like it is here in this place. How can human beings behave like this to other fellow humans? I glance to my side and get hit for my efforts. The wall feels cold and damp on the tip of my nose. I shut my eyes and try to think of pleasant things in order to survive the hours I am expected to be in this position outside the torture rooms. My ears will not shut out the sounds of fellow comrades who are in these rooms and suffering terrible fates. In the gaps of silence my hearing reverts to the guards who stand behind me. I must not weaken and collapse. I'm exhausted, hungry and thirsty. Fear seeps through the pores of my flesh and it takes every effort to prevent my body shaking which ultimately encourages my brutal assailant to seek revenge on the weakness of my body and spirit.

So far I've managed to refrain from giving information concerning Maria Müller and the organisation which has been set up and it seems that they are unaware of the full extent of my involvement apart from the initial unit which we started. It's essential I maintain this silence. The door to the side of me opens suddenly and I can hear a man being dragged out and taken along the corridor back to the cells. I get a kick on the back of my shins; I stagger and then am pushed in the direction of the room.

★

After what feels like eternity to me I sit alone on the cell floor with my back against the wall feeling very forlorn. My body hurts even to breath. I want to sob but I put my mind back to a song Anna and I used to sing together. In my mind I start singing

Thoughts are free!
Who can guess them?
They flee by like nocturnal shadows
No man can know them
No hunter can shoot them with powder and lead
Thoughts are free
I think about what I want
And what delights me
Still always reticent and as it is suitable
My wish and desire
No-one can deny me
And so it will always be
Thoughts are free
And if I am thrown into the darkest dungeon
All this would be futile work
Because my thoughts tear all gates and walls apart
Thoughts are free
So I will renounce my sorrows forever
And never again will torture myself with whimsies
In one's heart one can always laugh and joke
And think at the same time
Thoughts are free
I love wine, my girl even more
Only her I like best of all
I am not alone
With my glass of wine
My girl is with me
Thoughts are free[112]

---

[112] "Die Gedanken sind frei" or "thoughts are free" is a German song about freedom of thought. It is a popular protest song against political repression and censorship and various versions of it have been recited over many centuries. During his incarceration in a concentration camp Hans Litten recited the poem when guards ordered prisoners to stage a performance in celebration of a Nazi anniversary. He was a very brave man.

Werner remembers singing this song during the 1930s. There is a very good English version sung by Pete Seeger who Werner met in England whilst with some of his German friends.

The words of "Die Gedanken sind Frei" always help my resolve not to let the Gestapo win over my soul. My mind feels more at peace and uplifted remembering those happy times with my beloved and thinking of the words of the song. Mixed feelings well up inside me and I think of my little family. Where are they now? I'm sure my parents will help them as much as possible.

Then I'm jerked back to reality as I hear footsteps along the corridor. My body tenses involuntarily as I listen and wonder if they will stop outside my door. My heart sinks as I hear the clanking of the keys in my cell door. Surely they will leave a little more time between the interrogations. I know that a friend of mine within our organisation committed suicide last year as he could no longer take the torturing and he was frightened of betraying his colleagues. I really can understand that awful situation. So far I have not betrayed anyone and the Müllers and their group are safe but how much longer can I keep information away from the Gestapo? My body is racked in pain and my nerves are going.

"Keep thinking of that song Ernst" I mentally reprimand myself before my assailants arrive to destroy me a little more.

The door opens and despite the agony I am in, I jump up and stand at the back of the cell yelling out my name and prison number. To delay means that even more pain will be inflicted on me. I can feel my legs wanting to buckle under my weight. The corridor feels longer than before and I can't think straight but the direction we are going in doesn't feel like the usual interrogation quarters. This time there's a wooden chair in the corridor next to a door. Instructions are given in a crisp tone to sit on the chair and after what feels like an eternity, the door opens and I'm told to enter. I'm so mentally and physically tired and it looks as though my interviewer is in no rush to start interrogating me. After a few minutes of me standing, waiting and watching the man studying some paper work, the Gestapo officer finally looks up and closely studies my face with distaste.

"Well Stender, you're to be transferred to a remand prison" pauses, and then continues with the caveat "*for the moment*. This doesn't mean that we've finished with you altogether as who knows what else we will find out about from your friends" snarls my tormentor.

"You are to go to remand for the moment to await your trial and be witness at other trials" he continues.

My body feels like a huge weight has been lifted. Is the worst over?

★

I cannot believe how different my life becomes on remand. It feels like sheer luxury as no longer do I have to wait each day to see if I will be tortured. It feels like heaven but I'm sure that the purpose of this period is to heal any outside wounds ready for my trial appearance. Despite a lot of people knowing what sort of treatment people receive when they are arrested by the SS and Gestapo, these Nazis like the world to see the justice system seeming to be fair. Occasionally I even get the chance to go into the exercise yard. Although I'm not allowed to talk or show any signs of recognition to any fellow prisoners, I can't help by being so shocked seeing fellow "fighters" looking so ghost like in their appearance. Do I look like that? Who knows as there are no mirrors in this place and perhaps that's just as well.

If only I could receive letters from home so that I would know if Anna and Gretel are surviving without me. Rudolf at least is safe in Russia but what about young Werner? Is he being careful with his activities? He's so young with such a lot to learn. Is he managing to continue working at Daimler-Benz? His pathetic wages as an apprentice won't help our parents that much but it's better than nothing. I scratch another notch on to the wall just to keep track of the number of days I'm here waiting for my trial.

As spring arrives, my old fears flood back as the guards come take me to attend Frieda Hüffner's trial. It's a nerve racking experience as the prosecutor barks questions at me but I refuse to betray my friends apart from trivia information which had come to their attention.

On 8th May they transfer me to what looks like another remand prison. What will happen when my trial comes? Have my fellow resistance workers who have also been arrested managed to keep quiet. How much do the Gestapo really know?

Boredom along with underlying fear of the unexpected continues as summer arrives and then departs. There is still no news from my family as to how they are all coping without my support. Oh if only I could receive a letter from them, then I would feel so much happier. It is so cold in my cell now that winter is approaching. During the summer it was never warm in here but now the chill is seeping into my bones again.

The sounds of footsteps approaching my cell, alerts me once again. I sit in dread waiting to know if the owners of these marching feet are coming for me. The keys clank in the lock and I jump up, stand with my back to the wall opposite the door waiting to give my prison number.

"You're wanted for more questioning Stender" says one of the SS guard as he sneers at me. My heart sinks hearing the words. My trial is only a few weeks away so thankfully the physical abuse is not too bad. The emotional torture is still horrific and of course they still expect me to go through the exhaustive standing to attention with my nose touching the cold wall which is exhausting both mentally and physically.

"Well Stender, we may not have caught your eldest brother, but your youngest sibling is now awaiting his trial" smirks one of my tormentors with deliberate connotations. My heart skips a beat at the thought that young Werner is experiencing this hell? They'll take such pleasure in seeking revenge having failed to capture Rudolf. Werner's not quite nineteen years old and probably like me he might be languishing in Kolafu in between being "questioned". I mustn't show any emotion which would mean I am aware of his activities or that I want to protect him. Keep yourself impassive Ernst. I try to look surprised.

"What's Werner done wrong?" I try to ask innocently. I have some idea of his deeds but I don't want them to know that.

"He has been copying his brothers in traitorous behaviour against the state. Your parents must have indoctrinated you all"

Now I am really worried. Surely they wouldn't arrest Mama and Papa? Think hard Ernst.

I laugh, I hope convincingly. "What my parents – indoctrinating us? Why they spent their time trying to convince us to believe in the new way of thinking". I couldn't bring myself to completely lie, but perhaps I can convince the Gestapo that Mama and Papa have no political thoughts such as Rudolf and me. I cannot even say that Mama and Papa tried to talk us out of our "work" as then they would certainly arrest them for questioning for having any knowledge about what we have been doing.

"Well they will suffer for having such rebellious sons, make no mistake about that" says my hated foe with a leer from ear to ear.

Oh God, Mama and Papa don't deserve to be treated so badly.

"Please don't harm them" is all I want to say, but I know that would make matters worse. Will Lotte have the courage to support them? I mentally count very slowly up to ten, breathing deeply but say nothing.

"As to your brother Werner, we intend to ask that he receives the death penalty. That is unless you wish to tell us some more about your illegal activities. We might then consider revoking that idea."

"There is nothing else I can tell you. You have all the information" I reply. I know how these Gestapo agents work. That threat of the death sentence might be carried out regardless of what I might say. Oh please forgive me Werner, but I have to put our fight against fascism before family loyalty and such threats. How many times have I heard that they have put such intimidations before prisoners and at times this plan has worked and then others are arrested as a result?

Finally on 8th November 1934, nearly a year after my arrest, I'm summoned to the High Court in Hamburg charged with High Treason. This is the day I've been dreading.

I listen to the best of my ability to the charges but it's so difficult. The prosecutor is speaking so quickly and with my nerves playing games with my mind, it's hard to concentrate and fully understand what is happening. Fritz Lux's name keeps being mentioned and then I find out – he's dead. Oh God what happened to him? My poor friend, he was so devoted to our fight against fascism.

I don't know who has confessed to the information against me, but I know only too well how difficult it is to resist the tortures of these Nazis. We've at least managed to keep from these villains most of our set up which was put in place so hopefully others can carry on where we have failed. Thank goodness the Gestapo seem to know so little. A fleeting thought flashes through my mind. Why is L…, the courier for Karl Rattai and the fiancée to the arrested Rudi Lindau not being prosecuted with the rest of us and only seems to be a witness? I wonder if… and then I remonstrate with myself. Ernst you have enough to worry about so forget it.

Rattai and Willendorf are mentioned as having asked me to recommence work after Fritz had been arrested and it was hoped that we were safe for the moment. I wonder what will happen to my friends? "Emil" is also included in the trial but it seems we've all kept his identity quiet and also the reason for the existence of our group. I had made a statement that my intention had been to hear the views of the work force in other factories. Then my heart sinks as Alfred Karpinski's statement is given declaring that the group intended to bring the essential factories to a standstill should there be an armed uprising against the fascists. We had also been taking a special interest in the arms industry. Even this though is not as bad as it could have been. Poor Alfred must have been physically suffering to release this information under torture. Now I have to await my fate being accused of High Treason.

My heart pounds as I stand waiting. The judge barks out the sentences to one of the other of our little group of resistance fighters who have been rounded up. Ernst Rambow, who is forty seven years old, receives a six year sentence in the Zuchthaus[113].

My name is given along with Eduard Willendorf who was the leader of another section of the resistance unit.

"Three years Zuchthaus" barks the judge. I gulp and then bite my lip to keep control. It's a mixture of feelings between dread at being sent to such a place and yet relief that I might live to see Anna, Gretel and the rest of my family.

"Six months imprisonment whilst awaiting trial is to be taken into account" he adds.

---

[113] The Zuchthaus is a severe punishment prison and all who enter it do so with fear and trepidation.

I can hear other names being given out and their sentences but I know that they will receive more lenient sentences as they were not as involved as Eduard and I. I can no longer concentrate on their details. I can feel my body start to shake involuntarily in delayed shock due to the last year. I must just keep a low profile in the Zuchthaus and hope that I can survive these next two and a half years and that the Gestapo do not discover how involved I really was. Time will tell depending on who else gets arrested in the future. Oh how I hope that the group who are still free will be able to continue. Someone has to damage the power of the fascists but unfortunately it cannot be the Stenders as two of us have been captured and one has escaped so our efforts are for a while curtailed.

I have to count myself fortunate that I am only getting a further two and a half years. I have the feeling that this judge is not a committed Nazis. Some of the original judges have not been removed from office but I suspect that this will change.

A little part of me feels angry though that Eduard and I have only six months imprisonment taken into account. Is that all which has been recorded and not the eleven months? Perhaps the Gestapo have withheld that information as they didn't want the judge to know about the torturing. Perhaps these six months is from the time that I was put into remand after my time with the Gestapo. What a country our glorious Germany has become.

CHAPTER 20

Rudolf during 1934

Well the New Year is over and I've managed to get through my first season of festivities in my new adopted country. It's so cold here but after experiencing constant dangers in Hamburg where I was always expecting to be arrested I have a preference for cold winters as it is so wonderful to feel safer. Another comfort is that I'm not here alone. Due to the situation in Germany there are quite a few other refugees so life is reasonably tolerable.

I feel that if I can only master this difficult language, I can start to live again. Then I hear some news I have always dreaded. A comrade who has contact back home in Hamburg breaks the dreadful news that last November Ernst had been arrested. I don't know how many have been rounded up from his group and how much the Gestapo know about Ernst's activities. If they are fully aware, then he will not survive and like so many others, he will most likely be beheaded. Then there is poor Anna with her weak heart and their darling little girl, Gretel. I know that our parents will support them as will Werner and Lotte but it's the most terrible news especially as I cannot be there for them. Oh the frustration of it all. If only I hadn't left them to fend for themselves, but there again I know that if I had stayed then I too would have been arrested.

I shall have to write to our parents and with careful wording and using the name "Otto" I will let them know that I am thinking of them all. If I can send some more food to Anna that would be a positive move as without Ernst bringing home a wage, they'll be in terrible financial hardship; yes they are in an even worse situation than me.

I've been told that a job has now been allocated for me in an industrial city which is 85 kilometres east of Moscow. It's a place called Orechowo-Sujewo which is situated in a forested area by the

Klyazma River. The city is new, being established in 1917 when three villages of Orekhova, Zuyevo and Nikolskoye were merged. Travelling is difficult here so I make use of the train service to take me to my new home. What will my future now hold I wonder? I'm not sure how well I am going to cope with just working as a lathe operator in a factory but at the moment I have no choice. Let's hope that boredom doesn't take over.

I present myself to the committee running the Karbolit factory. It is a chemical factory producing plastic insulators for the first power stations in Russia. I know how desperate the situation is for power stations to be installed as this country is not only huge, but also extremely primitive in facilities, equipment and machinery. Without power, the massive factories which are being constructed all over the country cannot hope to function. However from my observations, there seems to be an administrative problem with the supply of raw materials and machinery so even if they do have power, the manufacturing line will not be able to produce essential items. It's all so different from our efficient German industrial country, but at least the Nazi terror is not here.

I'm determined to give my very best efforts to try and help this backward country. The working class here are in a worst state than in Germany from the point of view of quality of life but they all have hope that with a lot of hard work and dedication, this new society will eventually improve their lifestyle. At present the sanitation is thirty to fifty years behind other western European countries. The communist policy is to put all effort into building and equipping factories which is commendable but it is to the detriment of a clean and safe environment. It's a difficult situation and I'm glad that I'm not the person having to make the decisions.

Russia had been living in 'the dark ages' for so long during the period of the Tsars. Since the revolution people who are not used to being in government have had to make difficult decisions. Socialism is something completely new to this country. None of the people who are in power have experienced organising and running a country. There was very little education for anyone apart from the rich landed gentry which of course means the USSR is a backward society. It will take a lot of effort to improve life for the majority of people. The land is vast beyond most people's comprehension including mine with no proper infrastructure.

I just hope that with the experience of skilled immigrants coming in to help, we will make it possible for the new USSR to succeed. The extreme weather conditions hinder the improvements due to many people struggling to survive. I'm really looking forward to spring and some warmth to permeate the bones of my body. The whole structures of the buildings need warmer weather to make the dwellings more habitable.

Here at Karbolit, they're trying to construct a phenol neutralization plant and a sewerage collector to connect to the factory sewerage system. To my frustration, it can't be finished as we are unable to get the essential equipment and building materials. This means that once the chemicals have been used, they cannot be disposed of safely as there are no proper discharge points. They have tried to detoxify the high quantities of phenol which is being discharged in the river but I somehow doubt this has been successful. As with many other factories in the Soviet Union chemicals and sewage are released untreated into the rivers; this causes hazards downstream to animals and humans alike.

As a result clean water is difficult to obtain and without thought to other areas, one district is in direct competition with others for this golden nectar. At Orechowo-Sujewo which is a new city and my new home the sewage is collected and discharged downstream to the detriment of anyone unfortunate to live in that direction. The drinking water we use is collected upstream but might have sewage from somewhere else. There is very little attempt by the authorities to treat any effluent. In some places human and animal excrement is left on barren land to be washed away when it rains or will be absorbed into the water system during the spring thaw when it gets flushed away into local rivers.

I try not to get too angry at this situation as I am a guest in their country. This situation is really difficult for me as I believe in socialism but this country is only in its youth practising socialistic idealism. The USSR is in such a terrible state due to lack of investment during the Tsar dynasty. Not only is there no infrastructure but also the living conditions of the working class people is appalling. The rich were either ignorant of the distress the poor were in or they did not care but they themselves had a very comfortable life. Poverty here is far worse than it was in Germany and as for the archaic system of lack of rights for the ordinary citizens in the Tsar years; it is hard to decide where to start to change things. It is really impossible to try to rectify these things without properly thinking through policies. I hope that the new leaders are able to succeed as they have had no experience of governing a country let alone on such a gigantic scale. In the meantime day to day problems and environmental pollution will continue. We must strive together and get this country up and running.

I am now a member of the Trade Union of Chemists and with my engineering skills I know that they have put me in appropriate employment. If all the machinery parts arrive then electricity will be provided throughout this vast land.

As there are many other Germans here with me there is a lovely community feeling. We have meetings which I take part in and as the weather improves, I enjoy joining others in walking in the countryside but I know better than to go near any water or waterways.

I'm a little surprised to hear that Hanny Dünkel wants to come and live over here and initially would like to stay with me. I hope she realises the difficult living conditions here as the theory of helping a young socialist country develop both psychologically and physically and the reality can be quite different. The people here in the Soviet Union have never experienced democracy. Hanny wants to come and help educate the children and that is something this country desperately needs. The adults are working exceptionally long hours and they themselves are very poorly educated so it is very commendable that she is sacrificing the little comforts she had back home in Hamburg. Perhaps the strain of the family's involvement helping to fight the Nazis has played a part in her decision to leave Germany. I hope that it is not because I am here as I cannot forget Käthe.

I've been asked to give a reference to her suitability before she enters the country so I compose a note explaining the family Dünkel's connection with the resistance movement. Despite my reservations at having the commitment to help her settle here, it's lovely having someone around who comes from my past life. What does concern me are the books she has brought with her, which may not be suitable reading material for educating the children. They are very strict about such things. I try talking to her about this delicate situation.

"But they're school books Rudolf. I know that this country is lacking in such luxuries" is all she says.

"I know but like in Germany, the officials in the Soviet Union are very particular what you teach the youngsters. Social and political history is always subjective so one country's version of history can be interpreted completely differently in another. The U.S.S.R. is a very young country and sensitive about their past history. Promise me that you will never show anyone these books Hanny and certainly never let any children read them" I try to warning her.

I hear from various sources that my name is being mentioned in Friedrich Grüpe and Otto Borstelmann's trials. I cannot blame anyone admitting under duress any connections with me if we were working together in the resistance, especially now that I am safe out of Germany and the Nazis clutches. It is the sensible solution when being tortured to give a name of a dead person or one who has escaped the country keeping the interrogators off the scent of finding out names of people still in Germany. I should imagine that this will be two of many statements where I am accused of action against the Nazis.

News of people close to me back home keeps filtering through. I'm greatly relieved to hear that Käthe has not been taken into custody for further questioning after her month in Kolafu at the beginning of the year. It distresses me being told that the Gestapo frequently visit her at her home. I feel so guilty that she is being treated in such a manner when she is innocent. Receiving the news that she has divorced me is heart-breaking but I completely understand that my life style has been without doubt the reason. She has taken the only course of action open to her and now I hear she intends to marry Rudolf Wilhelm so hopefully the Gestapo will always leave her alone.

She doesn't deserve the unhappiness and stress I put her through. I wonder if we would be still married if circumstances had been different. Will we ever meet again in the future? Will this ever be possible? I sincerely hope so and maybe we will be good friends if I can tolerate her new husband. I know that I'll find that part very difficult as I still love Käthe.

There's still no news about Ernst and now I hear that young Werner has been arrested. He's so young for this to have happened to him. I've no idea what he's been doing but it's hardly surprising that he wants to fight fascism. He's grown up listening to our political discussions and I'm sure he has known that both Ernst and I have been seriously involved in the resistance movement. It's still a shock though as it seems our family is disintegrating despite being so emotionally close.

Our poor parents' nerves must be suffering so badly being so anxious about all of us. Their little Werner being arrested must have devastated them especially as his health problems have been a source of worry all his life. I know he has also given them great joy as they had not expected yet another son so late in their lives. I just hope the Gestapo do not act extra harshly towards him because of me. I just could not stand hearing that piece of news. Perhaps Anna, Käthe and Lotte will visit Mama and Papa regularly. Thank goodness for the young women in our family who we know we can rely on to support them.

A few weeks later, news spreads throughout the German population here that Hitler has instigated something called the "Night of the Long Knives". I know that the SA had always dreamed of using their long knives on their opponents but it seems that the SS have got their knives into them instead. According to the information which has filtered through to us, Heinrich Himmler told Hitler that the SA and their leader Röhn had been scheming to overthrow Hitler. Himmler had offered his SS troops to solve the SA "problem". Between 30th June and 2nd July the purge was launched. One hundred and fifty SA leaders were arrested and summarily executed. The SS execution squads had been kept busy throughout the weekend.

Hitler had also taken this as a good opportunity to dispatch people he had a grudge against so hundreds of people died that weekend. What a blood bath that weekend must have been as the fascists fought each other and the three Stender brothers not there to see it! Ernst Röhm had previously said that for every one SA man killed, twelve men would be killed in retaliation. As it turned out, his threat was not carried out. Röhm refused to commit suicide so he was executed. A comrade had told me that at the beginning of 1934, there were three million SA troops but I suspect many will now join the SS to save themselves. Will this slaughter develop into an opportunity for the annihilation of political prisoners?

We hear that President Hindenburg died on 1st August and Hitler is now Chancellor *and* President. All military ranks now have to swear personal loyalty to Hitler. He can only be removed from power by revolt or by death. Hitler on 2nd August proclaimed himself Führer and Reichskanzler.

A fortnight after this move there's a plebiscite for the public to endorse this rank. With all the intimidation outside the polling stations, how many people will stand up against the man? So many of us who used to organise resistance have had to leave the country, have been arrested or killed so opposition is becoming very weak. All hope of some kind of revolution against these moves to dictatorship is lost for the moment. It would mean a blood bath and with very little support from the outside world, it will be the antifascists who would be finished forever. It makes us furious hearing that at Hindenburg's funeral, Hitler spoke and all present raised their arms in salute at "Deutschland Uber Alles" then the sound of the Nazi Anthem "Horst Wessel". Can't the nation see the way things are going?

It is difficult hearing the news of my old country and knowing that I am so far away but safe. I should be doing something active in the fight against fascism. If I'm honest I've probably needed these months of just working hard, organising events for other ex-patriots and then relaxing during the short summer months taking walks in the countryside.

To bring this country to modernity means many sacrifices but I am still finding it upsetting seeing the poverty and also the damage being done to the environment. Mind you, education and the health services, although primitive are now free for everyone to use. Women at long last are beginning to get equal rights so there are great changes for the better. Infant as well as adult mortality is decreasing as the authorities immunise against typhus and cholera. If only the water and pollution situation could improve.

We hear some good news though as on 18th September U.S.S.R. is admitted into the League of Nations. At last my new country has been finally accepted on the world stage.

As winter starts to close in around us in Orechowo-Sujewa, we hear that the German army is being increased, U boats as well as two battle cruisers are being built and Göring has established the Luftwaffe ostensibly for civil purposes. The industrialist firm Krupps is developing tanks and guns and I G Farben scientists are producing gasoline and rubber chemically from coal.

All young men between seventeen and twenty five years old are forced to join the Arbeitsdienst (Labour Service) clearing ditches and making roads thus taking the young unemployed off the labour market. As military training is banned under the Versailles Treaty, Hitler decides that it will be to his advantage to introduce indoctrination to these youngsters from his men giving lectures. Posters are apparently everywhere so that people without realising the way propaganda works are being brain washed. Of course there are the fascist books to complete the programming of the populous. Much of the young folk's time is spent listening to the leaders glorifying militarism and soldierly virtues rather than discussing political and social issues. This is very clever as the future as we all know lies in the youth of society and if they can be persuaded to follow the Führer, then we will have little hope of winning. I'm horrified to hear that by the end of the year some 240,000 factories have been mobilised for war and yet the rest of Europe seems to look the other way and not object.

This escalation of German war preparations makes me feel very restless. Europe is becoming a very dangerous place and I have to acknowledge that this factory life is really not suiting me at all. When I look back at my past, although I have done both skilled and unskilled labour, I have always been active in the resistance in Germany working towards a socialist society. We have it here in the USSR but I feel uncomfortable with all the dogma and slow productivity stopping improvements to people's lives. I have had to 'bite my tongue' on several occasions. I need to do something else more suited to my abilities. I need to stop Germany falling into Hitler's trap. It all might be too late but perhaps I should volunteer my services to the authorities and return to Germany.

CHAPTER 21

Werner from 1935 – September 1936

It's so lovely sleeping on a bed at long last albeit a very basic one but it's not a straw mattress on the floor. Oh such luxury and it feels so much warmer being above ground level even though it's January. That basement cell had been torture in itself what with the cold and damp, the fear with the expectation of more 'questioning' and the pitiful noises from my fellow prisoners in adjoining prison cells. Now at long last I'm left alone by my tormentors as they want me looking presentable at my trial.

Just as I feel more at ease with the situation, a clanking of the keys in the prison cell door makes me leap off the bed and stand to attention waiting for the SS guard to enter. I yell out my name and prison number.

"You're wanted downstairs Stender. The lawyer who will represent you during your trial wants to see you."

Having been escorted unceremoniously downstairs I take my first good look at the person who might save my life. The solitary light bulb dangling from the ceiling exposes the bareness of the room. There are just two chairs either side of a table immediately underneath this light. The man sitting in one of the chairs acknowledges my existence by indicating with a nod of his head and a slight move of his left arm for me to take the vacant chair and I sit down. He doesn't look that much older than me but who would want to represent a prisoner being prosecuted for High Treason against the Third Reich? He looks up from reading some paper work. He leans back on his chair and looks intently in my direction.

"Ah Stender, I've just been reading the case for the prosecution against you and the statements from your so called friends. The trial is next week so I just need to get familiar with your case. I will be representing just you as your colleagues have claimed that they were under instructions from you so you are to be blamed for their plight."

He looks back and studies the paperwork again. I'm not sure if he expects me to reply but I will.

"I had realised that this would probably be the situation and as a result I accept that I will receive the heaviest punishment"

"You do realise that your situation is very serious as the Gestapo have every intention to apply for the ultimate punishment of the death sentence?"

He stops speaking and looks up from the paperwork in order to study my reaction having given me this piece of news.

"You do realise this don't you?" he asks looking me straight into my eyes.

I nod. "All that I can ask of you is if you can plead my case with emphasis on my age in order that I may receive a lighter punishment but if all fails, I do accept what will happen."

I try to sound as brave as I can but the dreaded shakes are just beginning to start again. I'm going to have to control this physical weakness by the time of the Court Hearing next week.

"The Gestapo have arrested about one hundred of your resistance movement colleagues, obviously from different groups, but they are interconnected. You are being charged with organising a resistance movement, printing leaflets and other material, calling on the German people to rise against the Nazis and attempting the forcible change of the constitution of Germany. Do you intend to deny any of this?"

"No what is the point? I cannot expect the Court to release me when the Gestapo have decided on my guilt. As I said just now, I can only ask that you try and reduce the intended punishment".

He nods his head in agreement to this request, shakes my hand which is something I had not expected and I get up to leave realising that the session has finished. My fate is now in the hands of this young man. Although he is a young Nazi, I have the feeling that he has some sympathy towards my situation. I might be wrong but time will soon show me whether or not this is the case.

On 17th January 1935 the day of the trial arrives. As a mere nineteen year old, it is terrifying being taken to the Hamburg Supreme Court of Justice and being accused of High Treason against my beloved country. I would never betray my country; only defend it against the fascist regime and the withdrawal of our democratic rights.

I look across the room and see my friends and fellow accused who are sitting in a separate area from me. They all look as scared as I am feeling. I can feel myself shaking with my nerves. It is difficult to concentrate whilst this fear envelopes me making it almost impossible to take in what is happening. Whatever the result, I must give the outer appearance that I am calm. It won't help the others if I look so frightened.

Just as the Court goes into Session, Erwin Wagenknecht leans forward to his lawyer and whispers something into his ear. His lawyer then stands up and asks the judge for one of his accused to make an additional statement. The judge agrees so Erwin stands up.

"I wish to make it clear to the Court that I would like to withdraw my statement as I gave it under duress".

Poor Erwin must be feeling that he is betraying his friends with his statement but I have no resentment about what he says. We all have been under a terrible strain with the questioning but he is very brave trying to counter his original statement."

An official tells him curtly to sit down and then the trial commences. None of us are called to the witness box. We just have to listen to the prosecutor. He goes over the past with how Werner Etter, Hans Schwarzmayer and I went to the meeting with Walter Knuth to discuss the reconstruction of our organisation in order to plan High Treason against the State. He then went on to explain our actions. What good news that so little has been discovered by the Gestapo. Each one of us is accused of different things but I'm the one accused of being the ring leader of them all. I can hardly absorb what is being said no matter how hard I try to concentrate. The voices are aggressive and the words are very crisply pronounced with absolutely no compassion. I glance over to my friends and see their white faces staring nervously at me and then to the officials and finally lowering their eyes to the floor.

After a while I endeavour to channel my thoughts to the judge as he is now summing up the Court's decision. He continues to speak.

"The accused here today are guilty of preparation of High Treason. These young people were influenced by their political organisation who was aiming towards a forcible revolution against the realm. There are incriminating statements concerning Hertha Winzer, Elisabeth Eberhardt and Carl-Heinz Rebstock although they are still juveniles. I have no doubt that they were involved with illegal publications but I do query Elisabeth Eberhardt's commitment in this organisation. The Senate's opinion is however convinced that they all knew what they were doing.

I can see no evidence that anybody took part in any activity after 1st May 1934 apart from Stender. The punishment with the new law is therefore only relevant to him."

I feel a cold chill down my spine. Hold firm Werner. I concentrate on the verdict which is being announced.

"Eberhardt is to receive the least punishment. She is to receive no more than six months suspended prison sentence which should be a warning to her in future not to be involved with such unsavoury characters.

The worst offender of the group is Stender who is the driving force of the sub-district. He enforced his views on these people and continued to be active at the beginning of June 1934 making ordinary punishment or sentencing insufficient. Under the new law such activities normally results in a two to fifteen years imprisonment in a zuchthaus. Stender's criminal actions have been working in an illegal organisation towards the groundwork for High Treason and the preparation of documents and their distribution in order to persuade people to take unlawful action against the State."

I'm beginning to feel a little relieved that imprisonment in a zuchthaus is the only punishment being mentioned regardless of the Gestapo's wishes for the death sentence but then the Judge starts to speak again.

"It is now possible in Germany that such a crime can involve the death sentence as punishment or to be detained for life in a zuchthaus. Prior to the new law the sentence used to be one to ten years zuchthaus"

He stops speaking and again I hold my breath. He continues glaring in my direction and out of the corner of my eye I see the look of terror on the faces of my friends.

"However... " he pauses again. "Stender was only eighteen years old in December 1933 and his criminal activities are obviously as a compliant tool of the top leadership of his organisation. The senate believes that the sentence we issue in this instance should be less heavy. Stender is given a more lenient punishment of two years six months prison and is not to be sent to a zuchthaus."

I grip the bar in front of me to steady myself. I can't believe it. The court is going to override the Gestapo's wish to give me the death sentence. The judge continues to finish his summing up.

"Now we come to Werner Etter who is a good friend of Werner Stender. He is older than Stender being twenty-one years old and therefore should have more understanding of his traitorous activities but he has given the court a confession showing his repentance. Because of this he is to be given a two years prison sentence which is considered sufficient."

Oh Werner, what a relief that you, my dear friend, will receive a shorter sentence. I want to smile encouragement to them all but quickly think better of it. I dare not antagonise a judge who is obviously being compassionate towards us. Surely he must realise that he is endangering himself in doing this. He continues.

"After admitting their smaller participation in traitorous activities having been influenced by Stender and also taking into account their youth at the time, Georg Kehnscherper and Erwin Wagenknecht will receive eighteen months imprisonment but one year is sufficient for Harry Schöning, Helmut Rohwer, Siegfied Volkmann and Walter Beyer. Herta Winzer and Carl Heinz Rebstock have both received nine months prison sentence at the youth court. As these two have already felt the consequences of their act by their imprisonment in a concentration camp whilst awaiting trial, we have decided that their sentence will be suspended unless they commit another offence and then they will have to receive the full punishment, plus any additional time due to a new offence. May this be a warning to you both". He glares at my friends.

"Protective' custody which the others received prior to the trial is to be taken into account now that a penal sentence is to be given. The following incarceration periods will be taken off the relevant prison sentences: Stender – seven months, Etter – seven months, Winzer – four months[114], Schöning – seven months, Kehnscherper – five months, Wagenknecht – seven months, Rohwer – four months, Volkmann – three months, four weeks, Rebstock – three months three weeks and finally Beyer – three months one week.

The Senate also expects from the accused that when they are released they will keep themselves away from future trouble." He glares at all of us. "This is a warning to you all. If you do not heed this advice, there will be no further sympathy towards any of you."

Finally he says "All the people being sentenced here in this court apart from Eberhardt are responsible for the Court expenses". At this he stands and makes his way to the exit. Out of respect, all the people in court stand until he has left the room.

I want to sink back down on my seat suffering from a mixture of shock and relief but without any delay I'm ushered out of the court and back to my prison cell for the night. Tomorrow I'm to be transported to my new prison but for the moment I'm still in a state of disbelief. Why were the Gestapo so expectant that I would receive the death sentence and yet the court held out against them and tried

---

[114] After a time and in spite of her first imprisonment and the terrible experience of her brother being badly tortured and given a life imprisonment sentence, Herta decided to take further part in anti-fascist activities. Although she hesitated, Carl Heinz (whom she later married) persuaded and assured her that everyone in the group was trustworthy. This new group called themselves "Versohnler". The members were young communists, social democrats, liberals and some Jewish members. They had study groups, read banned books and decided to build up a strong resistance movement. But the Gestapo infiltrated the group and everybody was arrested between February and October 1936. Herta was arrested on 7th May. She never forgot the tears of her mother when she was arrested for the second time by the Gestapo. She was sentenced to 3 ½ years' imprisonment. Karl-Heinz received a 5 years sentence.

to be fair to us and especially me? I know that in a democratic country our actions would not be considered illegal or treasonable but in a dictatorship it is different. Was it the intention of the Gestapo that I should be punished due to my brothers Rudolf and Ernst activities? Rudolf had especially upset the Gestapo having eluded arrest by escaping out of the country. It would seem we Stenders are a thorn in their sides. Whatever the reason, I feel very lucky and grateful that I should be given just a two and a half years imprisonment sentence.

The following day one of the terrible prison vans arrives which has tiny dark compartments for separating prisoners and this vehicle transports me to my new penal complex. I can hear shuffling and coughing in the other small dark cubicles and wonder if my friends are also with me in the lorry. This time though, my heart is lighter as for now the imminent danger has been lifted and I'm heading away from the concentration camp and the dreaded Gestapo. If I can just keep my head down, I will get through these next two years and hopefully will be released so I can go home to my family. I'm worried that poor Ernst will probably not have fared so well. I wonder if I occasionally will be able to see my family during my sentence and then I will find out exactly what has happened to him.

The van stops and after a few minutes my individual door opens and I'm blinded by the glare of daylight as I jump down from the vehicle. My body aches and I almost fall to the ground with my legs buckling underneath me through being in such cramped conditions. A large river flows uninvitingly by the side of the vehicle which I guess could be the Elbe and then I can see the island where I am to spend the rest of my imprisonment. The sign by the quayside displays the words "Hahnöfersand Youth Prison". This sounds quite pleasant by comparison to Fuhlsbüttel Concentration Camp, but I'm under no illusions of a stress free existence. It will be a strict labour camp for youth offenders who are probably between the ages of 18 years and twenty one years.

Standing outside in this cold winter weather makes us all shiver involuntarily. A boat without any cover waits by the river bank. It looks as though one of the prisoners who is closely watched by a guard, has been given the job of transporting us across the water. I know that the current of the Elbe is strong as the water is tidal so escape is something I very much doubt will be on my agenda. We scrabble into the boat and the prisoner who had been waiting aboard, pulls the cord to start the engine. It splutters into life, the tie ropes are released and the final section of the journey to our new prison takes place as we cross the water to the island. I try not to make eye contact with the other prisoners who as I suspected are my resistance friends. It pays never to show emotion as reprisals from the armed guards always seem to follow.

I have to think positively as the air is so much cleaner here and it looks as though I will be able to be outside rather than in a cold dark cell. My mind wanders back to those high walls in Kolafu which closed us away from society and for some people to life itself.

We reach the island, disembark and are taken to the reception area where we are registered in a book. Each of us is given a scarf which we have to wear at all times. I cannot help showing surprise that I am given a different colour to the rest of my colleagues. Once again it is inadvisable to show any expression as one of the guards takes pleasure informing me that the blue scarf is for the short term prisoner but I have been given a red scarf as I have a longer prison sentence. I nod that I have understood and then we're then given our billet.

Walter Beyer is in a dormitory in the upstairs part of the main building and I am taken to a single storey brick building. I study my new fellow prisoners looking for a familiar face but I don't know anyone in this dormitory of eight people. I hope that a good friendship will develop with them as time goes on. There's no heating but somehow it doesn't matter as I am at last with other people. These last seven months have been hell for me being in solitary confinement and with trying to prevent my mind becoming unbalanced or confused. I'm sure this had been my torturers intentions but I mustn't dwell on the past. I have a chance to be released at the end of this sentence.

It doesn't take me long before I get used to the new regime but it's certainly not as pleasant as I had initially thought. We have no toilets so first thing in the morning we relieve ourselves in buckets, and then we run around the square outside. This sounds fine, but put into the equation totally committed young Nazi guards who are in their early twenties and ready to physically punish anyone not moving quickly enough around that square, and then a more accurate picture is painted. I succeed in getting round the yard without punishment, despite my gammy leg and then we line up for the roll call and we 'new comers' are told to report to a particular person in the main building.

I hear the so called teacher who is present during this registration period encourage the young Nazi guards to punish us at any excuse. Over time he lectures us on his version of current events especially with regard to the Italian invasion of Abyssinia. It is so difficult for me to sit and listen to such a biased view on life. Some of the people here are criminals and I suppose that these youths will be the type of people he will influence with his indoctrinations. As for the rest of us, we are political prisoners and no amount of these lectures will change our point of view.

Forced labour is expected from us and despite my physical disabilities I have been assigned to be part of the road building team. Not being able to bend one leg makes it difficult as I have to hammer away at the stones and bricks in order to break them up into small pieces. These rocks are delivered to us by other prisoners who struggle from the weight of the stones on the carts which they push in our direction. Sometimes the carts, filled to capacity, come off their tracks and then the guards make this their excuse to beat the poor prisoners. Any of us who do not perform at the level the guards expect are severely punished. It really is slave labour.

Not all of the guards are so vicious towards us. Some are more mature in age who I presume were the old original guards. I notice at times they watch with unease at the level of the behaviour of violence towards any of us. The new unit of Nazis seem to be taking over the prison ousting the old sentinels who have compassion; a non-existent word known by any of these new younger guards.

I'm so hungry every day as we are doing such physical work. The food is not any better or worse than in Fuhlsbüttel but in there we were not exerting ourselves and therefore not using up as much energy. Some of the youths here are looking extremely gaunt.

Sheer exhaustion and pain is taking over my body so after a day's hard work I lay on my bed to rest. To my amazement and delight my closest friend walks into my dormitory. I almost fell on the floor trying to get up so quickly from my prostrate position, my energy having returned in a flash. It has been a few weeks since I have been here so I thought we were all in situ for our punishment. Seeing my special friend arrive here is amazingly good news for me.

Werner Etter laughs at my predicament and then we almost collide rushing to meet each other in a wonderful bear hug. We both laugh mixed with tears of joy falling down our cheeks.

"Werner how wonderful it is to see you here. I have to say that you are the last person I expected to see" I exclaim.

"Werner" he teases back as we always laugh and made fun of each other having the same name "I can honestly say that I am not so enamoured at seeing you in a prison, but I know what you mean. At least we are together again. It's my Mother we have to thank for this. She went to the authorities and begged that I be put into prison with my friends. Can you imagine how brave that was for her to do. I know that I am really too old to be in a youth prison but somehow with Mama's persistent begging, they relented. You know how my Mama can be when she puts her mind to a problem."

We both smile thinking of Werner's protective mother but I am really surprised that even with her persistence at asking for Werner to be transferred to us that such a thing can happen. Now my life is as near perfect as I can expect considering the situation we are in and to think that Werner has been able to join me in my dormitory. We talk for many hours that first night about our experiences since we were together last June.

However the next day it's back to the drudgery of trying to break up the stones and bricks ready for road building. This task is difficult for me as the hammer reverberates on the hard stone jolting through my right wrist, arm, shoulder and body. Having a straight leg makes this job nigh on impossible for me but I struggle on. What with my generally weak body through lack of food, the work is physically affecting me but there are so many of us in the same weak state. As I look around this little island, I can see that we will be doing road building for a long time. The present tracks are just mud and earth as the prison was an ordinary youth prison just for criminals, but now it's so full due to the increase in political prisoners such as me.

To escape from here is virtually impossible as the currents of the Elbe are so strong that it is dangerous to attempt to swim across even from the part of the island nearest to the mainland. It looks so close but only the strongest swimmers would ever succeed in getting across.

One day though Willi Hilwig did try to escape and he actually succeeded in his attempt. We could hear the wailing of alarm sirens starting on the mainland as all the local villagers are warned that there is an escapee on the loose. As far as they are concerned we are all criminals, so there is no hesitation in capturing this poor lad and he suffered dreadfully for all his efforts when he was caught. Willi came from the Kleine Geibelstrasse just round the corner from Gertigstrasse and although he worked with us, he wasn't actually arrested because of our work. He also helped the social democrats and it was this connection which became his downfall[115].

Just after roll call I am about to depart for road making duties when I am pulled aside and told that I am wanted for another duty. This cheers me up getting away from such hard labour but there can be more distressing things to do. A boat load of piglets have just been delivered at the quay and I have the upsetting job of unloading them. They are to be fattened up for slaughter and I have to pick them up by their rear legs and despite them squealing at the tops of their voices, they are thrown into a lorry and transported to their new pen. Those poor creatures should never be treated this way even though their life is very limited. My only consolation is that I have nothing to do with their slaughter. This renews memories of my childhood when Papa slaughtered the chickens in our yard but to see something as big as a pig ending it's days here… I'll never be able to be a farmer!

---

[115] Willi Hilwig eventually lost his life in the dreaded 999 Division when he was sent to fight in Russia. Many resistance fighters were conscripted into this Division and were used as "cannon fodder" or for land mine clearance amongst other similar suicidal duties.

Walter Beyer has a far better job than me, but I am a 'long term' prisoner. He has been given a very useful job of being the boatman for transporting visitors and prisoners to and from the mainland. It's a way of quietly observing the policies and daily life of prison and prisoners and reporting back to me any useful information.

He's just told me that at any time, I might be due a visitor as it will soon be my turn. If this is correct then it feels like Christmas has come early for me. Now it's hard to concentrate on anything. Each morning I get up earlier and am keen to do everything to the best of my ability as I do not want to risk any punishment being given to me which might mean losing the right of a visitor.

So Walter had been correct and finally joy of joys, for the first time since last June which is nearly nine months ago, I have been told that I am allowed a visitor once a month. So Walter had been correct. My wait is over as a guard approaches me. I'm covered in dust and dirt through hitting the stones as hard as I can.

"You have a visitor and she has just arrived Stender" he mutters. "Act sharp now and report to the main office".

Well I do not need to be told twice. I put down my hammer and rush over to the main building. Who will it be? The guard said "she" so is it Mama or Lotte? I try not to run, walk fast or too slow. I mustn't lose the right to see my visitor. I walk inside and to my utmost joy Mama is sitting on a chair in the main hall waiting for me. There are a lot of other visitors, some who are already busy chatting to their loved one and others are looking anxiously towards the door I had just entered through. Their look shows disappointment when I enter but I quickly glance around and instinctively get drawn into looking in Mama's direction. She holds out both arms towards me and within a few seconds her face is buried into my chest and I feel her sobbing.

Oh what joy it is to feel the arms of my beloved Mama around my waist. We just stand for a few minutes in this embrace before I realise that I will be separated by the guard if I do not unlock our clasp soon. Mama looks exhausted but it is not surprising as it is such a long journey for her to make by herself. Typically though she smiles and gives me every encouragement. Oh how I have missed her but

I have dared not think too much about my parents over these last few months as I have to keep strong. Our time together is over far too quickly but in that time we manage to exchange so much information.

"I've been told that I can visit you once a month Werner. Isn't that marvellous? I'm afraid that it'll only be me as Papa isn't strong enough to make the journey. You do understand don't you?"

She looks anxiously at me and then smiles encouragingly.

"You won't get rid of *me* that easily though. Everybody sends their love to you. I know that they would all love to visit but as it's only one visitor allowed, I've told them that I want to come."

I smile at that comment as Mama has always been my rock and if I'm honest, she is the one I'd rather see. There is such a strong bond between us which gives me inner strength and a positive attitude in life so I really need her to visit me.

"I have received loads of cards already from so many of my friends and also our family Mama." I pause not sure if I should tell her this but I continue. "After being so isolated for so long, it's absolutely wonderful having everyone's support. It was terrible not hearing from all of you whilst in Kolafu." I try to cheer up and add "Even my friends who received shorter sentences to me have lately been writing to me. I already feel stronger since I have been here and I am making good friends with people of 'like minds'. I've just got to keep a low profile and not upset the guards."

She looks to see if anyone else is listening and then says "I'm also working on helping you with regard to your life here."

I can't help showing surprise at that comment.

"I was telling your father's brother about where you are. You know Onkel Friedrich who lives just outside Hamburg near the Elbe? Well Carl, his son as you know is married and his father-in-law is one of the old guards here. News of your imprisonment is rapidly spreading and Carl is hoping that his father-in-law might make your life here a bit more pleasant."

"What a small world we are living in. Fancy that, but I won't be counting on his help Mama as the regime here is so strict. I know that the old guards are definitely kinder to us but they are restricted in their behaviour with these younger Nazi guards watching them. Tell him not to risk his own safety – I can cope".

She smiles at me and squeezes my hand reassuringly. It seems like only a few minutes of visiting time have elapsed before my beloved Mama has to leave. I know that our time in reality has been much longer but when our period together is so precious, the visiting hour just flies past. Walking out of that hall, my heart sinks knowing that I will have to wait another month. It's almost too painful to think about it but I have seen Mama at long last.

That evening I tell Werner Etter what Mama had said to me.

"Please Werner do not raise your hopes too much" was all he could say. I think he is also worried that the disappointment of not getting the promised help and perhaps not being allowed visitors again might shatter any raised morale. I should have had more belief and trust in Mama as some time later I meet Carl's father-in-law. He makes his presence known to me only when I am alone. He's a quietly spoken man but seems to be respected by all the other old guards. I notice that he keeps his distance as much as he possibly can from the Nazi guards. The different attitude towards us from the young guards and the old ones is immense. If the Nazi regime continues, I dread to think what is going to happen when the old guards retire or are replaced. As it stands at present the Nazis overrule the old guards in everything they try to implement.

One day after roll call, Siegfried and I are told that we have a new duty instead of building roads. Surely this will not involve the slaughter of those poor pigs! We follow the guard to the kitchen area. I can't believe my luck when we're given a job in the food store. This position includes distributing food to the prisoners so at long last I can do something to help the others. By cutting up a little extra dry bread and putting it on trays for the allocated prisoner to take back to his group, I make sure that there is a little extra food to help the desperately hungry prisoners. We have so little nourishment here especially considering the manual work undertaken. Some of the lads are losing so much weight that it really is quite worrying. I hear so many tales of people being beaten by the guards for not working at full pace but how can they when they are so hungry and weak. It is a vicious circle.

In March 1935 it is announced to us that conscription is being reintroduced. My friends and I are very concerned when we see officers from the army arriving at the prison. Surely they cannot even consider us to join a fascist army? Much to our relief the names of criminals in our age group are taken and they are told that they have to join the army as soon as they are released. At a roll call, the army officers speak to the rest of us. My friends and I are told with disdain and in very strong terms that we ought to be ashamed of ourselves. We are unworthy to be members of the proud Germany army. I cannot show any emotion at this remark but there are some bonuses to being enemies of the State!!!!!

Walter finally finishes his sentence and both Werner and I make a fuss of him the day before he is due to leave.

"We will be thinking of you. Somehow I very much doubt if you will accept the Nazi regime but if you do continue with resistance work please be careful Walter. I'm sure you will be watched." Walter looks at me and smiles. We have been good friends and he a trustworthy comrade and I know that if he continues with resistance work, he will be a very reliable member of a new resistance cell[116].

---

[116] On 18th June 1935 an agreement was made with England making it possible for Germany to build a number of *warships*. Walter worked on the large ships but after three weeks he was dismissed. He was told he was politically unreliable having tried to persuade younger workers that war means terrible casualties. Later in 1936 one of Walter's sisters was arrested. She was later sentenced to two years imprisonment. Shortly afterwards Walter and one of his other sisters were arrested and questioned and after a few days released. In 1941 he was again arrested and tortured by the Gestapo in Fuhlsbüttel and finally sentenced to 3 ½ years for planning High Treason. He was sent to many prisons but ended up in Schneidemuhl which was a forced labour camp. In January 1945 he was returned to Fuhlsbüttel Concentration Camp and then to Neungamme Concentration Camp. There they were marched through a gate "Arbeit Macht Frei" [work means freedom]. During the last few days before liberation, the prisoners were separated – some to the left, some to the right. In the morning he heard the SS throw hand grenades in the bunkers. Fifty eight men and thirteen women were executed amongst those women was Werner Etter's wife. Walter along with others survived and were force marched to Bergedorf and then taken by train to Barmbeck. On yet another train journey, Walter managed to escape.

Werner who had been observing both of us adds quietly "Perhaps you should do the same as me Walter. I have no intention of working with my friends again. I would hate to go through the same again as it is too much emotionally to worry about my friends in danger should I be arrested. Memories of what happened to us… " he pauses clearly upset.

"It devastated me thinking of you all being "questioned" by the Gestapo. Also I think we have to be realistic about our futures as the Gestapo were a little slow initially working out who we all were but now our friendships are well known to them and it won't take five minutes to round us all up. I intend to start in a completely new resistance cell with people who are only associates but have a sound background. Our friendship will therefore not be put at risk again"[117].

I can see the sense in this logic. We cannot consider a similar resistance group as before as we have to outsmart the Nazis. Looking back we were naïve thinking they would not know who our friends are. Even more frightening is that quite a few other people whom I had never met before seem to know about me. They'd been operating in different districts and it seems that despite true identities being kept quiet, my reputation is known.

Whilst being imprisoned in Hahnöfersand, there were some positive opportunities such as giving me the chance to make new friends who had been in other resistance groups. One of them is Siegfried Ortleff who is a member of the S.A.J. We decide that when or even if we are ever released from here, we will try and meet up.

---

[117] On 21st March 1944 Werner Etter was arrested and sent to Fuhlsbüttel Concentration Camp. In June he was told of the death of his baby son which devastated him. He was then sent to Neuengamme Concentration Camp. He was eventually tried in Berlin and sentenced on 5th January 1945 to death by beheading. This was carried out in Brandenburg-Görden when Werner was only thirty one years old. Werner Stender's best friend is now at Ehrenhain in Ohlsdorf Cemetery, Hamburg along with many other heroes of that time. His wife was one of those who were executed by grenade at Neuengamme on 20th April 1945. Her name is next to her husband's – forever together.

Let's hope that neither of us ends up in a concentration camp when our release date is due. It is never a certainty that we will be free men after our sentence has been served.

I had a surprise in October 1935 when Lotte came to visit me instead of Mama. Whatever is wrong for Mama not to be able to visit me? Is she poorly or is it something else? Whatever it is, my big sister is here and that is fantastic as I have not seen her for such a long time. I cannot help but give her a smile from ear to ear as I realise that it cannot ever be a pleasant journey for my family knowing that I am imprisoned here. That last section of their journey of sitting in the prison boat to cross the Elbe to our island must make them feel low. For me though it is marvellous to see my sister. She tries to put on a brave face but I know that there is something wrong. After a lot of persuasion, she finally tells me what has happened at home.

"The Nazis have accused our Father of helping Rudolf and Ernst in their attempts to destroy the Fatherland. At every meeting held by the Nazis in our area, it is repeatedly announced that no-one is to buy anything from our parents' shop anymore. There has been a total boycott as it is said that all the sons of the Stenders' are enemies of the Third Reich and therefore Papa's shop is to be treated in the same way as any Jew's shop. It is becoming dangerous for the regular customers to enter the shop as it is due to continuous observation by Nazi spies. Even Nazi guards stand outside the entrance so the customers are frightened to show any sympathy towards us. Several old customers have met our father privately and they have expressed their sorrow but they cannot risk the danger of entering the premises. Papa is therefore lucky if he makes 2 RM per day. I am sorry I am burdening you with this problem, but I do not know what to do to help them."

No wonder Lotte looks so worried and there is no-one she can turn to for support. She needs to share her worries with me as I can see the effect all this is doing to her nerves. She says she doesn't want me to hear all this information about our parents from other people, which is quite sensible as sometimes the information given third party is not quite correct and that can cause more worries. However, her final update shakes me to the core.

"Opa is now under suspicion as he was a social democrat and has given support to all his sons, which is the natural thing a father would do, but the Gestapo as a result come night after night to his home and shop and they throw everything about searching for items to incriminate him. And now our parents are being forced to sell the business for 500 RM. It is being sold so cheaply because according to the book work, there are no customers. The fact that the Nazis have frightened people from entering the premises obviously has made the business worthless. I hate to say this but our Papa has in fact contemplated suicide."

"What? This is terrible news Lotte." For a while I am unable to speak. Our lovely parents who have only wanted to help and support friends and family alike and now they are suffering because of us. As for his sons where are we – one in Russia, two in prison and one... well! I do not know what to say to her as I feel that we have let our parents down. I grip her hands tightly and then Lotte takes a deep breath and continues speaking.

"Werner, we are lucky as our relations are standing by Papa and have prevented him from trying to finish his life by giving him courage for the future. He's even had to claim for financial help Werner. The trouble is that I am just keeping afloat financially so Hans and I cannot help them. That private pension he'd paid into for all these years he'll now be getting less of a pension than he had hoped as he has had to start it early at sixty one years of age. It was agreed to release it because of Rudolf, Ernst and your situation. I suppose that they felt he would get hardly any financial support from his offspring."

No wonder poor Mama just can't face the long journey to see me. She has so much to cope with at our home.

"Rudolf has even written from Russia at his disgust at Hans Stender and Carla employing our mother mending their clothes and paying her 1 RM. How can Hans do this to Mama? Why won't they automatically support our parents in their hour of need, go round and let them know that their only son who is a free man will be there for them" remarks Lotte.

"Look Lotte, we can't help how Hans behaves, but as soon as I am released, I'll be able to help them".

"I know Werner. I shouldn't be worrying you about all of this. There's absolutely nothing you can do but I was frightened you would hear of our problems from elsewhere, particularly from the Nazis. If that happened you would not know the actual truth and be in extreme depression at the news. Just keep a low profile here and hopefully you'll be released on time. We need you home."

I squeeze Lotte's hand again. I would love to give her a brotherly hug but I do not want the guards to prematurely end the meeting.

"There is some good news though" she adds with a smile "Despite Hans' behaviour he has had to contribute by law towards our parents' upkeep".

"It is Hans' opportunity to help our parents now there is no-one else apart from you. Perhaps it'll make him more responsible" I add positively but with nagging doubts in my mind. Perhaps that is why they are sending them their clothes to mend – either because they are annoyed to have to provide some money or in their twisted thoughts, they think they are helping them by employing Mama to work.

After Lotte had left, I feel shattered not knowing what I can do to help. I just can't get out of my mind this awful situation at home. I am still in prison and I am not at all confident if I will ever be released. Will I be sent on to a concentration camp after my sentence comes to an end? I have heard that other people have suffered this fate. I feel devastated after hearing the news about Mama and Papa. Papa has always been an independent person and self-employed. He has kept that shop financially afloat since he moved into Gertigstrasse in 1899. As it is below the flat, he will be reminded of his loss every waking moment. Our poor parents have not only lost their livelihood, but one son has had to escape to Russia to save his life and two other sons are in prison having been charged with High Treason against the Third Reich. If they didn't have Lotte to support them emotionally, how will our parents survive?

The month prior to this, Mama had been to see me in prison and yet she had said nothing. Her face was full of smiles and encouragement. Mama had mumbled excuses why it was she and not Papa here to see me. I knew that it is all too much for Papa and yet I had no idea just how bad it has been for him at home. Mama had sat at the table opposite me and had leaned forward grabbing my hands and talked of the good times we had had together before the Nazis had destroyed our happiness. If ever I get out of this terrible place, I will try to help them as much as I can.

The day came for Werner Etter's release. I am now the last one of our old group left at Hahnöfersand. It's sad that I am left behind but in a way I am pleased that the time hopefully will come when I will be released. I have made so many new friends during this time and received much support from my friends and family who regularly send me postcards to let me know that they haven't forgotten me which makes life bearable. I watch as Werner Etter gets into the boat and leaves the island. I hope that this means that he will be released and not sent on to a concentration camp as I know this is happening now.

I walk into the dormitory that evening feeling very low about losing the company of my friend, but also happy for him. Everyone looks up when I enter stopping their intense conversation. I have no idea what is going on but did not really feel like asking. Come on Werner, pull yourself together as you will be leaving here in six months.

"What's happened? Is Hitler dead?" I ask hopefully.

"We've just heard that Hitler became President on 29th June 1936" says one of my comrades."

How much worse is life going to get?

CHAPTER 22

Rudolf from 1935 – September 1936

Obviously I cannot return to Hamburg as I am too well known but I am prepared to be sent anywhere if it means fighting fascism. I have little doubt that reports from the soviet party have been made about me and these can only be positive as I have proved during this last year that I am trustworthy and loyal. After my interviews I've been told that I will be going to Berlin and not Hamburg which is very sensible as I am too well known in Hamburg. As expected they think my expertise in explosives will be a useful weapon against the fascists. Every part of my body is geared up to make this return even if I will not be in the city I love the best.

Having left my Russian passport with the authorities just before the borders of Germany I clutch my new false identity papers in my hand, memorising the details in them and head for Berlin. If the purpose of my mission wasn't so serious I would be smiling at my passport photo as my hair and facial expression is so unlike my usual appearance but it is important to look different as it'll help me not being recognised. After all I am very much a "wanted" man. Although it is January, I can hardly feel the chill wind having experienced such harsh Russian winters. I doubt if any part of Germany suffers similar severe weather as my new adopted country. All I know is that I will never complain again about the cold in Germany.

One of my targets I have been given is the regional court in Berlin, whether or not the Untersuchungsrichter bei dem Landgericht (Examining Magistrate at the Regional Court) will be present at the time is irrelevant. Whatever happens after my efforts on 9th January I shall continue my subversive activities for as long as

I can before the Gestapo catch up with me. When a warrant is made for my arrest by the Berlin Gestapo on 21ˢᵗ February I decide to retreat by making a quick exit back to the Soviet Union. There's no point bringing other people's lives into danger.

I find that it is so frustrating seeing Hitler's progression of power. In January France hands back the Saarland without demanding any concessions and in March Hitler introduces compulsory military service in order to bring the Army up to one million soldiers. Why do the democratic countries in Europe let this happen without it seems much protest? Do they not see that there can only be one reason for his increase in military power? Do the European leaders see the U.S.S.R. as a bigger threat to democracy than fascism and therefore live in the hope that Hitler will destroy my new home?

When I return to the Soviet Union, spring is beginning to appear and the snow finally begins to thaw. As I try looking out of my still frosted glass window I realise that it is time for me to take another turn in my life. I have been a Soviet Citizen for over a year now but I feel that I am wasted working at the Karbolit factory. This country needs to protect itself from Hitler's military might. I sigh deeply as I turn to sit down at the kitchen table and with a pen and paper put in my request to the German section of the commintern for military training. Oh how I hate all this ridiculous officialdom but it has to be done. I write the date which is 14ᵗʰ April. My mind wanders back to my family. It's the day after Ernst's birthday. Poor Ernst – if only I could help him.

Carefully I write details of all my military experience from 1914 when I was in the Great War, finally leading up to the time when I had to emigrate from Germany to the USSR. I decide to put Heines Meier, Herman Schubert, Hans Meins, Max Magdalena and Gustav Gundelach as my references. Finally I write about my family so that the authorities will understand my background and commitment to the 'cause'. I put down my pen and read back all seven pages of the information I have written.

"Well done Rudolf" I congratulate myself and then smile, pleased at the effort I have made. Let's hope I'm successful.

It was lovely receiving a letter yesterday from Hanny asking me to send all her items she has left with me as she has settled in her new home in Odessa. I'm so pleased that she has found suitable work teaching at a school there. At long last the school books will no longer remain with me as I am aware they are of no literary value for use in this country. I presume she only wants to keep them for her own reference but really I hope that she destroys them. I'm sure that her new life in Odessa with her Russian husband will be happy as he seems a lovely fellow.

It feels like eternity to me but in actual fact it doesn't take long before I hear that my destiny is with a scholarship at the Yu. Yu. Markhlevsky Communist University of the National Minorities of the West and not military training. This university is based in Moscow. Before I go there I am advised to change my name to Karl Klug. I suppose that it is a safety move as there are so many people attending this university including comrades from Germany and many will eventually return there. If these comrades are later arrested and tortured then it is more than likely that they might reveal names of the people in attendance at the university so I have to have another identity! My patronymic name is Rudolf Rudolfovich, my local name is Karl Klug, my name when I arrived here which was Otto Kammers and then of course my real name. I hope that I am not asked my name when I have had a drink or two!

The name of the university fascinates me so being a naturally inquisitive person I decide to find out why the university is so named. Apparently Marckhlevsky was the first head of the university or KUNMZ as it is otherwise known. This gentleman served there from 1921 until 1925 and he was obviously a great man as it is a great honour to have a university named after you. How will I cope with being at a place of further education? Apart from an apprenticeship, I left school some twenty years ago.

It is therefore with some relief that I will start initially at a reception course as from May before continuing on a two year course but my heart sinks as I have once again to write about my life. Yet another five pages about me and then my family. I'm really feeling frustrated at all this bureaucracy. Once again I give references and this time I'm able to put Robert Dassau's name down. I wonder if Ernst realises that Robert, Rudi or "Munki" as he is known, has managed to escape arrest and is now with me. He has been able to update me with information about Ernst and I can feel my chest puffing out with pride knowing what good work Ernst had done before his arrest. Is he alive still after being in the hands of the Gestapo? He is not a physically strong man but I know he has boundless mental determination to withstand their 'questioning'. I wonder how the rest of my family is surviving.

Moving to Moscow changes my life for the better as it is rewarding living with so many friends who I know from my days in Hamburg. It irks me somewhat to also admit that I feel happier living in Moscow. Outside this huge city accommodation can be so primitive and very overcrowded. There are outhouses where human waste is disposed of in cesspits. In some places people have no indoor running water so it has to be collected from street pumps or wells. Domestic tasks then become time consuming and exhausting. After a long day of heavy physical labour working in unheated factories and coming home to no heat again after a long gruelling walk due to public transport being inadequate is indescribable, especially in the severe weather experienced during the winter period.

In Moscow there has been considerable progress and is the show piece of socialism improving people's lives. It is an eight hundred year old city and as a consequence, there are still many wooden, brick and stone residential dwellings, some of which were built as far back as the 16th and 17th centuries. Due to the haphazard layout, there are a lot of twisty lanes. However, the Moscow Metro which has taken three years to build finally went into service on 14th May. This structure is a sight to behold, and provides quick, cheap and efficient travel for the masses. The citizens should feel proud of such a wonderful soviet achievement. Another brilliant piece of engineering is the Moscow Volga Canal which is still under construction. The labourers are prisoners so is it appropriate to acknowledge that it is being constructed through forced labour or should I say that it is making good use of prisoner's time.

There are two forms of money, the rouble and the ration card. The workers are given a small amount of cash which they can spend in the co-operative or government shops where prices are low but there is very limited choice of stock. Any surplus money, they can spend on the free market where prices are fifty times higher. At least having alternative ways of purchasing food people have a chance of bringing home the basics at reasonable prices but for the luxuries of course you have to pay a lot more. When I arrived in Russia, there had been a shortage of bread but rationing made it possible for it to be shared equally although not in sufficient quantities. Without rationing and price control, the price of bread would have soared out of reach of the poor and starvation would be the result. At long last it's good to see a fairer society.

Thankfully a commission has been set up to reconstruct the old Moscow. The master plan is to expand the city's area from 285 to 600 square kilometres. It's a massive scheme devised by Lazar Kaganovich and co-signed on 10th July by Stalin and Viacheslav Molotov. The new buildings will be at least six storeys high but on the more desirable streets they will be seven to ten or even fourteen storeys high. The embankment is considered a first class housing area. The low cost housing will be built in more remote areas but most of the funds have been diverted to the new expensive projects. I do feel a bit uncomfortable about this but these people have accepted me into the Soviet Union and this is still a young socialist country trying to recover from poverty and degradation. The people of this country are desperately trying to modernise and bring themselves into the 20th Century despite having very few luxuries.

Life feels good for me at the moment. I love going to the university and mixing with fellow Germans and I study hard. We all mix well together and socialise a lot. I've met another member of Ernst's resistance group. Wilhelm Bahnik's family are over here as well as Wilhelm himself. It's so nice to be able to talk to someone else who knows Ernst. If only Ernst could have escaped to the U.S.S.R. and then we would be together again. I know though that he would never have left Anna and Gretel and Anna would not have been able to make the journey let alone survive in these harsh living conditions. I do envy the people who have been able to bring their families here. I miss mine so much.

I often think how wonderful that my Käthe still writes to me even though we are divorced. There are many friends and comrades here but none the less I feel low as I know that she is the only woman, apart from my family members for whom I've ever had strong feelings. If only she were here with me now. If times had been different, we'd still be together. As it is, I will just have to accept that life has changed forever and that she has remarried. We do though still have our son so our links I hope will never be broken.

Her last letter worries me though with her comments about our Rudi. It seems to me that he like so many other young people, is being influenced by the Hitler Youth Organisation and shows signs of disrespect to his mother because of our anti fascists beliefs. I know that it's difficult for Käthe to discipline him as like most youngsters in Germany, they are being taught to inform the authorities if their family has similar views to us. I'm reading between the lines with her comments as there's a high possibility that both our letters are being intercepted by the Gestapo even with me using the names Otto and Karl. I read Käthe's letter again. Does Rudi not want to learn ordinary subjects or is his only interest the Nazi philosophy? Is there a lot of anger and hate simmering within him as his mother has remarried and from his perspective his father deserted him and a traitor to the Reich? I have to try and write a careful reply to Käthe to see if I can help her. I really do feel very guilty not being able to support her more[118].

"*Thank you for your letter. I know that you are worried about the boy but I will have to leave everything in your hands as I know little about the present situation. I have only one wish and that is that the boy learns and learns again. Whilst he is young, learning is easier. If he leaves it to until he is older, he will find it more difficult.*"

At this point, I pause with my writing. Yes, learning as I am now doing comes very hard at my age of nearly 36 years old. I should have concentrated more when I was at school as it does affect future prosperity and an altogether better life.

"*Käthe I would love a picture of you and the boy as I have none. Let the boy write a letter without your help so that I can try to comprehend what his thoughts are. Greetings from Otto*".

I put down the pen and went to get a glass of water, pondering how I would write to my only son whom I no longer know. The poor lad is probably very troubled with his family background and

---

[118] Words in italics are translations from letters from Rudolf

even angrier with me. This is such a difficult situation for both of us. I'm not enjoying using the word 'boy' rather than 'my son' but I must not let anyone know who it is writing this letter to Käthe as I do not want the Gestapo to know where I am.

A little while later I am pleased to receive the hoped for letter from Rudi. I would love to write freely and lovingly to him but I know it is too dangerous.

"Dear friend" I write. Oh if only I could put *"my son"* and give him some honest advice.

"Your mother has written to me that sometimes you come home like a filthy sparrow. Is that right? Can't you keep clean when you play in the road? You write that unfortunately your holidays are over. Have you no desire to learn? It will be interesting to see who is quicker to read and write – you with your German or me learning Russian. If you agree I would love for you to write more letters to me. What you are learning now… " I pause wondering if I am making it clear that I disapprove of the Nazis doctrine my poor son is learning at present *"you will not need. However you must learn many things otherwise you will not earn much money when you are older. Greetings from your friend Karl."*[119]

I read through the letter I'd just written. Have I been too hard I wonder? It is so difficult understanding the situation from a distance but is does sound as though he needs a firm hand so as not to waste his education and Käthe is finding it hard disciplining him.

One evening Wilhelm Bahnik and Rudi Dassau called round along with other German friends to my apartment for a meal. I really love these occasions when we can chat freely about politics not only here in the Soviet Union but in Germany and the world. We are all displaced people and yet still remain active in our thoughts and aspirations. We are all happy at being free at long last, provided we do not query policy decisions made for this country. Our chats are also a way of catching up on news as newspapers here can be biased but we are used to this as for so long newspaper censorship has been a feature in Germany.

"Did you know that on 15th September, the swastika emblem is now the German national flag" asked Rudi Dassau.

---

[119] Words in italics are translations of letters from Rudolf

We are all flabbergasted at this news. Political beliefs have become more important than our national identity with regard to our state ensign. I also had some disturbing news to pass on.

"As from the beginning of the year Hitler has taken the Saarland back and the neutral buffer zone of the Rhineland. France has signed a mutual assistance treaty with the USSR just like the treaty they had prior to the Great War. Great Britain has made no protest about all of this and France has given Hitler the additional excuse for taking up rearmament in a big way. France has put thirteen divisions of the army at the German border and Hitler has built the Siegfried Line."

"So he's showing again his aims and yet is the League of Nations that concerned? What sanctions are being taken against Germany with this rearming taking place?" asked Wilhelm. "Are they not aware that Germany has started compulsory military service bringing the army numbers up to one million soldiers?"

"Have you also heard that on 3rd October, Mussolini attacked Ethiopia? This crisis feels very similar to prior to the Great War. The world is becoming a very unstable place and I have to say that I am feeling a little bit restless living here as I am sure that I could do something more useful" I add.

Rudi Dassau smiled at this comment. "I am sure that you will be putting yourself forward for more action Rudolf, but first you should finish and qualify at the University."

"I know, I know. I must admit that I am enjoying my time there even though it is hard work."

"You always were an "action man" Rudolf" Wilhelm teases me.

We all laughed each picking up our glasses of vodka and with a clink of the glasses shouted "prost".

Living in Moscow is safer than we have felt for many years but we still cannot help worrying about the future. Most of us have experienced the trauma of the Great War and realise that the next world conflict will be much worse. Somehow I feel that my future will not lie in remaining in the Soviet Union. With my training at the university and the military experience I have gained, I know that my destiny will be fighting fascism somewhere in the world.

One day a letter arrives for me and as I open it and read the contents my heart starts pounding. It's from Kader-Abteilung. I wondered if in some way this might occur, but I had put it to the back of my mind in the hope that it would never happen. The letter is dated 29th September but it has only just arrived. The books which Hanny Dünkel had brought with her from Germany have finally caused her and now me, a massive problem.

I know she thought any educational books would be useful to children starved of literary knowledge but why on earth did she bring those ones with her? Surely she could see that the contents were biased in a Nazi way and in this very politically sensitive country, such items would offend and even threaten the stability of the Soviet State. I warned her not to let anyone see them and now it seems she has ignored what I have said to her.

She has been officially warned not to show these books to anyone and that they cannot even be kept for personal reference either. It seems that the authorities are insistent for an explanation as to why I brought these books to the U.S.S.R. Why would she try to put the blame on me? She must finally realise the serious situation she is in but I am surprised she should mention my name in all of this. I am going to have to be very careful how I reply as if I do not watch out I will be in trouble despite having done nothing wrong. I suppose from the authority's point of view I had given Hanny a good reference with regard to her character so I have to expect that I may come under suspicion now. Once again the pen and paper comes out and I sit for a while looking at the empty sheet. I put the date of 9th November and Moscow on the top right hand side, ponder for a few minutes and then start writing[120].

"As regards the books.

Reading your letter, I have the impression that you think I had brought these books with me when I arrived. That is certainly not correct. They are school books which Hanny Dünkel brought with her. All the time that she stayed in my home, nobody read let alone saw the offending items. As soon as I was aware of these books I told her not to give them to anyone. In May of this year, I sent all her belongings including the books to Odessa where she now lives. I can see in your letter that she was informed not to show them to anyone. I did not know that she was not allowed to retain books for private use.

---

[120] The words in italics are translations from Rudolf's statement

As she belongs to a proletarian family and has answered correctly any questions I asked her, I believed that she would obey my instructions."

I put down my pen and read the statement carefully. Would they accept my explanation I wonder? Will I now be under suspicion because of Hanny? Her father and I were always very close and I feel a sense of responsibility for the welfare of his daughter but anxiety as to the repercussions of her behaviour. This is not a country to behave in such a careless and carefree manner. She may not have said that I brought these 'sensitive' books to Russia. Perhaps it was insinuated by some official with the idea of trapping me to confess something. I've heard that this is happening lately, but I have not experienced it myself until possibly now.

Because of the political upheaval to a new socialist country, life can get very tense. Words and deeds can be intentionally or unintentionally misinterpreted. I do not know what to think when I hear that Hanny's has been dismissed from the Institute in Odessa due to her behaviour. Then all contact with her is lost. I do not know if I should write to her father about her disappearance or wait until I have more information. Even then I must be careful as this could be misconstrued by the secret service as me being implicated in what she may have done. Why didn't she listen to my warnings![121] I had such high hopes that at long last a true socialist country can be formed which would give a very backward country a chance to prove itself amongst its capitalistic neighbours. I still have faith that this man Stalin will either soften his outlook or will be replaced by a true socialist leader.

Winter has well and truly arrived now. The windows become full of ice on the inside as the temperature rarely rises above freezing the flat. The running water is no longer available as the pipes are frozen, electricity is often cut off due to power failure and the electric tram cars are often not available outside the usual hours to get workers to and from work. Many offices have only paraffin lamps for lighting and the workers wrap themselves up in quilts. Clouds

---

[121] Hanny and her Russian husband 'disappeared' during the Purge and her family in Germany never heard from her again. It was a dreadful period of soviet history when too many innocent people were either arrested and shot or finished their days in concentration camps which were called Gulags.

of condensed breath are clearly seen when people breathe. Oh how I hate this cold but hopefully if our soviet comrades can improve the electricity supply and the quality and insulation of the buildings, life will become more tolerable.

It feels at times an almost impossible task because appalling conditions have always been in place for the working class under the Tsar dynasty. I just hope that Stalin has enough capability and determination to improve life for these people. Certainly the master building plan for Moscow is a chance for this to happen and the old dilapidated buildings are rapidly being pulled down and better ones being built. I know that I am luckier than many other Moscow citizens but I have always tried to help others less fortunate than myself.

At long last Rudi writes me a letter but it is a short reply to a previous letter which is frustrating. I cannot seem to get to the real problem so this time I shall write a bit about our life here. Out comes the wretched pen and paper again!

Moscow
December

Dear Rudi

I have received your letter, but why do you always write so little? I take it that you are able to write, so you should be able to write a long letter.

Here it is cold at minus 17 degrees and already we have a lot of snow. In January we expect to get minus 35 or minus 40 degrees Celsius but it will not be so cold where you are. We always get a lot of snow so the children go out with their toboggans. Have you any snow yet? Have you used the toboggan this year?

Every free hour I go in the cultural park to ice skate. This is a large park and all the open areas and paths are used as ice-skating rinks.

Do you remember little Röschen when you were in the nursery? She is thirteen years old now and in the Soviet Union with her parents. She is always outside and goes fast on her toboggan. At present we always have clear frosty weather.

Rudi you write that you have got the results of your exams. What marks did you get? Are the results so bad that you cannot even write about them? I certainly would like to know.

You write that you sometimes go to Oma and Opa. Do you play there with Halma? Rudi now it is already Christmas and we still have not seen each other for a long time. Hopefully you are content with your presents as you know that there is very little money in the family. They cannot give you much and I am not able to send anything from here. Please do not feel too upset. Here we have no Christmas celebrations and the children also get nothing. As Gretel's Papa is also not around at the moment, Gretel will probably have no presents.

Rudi be happy while you are still young and learn as much as you can. It is easier to learn when you are young so when you grow up you can then buy what you want.

Greetings to your Mama at Christmas and don't worry or upset her.

Greetings from your friend Karl.

Rudi when are you going to answer all my questions?[122]

I put down the pen and read the letter I have written. I must actually practice what I preach and continue studying as hard as I can. I would have loved to have told Rudi the friends who are here with me in Moscow, but I hope that he will understand that I cannot say for everyone's safety. Perhaps Käthe will remember little Röschen so she will know who her parents are. There are times when I feel empty inside. If only our marriage had survived and Käthe and Rudi were with me, but life is hard here with even less luxuries than in Germany. Anyway it was my fault that our marriage ended. I know I put the fight for freedom and justice before my family. They're better off without me. I should never have put Käthe through so much but at least she still loves my parents despite the harm I must have caused her. There are times when I feel envious of my friends who have their families with them.

With all the events taking place in Germany and the concentration needed for my studying, I haven't really been fully involved or seriously concerned with the developments taking place within my

---

[122] Words in italics is from one of Rudolf's letters to his son

adopted country although I have volunteered my services and spare time to the party. I have noticed though that people are becoming more furtive and nervous and it is common knowledge that we all have to be careful who we talk to. Despite this, I just keep telling myself that things will right themselves in time and we just have to be patient.

It therefore comes as a bolt out of the blue when we're told during a lecture that the Executive Committee of the Communist International Secretariat (EKKI) has made the decision that our university days are over. What is behind this momentous pronouncement? Is it because of the escalation of Hitler's military ambitions is causing a lack of trust towards us immigrant Germans? We came to this country for sanctuary against fascist persecution and also to help build a socialist state. There are times when I feel uncomfortable with some of Stalin's policies leading me to wonder if he is a socialist or a tyrant. Are his final aims for a socialist democracy? All I know is that fear is permeating everywhere. Things were different when Lenin was the leader. However the abject poverty and degradation from the Tsar dynasty is being eliminated.

Some decisions being made by Stalin makes me wonder if it is going to become unsafe for our countrymen to remain in this country. Will we become the scapegoats for Stalin just as the Jews and socialists were with Hitler? My friends and I are feeling uneasy.

The same day as we are told that the university is closing I receive a Certificate from the university rector. I glance down at the sheet.

History of the USSR people – excellent:
General History – excellent
Economic and Political Geography – excellent
Russian – satisfactory
National language – good
Mathematics – excellent
Physics – satisfactory
Chemistry – excellent
Biology – good[123]

---

[123] Information found in Russian State Archives

The personal report concludes that I have shown self-restraint and discipline, have taken active part both socially and in 'party' work, and I am an excellent student and politically well developed. What a relief to read this. Well my hard work has proved that I am a reasonable student. I only wish that the university is not closing down.

My mind strays for a second or two wondering if my son's report is as good and then I smile to myself that I should even compare myself with Rudi as he is still only a young child.

"We are writing to the Party Committee of the "Karbolit" factory in Orekhovo-Zuevo to see if we can send you back there to work" said Rector Frumkina.

I try not to show my reaction of horror on hearing this information. I had worked there for a year and I had ended up so appalled with the petty squabbling of why spare parts were not available and therefore impossible for the work to be completed. There is a really serious problem with production of goods in these factories. I cannot go back and spend the rest of my days there. I have so much expertise of fighting and use of weaponry that I would rather do something militarily useful against Hitler or some other fascist leader.

Perhaps I'm not the only one thinking that my talents can be put to better use as unbeknown to me I discover that investigations are being made about my character. The EKKI have been writing to Hans Hagen and Richter along with the rector of the University for Information about my abilities.

Finally my fears of returning to "Karbolit" rescind as at long last I am asked if I am willing to go to Spain. The elected Republican Government in Spain is having problems with the nationalist party which is a fascist organisation. Without any hesitation I agree to go even though I know that it will be a dangerous assignment. I am given a Norwegian identity in the name of Sigmund Nielsen but I have to do some military training first.

Once again another blank sheet of paper is handed to me as I am asked to write out my past military and resistance work. This time for security reasons I have to use my new identity.

In mid-July I receive a letter from Fritz Weber who is the German representative of the EKKI. I open the letter, start to read the contents and involuntarily cannot stop myself from groaning.

"At a family celebration of comrade Ernst Ottwald you made the following remark about comrade Will Bredel. "In Bredel's past there is one dark spot and that is the Hamburg uprising which I will one day clarify with him." We ask you immediately to give a full explanation."[124]

I'm really annoyed with myself firstly that I had made this comment on that enjoyable evening and secondly that someone, supposedly my friend, must have reported my comment to the authorities. Really I should have known better than to make any such remark, however true, as so many people in this country are quick to report such statements to the authorities. Why did I drink so much that evening? I think that I shall just ignore the letter as I know that I am destined to leave this country in the near future. Perhaps I'll have gone by the time they chase me up on this. I do not want to be responsible for any arrests, let alone mine even if the comment I made was true! Sometimes the truth is best kept to oneself.

My personal thoughts and worries are overridden hearing that Franco is making an attempt to overthrow the truly elected government in Spain. The non-intervention policy which has been adopted by the French and British governments is, in my eyes, unbelievable. Germany, Italy and the Soviet Union have also agreed not to intervene, but as expected Germany and Italy are underhandedly backing Franco. This will mean civil war in Spain is inevitable. Whilst this non-intervention policy will starve the Republican government of weaponry and financial support, Hitler and Mussolini are able to supply Franco with all kinds of help virtually unhindered.[125]

Are the people who hold high positions in the British government secretly supporting the fascists against the republicans? I know that Britain inherently has a fear of left wing governments and socialism. Thank goodness Mexico is refusing to sign the non-intervention pact and has sent 20,000 Mauser rifles, 20 million rounds of bullets to stop the fascists advancing on Madrid.

---

[124] Words in italics are from a translation from documents in the Russian archives
[125] In my opinion this policy was a major reason for the defeat of the republic.

That will not be enough though if other countries, including America sell military equipment to Franco.

From sources within Spain, news is filtering back to us about the atrocities being carried out by the Nationalists. It seems that their nationalist enemies are anyone who sympathises with the government and who voted to improve the standard of living for the poor, especially to improve education for the illiterate population. The nationalists seem to be taking over more territory, their intention being to 'cleanse' the country of anyone wanting a true democracy. I'm so angry when I hear that the military has the blessing of the Catholic Church thus encouraging the nationalists to stop the republican government improving the 'lot' of the poor.

I know that by going to Spain, my life will return to being a resistance fighter just as I was in Hamburg. The republicans have no idea yet how vicious and dangerous fascists can be. Some parts of southern Spain have already suffered from these extremists and now have a taste of their future. When the nationalists conquer a new stretch of land, they terrorise the neighbourhood by 'cleansing' the area. Union leaders, representatives of the republican government and loyal republicans are shot on the spot. As the troops advance on to the next territory, I understand that the Falange establish themselves in the occupied district. We have received news that they are even worse than the army as they apparently are 'purging' the civilian population of people who are suspected of voting for the republicans. People are being buried in mass graves.

In Teruel, corpses are being disposed of in the 84 metre deep wells, without any thought of the innocent people they are killing or the water system being poisoned. There are so many anti-fascist people who are being slaughtered for their beliefs. Something has to be done to stop this murdering and pillaging.

Dark clouds are forming all over Europe. It is as though the horrors of the Great War have been forgotten. If I cannot do any more to stop Hitler, I can help protect some of the population in Spain before the whole of the country capitulates to fascism.

Will the USSR respond to Spain's need for military help? Trotsky, who has been exiled from the Soviet Union, has always advocated worldwide revolution. He thinks that the Soviet Union will never prosper if its neighbours are capitalists. However Stalin believes in not worrying about socialism in other countries and this policy was adopted in 1927. As a result no real help has been given to other countries that have been in trouble, such as China where the communists were sacrificed to Chian Kai-Shek's army. The Americans approved of this decision and Stalin gained recognition from them. Is this something to be proud of?

I know that the Spanish government has requested modern armaments and ammunition but the Soviet Union decides not to get involved. I can't understand this policy and now I hear that Trotsky is accusing Stalin of betraying the Spanish government and encouraging the fascists in overpowering the elected government. Surely Stalin will change his mind about his disastrous policy. He has seen the demonstrations which have taken place all over Russia on 3rd August, in support of the Republican government. Even the factory workers are making voluntary contributions to send to the democratically elected government.

Surely this lack of support cannot continue. With great relief I hear that the Comintern at the beginning of August decide that they wish to give Spain some form of military support but are waiting for a decision from the Kremlin. Will something positive happen now?

At the end of August I receive another letter asking for an explanation of my comments about Willi Bredel[126]. Will I be able to leave the U.S.S.R. before things start getting unpleasant? Spain is calling me.

At long last on 18th September Stalin decrees that there should be a resolution supporting the Spanish struggle against fascism. Volunteers with military experience are being encouraged to leave the USSR to go to Spain. Without hesitation I now put in my application for permission to leave the Soviet Union. Due to the delicacy of my mission and the

---

[126] Willi Bredel was a German writer. In 1923 he participated in the Hamburg Uprising (as did Rudolf), was arrested and sentenced to two years imprisonment. In 1933 he was arrested and sent to Fuhlsbüttel Concentration Camp and released in 1934. He then went to live first in Czechoslovakia and then Moscow. Whilst in Moscow he published in the Deutsche Zentral Zeitung, a German language newspaper, accounts of his experiences.

enquiries about my loyalties to my adopted country I have just requested to leave as my university course is finished and I wish to go to France. It sounds a reasonable request so I hope the authorities accept my explanation. I just hope that they will ignore the enquiry taking place about my 'loose' talk. I might also be of more value to them in Spain than being arrested along with so many other poor souls. I must keep calm and wait. At least I feel that my present training would soon be put to good use if my request is granted. Fascism must be stopped in its tracks no matter in which country it raises its ugly head. Hopefully my friends will be able to join me in Spain if they too can leave.

Somehow I suspect that Stalin will be pleased to see so many of us strong forthright individuals who came to the Soviet Union with socialist political convictions now leave his country. Lately arrests have taken place of people whom I think Stalin feels are a threat to the stability of the USSR. I'm not convinced that these beliefs are justified but I know that I am of better use fighting for my socialist ideals in Spain.

If only I can leave before I get arrested.[127]

Photo found in the Russian Archives – was this for the passport in 1934?

---

[127] It has been recorded in Stalin's minutes on 20th July 1937 that "*all* Germans working in our military, semi-military and chemical plants and in electrical power stations and building sites in every region are to be arrested. Later German citizens wherever they worked and also former German citizens who had acquired soviet citizenship and had previously worked in defence establishments are also to be arrested.

CHAPTER 23

Ernst from 1935 – September 1936

In a strange way, life is becoming routine in the zuchthaus. I have to accept my situation and try desperately hard not to think too much about my family. What good will worrying about Anna and Gretel do for me. It would destroy my morale and then mentally I will not survive my imprisonment. I've seen it with others in here who devote too many thoughts to their loved ones. In my heart my dearest wish is to have contact with my family, but that is forbidden. A cruel decision for all of us imprisoned here but it is no good dwelling on it.

Oh how I wish that I could get warm which would then mean losing the pain in my joints. As it is February, the weather should be getting a little warmer in about eight weeks' time which will make these cold prison cells slightly more bearable.

I'm beginning to feel safer but how foolish to think that the Gestapo will leave me alone, especially when I know that they haven't rounded up the rest of our organisation.

"Be positive Ernst – they might not" I quietly say to myself.

"Stender, you're wanted for questioning in Berlin" announced one of my guards coldly as he leaves the door open. I can see that two other SS guards are waiting in the corridor for me. As it is not good to hesitate and upset them I walk quickly through the gaping exit.

My legs start to give way as I'm 'frog-marched' along the echoing corridors to the main office where I receive my travel papers. My mind is in a whirl. Why am I being sent to Berlin and not to the Hamburg Gestapo headquarters? Who has been caught? What has been said about me? Will I be implicated in more serious "crimes" and how much more have they discovered about our plans?

Walking into the Gestapo building in Berlin makes my blood curdle. The huge swastika flags hanging down along the entrance has the desired effect on all of us. It intimidates and terrifies all who enter. There are so many connections I've had with Berlin and if it's concerning any one of them, then I'm in serious trouble. Once again, I can feel my nose touching the cold hard surface of a wall in the Gestapo headquarters and there is the heavy breathing of someone behind me, just waiting for me to collapse or even move.

"Keep still Ernst; don't let them know how frightened you are" I remonstrate mentally with myself.

Finally I feel the butt of a pistol in my back and I'm ushered into a room containing a table and chair. Occupying the chair is someone from the Gestapo and behind me stands two SS guards waiting for an opportunity to inflict pain on my body. The man from the Gestapo is busily reading some sheets of paper. After several minutes, he puts the paper down and slowly lifts his eyes in my direction. Fear and dread is spreading in my body but I will not let my true feelings show. I will not give him that pleasure.

"Are you enjoying your stay in the zuchthaus Stender?" He enquires, almost with pleasure.

"I have only been there for three months. I have a long time yet before my sentence is finished" I reply trying not to be too antagonistic with my answer. It's never good to annoy these people.

"A friend of yours has been arrested for questioning". He watches my face closely.

"Who is my friend?"

"Helmut Werner is helping us with our investigations." He pauses for a short time and then "you know him of course?

There's no point in denying the association. Acknowledging some facts is always a good thing if it side lines the fascists away from the real purpose of our resistance work.

"Yes sir, I know Helmut Werner. We have met once or twice in Hamburg".

"He says that you recruited him for your organisation" he snarled at me.

"That is not strictly true sir. I *tried* to recruit him but he refused to work for me".

The Gestapo man stands up and walks round and then behind me. I hate it when they do that as I'm never sure if I'm about to receive a blow from behind. The unknown is the worst part of being scared. This time I'm lucky as he continues to walk back into my eye sight. The questioning seems to continue for hours but to my relief it appears as though only Helmut Werner has been arrested as no other name is mentioned although they keep asking me for names. Thank goodness they haven't broken into our real set up. I gather by his questions that the Gestapo have no idea of the connection and that Helmut has managed not to reveal anything apart from him financially supporting the organisation. This is something which is not worth denying.

Helmut has always been financially secure and has helped us frequently with the funding which we need. Let them think that he knows nothing else and then we can all live for another day. Knowing that this is the full extent of their knowledge, the tension in my body is released and the headache starts to abate.

After being returned to my new prison cell I sit for a while on the damp cold floor but the chill inside me returns to make my body ache. I start trying to move about but that is almost impossible as the area is so small. I can hardly believe that I am only in my mid-thirties and yet I feel like an old man. Although it has only been thirteen days that I have been here, it seems as though I have been here for weeks. My ears pick up the noise of someone approaching along the corridor outside and then I hear the dreaded footsteps stop outside the door. Once again, I can feel my body tense but I try to breathe deeply to keep calm. Keeping my nerve is so important. I don't know where my comrades are or even if they are still working in the resistance. Without being told anything, I'm shuffled out of the Gestapo headquarters to where I do not know. Is this my end?

After a long journey the prison van stops, the engine is switched off and then silence. Suddenly the door opens as I'm told to get out immediately. Every part of my body feels as though it's floating as my spirit rises when I see the zuchthaus where I had been serving my sentence. So they did not have any further information about our real activities. I wonder where everyone is. Are they still in Germany? Are they still fighting the fascists? Where is my dear friend "Munki"[128]. Did Michael Blöth manage to take over from me as we had previously arranged?[129] Are Herbert Wöhrlin, Wolfgang Koglin, Maria, Alfred Barthel, Benno Dohrn and all the others safe? The Gestapo know that I have been involved in 'criminal action' with 'Jensen' but they have no idea who this is.[130]

I do not blame any of them for abandoning the fight. We all know that we might not survive when we are caught and the torture is unbelievable. What will happen to our country though if we do not defeat these fascists? What will happen to the world? As for me, if I can just keep my head down then I can get through this prison sentence and perhaps I may be released. I know that the release is not a foregone conclusion as many fellow prisoners, I have heard, have been sent to concentration camps and to what fate? Oh Anna are you ok?

---

[128] Rudi Dassau also known as 'Munki' is in Moscow with Rudolf at this time.

[129] Michael Bloth was arrested at a meeting in Berlin on 12th March 1934. Details of the events afterwards are given in the next chapter

[130] According to information in the Berlin Archives, 'Jensen' is Gustav Gundelach – once again, someone both Ernst and Rudolf have close connections with.

CHAPTER 24

Ernst from 1937 – 1939

There have been sounds of laughter from the guards these last few days. By my calculations of scratching marks on the wall, it must be because the New Year has begun and that must make it 1937. Will this be my last Christmas and New Year in custody? There has been no further 'questioning' by the Gestapo so does this mean that the others are still operating successfully or have they left the country? With a bit of luck I might get released if nothing further is discovered. Dare I even hope for this possibility? The alternative so I have heard could well involve being transferred to Neuengamme Concentration Camp.

I shudder involuntarily at this thought. I might never be released if I end up there or may even receive a worse fate. These camps are not only to persecute and oppress the political opponents of the Nazi Regime, but also to intimidate and warn the population that they too can become incarcerated in these places if they do not support the Nazi party.

A few days later[131] my thoughts are shattered by bolts being shot back across my cell door and then the noisy jangling of keys as a key turns in the lock. Has my fate been decided? The door is flung open but I manage to jump up in time and run to the furthest wall of my cell with my back against it just as the SS guards enter the room.

"We're transferring you back to Kolafu Stender. You are then wanted for questioning at Gestapo headquarters" says one of them in a crisp manner.

I feel at my lowest ebb, having struggled through a tough sentence with the unpleasant treatment but being left alone from the Gestapo sadists has made my prison sentence almost bearable. I

---

[131] 8th January

should not have put the thoughts of possible freedom into my mind. How can I even contemplate such a thing? The following day I am back at Gestapo headquarters and after the usual standing to attention with my nose to the wall, I am finally ushered into the interview room. I'm asked if I have anything to tell them which I answer in the negative. He studies my face thoroughly and I can feel sweat beginning to pour down my face. I am right to feel worried.

After all this time, the Gestapo seem to be aware of others connected to the group I worked with. Question after question is thrown at me about Wolfgang Koglin. I finally make a statement saying he rejected my approach and was unwilling to supply information to Fritz Lux. I admit I knew his employment and that I think he knew 'Munki' who escaped from Hamburg. I just try to be non-committal. I must not show that I know anything about Koglin's resistance work otherwise others will be arrested.

Then the worst scenario is realised when I am told that Maria and Wilhelm Müller have been arrested along with Walter Stiller, Helmuth Werner, Benno Dohrn and many others. Is this the end for us? Am I strong enough to go through more Gestapo treatment which the SS seem pleased to assist with? I hope my comrades have been sensible setting up contingency plans in order for the resistance to carry on without them. If our group totally collapses it will be terrible. I feel proud though that these comrades managed to continue for so long after we were arrested. They have shown such strength of character and dedication trying to defeat the Nazis. After all this time of withholding information, I cannot expect my name to be kept out of their confessions. It would be too much to hope for. I must stay strong by trying to only give the barest information about our work. That way we all might survive. Perhaps some others have not been discovered or even managed to escape.

Will anyone be able to carry on fighting the Nazis? When they 'question' me[132] about Maria, I decide it is best to admit something so I say that I tried to recruit her in 1932 but she declined. I say I cannot remember what I wanted her to do as it is so long ago. My

---

[132] 23rd January 1937

heart sinks as I am interrogated four days later when Alfred Barthel or "Emil" from Berlin is mentioned to me. This does not bode well for any of us. Has he managed to escape? He is such a major part of our organisation. This is a catastrophe. Oh I hope the true extent of Maria's work is not discovered. How long will these fascist thugs be able to keep me conscious this time?[133]

Finally I can feel myself being pulled along the corridor by two men holding me under my armpits but I am beyond caring. Is it possible that my poor exhausted pain ridden body can take any more of this treatment? Is it worth struggling on to receive yet more from my tormenters or shall I just succumb to the feeling which is beginning to envelope me which is to just let life slip away and then I will be at peace?

Cold air rushes across my face and then darkness as I realise I'm on a seat as a door bangs shut. My forehead is pressed against a cold wall, stopping me from falling down; my arms are limp and my hands touch the floor. I can feel movement as the ground seems to jerk into life. Will this be the end? Have they finished with me and now my fate sealed? The vehicle comes to a stop and I'm dragged back to my old cell in the Zuchthaus. So after twenty two days, I am free from Kolafu for a while. As dark falls, I curl up into the foetal position on my hard bed with the freezing cold air sinking into my bones. I can feel my body shaking with both cold and fear. What will happen next I wonder?

After a night's fitful sleep, I somehow seem to pull myself together thinking of my two beautiful girls, Anna and Gretel, who must be worrying about me. I can't let them down so I must try to keep going. My life continues in the Zuchthaus. I wonder if we have managed to succeed in foiling the Gestapo. How foolish is that thought as once again, a month later[134], the cell door opens and I'm on my way back for more 'questioning'. Oh how silly of me to think that I might be released at the end of my sentence.

---

[133] On 27th January 1937 at the court hearing for Wilhelm Müller, Ernst admits that there is a possibility that he gave instructions to Wilhelm which he got from Barthel.
[134] 25th and 26th February 1937

There are times when I sit in my tiny "hell hole" in total despair. I have no rights, no certainty of release or of life itself. Has this strain I have put Anna under damaged her health irretrievably? I'll never forgive myself if this is the case. Now they have some of the main "players" the situation is extremely precarious for all of us let alone the resistance movement. Maria Müller having been arrested is a great blow for all of us. I'd tried so hard not to give any information which would destroy our hopes of dismantling the Nazi movement.

With great effort I try to hide my dismay when with a great deal of satisfaction the Gestapo informs me that Maria has admitted knowing Wolfgang Koglin and that Wolfgang provided important details about firms and their latest innovations and inventions and this had been passed on to me. There's no point denying knowledge discovered by the Gestapo – why go through torture for no reason. Poor Maria must be having a terrible time with her interrogation. Please, please let us hope that she can survive the 'questioning' without revealing too much information but if not I cannot blame her. I know only too well how difficult it is to withhold information from the Gestapo. It seem as though our "cell" has well and truly collapsed.

Will they find out any more information about Wolfgang Koglin? He was useful to us as an employee at the company Carlowitz as they exported material to East Asia. Thoughts flood in of the times when I was active in the resistance and Koglin had been able to give regular reports on the trade deals of armaments between Germany to China and Japan in exchange for raw materials. He'd also given me details of the routes used for these transactions including the railway network. Our country gave so much help to China to build major new railroads between Nanchang, Zhejiang and Guizhou. There was a reason why our country did this as building those railroads gave Germany access to more raw materials but without the delays.

Germany had been providing expertise and equipment in setting up ventures such as the construction of the central steel and machine works and the development of power plants and other chemical factories. To lose Koglin from our network is without doubt a major setback. A lot of Germany's shipping companies who trade with various countries have been infiltrated by our agents and this information has been passed on to 'friendly' countries. Hopefully this will stop the fascists from aggressive intentions. Will the Gestapo discover the extent of our penetration into their security? I've tried so hard to make them think how ineffectual we have been but will they now find out the truth?

After two days I'm back in my cell. I never thought of this tiny cold room as a sanctuary before, but it's certainly a safer place than being with the Gestapo! I hear the noises of pain and despair from fellow prisoners and this haunts me. Sometimes I lose heart. I'm not allowed contact with my family and this is soul destroying.

My heart lifts a little when spring arrives – I can feel the change in the air when I'm out of my cell. What is going to happen to me? Will I see my family again? "Keep your nerve Ernst" I keep telling myself.

One glitch of light falls my way when I overhear a conversation[135] that Maria's interrogation is over and she is put into custody. I am so relieved for her. I know only too well how terrifying and exhausting it must have been for her. But my heart sinks again as I yet again get bundled into the prison van and taken to Gestapo headquarters. This time though a piece of paper is thrust in front of me and I am told to sign it. I start to read it but feel the aggravation simmering within the Gestapo agent so scan the words quickly before signing the paper. Apparently I am completely happy with the treatment I have received. To refuse to sign would be utter madness but my reward of conceding to these lies is beyond belief. I am to be released. Oh joy. I would sign that paper again and again just to be told this good news. The door is opened behind me; I look round to see that I am expected to exit the room. I'm escorted to the entrance door of Gestapo headquarters and given a shove into freedom.

The daylight hurts my eyes even though rain is pouring down, splattering on the pavement forming huge puddles. Freedom is a wonderful experience but are the Gestapo watching from behind ready to call me back and arrest me again? Such cruelty I have come

---

[135] 14th April

to expect from them after these 3 ½ years of incarceration. I must keep walking at a steady pace, not look back as I must not tempt fate. Just as that moment, as if from a dream from my past I hear two familiar voices call out my name.

"Ernst, we're here. Stop, stop for a minute."

I stop and looked over the road slightly to my right and see Lotte and Werner trying to catch up with me. It's such a wonderful surprise to see them both almost running towards me in the torrential rain. I glance behind to see if I'm being followed but the street is empty. It's late in the afternoon but still too early for people to finish work.

Feeling their bodies, strong and comforting against me is like heaven as they give me a brotherly and sisterly hug. I must look terrible as the expression on their faces show great concern, but this is quickly masked by their smiles and hooking my arms into the security of theirs we walk towards Rebenstrasse Boat Station on the Alster. I can feel a lump in my throat with the emotion of being back with my family and especially seeing young Werner. When the Gestapo during one of my interrogations told me that they had arrested him and had intentions of giving him the death sentence, I had tried desperately hard to put him completely from my mind. I had to do this to keep my sanity and now here he is looking so well and very tall. He has certainly grown up since I last saw him into a mature young man. I keep looking at him unable to speak, but I know he understands my reactions as I feel a tightening grip of reassurance from him.

We climb on board the canal boat and it starts its usual journey to the other side of the Alster crossing north east to Alster Park, west over to the original side and finally north east again to the other side in order that people can embark and disembark before it reaches Langer Zug and the start of the Osterbek Canal. It is a journey we all love in normal circumstances but it seems a dream today and I cannot see any of the beauty surrounding me. There's general chatter from the passengers as they continue their lives without any knowledge that on board one man had with his experiences just left hell, an experience so many of us resistance workers are aware of. I can't stop worrying that Anna is not here to meet me. The lake is so beautiful and the parks and embankments so enchanting to see again but where is my Anna? Lotte and Werner must have read my thoughts as Lotte starts talking gently to me, holding my hand.

"Ernst, your Anna is in hospital with heart problems."

A mixture of feelings envelope me as I try to take in what I am being told. She is alive thank goodness but how ill is she?

"We take it in turns to regularly go and see her and we always take Gretel with us. Anna has really been very poorly this last year and has spent most of her time in hospital. Mama and Papa have been looking after Gretel so never fear as she has been given lots of love in order to make up for not being with her parents. We haven't told Gretel that you were due to be released today as we didn't want to break her heart if it didn't happen. That's why she is not with us now".

I bite my lip trying not to show the world my real feelings, nodding that I have understood and try to smile, but it just doesn't happen. Tears start to fall down my cheeks and I quickly rub my cheeks. Oh what have I done to my family? Anna's had heart problems for so many years now but somehow she had kept going with my love and support. I wouldn't have put it past the Gestapo to inflict fear into her whilst I was away. I must never do this again to my lovely wife. Anyway, my nerves, I know, have gone and I will be a hindrance to the movement now if I became involved again.

As we disembark at Mühlenkamp and start walking along Gertigstrasse, I can't believe the person staring back at me in the shop window is me. There's an old man with grey hair, no longer walking upright and purposeful but walking very warily like a wounded animal. I look just like the other people who have been released after being incarcerated in the Gestapo headquarters, a concentration camp or a Zuchthaus. I'm only 36 years old but there isn't any sign of this fact in my reflection.

We finally stop as the familiar double doors of no. 56 seem to welcome me but why has the sign changed over Papa's cigar shop next door?

"What has happened to Papa's shop?" I ask Lotte.

"Don't worry about that now Ernst. We'll explain later. Right now you have your daughter waiting for you in our parents' flat" chides Lotte.

I didn't need telling twice and from nowhere, my strength appears as I take two steps at a time up to the first floor inner door of the flats, open the heavy wooden entrance and head to the left and into Mama and Papa's flat. In the lounge, playing a card game with Mama is my precious little girl Gretel. She has grown so much in these 3 ½ years being ten years old and looking more and more like my wonderful wife. Gretel looks up as she hears all the kerfuffle of the three of us entering the flat. I hear Mama making pleasant but nondescript sounds of joy but my eyes are only for my little girl.

"Papa?" queries Gretel with some doubt in her voice, obviously not really recognising me with my changed appearance.

"Yes my little Mädchen. I am home at last" and we collide into each other in our rush to hug one another. After several minutes of laughter, tears and a rolling hug, I glance up to see Mama looking at both of us, and she is also in tears but with a huge smile on her face. I hold Gretel's hand and give Mama a hug. No words pass our lips as there is no need. What a special moment for me but to be without the other precious love of my life is mortifying.

At that moment Papa walks into the room and there is more hugging, tears and laughter. Mama scuttles off into the kitchen to prepare some food and I sit down on the settee next to Gretel. I want to talk but I can't. It's all too much for me. All I want is my family near me. I suppose 3 ½ years is not so long but it feels a life time when nothing is certain as to whether you will live, die or have more torture. I think that it must be impossible for anyone who has not suffered in such a way to ever truly understand how I am feeling. I glance over to Werner and I can see it on his face that he understands fully the emotion I feel at this moment. Our eyes lock and I can feel his warmth and love for me. Oh what suffering has my poor little brother been through so young and yet I can see now he really is an adult. After eating some of Mama's wonderful food, Papa starts to speak very gently to me.

"Son I will take you to see Anna. I'm sure Lotte and Werner have told you about her health but we all hope that now you are back with us, she will start to improve."

"Can I come with you Opa" Gretel asks Papa.

"No my child not today as I think your Mama needs time alone with your Papa. Tomorrow I am sure will be fine for the three of you to be together". Papa rests his hand on Gretel's shoulder as she hangs her head, full of disappointment. After a few seconds though, like a child can suddenly do, her emotion changes and she looks up, smiles and gives me a wonderful hug, obviously making sure that I know how much she has missed me. Three and a half years for a ten year old must feel like a life time. Gretel must have realised how ill Anna has been which has meant that she lost both parents at the same time. At least she's had stability and love with my parents caring for her.

I feel restless as I need to go to Anna and see for myself that she is still alive. Papa keeps reassuring me that as soon as visiting times start, we will be there waiting at the hospital ward door. He keeps his word but I think both Anna and I are both shocked seeing each other's appearances when we finally meet that evening. Almost immediately though her reaction changes as her face breaks into the loveliest of smiles. She looks so weak and I can't help remonstrating with myself at being the additional cause of her heart problems. She lifts her left hand out towards me. I gently hold it and then we are in each other's arms, blissfully unaware of anyone else present. What joy to hold Anna and to talk to her.

In her usual stalwart manner, she smiles lovingly at me, tears falling down her cheeks and says that the past is over and it is the future we have to look forward to. Despite her comments we have both aged since we last saw each other. I know she has a heart problem, but it's been my fault that she's deteriorated through worrying about me. After a while, she starts to speak in a weak but determined voice.

"Now Ernst, I will not hear of you taking the blame for our circumstances. We both know who is really to blame here and that is the fascists. We both discussed whether you should join the resistance movement and you had my blessing to do so. You know we couldn't just sit back and let the Nazis take power without trying to stop them. We couldn't live with ourselves if we had done that."

She slumps back down, head on the pillows, totally exhausted.

"I know you are right Anna, but I think that it is time we tried to recover from our experiences and put your health first. We must also give time to our dear little daughter as she has not deserved her life either."

She squeezes my hand and says in an even quieter voice so that I had to put my head close to her in order to hear what she is saying.

"None of us have, but we'll get over this Ernst. Now I know that you are safe and back with us that strain is no longer with me."

Her eyes close but her smile remains. I kiss her gently on the lips and stand up to leave. How can I tell Anna that I think worse is yet to come now that many of my colleagues are being "questioned"? I can't even think about escaping and leaving the country as my great friend "Munki" has done. I know that there would be repercussions towards not only Anna but also to my parents. If Anna was fit, then I might even consider trying to take her with me; away from the dangers but that is out of the question with her heart condition. Feeling exhausted, frail and full of guilt that Anna's heart has not been strong enough to survive my resistance work, I leave the love of my life in her hospital bed and head for home.

Papa and I sit quietly on the tram as we make our way back to Gertigstrasse, each deep in our own thoughts. As we disembark and start walking home, I decide to take the opportunity to speak to Papa about his shop. I'm very exhausted as it's been such a long day, but I don't want to have a sleepless night tonight worrying about anything unnecessarily.

All Papa does is shrugs his shoulders and tells me that he's tired of working long hours for little return and changes the subject. By now we're ascending the steps to our flat so I give up cross-examining him as he obviously does not want to discuss this with me at the moment. I shall have to concentrate my mind now to my little girl who desperately needs me to give her some of my time. She has been deprived of both of her parents through no fault of hers.

She must have been sitting on the large lounge window sill overlooking Gertigstrasse because I didn't even need to find the keys as the front door is already open. There by the door is my wonderful Gretel with her dark brown wavy hair having been tamed by a hair slide and her young face is lit by an enormous smile.

"Hello Papa. Is Mama all right? Did she ask about me?"

Oh my Gretel. How lovely to hear her voice again.

She continues "Oma says that as our flat is not aired at the moment with Mama being in hospital you must also stay the night with us. I've been staying here with Oma, Opa and Uncle Werner."

"Now that sounds a lovely idea Gretel." Turning to my mother, I meekly add

"Thank you Mama."

Mama just smiles sweetly at me. She's already clutching sheets and blankets to prepare my bed.

"I can see how tired you are son, so please don't think you should stay up with us. In the morning I'll come with you and Gretel over to your flat to help you make the beds up and to give your home a spring clean and then I will leave the two of you alone as you need some time together. I'll bring some food over as well."

I have to say that I slept well that night being totally exhausted both physically and emotionally. For the first time in years, I have freedom to get out of my bed and walk into another room and yes go to the toilet. No more waiting for those footsteps along the corridor, the turning of the lock and for the cell door to open to unknown fate. After a few days, my life is beginning to return to some semblance of normality and I manage to find employment at T H Schule in Hammer Deich as a dreher[136]. It seems a life time ago when I did such work but it's up to me now to keep working and bring in a wage for my family.

Mama and Papa once again are there for us as Gretel stays with them during the day after school and I cycle back to Gertigstrasse to pick her up. Her little face is always so excited each time I arrive back at no 56. Mama kindly cooks us both a meal and then it's that special time for Gretel and me as we make our way back home. Anna will be back with us soon and then we will quietly spend time together so as not to over exert my lovely wife.

Just as I start planning our future, our lives fall apart again. Why do I always make the mistake in thinking that our lives will ever go

---

[136] Lathe operator. There are many levels of ability to this profession and Ernst was a skilled dreher

back to how it was before Hitler! Just nineteen days since my release, there's the dreaded knock on the door and I'm arrested again and this time taken to Berlin. The Gestapo seem to know about so many of us and what important positions we have all held in the resistance. How many more times will I be arrested and when will they decide that I am not to be released. The future looks bleak. Will I ever be allowed to live a "normal" life? By some miracle I'm released a while later but as I look at the tarnished mirror in our bedroom, the reflection looking back at me has white hair now. It's all too much strain and I can see the distress in little Gretel's eyes to find her Papa has aged even more.

The only good news is that the Gestapo have confirmed that Rudolf is still in Spain. I had not really been surprised hearing that he has taken up arms again. How do they know about where he is? That is very worrying. As for Rudolf it is not in his nature to sit quietly having a normal job when he can be fighting fascism. Oh how I miss him. We used to have such a close relationship and many hours were spent discussing politics and also how we hoped to stop Hitler in his tracks.

At least Anna is home at long last and with love and care, I hope she will regain strength. She looks a lot more relaxed and happy now that we are both together at last. I am going to have to make sure that nothing separates us again. I fear that this will not be easy as my complicity in resistance work and the position I held has only been discovered this year by the Gestapo. Who knows what the consequences will be. I know that I will be arrested at some point and may not return.

It has been difficult making the decision not to tell my family about my 'interviews' at the Gestapo headquarters and the reason I keep being interrogated. Anna and I spent several evenings trying to decide whether our family should know but I can see the strain on Mama and Papa's faces. They never say anything how they are feeling with Rudolf being involved in the Spanish Civil War and I know they are hoping Werner will not restart his resistance work. How can I tell them that worse may yet occur to me now that my comrades have been arrested?

My darling daughter has been burdened with more secrets not telling anyone about my arrests and knowing that she cannot get support from her grandparents, the people most children would naturally seek comfort from. It is not fair that someone so young should have these worries on top of living an uncertain life due to Anna's weak heart. It has been so difficult making this decision but my parents; especially my father is finding life very hard as the years' progress.

His escape from worries is his visit to the Stadtpark where he goes to the garden area opposite the Landhaus Café. Here he meets his friends and they play cards and chat which is therapeutic.

One evening whilst enjoying the tranquillity of reading, a quiet knock on the door jerks us both into a tense alertness. Anna is up out her chair before me and when she opens the door, the familiar frame of my youngest brother fills the doorway entrance.

"Come in Werner. How lovely to see you here" Anna exclaims giving him a hug, pulls his head gently towards her and gives him a peck on the cheek. We all laugh at this as Werner has grown so tall and slim.

"Is it all right if I come and speak to you both? I don't want to disturb you from your books."

"Don't be silly. I can think of no better interruption" remarks Anna who already is making her way to the kitchen to fetch a drink for us. After a little while, Anna leaves us as she says that she wants to lie down and rest.

I study Werner's face closely. He was still a young teenager when I was arrested but he has grown up so much since we last had contact with each other in 1933. I can understand why he's changed, both of us having been in the clutches of the fascists for some time.

"Werner do you know why Papa no longer has his shop? I have asked him but I feel that he hasn't given me an honest answer".

Werner looks down at his drink and is thoughtful for a few minutes before answering.

"It all happened whilst we were both under arrest. Our parents will not discuss the situation with me but I had an explanation from Lotte who has been brilliant in her support for them. I understand that they were persecuted by the Nazis who treated them in the same way as they do to the Jews. The regular customers were warned not to purchase items and guards were constantly standing outside Papa's shop to deter anyone who felt brave enough to override this order. Some of Papa's regular customers managed to speak to him when he was away from Gertigstrasse. They felt awful at betraying Papa but were too frightened that they would receive similar treatment themselves if they defied the Nazi order and entered the shop. Papa had to sell the business and as hardly any customers were shown in the ledger books, it was not a financially secure business so sold for next to nothing."

"But that has been Papa's sole income since they were married, apart from when he was "called up" in the Army" I exclaim in horror.

"He won't talk about it as he doesn't want either of us feeling guilty about it. I feel so angry that they should be treated in such a way but what can I do?" Werner looks upset.

"I had suspicions that some terrible fate had befallen our parents due to the three of us being in the resistance. It's typical of Mama and Papa taking this punishment without telling us."

This is all I could say to Werner on hearing this information and then we fall into a silence for a while, each in our own thoughts. Finally Werner begins to quietly persuade me to talk about these last years. I can't tell him everything as I can't bring myself to accept what has happened. The brain seems to put a shutter down against the worst memories in order to survive, but I know Werner understands how I'm feeling. Only someone who has been through such fear and pain can truly understand another person's emotions. I have no idea how long we talked, cried, sat in silence but that evening helped me release many anxieties and feelings.

Werner also comments that perhaps it is time to consider that I have done enough resistance work and should put my health and my family first. We have never talked about what either of us has done as even after our sentences have been served, lives can be put at risk if we mention to anyone, including family, any names and what we did. It seems we are still both withholding more information from the Nazis. I suspect Werner being so young at the time was not involved in the same dangerous espionage as me but a youngster can still be meeting very important people and provide the backbone of resistance work. The fear and consequences of being caught can be the same as the rest of us more highly involved members.

I wonder if Werner will lead a normal life again or will he return to resistance work. I cannot advise him either way as he is a grown man now. He has not met a special girlfriend yet but potentially we will have heart-broken parents if he gets caught again. Also if he is rearrested, the Gestapo will not be so lenient towards him. Time will tell what he decides. The next morning, although mentally exhausted, I feel I can face things a little more easily.

It's strange never chatting socially to my colleagues at work. Just keep your head down Ernst and don't get involved I keep reminding myself. There again, I've noticed that people don't really want to speak to me as they know that I've only just been released from prison but keep being taken back to Gestapo headquarters both in Hamburg and Berlin. Thank goodness I've still managed to hold back from giving the Gestapo the information they really want to know. How much longer will this go on for? How much longer will I be able to keep the truth from them? I think the Gestapo are becoming aware of how dangerous our movement has been and how much we managed to infiltrate and obtain highly sensitive information from business and the military. Hamburg docks are important strategically and we had a brilliant set-up with so many people within the area who were willing to provide information to us.

I'm really lucky to hold down this job but if I wasn't any good as a dreher, then I would have been dismissed a long time ago and then would I find other employment? I have to repay the benefits which had been given to Anna and Gretel whilst I was in prison. Will I ever earn enough money to give my family any luxuries? I think that the Nazi party intend that I shall keep on the lower financial level forever.

Once again the Gestapo arrive[137] to collect me for more 'questioning'. This time it is about my contact with Herbert

---

[137] 29th July 1937

Wöhrlin. I manage to keep everything back apart from meeting him in the summer of 1933 when he told me about a cargo being loaded to the Soviet Union.[138] I tell them that I cannot remember anything else. I am then 'dismissed'. I must carry on and try not to worry.

As it's a beautiful August Sunday morning Gretel goes to play with a friend and Anna is busy cooking our lunch. We are not expecting visitors but are pleased when Werner unexpectedly arrives to see me. He's in a very cheerful mood as Papa has at last been given a job, albeit a very menial one, but at least it will give him a feeling of self-respect.

"Hans has persuaded his employers to let Papa earn some money doing odd jobs such as sweeping the factory floor. I have been so concerned seeing Papa's health deteriorating especially mentally."

He has never quite recovered from losing his shop, Rudolf having to escape the country and Werner and I being arrested, let alone the effects of the Gestapo's regular visits when we were both in prison. It's all been too much for him. He became a changed man after the Great War, but life since has continued to be cruel to him. He never aimed to be a high achiever, but he's been a hard worker and a loving father and grandfather. Hopefully now, he will feel part of society again, however menial the job is.

I study Werner's face and can see that something else is on his mind.

"Well come on Werner. What else have you to tell me? Have you met a nice young girl?" I tease.

Poor Werner blushes at that comment. I know he has a lot of friends of both sexes, but the next step of having a girlfriend seems to be a hurdle for him. How can I criticize him though when I had the same problem at his age? Shyness is a dreadful thing to conquer and neither of us have Rudolf's way of charming the fairer sex.

Werner shakes his head. Perhaps he wants to talk about something else.

"No it is nothing Ernst, honestly."

Does this mean that Werner is working in the resistance again? He's just finished his apprenticeship and is finally earning reasonable money which will help our parents.

---

[138] I am not sure if this has anything to do with Rudolf escaping from Hamburg to the Soviet Union

As Werner prepares to depart, I can't stop myself going over to him, giving him a hug and saying "Be careful Werner". My young brother just smiles back and nods as he leaves the flat.

It's awful to think that these lovely summer days are rapidly coming to an end. The sun warms our bones making the world feel better and it is wonderful not having to clench our muscles to try and keep warm due to inadequate clothes and heating. The three of us spent the early evening in the Stadtpark and have promised Mama and Papa that we'll call in on our way home.

Even in the Stadtpark we have to be careful. I've always made sure that I avert my eyes from the SS as they strut around the Stadtpark ruining ordinary citizen's relaxation time. They now wear dove-grey tailored uniforms and I can't help but shudder at the sight of them with their very self-assured manner. I glance at Anna and Gretel who seem oblivious to these people. I used to be more measured in my outlook but now my nerves are not the same any more. Anna feels my glance and looks at me, smiles reassuringly and squeezes my hand.

"Come on Ernst, Gretel wants you to throw her the ball."

I smile back at Anna, pull myself together and say to Gretel as I start running backwards "well come on Gretel, let's see who can last without dropping the ball."

After much laughter and frolicking around, my rejuvenated body and soul feels up to visiting my parents. I know how important it is to show them that I am all right now. As we walk into no. 56, I hear no sound at all. Mama and Papa are just sitting in the lounge, neither of them talking, just sitting staring into space.

"Whatever is the matter" I ask, but somehow I know that it must be about Werner. Still no answer from either of them, so Anna disappears into the kitchen to fetch them some refreshments. The place looks a mess which is unheard of when Mama is in charge.

"The Gestapo agents have been again but this time they came to arrest Werner. They're furious as he seems to have been given a "tip off" not to come home after his work."

So I was right in that Werner had taken up working for the resistance again. This time, if he is caught, he will be lucky to survive.

I know that they had threatened him with his life last time and that it probably has not helped having two older brothers outwitting the Gestapo. I hope he has someone able to help him escape otherwise I would not bet on his chances of survival.

Gretel went over to her grandmother and gave her a cuddle.

"Onkel Werner will be all right Oma, I know he will. He's my special Onkel and he is very clever."

Oh how strong Gretel is and then I can see the tears rolling down her face. I'd forgotten how close she is to my brother. Probably due to his age being eleven or twelve years older, they have been more like big brother and little sister than Onkel and niece. I stay late that evening with my parents. Anna and I help Mama tidy the flat up after these thugs had terrified Mama and Papa and then turned their anger on our family home destroying their furniture and belongings. I want to find out if Werner is safe but the last thing I should do is start going to my old sources to see if Werner is in a safe house. I'm sure we are being watched so we must not make any ill-judged move.

I hear that poor Lotte received the same treatment as the Gestapo are intent on "visiting" all our family and close friends in order to try and find out where he is. As the days progress, news does filter back that Werner is in hiding somewhere in Hamburg but we must all act as normal as possible so as not to attract suspicion to anyone. The Gestapo question my parents incessantly along with poor Lotte to try and ascertain where Werner has gone. They were told that should there be any news or post from abroad or wherever, they had to get in touch with them at once. If they fail to comply with this, they must accept the consequences. Yet more heart breaking worry for Mama and Papa.

If we felt that matters could not get any worse the Gestapo arrive to arrest me[139]. They feel they have sufficient information to take penal action against Karl Rattai, Wilhelm Timmerman, Karl Sandmann and myself. So now they have finally found out more information about our set-up. What will happen to us all now? I will not try to escape – how can I leave my Anna?

---

[139] 29th September 1937

It seems that they know about the connections between the Müllers, Wolfgang Koglin, Benno Dohrn and Herbert Wöhrlin. They're accusing me of discovering a great degree of information mostly through Maria, about armaments, state secret designs and innovations of the new weaponry within Germany and in particular of the aircraft industry which I had passed over to a foreign country. Therefore I am considered a traitor for persuading the Müllers to become armament spies and acquire State Secrets and that I have a well-known reputation as a leading figure in the Communist Intelligence Service. That is what they now say so have I any chance of surviving?

That word 'traitor' is alien to me. I am not a traitor as we were trying to let the world know what Hitler intends to do. He and his henchmen are the traitors to world peace and to our country, and unless people such as our movement warn the rest of the world, then what will be the future for any of us?

I know we have done the right thing but now what is going to happen to us? My body is wracked in pain and I feel almost dead within my mind. I should have more faith though. To the Gestapo's fury, the courts decide that they cannot put me on trial twice for the same crime. The fact that they have so much more information incriminating us seems to be irrelevant to the judges.

My whole body starts shaking as the realisation that I might survive begins to dawn on me. That's twice now that the courts have overridden the Gestapo concerning my family's fate. They saved Werner's life in his trial for High Treason and now me. So there is still a justice system overruling the Nazis. I know that most courts are run by Nazis but I hadn't realised that there are still some very brave judges still willing to stand up for the Rule of Law. I wonder how much longer they will be able to do this and what will happen to these brave men?

Before I leave the courts my "interrogators" stand deliberately in my way with expressions beyond the angry stage. They look at me with such hatred and one of them said "We will get you Stender – one way or another your luck will run out and then we shall wreak our revenge."

I lower my eyes and wait for them to clear a route for me to walk out of the court house. I know they're right unless someone in the world manages to stop these fascists before we're all annihilated. I feel so much that I am now on "borrowed time". Rudolf is in Spain and Werner by some miracle I hear reached Czechoslovakia but I am still here, not able to leave because of my precious darling Anna. I have to take my chances. As to Werner, his new home is a bit of a poisoned chalice as he is surrounded by fascist countries so what will happen to him if Hitler invades Czechoslovakia? Still I mustn't worry about things that haven't happened.

How pleased and relieved I am that Werner escaped when he did. For my parents, their life fell apart when their "little Werner" was put in a similar position as Rudolf and me. Anna later told me that whilst I was 'away' Werner had called to say that he was leaving. I am pleased that he spoke to her and that she was able to wish him well. He could not say goodbye to Mama and Papa as it would not have been safe and despite that danger, such a meeting would have been too distressing for everyone. Our parents do not deserve this happening to them as they are such loving parents. Lotte found out that Werner had passed his exams and had achieved top marks above the other students. In his hurry to escape he left behind a wonderful new coat which he had bought for the winter but Papa will be able to make good use of it thank goodness.

Papa is now under suspicion as he was a social democrat who supported all of us. The Gestapo come night after night to his home and throw everything about searching for items to incriminate him. Mama and Papa suffer in silence. It is only because I am still in Hamburg that I found this out from Lotte one day when she broke down with the stress they were going through. Oh I wish I could change things for them.

During the night of 9th/10th November, a shocking event occurs throughout Germany as the SA thugs turn their hatred on the Jews. In Hamburg the large Bornplatz Synagogue is badly damaged and the shops owned by the Jews had their windows broken. People are calling it Krystalnacht and I think it is the final straw for many of the Jewish population that life is becoming very unsafe for them to remain here. Many decide that it is wise to leave Germany. Others either cannot or will not be terrorised out of the country they love.

All these years, we, as ordinary German citizens have fought fascism and many thousands have been tortured, put in concentration camps or executed. Others in the resistance who were able to escape from Germany when they were about to be arrested, are now fighting fascism elsewhere. As a result, we have been weakened to the point of not being able to help our Jewish friends.

Anna and I have spent some time saving money to buy Gretel a mandolin and lessons for her Christmas present. Seeing our daughter's ecstatic face when she opens the parcel and there is her own musical instrument, was worth all our financial struggles. The joy somehow blots out the mental pain within our family. Whatever happened to those lovely family Christmases? They seem to be a life time ago.

January comes and goes and then on 8th February once again the Gestapo come to collect me as I have to appear in yet another trial, this time in Berlin and it starts 15th February. This is for Elizabeth Fenske, Herbert and Martha Wöhrlin, Julius Grönwold and Paul Stiller. The prosecutor keeps talking about Michael Blöth who took over from me in November 1933 and is now "deceased". I wonder what happened to him.[140] The prosecutor continues speaking giving so many details. Most of it becomes a blur but some things I can still recall.

According to the evidence it seems that Alfred Barthel, having taken over from Michael Blöth managed to escape which is excellent news. Alfred Barthel or "Emil" was an important member of the

---

[140] There is a letter from Gestapo Headquarters to the Courts Volksgerichtshof on 9th March 1938 stating "I send you details with the notification that Michael Blöth on 13th March 1934 committed suicide. He was arrested on 12th March 1934 at a meeting in Berlin and during the questioning the next day, 13th March he used the opportunity to jump out of the window of the 3rd floor which is at Dienstgebäude Prinz Albrechtstrasse 8, Headquarters of Berlin Gestapo. He landed on the pavement and died instantly. Blöth is a member of the M School in Moscow and a functionary of Central Germany. He was in the Central Leadership of the M Apparat and was known as such. (A photo of him was enclosed; one when he was alive and one when he died).

resistance and I know worked very closely with Maria Müller. "Emil" sometimes came by car from Berlin and Maria accompanied him on his missions. I remember this happening. This did cause some problems between Maria and her husband as Wilhelm was suspicious of "Emil" with regard to a possible personal relationship with Maria. I have no idea if this relationship did develop, but I thought it prudent to keep out of the situation and not get involved.

"Emil" also asked Herbert Wöhrlin to find out more information concerning the bacterial cultures being made in Germany. From Mühlbach he obtained details concerning four cultures and gave details of their intended destinations.

Paul Stiller, who worked on the ship D "Margaretha" which belonged to the Mathies Shipping Co., took letters over from Herbert Wöhrlin and Elizabeth Fenske to Sweden where he posted the letters to other countries. Elizabeth Fenske went to Amsterdam often with her driver Martha Naujoks with, according to the trial, treasonable information to pass over to a man known as "der Dicke"[141].

When Eduard Beckel, Station Inspector of Altona-Bahrenfeld, was arrested, he was about to visit Elizabeth Fenske at her dwelling, but she had already been arrested. On a body search, they found a crumpled note which Eduard had pushed under his suspender. In this note, Eduard had written[142]

"From the Central Committee of the KPD, Hamburg to Herman Schubert, Moscow. The rail road men ask you to transfer our modest contribution to the heroic Spanish women and children. Despite the terror[143], we stand by our heroic and courageous class brothers and wish them a full victory. We know and sympathize with them each day and hour in the hope that they can defeat the fascist beast.

Long live Red Spain.

From the Railroadmen in Alton and Hamburg".

What a shame that this note never arrived at its destination and now I finally find out more details about another important document. The prosecutor starts reading it out to the court.

[141] According to Berlin Archives, this was Willy Goldberg
[142] Translation of documents from Berlin Archives regarding the trials
[143] Fascism in Germany

"How Is the Situation in Spain"[144]

German workers solidarity with the Spanish People.

… *throughout Germany there is an underground wave of enthusiasm in support of the fight for Spanish freedom, a wave of international solidarity. The German people now build cannons thanks to Göring rather than making butter to eat*[145] *and we now use German poisonous gases and German bombshells to murder the wives, children and the freedom fighters of the Spanish Popular Front. The German people have been forbidden by Hitler, Göring and Göbbels to openly show their feelings of support towards the Spanish freedom fighters but would give them hope for victory which would also mean a heavy defeat for Hitler.*

There is active solidarity within the factories towards the Spanish freedom fighters. It is so strong that again the Gestapo has been assigned to investigate and suppress it. Even Göbbel's press admits this. A few of their articles have been copied for you as follows.

In mid-November, the Nazi press announces "The Gestapo gave orders that about 90 workers of the Adlerwerke in Frankfurt/Main must be dismissed without notice. The police have accused the workers in the car factory of collecting money for the Spanish workers. In the workers suburb of Frankfurt, known as Rödelheim, forty-two workers were arrested for 'carelessly' having their names on a list to collect money for the Spanish workers."

At the beginning of November 1936, the Berlin Correspondent to the Prager Press announced mass arrests at the Siemens factory in Berlin. These people were accused of making lists for collecting money from the workers which would then be sent to the Spanish Popular Front. The correspondent reports of the comments and attitude of the workers with regard to the Spanish question.

The workers say that "The German newspapers and radio have systematically backed the fascist General Franco to the hilt and insulted the official Government of Spain. The German workers however sympathise with the defenders of the Spanish Republic. Very little is said in Germany about the foreign broadcasters who are reporting about the fighting to save Madrid".

---

[144] Translation of documents from Berlin Archives regarding the trials
[145] Göring used the phrase "Guns before butter"

In the Public Relief Office of Ratibor, an exciting incident occurred in the middle of September. A large number of unemployed people whilst waiting in the queue for their unemployment benefit shouted out loud "Long Live the Spanish People's Front. Down with the rebels[146]". An excited discussion developed immediately. The officials called the police who arrested some exhausted workers.

A Ruhr mining industry enterprise had been illegally collecting large amounts of money for Spain from the staff. Seventy three marks had been collected and a representative of the staff had taken the money over the border with a letter which said "transfer the money immediately. It is not much but is given with pleasure in order to help the Spanish workers in their fight. Our staff show great interest for the Spanish fight to keep democracy and nearly everyone, even the SA people when informed about the situation which is happening there, hopes for the victory of the workers and farmers… Likewise the thought of the workers here is that they are not misled by the Germans who are in Spain who are in truth fascist subversive seducers.

An illegal group of trade unionists, who are citizens of Berlin and work for a metal firm, collected from the employees 50 Marks to be used for the Spanish Popular Front. In an accompanying letter, they stated

"We are particularly pleased to immediately make a collection when we discovered that the Government of the Hitler regime undertook an air raid against republican Spain. We have collected money from the public in solidarity of the people".

The workers who have given information on exact data of the extent, time and type of German war supplies sent to the Spanish Rebels [Franco] have provided a lot of practical help. Such information leads us to the knowledge that weapon transport can be stopped and then prevented from continuing the journey. An example of information we have received is shown in the following letter from a Hamburg worker to republican Spain.

"We wish to tell you comrade, our Spanish brothers, that we are supporting you by sending you combat greetings. We are unable to help very much as we always have the Gestapo watching us. However, we can cause some problems for them. Everything that we find out about weapon transport to the fascist in Spain, we will inform to you. Unfortunately we have not sufficient strength to prevent these transportations.

---

[146] Franco's army

Leaving Hamburg docks in the next few days is a cargo ship containing weapons heading for the rebel rouser in Spain[147]. Amongst the cargo are weapons and ammunition for Spain. The machine gun cartridges are not from ammunition factories here, but are direct from the military depot and are as follows:

	Pieces	Tons
From Berlin 100 crates	*2,500*	*17.2*
Furthermore from Berlin	*1,500,000*	*46.5*
From Grüneberg	*500,000*	*15.5*
From Hanover 30 Crates	*2000*	*12.0*
From Magdeburg	*2,000,000*	*60.0*
From Wolfenbüttel	*500,000*	*15.5*

These are only some details. Altogether there were 2334 crates of 109.745 kg. We are not sure of the name of the cargo steamer on which the material will travel, yet we will endeavor to discover this. We can say with fair certainty that it is the "Monte Saraiente" of the Hamburg-Südamerika-Dampfschiffahrtsgeselleschaft [Hamburg South American Steam Shipping Co.]

When the Steamer "Usuramo" left, it took 28 heavy bombers. Three sailors refused to travel on the ship. They were arrested and are now in a fascist prison. Red Front"

I listen enthralled as a mixture of feelings goes through my mind. How wonderful to hear that there are still people out there continuing to work against the fascists. What a relief to think that all is not over, but it is horrific to realize that this weaponry is being provided by Germany for Franco against the Republicans and people such as Rudolf. Is Rudolf all right?

Oh how marvelous so many workers are standing up against Hitler *and* trying to help the democratically elected republican government in Spain. Yes it is incredible to think that despite struggling to fight the Nazis there are many people in Germany who think of others in Spain who are also fighting fascism.

---

[147] Franco

I wonder when this was written. Were those bombers were the ones destined for Guernica? Oh I hope this communiqué actually reached Spain. If only we had sufficient strength to have stopped that shipment leaving Hamburg.

It was Herbert Wöhrlin who had discovered about the steamer "Usuramo" and its contents of 28 heavy bomber planes. He had passed this information on to Elizabeth Fenske who gave it to Maria Müller or vice versa. My head was starting to ache and it is difficult to keep concentrating. The document had been intercepted in Paris so it looks as though it never reached its destination. What another disappointment hearing this news being read out in court. Herbert and I had worked so well together before I had been arrested in November 1933; he's a good man.

They even know about Julius Grönwold who worked on the steamer "Wiedau" and had agreed to take letters to England and also bring back printed material for distribution amongst the working class. The trial continues with one accusation after the other and I realise what a wonderful job everyone has done. These accusations along with many others are announced in court. Some of our activities have now been exposed to the Gestapo but I have no doubt in my mind that the largest part of our work will never be known.

Elizabeth Fenske, I hear, received life imprisonment and Herbert Wöhrlin twelve years with the loss of any civil rights for ten years. I know what these sentences mean. The treatment in these places is harsh to put it mildly.

Now my friend Wolfgang Koglin's trial starts in February. Will it ever end? I seem that I will forever be brought back for questioning.

I manage to have some peace of mind seeing the joy Gretel is getting with her mandolin we gave her for Christmas. We also paid for her to have three months of lessons so it is not long before she is able to play with us – me with my mandolin and Anna with her guitar. Such pleasure for the three of us and I shall treasure these moments for the rest of my life.

As the year ends and 1939 commences, a small statistic is put into the newspapers which is supposed to be good news for the

German people. In 1933 there were six million unemployed, in 1935 one million unemployed and now in 1939 there is a labour shortage. Is everyone so blind that they cannot see that the sole reason for the unemployment is the preparation for war?

As for me, I'm sure that the Gestapo will get me one way or another. Those judges who refused to let the Gestapo put me on trial again are doomed to have a terrible fate and my time will come too. I am sure of it.

CHAPTER 25

Werner from
October 1936 – February 1939

I'm beginning to get very nervous now. My prison sentence is nearly finished which hopefully means being released. I have kept my head down and tried not to cause any trouble – I want to survive. As the day arrives there is no sign of me being released. What is happening? I'm really feeling very edgy and nervous as I have heard how some people are never released but are sent to a concentration camp and an unknown future.

Three days after my date of release[148] I am told to prepare to leave but to my horror I'm taken to Gestapo headquarters. I try hard not to show my fear but I can feel my body shaking from head to foot as memories come flooding back of my last visit there. Will they let me go? The thought of more torture from the Gestapo makes my pores open with sweat. What is going to happen? I know that the reduced sentence the judge gave me is not the only reason why they feel angry, but one of my older brothers evading arrest and one of the others being part of the resistance, so how are they going to deal with this situation now?

It feels as though I'm reliving a nightmare being force marched into a large room in the building of torture. It is empty apart from a table placed at the end right by a window with bars across it. There is only one chair and this is occupied by a man who is

---

[148] On 17th December 1936

reading from a sheet of paper placed on the desk in front of him[149].

"Stand to attention" barked one of the two SS guards who is standing behind me. Every sinew in my body goes into overdrive as I stand as upright as possible.

After what seems an eternity, the Gestapo man sighs and looks up at me with an unpleasant sneer on his face.

"Well Stender, I see that your sentence has been completed. What reason can you give me as to why you feel that now you should be released?" he asks menacingly.

I shudder inwardly. The answer I'm about to give could mean life or death.

"I have had time to reconsider my actions which I took when I was just a youth, sir. I now fully intend to try and become a useful citizen by hopefully going back to the Daimler Benz factory, completing my apprenticeship and earning a wage to support my family." It is so hard trying to avoid speaking the truth about my real feelings of this evil government, but I'm desperate to be released and to try and help my family especially with Rudolf in the Soviet Union and Ernst still in prison.

"Ah your family" he answers thoughtfully and with malice. "Your father seems to have brought up three disobedient and disrespectful sons who seem intent on trying to destroy our country." He pauses

---

[149] Unbeknownst to me, the Oberinspektor (person in charge) had written a letter to the Gestapo on 10th December 1936. He wrote that *"Werner Stender, born in Hamburg has served his sentence in Hahnöfersand Youth Prison. He was sentenced by the High Court to two years and six months prison. He had no previous convictions. Here in prison his behaviour has been excellent. The last one and a half years he has been assigned for duty to distribute food. He did this willingly, is reliable and helpful. Stender at the age of 16 years became involved in radical ideas. The court decided in Stender's favour and that he had become a tool for leaders of unfavourable organisations. I [the Oberinspektor] have the impression at the end of Stender's sentence that he had tried hard with good will to correct his mistakes and that he will behave when he is released."*

I feel in hindsight that this letter saved me from going back to a concentration camp and perhaps to my death. I also have a feeling that this letter was written thanks, once again, to the father-in-law of a cousin of mine, who was a prison warden there.

and just stares at me. I can feel myself starting to involuntarily shake with fear. "However, you have had a good report from the youth prison." He starts drumming his fingers in quick succession and studies my face for any reaction. I try to give him an unemotional blank expression just in case I might offend him.

It must have been a few minutes but felt much longer. The silence is broken by "I will release you *this time*" he emphasises, "but if ever I hear your name mentioned with regard to any illegal activities, I can guarantee you that I will have you back here and the result will not be so good."

I feel like collapsing when I hear him telling me that he is about to release me. Surely he would not be so cruel by bluffing just waiting for me to do something wrong.

"Thank you sir"

He pushes some documents in front of me telling me to sign them. I know that I mustn't spend much time reading them as he will lose his temper and perhaps change his mind about my release. However I glance quickly at the writing and notice that I have been happy with the treatment everywhere I have been imprisoned and that I have not been maltreated in any way. What sane person would refuse to sign these documents? With a shaky hand I sign my name along the dotted lines and to my relief, I'm released.

I walk out of the office trying not to run towards the open front entrance door. It is 15.15 hours. Oh how I want to run but I have to keep myself in complete control. I must not let myself down at the last minute. It is just getting dark, but to my utmost joy, I see the familiar shape of Lotte in the dusk light. We hug each other with such untold pleasure followed by equal tears and laughter. Whilst we are locked in our embrace, I make a detrimental remark about the Nazis and then see the worried look on Lotte's face. She holds me firmly by my shoulders and at her arms length looks straight into my eyes.

"Please Werner, you've only just been released. If someone hears you, you will be back inside in no time and they won't be so forgiving next time."

I know that she is right but my beliefs are the same as before.

My first priority is to support our parents being the only offspring left at home. Also there is my apprenticeship which I need to finish – that is if I have a job to go back to.

We make our way back to Lotte's place. To be honest I'm a little disappointed as I'm so looking forward to seeing Mama and Papa, especially as I haven't seen Papa for two and a half years. As Lotte opens her front door, it all seems very quiet. So Mama and Papa are not here waiting here for me as I'm sure Mama would be hugging me by now. What is wrong? I open the lounge door and the whole room is packed with all my family; a sea of familiar, loving faces all smiling and suddenly bursting into conversation and laughter now that the surprise is over. The only people missing are my two brothers – Ernst still being in prison and Rudolf in the Soviet Union. Käthe, Rudi, Anna and Gretel though are here to help make up for their absence. Oh my goodness – Anna looks so unwell, but I know that she will not want her health discussed at such a time. I will have to find out afterwards about her situation.

Mama on the other hand looks as though a great weight has been lifted as her lovely smile lights up the room. Poor Mama – what a terrible few years she's had to endure seeing two of her sons arrested and another escaping the country in order to survive. Where's Papa? Then I really feel guilty when I see his face at the back of the room. He has aged so much which in truth we all have to take responsibility for. I have been the one he'd hoped would keep out of trouble with the Nazis, being so young, and yet even his youngest cannot be kept safe. I think they all can read my thoughts as I squeeze past everyone and give Papa a hug. He takes out a hanky from his pocket and blows his nose hard, quickly wiping away a tear. In his old fashioned beliefs it is unmanly to show such emotion.

I squeeze his hand acknowledging his feelings; he grunts a few words of greeting which is more than enough for me to know how much he loves me. I smile and in return there's a flicker of a smile on his face. I must spend time with him when we get home as I know he's desperate to be near me, regretting bitterly how he was never able to come and see me in prison. I understand how difficult it has been for him and I need him to know that. As for now, we all are together and it's wonderful to be back with my loved ones. How incredible it feels to be a free man. I have missed such an important stage of growing up as now I am twenty-one years old.

"Lotte, who's the young lad 'helping' Mama?" Lotte smiles at me with absolute pleasure and walks over to the youngster who must have been no older than two or three years. She takes him by the shoulders and leads him over to me.

"Meet our son, Walter." I look at her in disbelief. I have been away, I know but not that long.

"Hans and I decided to adopt when we accepted that we cannot have children. Young Walter here came to live with us earlier this year and we have been lucky enough for Walter to officially become our son."

I had always wondered why Lotte never had children as she always loves being near youngsters, but equally I'm so pleased that she and Hans have done something about it so that she has someone she can call "her son". I bend over and hold out my hand to young Walter.

"How do you do Walter? I am your Uncle Werner. I am very pleased to meet you."

He timidly shakes my hand and when I glance up at Lotte, she has tears in her eyes but a very proud smile on her lips.

★

My parents, forever supportive of me, had been in contact with my old firm Daimler Benz to ask the management there if they are prepared to re-employ me. Apparently the manager and directors then asked all the employees if they would work with me again. Despite what I had done, not one person objected so this is my chance to finish my apprenticeship.

After a very joyous 21st birthday and Christmas celebration, I return to work on 4th January 1937. Considering nationalist sympathies and rhetoric against people like myself, the behaviour of all my working colleagues is marvellous and they all do their best to help me pick up my trade again. It feels wonderful to be able to be a normal free person.

If only the nightmares would stop. Whilst I am awake, I can control my memories but the moment I fall asleep, my brain releases all the fears and scenes I have witnessed these last two and a half years. Without doubt I'm still very shaky after my last few years' experiences.

I keep myself very informed during this time, of the political situation. I know that the outbreak of war will only be a matter of time unless the whole world unites against the aggressive moves of Germany. It is only too clear that the majority of the German people have been taken in by Hitler's propaganda and therefore hope that Hitler's demands will be acceded to. The population seems so easily pleased as unemployment is no longer a problem along with their own personal financial position improving. The dockyard Blohm & Voss works day and night building war ships and war planes. Factories are busy day and night making armaments. Even when at times there are food shortages, Goering just says "Guns are more important than butter".

It is a depressing time for left wing opponents and pacifists. I know that the resistance movement is carrying on with our fight against evil but will the members ever be able to prevent the coming war? After all, the reaction of all the nearby democratic countries concerning the dangerous developments in Germany shows how it suits people in power to 'bury their heads in the sand'. Are they hoping that Hitler will be marching against the Soviet Union as described in his book "Mein Kampf" where he says that "Germany's future lies in the East?" I know that many so called democratic countries consider communism more dangerous than fascism so is this the reason why the other countries are doing nothing? Are they considering it more important for Hitler to destroy Stalinism, therefore resolving the so-called threat of that country? The newspapers have been printing propaganda to the German people into believing that we have to re-arm as our country is encircled by enemy states which will try to destroy our Fatherland.

Despite all of these worries, I know I have to concentrate solely on the final examinations of my apprenticeship. It's a difficult decision for me but I take no further part in so called 'illegal' activities.

Compulsory conscription starts and young people are expected to build Autobahns for the preparation of war and troop movements. Young girls go and help farmers work on the land. As succour for all their efforts, Hitler organises holidays for the workers through the Strength Through Joy Movement. Many people feel that they have never had such a good life as they have now. How can we compete with all this propaganda from the fascists?

When Ernst was arrested in November 1933, just seven months before my arrest, Anna had become very ill with heart trouble. Gretel moved in with my parents whilst I was away and Anna then spent most of the last year of Ernst's imprisonment in hospital. As I grew up I enjoyed being part of a large family so it feels good having her around. Gretel always treats me as her big brother as she is an only child. It was not surprising that Gretel turns to me and I just can't resist this lovely little girl who is my special niece. As there is such a big gap between me and my older siblings, it's lovely to return the love to her acting as 'her big brother'. When together with Gretel her mother and father make an incredibly tight unit so she really misses them. One day, we decide to go for a walk in the Stadtpark. She asks to sit down on one of the benches by some of the beautiful rhododendrons.

"Uncle Werner, I love my Oma and Opa so much, but why am I such a horrid and selfish little girl to them?" she asks.

I put my arm around her as she seems so lonely and upset. She continues "I know that Oma and Opa have no money as they no longer have the shop. Why then am I so selfish and demand a new dress. They explained the difficulties that they cannot afford to buy me one but I was horrible to them. I stamped my foot and shouted I just answer "but why – I want the dress!""

Poor Gretel – she is only ten years old. She has been brought up knowing that her father is doing something very dangerous but didn't know what and she knew that she must never say anything. Her mother she senses is dangerously ill and much as she loves her elderly grandparents the expectation for her always to be good is too much for a little girl. It feels quite natural to me for her to feel angry at not having a normal life.

"Look Gretel, Oma and Opa understand why you get so frustrated. They just want to help you as much as possible. When you see them upset, it's not always you that they are upset with, but they have so many worries of their three "boys".

Gretel looks up in surprise at this.

"Yes" and laugh at her astonishment "Believe it or not your Oma and Opa still count Uncle Rudolf, your father and myself as their "boys" and we always will be. Let's try and work this through and we will all try and help each other".

Gretel gives me a huge hug and we both laugh. I suppose as I am so much younger than my other siblings this makes me the confidant between the adult world and herself. I resolve to make more time to be with her in order to make her feel secure.

Regardless of my inactivity in the resistance movement I keep catching up with the news about my old friends. I discovered that one of Walter Beyer's sisters was arrested last year whilst I was still in prison. She had been sentenced to two year's imprisonment. Shortly after this, Walter and his other sister were arrested and questioned but thankfully after a few days they were released.

In his amusing way Walter Beyer tells me how he had found a job at the Deutche Werft dockyard working on large boats. It doesn't surprise me to hear that he made good friends and a few young ones had similar views to his. I had to smile hearing this as Walter is such a plucky person. Unfortunately after three weeks he was sacked as he was considered politically unreliable. Walter will never change his opinion about fascism.

My "junges Mädchen" as I call Herta who at the tender age of sixteen had been arrested with the rest of us, had received a suspended sentence. Her boyfriend and fellow resistance worker Carl Heinz had also received a suspended prison sentence as he was only seventeen. Despite being aware of the punishment Herta's brother Fritz[150] had received, she still has anti-fascist feelings. I hear that Carl Heinz persuaded her to take part in another resistance movement. He felt

---

[150] Fritz Winzer was arrested in December 1933 and until 1939 he spent his time in Fuhsbüttel Prison and then afterwards until 1945 in Sachsenhausen Concentration Camp when he was finally liberated. He would never give up his views and worked very hard when released to convince the young people that any war meant terrible casualties.

that everyone could be trusted within the group. They called themselves the "Versohnler" and the group had young communists, social democrats, liberals and some Jewish members. They held study groups, read banned books and decided to build up a strong resistance group. The Gestapo had other ideas as they infiltrated the group and between February and October 1936 everyone had been arrested.

It's such a shock when Herta's parents tell me this information when I call round to see them one evening. Her mother is in tears as she speaks to me and I feel that apart from trying to give words of sympathy, I can do little to comfort them. Until we can finally defeat these Nazis and stop them from taking our wonderful country into oblivion, we shall have no alternative but to try our best to deter them. This might mean that many of us will perish, but what else can we do? I am beginning to think that I have been sitting around for too long not helping my friends.

"I couldn't stop crying when the Gestapo came. My poor little girl has been arrested once again. They found an illegal newspaper in Herta's pocket. Now both my children are in captivity. What will become of them?"

I honestly didn't know how to answer Frau Winzer. As both Herta and Carl Heinz had received suspended prison sentences when we were originally arrested with us, they would now have to serve those sentences along with any additional punishment.

In May 1937 I hear the news that Carl Heinz has been sentenced to five years imprisonment and Herta two and a half years plus the suspended sentence which makes it three years in total.[151]

In the spring, I met a friend in the Geibelstrasse. He is wearing an Air Force uniform as he has been conscripted in the Condor Squadron. He came to ask me what he should do. I knew that I had to be careful, but all the same, I tell him of the situation in Spain. It is up to his conscience but I remind him that the people he would be bombing were fighting fascism and for the freedom of Spain.

It breaks my heart listening about the Spanish Civil War. We have

---

[151] After her sentence was finished, Herta was sent to Fuhlsbüttel and put with criminals so she had a tough time. Eventually after they were both released, Carl Heinz and Herta married.

been listening on the Moscow Radio whilst we visit a friend at their flat. It seems that the fascists are trying to defeat the democratically elected republican government. Hitler is just using this civil war to practise ready for his expansionist aims and yet this danger does not seem to be recognised by western governments.

Georg Kehnscherper who used to be in my original resistance group approaches me one day. He is concerned that his younger brother has volunteered for the Condor Legion. It is so difficult when family members of our friends have such beliefs, but apart from very carefully trying to educate them as to Hitler's intentions, there is nothing else we can do. Even then, we are risking our lives as they could report our anti-fascist views to the authorities. It's strange that in one family, the father is in prison due to belonging to the Rote Hilfe, Georg joined our initial resistance group and yet the younger sibling is joining the Condor Legion. This is not the only family having these contradictions in belief.

The Moscow radio station is very useful to us as it is the only verbal source of information to update us about world events other than the Nazi propaganda. The broadcast is in German and I know that many German exiles from Nazi oppression have escaped to the Soviet Union, just as Rudolf did. We are desperate to know what is really going on in the outside world.

Anna has come home from hospital for a little while, so we have high hopes that her health is improving and of course young Gretel is ecstatic with pleasure. One day Anna decides that she is well enough to visit my parents as she is so close to them. When I finish my day's work, I offer to walk Anna and Gretel home. Just as we arrive at the apartment, Anna starts to have severe chest pains. I cannot believe that this is happening. Gretel is distraught seeing her mother in such a state but I manage to calm her down and instruct Gretel to run to the doctors to get help. I stay with Anna to try and keep her stable but once again Anna is rushed to hospital. I am beginning to doubt if she will survive this awful situation of a weak heart and with the strain of Ernst being in prison, his life always being in the balance of life or death. Will he ever be released or is his future to be another Concentration Camp or even worse?

The day of Ernst's release from prison finally arrives. On 8th May 1937, Lotte and I wait anxiously in the pouring rain near the Gestapo headquarters. Will he be released and finally a free man? Eventually at 16.05 hrs we see him leaving the building. After three and a half years of imprisonment, it is difficult to recognise him as his hair is grey. He looks like an old man although he is still only 36 years old. Imprisonment has taken its toll. His face shows the strain he must have been enduring. I have seen that look so many times before whilst I was in Fuhlsbüttel and having experienced perhaps only a little of the treatment Ernst must have had, I can empathise with him.

We walk to the Alster and board a canal boat from the Rebenstrasse boat station and head towards Muhlenkamp. Ernst is very quiet but looks at the beautiful scenery. Hamburg is such a stunning city, but it is marred at the moment being ravished by evil. As we disembark at Muhlenkamp, Ernst turns, looks me straight in the eyes and asks "Where is Anna, is she all right?"

What can we say to him? Anna is the love of his life, along with his daughter and yet Anna is dangerously ill. Lotte and I find the next conversation so difficult to update him with the terrible news. He is completely silent as we walk together along Gertigstrasse arm in arm but lost in our own sad thoughts.

I am so worried about him. On 27th May Mama and Papa tell me the bad news that Ernst had been taken to Berlin for some reason or another. The treatment I had received was bad, but I know that Ernst had been through a far worse experience than me. He needs to talk to someone and he obviously cannot speak to his very ill wife or his young daughter so when he returns from Berlin, I call round to see him one evening after work. If only Rudolf was here. They were so close and I have the feeling that their work in the resistance had been interlinked. We never have spoken about our work for fear of being tortured at a later date by the Gestapo. We would never risk betraying anyone if we could help it. I'm shocked though when I walk into his flat as his hair is now white. Whatever has happened to him in Berlin?

Gretel opens the front door to let me in and gives me a huge hug as usual. Ernst is sitting down, quietly reading a book. He looks pleased to see me. The evenings and nights must be the worst for him when he has time to think about what has happened during those days when he had been so badly tortured. I can sympathise as I have nightmares of my time of being 'questioned'.

"How are you Werner? I'm so pleased to hear that you have finished your exams and that you hopefully have managed to finish your apprenticeship".

I sit opposite him and stretch out my legs. It is so nice that he is home.

"As you know I was very lucky when I was released as all the workers in the factory said they had no objection to working with me. I'm just so grateful that the employers agreed to take me on again. Mind you, I have Mama and Papa to thank for all their efforts to get me re-employed. Now I just hope that I pass my exams".

"I think it is your character which has made it possible for your return there. You always seem to get on with people and you have also worked hard. I'm sure you will have good news soon about your exam".

He smiles encouragingly, but those blue eyes of his look as though they have seen things no man should see.

"Ernst, I know that I can't have experienced the same evil things as you, but I do understand to a certain extent how you must be feeling now. I'm not the young Werner from 1933. I've done a lot of growing up and seen a lot too. I know that you can't talk to our parents about your imprisonment, but if you want to talk to me, then I am here for you".

"I know that Werner. I have also seen your eyes and behaviour since I have been home. You are right, you are no longer our little Werner. The last few years have been indescribable for all of us."

Ernst interrupts himself as he tells Gretel that she really ought to prepare for bed. Gretel looks crestfallen but I know would hate to upset her father. She gives a little sigh and gives both of us a kiss, wishes us goodnight and then leaves the room.

He continues "Sometimes I wonder what we have achieved as Hitler is still in power and we can't seem to motivate the general public in understanding the horrors to come if fascism continues. In the meantime, look what the Nazis have done to our family and friends. I know that we are nothing in the "bigger picture", but so many people have already suffered and too many have died."

He is right but it is depressing to hear that from him. We talk for hours that evening. It must have been a great weight off Ernst's mind to do this. Neither of us discusses our resistance work; that we would never do. I can't believe how terrible his interrogations have been. How can people be so cruel?

"There is some news I have for you Werner. During one of my 'grilling' I was told that they believed that Rudolf is now fighting in Spain".

"Spain? How did he get there? I wonder if he is fighting in the International Brigade." I exclaim incredulously.

"That's quite possible knowing our brother" he replies.

"If that is the case, he might have been protecting Madrid and I hear terrible tales about the conditions they are in. It makes my blood boil thinking of acquaintances who signed up for Hitler's Condor Legion. They must have been bombing, killing and maiming the people of Spain, the republican army and the International Brigade. I shall continue to ask the new recruits of this legion to think seriously about their conscience".

"Be careful Werner" warns Ernst. "We believe in the same thing and I know that you speak tactfully but don't take risks. If you are back in the resistance it is better to keep your thoughts to yourself so that you can do more useful work".

"Lotte has also told me something else about Rudolf but please keep this quiet" adds Ernst. I nod and wait in apprehension but also excitement.

"Apparently whilst you and I were in prison, the Gestapo turned up once again at our parent's home looking for Rudolf. It was back in early 1935. They said that Rudolf had used explosives and tried to harm the Untersuchungrichter bei dem Landgericht, Berlin[152]. Apparently Rudolf's name is on a list as a citizen of Berlin. I've got no idea if he has access to return to Germany from the Soviet Union to do this resistance work against the Nazis".

---

[152] Judge at the Court of Justice in Berlin

This totally shocks and surprises me as I have always thought that Rudolf at long last has been safe from our enemies; on reflection, perhaps he hasn't been accepting a quiet life. Who knows if it is true and also the circumstances surrounding the case. He would never do anything without a just reason. We chat for about another hour talking about this and other memories of our much loved and missed brother.

In June 1937 Helmuth Prosche[153] approaches me. I know him well as during 1933/34 he had been responsible for the finance of the youth organisation for the whole of Hamburg. He tells me that his contact in the resistance had been arrested and as a result Helmuth is now in danger and has to leave Germany.

"Werner I know how trustworthy and reliable you have been with organising your group in earlier times. I also appreciate that if you become involved again, should you ever be caught, your life will be at risk. We do need you though as so many people have either been arrested, whilst others have had to leave the country as I am about to do through no choice of our own. Will you please consider taking over my position as I know that you are capable and experienced."

Can I honestly live with myself ignoring the situation of the fascist dictatorship control of our previously democratic country? I really am torn by a dreadful guilty conscience knowing the effect on my poor parents should I be arrested by the Gestapo. Mama and Papa have been through so much and it is very possible that three of their sons might die fighting fascism. As I had already been told by the Gestapo in 1934, it is now within the law to execute resistance workers. I'm acutely aware this time of the dangers involved, if caught. My experiences are mild compared to the treatment Ernst received from the Gestapo and his imprisonment in the concentration camp. Some people have not survived their 'questioning'. I've finally finished my apprenticeship which is wonderful news but perhaps I should now concentrate on other things.

---

[153] Helmuth Prosche escaped to Denmark, fought in Spain in the International Brigade, imprisoned in Camp Vernet, France, handed back to Germany 1941 and murdered in 1945 whilst at Sachsenhausen Concentration Camp

If I replace Helmuth, I will really have to be careful as the Gestapo have previously infiltrated the movement from the top and rarely the other way around. Another way of destroying a network is the Gestapo placing an arrested person who they know has a prearranged meeting with another resistance member and surround the area in the hope of catching the next person in the movement. One prisoner was known to jump in front of a tram rather than betray a comrade. Another such ambush was a friend of Walter Beyer but he managed to jump into the river in Berlin when he spotted his contact arriving, thus saving the other person's life. After sleepless nights, I finally make up my mind to return to the resistance and to my destiny whatever that may be.

I have no idea of most of my new contact's real names or where they live. Having experienced Gestapo interrogations, I realise it's vital we operate in such a way. I do make one exception though with asking Siegfried Ortleff to join me. No-one else knows he is involved with me so hopefully he will not be arrested should the rest of us be detained. We became good friends whilst we were imprisoned in Hahnöfersand youth prison. We had both ended up working in the kitchen. Although we come from different political organisations, we had learnt that it was more important to stand together and fight fascism whatever our political beliefs. This is something perhaps many of us should have done in the earlier days. That way we might have stood a better chance of defeating fascism.

My best friend, Werner Etter has also taken up resistance work again, and he has kept to his decision not to work with any close friends. It upset him so much when we were all arrested by the Gestapo. I can certainly understand his decision and am relieved he feels happier now he works with acquaintances.

My resistance work will become far more involved and dangerous. I am no longer a youngster and the strength of our opponents is obvious to us. Before Helmuth Prosche leaves he gives me full instructions of how the "cell" operates. Our main task is to inform our contacts in Denmark about the detailed war preparation which is taking place in our factories and other premises. Helmuth tells me how to compose a letter and I have to use the name 'Reichstag' in the correspondence so that our contacts in Denmark can decipher the information and recognise the source is safe. Special chemicals have to be obtained from the chemists and these are used to write information invisibly on writing paper. It's a very clever way of sending secret information, having written the words in-between lines of ordinary writing. It's also extremely difficult to use the system but this where Siefried shows his remarkable abilities. We work together coding the 'Reichstag' cipher into the information and he writes very neatly the new letters in the special ink. When it is impossible to see what you are writing and it does not make sense without the code, it's such a complicated task but he's brilliant at it.

I have many friends and contacts with people who are working in various factories such as Blohm & Voss. I never ask anyone to betray secrets, but I make sure that I am around these friends when they are relaxing and talking amongst other employees. A friend I work with in the Daimler Benz factory does not belong to our organisation, but he agrees to receive correspondence from Denmark and therefore has become the safe postal address between Denmark and ourselves. This is a very brave move, as should he be arrested by the Gestapo, he would be in as much trouble as us.

Of course we still print illegal material and distribute papers plus we encourage sabotage to take place in the factories. This to a certain degree is successful.

With Siegfried doing most of the writing, and my organisational skills we seem to be fairly well organised. I know that the rank and file of our organisation are all right but I hear that arrests are starting from the top of the leadership and even include some people who return from Czechoslovakia or Denmark. It is a very worrying time. We must not let the fascists infiltrate us otherwise we will be finished, but the Gestapo seem to know who is returning to Germany from Denmark before they had even left Denmark. We are becoming so nervous about any contact with people returning from Denmark or Czechoslovakia that we decide we should not have any more contact with them. After this, we find for a short while that things improve. Why though do I never receive a reply from Denmark?

"What do you think has happened to our contact with Denmark?" I ask Siegfried one day at one of our prearranged meetings. "I am really getting worried now that we never have feedback or instructions from Denmark. I have a nasty feeling that the Gestapo are getting hold of our letters. Perhaps they are preparing to make a swoop on our group"[154].

"I have the same feeling" agrees Siegfried, "but how can we be sure that we might be betrayed?"

"I know someone who was in my original group in the early days and had only received a short term of imprisonment. She is very reliable but decided not to become involved in any further resistance work. I hear that she is going for a "Strength through Joy" holiday to Norway through her firm. I think that I will ask her if she will help us by taking a letter and posting it in Norway."

"Brilliant idea Werner" agrees Siegfried.

I meet Elizabeth Eberhardt the following day and ask her if she has five minutes to take a walk in the Stadtpark with me as I have a favour to ask. We had been good friends in the past and she knows that this request will probably involve something dangerous. She answers that she is meeting someone in half an hour, but as it is such a lovely day, a walk in the Stadtpark sounds a wonderful idea.

We chat idly as we wander into the park. Once out of general ear shot I explain to her what I would like her to do. She knows the risk, but she smiles and answers "of course I will Werner, but let's hope nothing goes wrong as I will be marrying my fiancé shortly – I hope".

I write a letter with the usual gap between the lines and then in invisible ink write in code explaining the situation we are in. She takes the letter with her to Norway and I sit and wait for a response from Denmark.

Siegfried and I are really very concerned now so we decide to take a trip up to Flemsburg, which is right by the Danish border. Siegfried has contacts there that are in his organisation and have been useful in getting people illegally over to Denmark. I mention to Walter Beyer that we need to go to Flensburg and instantly without asking why, he offers to take me on the back of his motor bike. He is always a good loyal friend and he asks one of his comrades to take Siegfried.

---

[154] *If you are able to understand German I recommend that you read page 70 of Skandinavisiche Erfahrungen erwünscht?: Nachexil und Remigration* by Michael F Scholz

When we arrive at the ex-social democrat pub, Siegfried enters alone to find his contact. After about ten minutes he reappears alone, climbs onto the bike and suggests we leave. After we have driven for five or ten minutes he asks his driver to stop.

"My contact says he's no longer getting people across the border. It is too dangerous. He has not suggested any other contact so it does not look good if we need to escape" he tells me.

My heart sinks at this piece of news as I certainly have no-one to help us. Let us hope it will not be necessary to leave the country in a hurry. I then have a contact meeting with Schmidt[155] who Helmuth Prosche had introduced me to before he escaped. Schmidt is Helmuth's girlfriend's brother and an emergency contact for me. I get off my bike at Hamburgerstrasse, Barmbek on my way home from work and stop to talk to him. I'm totally shocked when he tells me that I am not to go home anymore and that he has arranged for me to go into a 'safe house'. The Gestapo have started arresting the group. I almost don't hear him continue to speak as panic and realisation hits me of the consequence of this news but he says something about the fact that there is too much at stake and the organisation has to be safeguarded.

My world finally crashes down around me. If I am caught by the Gestapo, my life will be over. I have to escape and leave everything and everyone I have ever known. I can't even say goodbye to my parents and let them know that I have to leave. They won't know if I am dead or alive.

My poor parents – what have we done to them? They have seen me struggle to adulthood with all my illnesses, watched Ernst and I being taken for 'questioning' by the Gestapo and seen all three of us at different stages of our lives sentenced and imprisoned for our fight against fascism. As a result of our beliefs, Mama and Papa have been punished by having their shop boycotted with SS standing guard to discourage customers, seen Rudolf escape for his life and now I am about to do the same thing.

I have no choice though. I just hope that I can escape the country and let them know that I am safe. Ernst is taken in for more

---

[155] I think it was his name

questioning so are they thinking he knows more? He really needs to escape this country but he is determined to stay. What a terrible predicament as he will not leave poor Anna as she is so ill and anyway what would happen to Gretel? Oh I wish he would come with me.

I am sure that Lotte will be able to continue supporting our parents and Ernst with his family. What a treasure she is – my beautiful loving sister. I pull myself together and try to concentrate on my situation.

It is amazing how efficient the network is which has been set up to help people who have to go into hiding. I have never known who or where they are until now; such is the secrecy needed to avoid betrayal. It's so easy to criticise people for betraying others under torture, but I fully understand the pain, fear and mental torment the Gestapo puts any poor soul through who has been captured. The only way to avoid 'safe houses' being exposed is by keeping the knowledge about them to as few people as possible.

I'm therefore amazed to find that my 'safe house' is the home of one of Walter Beyer's sisters. I'm sure that even Walter does not know that Elly Hackemesser[156] has decided to risk her life in taking on this task. Yet again, proof of the Beyer family's commitment to our cause.

---

[156] Walter Beyer was a wonderful comrade and he comes from a very brave family. Elly's husband was in the German Army during the War and was captured by the Russians. After a long imprisonment, he was finally released and returned to Germany. I cannot be 100% sure which of the sister's helped me and I only told Walter of his sister's activities in our 80s and so it was too late to confirm that it was her and not one of the other sisters. Another of Walter Beyer's brothers-in-law "Arthur" had twice succeeded in evading the Gestapo but was captured in Czechoslovakia and died after brutal torture and questioning in a Gestapo prison in Brandenburg. Another sister Hertha Michel had been arrested and spent some time in prison. Martha then had to leave Hamburg immediately to avoid arrest by the Gestapo. She was married to Robert Dassau aka "Munki", Ernst's courier. Munki went to Russia and then Denmark to carry on with resistance work. He was eventually arrested when the Nazis invaded Denmark. After the war he returned to Denmark where he lived out his days with his son, Sven and Sven's mother.

"You know that Walter does not even know that my home is used as a safe house," confirming my thoughts as she gives me something to eat and drink. "The least we know of each other's activities the safer it is for all of us".

I nod in agreement. There are so many people risking their lives and yet we are still not able to overthrow the tyrant. Why is it that other countries are not concerned about the increased threat of yet another war I ask myself? Surely our allies in Britain wouldn't be keeping quiet hoping that Hitler would carry out his intentions he wrote in "Mein Kampfe"? He had stated that Germany's future lies to the east. If that were to happen then the communist government of U.S.S.R. would be threatened without the west lifting a finger. I shudder at such a cynical thought as if it was reality. These European countries must be naïve to think that Hitler would stop with victory of the U.S.S.R. He wants world domination.

Walter's sister knows only too well how worried I am about my parents so she kindly takes a risk and makes arrangements to inform them that I had to leave but I am safe. It's awful being unable to ever go home again; who knows where I will be sent and if it is possible for me to escape. I start going back over the last few weeks to work out how our group had been discovered. There must have been 'a rotten apple' somewhere connected with Denmark. I had not been aware of anyone being 'questioned' from our group.

Alfred Drögemüller, who had been remotely involved in the earlier youth resistance group, had managed to escape capture and I think is a member of the resistance in Denmark. Had he seen my last letter which I had sent with Elizabeth to Norway? Had he realised that it was me who had sent it? Perhaps he feared that there must be a traitor in the link between Denmark and Hamburg. Had he managed to contact Schmidt in order to warn me of the danger I was in? Who had arranged my 'safe house'?

So many questions and no answers, but I shall always be grateful for my friends who are trying to help me escape. I will have to leave everything behind and as for my future – what will my prospects be; a different country? Where? Will I be able to understand anyone as I never have had the need to speak any other languages – until now!

I also have nothing apart from the clothes I have been given. I decide to take a risk and visit my brother Hans who lives in St George. I think he has no connections to the resistance, so it might be safer to see him. Before knocking on his front door, I spend a little while casually walking down his street, always ready to quickly divert into a doorway or disappear down a street should I feel that his place is being watched. Eventually I pluck up courage and tap the door making my usual 'rat a tat tat' noise. Hans opens the door having recognised my 'signature' knocks.

He glances behind me to see if anyone has noticed my arrival and pulls me inside, shutting the door quickly behind me. He gives me a hug which is quite unusual.

"Hans, I'm sorry to cause you any concern and I do not want your safety put at risk, but I have to leave Hamburg. I have no money as I cannot go home and I had nothing on me at the time when I was told to go into hiding".

Hans and I were never really very close, but to my great relief, he gives me some money. He tells me that Lotte had been to see my close friend Werner Etter as he and some other of my friends had also collected a small amount of money to help me when they guessed what had happened. It brings a lump in my throat realising how lucky I am to have such good friends and family. Hans gives me some money and I suggest a way that my friends' money can be passed over to me and leave as quickly as I can. I do not want any more of my family to suffer because of me.

Even though I am the only one who knows Siegfried is involved in the resistance, he decides that it isn't safe for him to stay. The Gestapo might just guess that he is connected with me as we were friends in Hahnöfersand. He manages to get word through to me via my family about his decision. In a way, I am pleased as I won't have to face the unknown alone. I make a very quick visit to say goodbye to Ernst but he is not there. Anna though gives me a hug and such encouragement that I am doing the right thing in going. Oh if only Ernst would come with me.[157]

---

[157] Is this during one of Ernst's arrests? Neither Anna nor Ernst told us how many times he had been arrested. Even poor Gretel kept quiet so as not to worry us.

After a few days, we are told that it has been cleared for us to leave Hamburg. Schmidt who had warned me about my imminent arrest knows he is at risk now so he is also going to try to cross the border with us into Denmark. We go by train to Flemsburg which is on the Danish border. We all look tense but I hope that we do not show this to others who do not know us. It has been arranged for us to meet up with a contact resistance worker who hopefully will get us over the border. We wait and wait, but he does not appear. After a while, as we have the name of a person we could approach if there is a problem, we decide to risk this visit. Our worst nightmares start unfolding as we discover that arrests have started to take place around Flemsburg. Is our whole network now at risk?

Schmidt has a passport so he decides to take a chance to cross the border by himself. I am beginning to have nagging doubts about Helmuth's girlfriend who is also Schmidt's sister; could she be the suspicious link in the chain? I'm in too dangerous a situation myself to start investigating further but this all makes me very wary.[158]

I am running out of money again, so we decide that it is not a good idea to stay in an area where we were strangers and are therefore looked at with suspicion. We feel safer in Hamburg. When I see a telephone box I telephone Hans at work. He gives me the address of a tobacco wholesaler (who my parents know and trust) who lives in Schleswig-Holstein. He had helped Rudolf, I know, when Rudolf had to escape. This man will be forever in my debt as he helps us out and we manage to get back to Hamburg. I return to my 'safe house' and start to think about our next move.

Siegfried and I decide that we should try to escape south through Germany and try to enter Czechoslovakia where perhaps we might have a chance of survival. By this time, my best friend Werner Etter has been told that he must leave as well. He has a chance to survive

---

[158] This lady left Hamburg at a later date. Schmidt decided to join the International Brigade and was questioned by Rudolf upon arrival in Spain. He told Rudolf to warn me not to have any contact with the sister as she was mixing with "bad company". She had been the girlfriend of Helmuth Prosche just before he had escaped to Denmark when his contacts were being arrested so it does all seem highly suspicious but these are my private thoughts.

and together we could make a new life in a new country. Lotte's husband, Hans through contacts brings me a bike from my parents and he also manages to bring me a pair of SS trousers and Nazi boots. I smile when I remember that these were legally bought by me when I was affiliated to the Hitler Youth in order to infiltrate the Sports Club and now they are to be used for my escape!

The day comes when the three of us are to meet and make another attempt escaping from Germany. Siegfried turns up but no Werner Etter. Siegfried breaks it gently to me that he had heard from one of our friends that when Werner's mother had discovered that her son intended to leave Hamburg she made such a scene and begged him not to go. I'm devastated but I can't do anything about it – I have to leave my best friend behind[159].

We start peddling down the streets in a southerly direction. "We've only been out of prison for ten months Siegfried" I puff.

"I know Werner, but at least we did everything we could to fight this evil government. Perhaps our time will come in Czechoslovakia IF we make it there. We will just have to hope that we don't get stopped en-route as all we have are our identity papers." I can feel him looking in my direction so I quickly glance at him. He smiles at me. "Mind you, with your outfit, perhaps they will just look at us thinking that we are "off duty" he exclaimed. "Your blond hair and blue eyes shows the world your Aryan purity" he adds sarcastically.

We laugh together trying to hide our apprehension. I know that I have the colouring of the Aryan race which Hitler is so proud to promote although he is the complete opposite in his own looks.

"I wonder if he looks at himself in the mirror or does he have sight problems!" I reply. We laugh again.

It is late October, so it is not hot weather which is all good news with all the physical exertion we are doing cycling such a distance. We have no change of clothes so it will be difficult to explain if we are stopped, as to why we are travelling such a distance from

---

[159] Werner Etter decided not to leave his mother who was a widow. He continued to fight in the resistance but was eventually arrested and beheaded by the Nazis. Such a terrible tragedy which still upsets me to this day

Hamburg on holiday without any other clothing. The first night is a very cold and damp experience as we have to sleep in the countryside. We decide that it is better not risk looking for any overnight accommodation as we could be reported.

We have a small amount of money for a train journey, so we decide to buy a ticket to Dresden. We sit in the carriage of the train, trying to look as relaxed as possible and hope that our hygiene is reasonable having only been able to wash in a pond earlier in the day. What a difference that train journey makes though. With a bit of luck we might get to the border before nightfall.

The train pulls into Dresden station, and we disembark, making our way to the goods compartment to collect our bikes. As we queue at the gates to show our tickets, we keep a low profile as we do not want to draw any attention to ourselves. We succeed to mingle with the crowd and as soon as we are outside, we start cycling south east using our compass. We begin to breathe more easily as we leave the city.

Having lived all my life in the north of Germany, I cannot believe seeing the hills and later the mountains which appear before me. How exquisite and absolutely totally breathtaking the countryside is. However it is not ideal for people using bicycles especially two people desperate to escape Germany for the safety of Czechoslovakia. I hadn't realised how difficult the cycling would be!

"I hear that this part of our country is called Sächsische Schweiz[160]" puffed Siegfried as we struggle up one of the inclines.

We are absolutely exhausted as we approach the Erzgebirge Mountains. I had seen photos of mountains, but this is my first experience of them. The roads are steep and although our bikes are not very old, cycling up mountain passes is certainly not easy.

"It's no good Siegfried; I'm giving up and going to walk up these inclines".

"I'm glad you are admitting the difficulty" laughs Siegfried as he gladly hops off his bike.

"We mustn't get too complacent though" I add. "We've travelled all these miles and have not been stopped even once and questioned.

[160] Saxon Switzerland

I'm sure these border roads must be checked by Nazi patrols but I've got no idea where the actual border is now. Have you? Our compass and map is not much help with all these thick woods and winding steep roads"

In actual fact I am really scared stiff that around one of these corners a vehicle full of Nazis will be travelling or even a foot patrol where we might not hear them approaching. We are so close to freedom.

As we come over some mountains and into a valley we notice that there is a footpath to a fast running river but no road bridge. The footpath is in a south easterly direction which is where we need to go. On the other side of the river there looks like a roadway running adjacent to it. I wonder if this could possibly be the border.

Although the weather is chilly and the water absolutely freezing, we carry our bikes across our neck and shoulders and wade across the river. I can't tell you how cold we both feel at this point, but we just have to carry on. It is nearing the end of the day and travelling through this terrain in the dark without torches will be impossible.

We reach a road, but don't actually know where we are but in the distance we see a village. As we approach in that direction a signpost with directions in Czech confirms that we have finally crossed safely into Czechoslovakia. For the moment we are safe but we are too tired at this point to give an excited cheer. All the fear of the last few weeks has left us feeling numb. We continue along the road until we see a public house which has a poster outside advertising the Social Democratic Party (S.P.D) of Czechoslovakia. We stop cycling and look at each other. Poor Siegfried looks exhausted but I can see he's looking with concern at me.

"I think we will have to take a chance and go in. There's a possibility that we might be treated fairly decently if they have S.P.D. beliefs" said Siegfried.

"I agree. We can't just keep cycling and hope that someone will help us. I hope that they will understand German though." I anxiously answer.

We walk in and everyone looks up at us entering the building. Being a village public house, there is no possibility of not being noticed. To our relief, as they are so close to the German border, they all speak German as well as their native tongue. We explain briefly how we are refugees of Nazi oppression and are trying to get to Prague. After these few sentences, they are so helpful and kind to us. They can see how exhausted both mentally and physically we are. First of all, they give us a wonderful meal and then we are offered to stay the night at the pub. I can't tell you how wonderful it feels being warm, dry, well fed, and above all else, safe. We collapse into our beds and are oblivious to everything until the following morning.

We awake to the autumn sun shining through the window. Where am I? Am I about to be arrested? I hear regular breathing of someone in the room. Who is that person? Oh think Werner – where am I? Then the memories of last night flood into my head. We are safe out of the reaches of our enemies. I try stretching but every part of my body aches. The two day journey has taken its toll on me and my poor old knee really is painful. I gently wake Siegfried who initially has the same reaction as me, jumping at my touch and looking at me with fear in his eyes. Recognition of who I am changes his facial expression.

We quickly wash and dress as soon as we smelt the wonderful aroma of coffee coming from downstairs. We are greeted with smiles from the owner of the premises and are presented with the most wonderful breakfast.

"I've been busy whilst you two have been in the land of nod. I've been in touch with an organisation in Prague and they will meet you at the clock face in Prague Station. I will take you to our railway station and pay for your tickets".

"We just can't thank you enough for your kindness" I answer. I'm already feeling a warm glow about Czechoslovakia. He smiles at me and continues tidying up the pub after last night's drinking.

We put our bikes into the goods compartment of the train, saying our farewells to the kind owner of the pub and climb into the passenger compartment, only to be almost completely knocked out with a very strange smell. It seems that the whole train plus passengers are giving off this smell. What on earth is it? We discover very soon that the smell is garlic and not long after eating the same diet as the locals, we do not notice the smell as we end up walking garlic ourselves!

Arriving at our destination, we head for the clock face in the station where we meet some Germans who had been waiting for us. Later that day Siegfried and I went our separate ways as we belong to different organisations. I find this rather disappointing that we are being separated as Siegfried and I have been through a lot together from our imprisonment together to fighting the common enemy as resistance fighters.

We'd overcome this problem of party politics over time when we knew that we must work together in order to succeed. It never mattered what our political beliefs were as fighting fascists was more important. My new friends though in Czechoslovakia are amazed hearing about our co-operation and friendship. They say that it's the first time they've actually seen such a successful liaison between two different political view points and congratulate us. To me it had been an obvious progression of resistance work.

I'm taken to an old factory building in the Strašnice area of Prague. The disused working area of the huge factory is now covered with iron beds with a mattress and blanket on each. In the smaller rooms are bunk beds. There are over one hundred people in this hostel. Privacy for us refugees is non-existent but to me it is a place of safety after all the years of fear and danger in Hamburg. It looks primitive habitation but clean. Just off the dormitory is a large kitchen where some of the refugees have volunteered to prepare all the food. There is a large dining hall which also doubles for meetings once the tables and chairs are cleared away. Everything is well organised and everyone does his or her best to keep it up to standard.

My new friends supply me with different clothing as I certainly could not go about Prague in Nazi boots and trousers anymore! I wash and change my clothes; it's wonderful having fresh clean ones on. I hate untidiness, dirty clothes and unhygienic conditions. It leads to disease and low morale. After I am given something to eat, I'm taken to a small room within the warehouse. There are a few other refugees in the room but it is obvious that they are in charge of the organisation within Czechoslovakia. Naturally they need me to prove my identity as a genuine refugee so for hours and hours I'm thoroughly interrogated. It's however a far more pleasant experience than the 'questioning' I had received by the Gestapo and I fully understand this necessity. The last thing anyone wants here are Gestapo spies.

I know nobody in Czechoslovakia as all my colleagues had escaped via Denmark. Mind you, I count myself lucky that I know enough people who are in other countries and are able to guarantee that I am not a security risk. I give my interrogators my cover name and my code which is "Reichstag". The meeting ends as they now have to contact the organisation in Denmark to discover if I am genuine. As I believe that Rudolf is in the International Brigade in Spain, I give him as a reference as well. His standing in the resistance to fascism is well known and respected.

After a few days, my identity and non-security risk is confirmed and I am accepted into the fold. I still have to face one small problem though as I had crossed the border illegally without any paperwork. This normally means a short time in prison followed by being returned to your own country. The thought fills me with horror but to my great relief, this matter is settled quite quickly as my new friends have a very good relationship with the police. On 27th October, the refugee organisation pays the very small fine of 10 Krona for me, but as I am not given permission to work, the only income I have is a very small allowance from the refugee fund. I have no problem that each time I leave the building and return I would let the people here know. This is a small price to pay for freedom.

Pangs of guilt re-emerge as I write a letter to my parents and Lotte making sure that they know of my safe arrival. I know that the news would then be spread to Werner Etter and our organisation. I sit down and spend a long time composing, scribbling out the phrases and starting again. It has to be written emphasizing and apologising for not letting them know that I was leaving Hamburg and that I had made the decision to fight fascism despite their appeals against me doing so.

My mind wanders back to my home. I wonder how my parents are. They must be worried sick about Rudolf and me. Has Ernst told them that Rudolf was in Spain fighting? They probably thought that he was relatively safe in the Soviet Union. Is Ernst being taken to Gestapo Headquarters or Fuhlsbüttel Concentration Camp to be 'questioned'? If only he would leave Hamburg, but I know he can't as he won't leave Anna and Gretel behind and Anna is too ill to leave with him. Thank goodness Lotte will be there for them.

"Concentrate Werner" I admonish myself.

I finally finish the letter to my parents and Lotte. As I drop the envelope into the post box, I desperately hope that the content of the letter is sufficient to stop the Gestapo seeking revenge on them.

I lie back on my bunk bed in deep thought about my family and my old home but a familiar voice distracts me. I glance in the direction where the conversation is taking place only to see my old acquaintance Gerhard Hinze[161] talking to a friend of his. They too are relaxing on their bunk beds obviously enjoying the knowledge that we are all here, hopefully safe from Nazi spies.

I am genuinely surprised to meet him here in Czechoslovakia. "Hello Gerhard, fancy meeting you here. Did you also have to leave Hamburg?"

The conversation stops as Gerhard's body freezes as he glances nervously in my direction and then his whole demeanour relaxes.

"Well if it isn't young Werner. How are you? Yes I believe that I left before you. I had to go into hiding in March 1933 having got into a slight fracas with some SA thugs at the Altona Schiller Theatre. I don't really have to explain more do I?"

I shake my head and answer "Who hasn't had problems with these Nazis!"

At this we all laugh in agreement.

He continues "I've since been working all over the place joining left wing theatres and spreading "the word" warning of the future if we don't stop fascism. I've even been in the Soviet Union but like many other Germans, had to leave there as well."

---

[161] He changed his name to Gerard Heinz, the actor. He also later became a film star and appeared in many television plays. Ironically he was often given the role of SS officers. He was in the Heroes of Telemark and many other films.

"Oh you didn't see Rudolf my brother on your travels did you as he went there in 1933?"

"You do know that many of us anti-fascists, who emigrated, or rather escaped to the Soviet Union, have changed their identities just in case any spies report back to the Gestapo? If I did see him, it is always better never to admit it. I can tell you though that when we arrived in that Odessa, we were all arrested and questioned for security reasons but many of the anti-fascists were angry at this treatment and banged on their prison doors insisting on seeing people in higher places and their nerves were at breaking point. It was such a disappointment for people having fought and suffered in many ways from the Gestapo. It is a frightening experience to find oneself back in prison."

At this piece of news, I am not sure how I feel. Is Rudolf safe or not?

A few days after my arrival, a meeting of all the refugees takes place in our hall. It is concerning the present deteriorating situation in Germany and what the consequences might be for us and the world. After such a long time being unable to meet others for open discussions, it is such an energising feeling being amongst fellow freedom fighters. I feel re-energised not having the fear that the meeting might be broken up by Nazi thugs. To make the meeting perfect, we end with music and songs of the working class and freedom. My feelings at this point simply overwhelm me and I can't stop tears welling up into my eyes. I try to take great gulps of air to control myself. Four years of oppression and then at long last freedom makes me so emotional.

For the first time in my nearly twenty two years of life, I have freedom. Siegfried and I manage to meet up and explore the wonderful city of Prague. We have very little money but who needs that when we feel safe to walk the small, hilly streets with such beautiful historic buildings and there is nobody wanting to stop and arrest us. It is absolutely sheer bliss. I actually feel young again or to be truthful, my real age.

We stop and watch the River Vltava which runs through the centre of Prague. There are one or two tiny little islands along the river. I can't believe how wonderful the Charles Bridge looks. Later I read old tourist books which I have been given. It had been ordered by Charles IV on 9th July 1357 by a master builder who was just twenty seven years old and had built Prague Cathedral. I ponder on how someone just a bit older than me can build a Cathedral and also this 600 yard long beautiful bridge. From here are the loveliest views of the Castle. I love my home city of Hamburg, but this city is completely different.

To see the Charles Bridge at night is magical as there are lamps shining in-between the two rows of statues which make me feel that I am walking down an avenue of fairy tale figures. These figurines were neither built at the same time as the bridge nor in the same style but the effect of it are absolutely exquisite especially as they appear through the autumn mists.

From the bridge I can see a little Vltava river steamer making its laborious way upstream, hooting a doleful warning as it drops its funnel to pass under a Prague bridge. What an unusual sight as the ferries we use in the Alster and the canals in Hamburg are designed in a different way and although they were constantly going underneath bridges along the canal, they did not need to move their funnels. I could ponder for ages on which are the best parts of Prague but this will never do. I must try and consider what I should do now with my life.

As I walk back into the refugee hall of residence, I'm handed a letter addressed to me. At a quick glance I can see it is the letter I have been desperate to receive as my Mother's handwriting is on the envelope. I open it, my hands trembling in excitement and start reading the contents. Oh thank goodness, she, Papa and Lotte are all well. I then smile to myself as she writes how surprised they are after my sudden disappearance to find that I now live in Czechoslovakia. She obviously has read between the lines as to the real purpose of my letter. Mama always did have her wits about her all the time and that is just as well as poor Papa is struggling mentally now to cope. I continue to read the letter.

Oh no, my cousin Kurt Bittkau had caught typhoid and died. What dreadful news and a complete shock as he was always so fit. I suppose that he caught that terrible illness from the canals. He spent so much of his spare time in his canoe paddling round the miles of wonderful picturesque canals, but it was a risk with the sewage being discharged untreated into the water. Poor Tante Meale, she must be devastated. When I think of the number of times I had swam in the canals, it makes me shudder to think that it could have happened to me.

Later another letter from Mama arrives but this time I notice that the post mark on the envelope is not from Hamburg. She must have made a point of visiting Papa's cousins in the country and posted the letter there. Being miles away from home territory, the local Gestapo would not be aware so correspondence from Mama might not be opened before it reaches me. I have to smile when I read it as she has a forwarding address for Rudolf in the Soviet Union. She writes that there is a professor in Moscow Rudolf knows and this man can be used as my brother's contact address. His name is J Karst, Gorkisterasse 39, Hotel Sojusnaja, Moscow. She had hidden Rudolf's letter away just in case the Hamburg Gestapo should discover it and she is the only one who knows about the contact. How lucky we are to have such a special mother. I decide to write to this professor and he confirms that Rudolf had left the Soviet Union in the latter part of 1936 and is now fighting in the Spanish Civil War. So Ernst had been given correct information from the Gestapo. How did they know? Have they got spies amongst our friends? We must all be careful but I really would love to contact my eldest brother.

Life continues in my new adopted country but I have a wake-up call one day when the leaders of our organisation warn us that the Gestapo are sending agents across the border so it seems nowhere is safe. Our fears that our organisation may have been infiltrated are confirmed. One person, who I met when he first arrived in Prague, could not give a correct password so he was questioned more 'intensively'. He finally admits that he is a Gestapo spy having been accepted amongst genuine refugees. I hear that he has been taken to the Czech police. It proves that we cannot take any risks which would endanger our organisation.

Later more Gestapo agents are discovered. Their photos are taken, and the agents are handed over to the Czech police where they were usually imprisoned as spies. How many more manage to escape detection I will never know, but I am sure that not all are discovered.

It is especially important to be vigilant as our organisation has been working hard to train volunteers to return them to a different area of Germany from where they had originally come. With so many of us having to leave to avoid arrest, it is important to have retrained recruits prepared to carry on the resistance movement. For obvious reasons it is usually too dangerous to return anyone to their same area.

Christmas is approaching and winter is really settling in. Despite it becoming very cold, Prague still manages to look wonderful. I have gradually been making friends with my fellow refugees and life is really beginning to feel good. I have been worrying that I will find it very lonely and difficult living in a different country. Christmas with my family has always been special and now we are miles apart. These last years have never quite been the same since Rudolf is no longer around and then my family were minus Ernst and myself when we were imprisoned.

My fears of loneliness are unfounded as some of the population of Prague decide to adopt a refugee for Christmas and I am one of the lucky ones who have been invited to stay in a Czech house Christmas Day. The family provided me with plenty of food and drink. How wonderful to be amongst a family again and to top all of this I am included to take part in my favourite pastime of singing after our meal. Unfortunately they do not speak German and I cannot speak Czech but they make me feel most welcome. For the first time in my life I have a drink of coffee with rum added to it. I have to say that it is most enjoyable. Later that day, the daughter of the household and her husband join us and to my relief, he can speak German. That evening they invite me back to their house so I will always remember the festivities with great fondness.

After Christmas I have the most wonderful surprise as a letter arrives from Spain. I recognise Rudolf's scrawl on the envelope. His writing has impatience along with an assertive character in the formation of his letter; not at all like Ernst and my neat detailed writing. So now at long last we are able to write to each other and I am able to let my parents know that Rudolf is fine. Rudolf and I can now write as frequently as we are able and he sends me lots of pictures of his friends in the International Brigade. It is so wonderful that this contact is possible and I can be useful as an intermediary between my family in Hamburg and Rudolf in Spain. I still use his pseudonym 'Otto' when giving information to Hamburg. My life is improving with each day and I am beginning to wonder if this country will be my permanent home.

It's February and as I walk along the Vltava, Prague still seems full of life despite the cold. There are floating islands of ice around the bridge piers which are fascinating to watch. A little passage has been cut into the ice for some fishermen to attempt to catch fresh fish. Prague is still so beautiful despite this bitterly cold weather with the snow falling but what is going to happen to us? Will I be of any real use to the organisation?

The snow begins to melt in southern Bohemia and I notice that the water is yellow. Not so pleasant a sight but a sign that spring is just around the corner. I feel restless as I am not used to having time on my hands. Over the winter some of my friends have been helping with duplicating leaflets ready to be distributed in Germany as these are often difficult to produce back in my home country. There was always the fear of a raid on the premises and also we lacked sufficient paper and ink so it is usually done in very small print and on small pieces of paper. I remember being very grateful when documents arrived from abroad. For the German population it is dangerous to listen to oversees programmes on the radio so to get information to the masses, leaflets are the only real alternative.

One day just as I arrive back at our hostel, I'm stopped by one of the leaders of our organisation.

"Ah there you are Werner. I wanted to catch you to see if you can help us. We have a young lady who is willing to become a courier between the resistance movement here and part of the resistance movement in Hamburg. The only problem is that she comes from a wealthy background and has no idea how to speak "low" German. The part of Hamburg she will have connections with is the poorer part and as you can imagine, her German accent is not at all the same as where she will be going. She also does not have the north German accent. Can you teach her the "low" German and let her listen to your Hamburg accent?"

"Of course" I reply. "I will do anything I can to help but I had not realised that I had a strong accent".

My comrade smiles at me so I can only assume that I must have a true northern lilt to my speech.

My pupil is a lovely young lady, in her early twenties and obviously comes from a well-educated background. They were quite right that she would 'stick out like a sore thumb' if she didn't learn to speak in a slightly different way. I start giving her lessons. I never thought that my background of coming from a poor district would be so useful!

I suggest to her that we take advantage of the improved weather whilst educating her about a different Hamburg to the one she might know. The warmth of the sun is finally finding its way through my clothing to my body. Late spring is here and there are bulbs in full bloom, bobbing their heads up and down in the light breeze. I glance up at the castle area and admire the scenery. Once again my mind starts wandering to some of the history I have read about since I have lived here. For a thousand years the most significant events in the life of the Czech people have taken place on this little hill above the Vltava.

My companion laughs at me as she studies my face. "You're back in the past, day dreaming about Prague's history aren't you."

I look sheepishly at her. "I know, but there's just so much history here and I love trying to understand what makes a nation exist. Social history is my passion. Anyway we're nearly at the landing stage for the rowing boats" I reply trying to change the subject.

We pay for the hire of a boat and I start rowing across the river. It brings back memories of rowing along the canals back home except here there is a strong current which makes it much harder. Once offshore and away from prying ears I stop rowing, regain my breath and start talking.

"At last, now we can start practising your "low" German". It is the only place I really feel that we can talk uninterrupted and in safety. I don't want other people to know what we are doing. We both know that security is the utmost importance in case any spies should be around to threaten her future safety as it is obvious that there can only be one reason a cultivated lady would want to learn "low" German. Anyone connected with her would automatically know that she is aiming to return in some clandestine role so a spy within our midst would watch her closely. At present we appear to be a courting couple out for a pleasurable boat excursion.

She is a quick learner of "low" German and is soon ready to start her new destiny[162].

At one of our social gatherings, the refugee committee decide to put on a Shakespeare play, but it is all to be spoken in the Czech language! They want me to take part in the play but it really isn't me at all and I have always hated performing to an audience. Anyway I find the play totally confusing!

I did have another duty whilst in Prague. Some of my fellow refugees from Germany escaped here with their children. These children are between ten to fourteen years old, so I'm assigned to keep 'an eye' on them. At least I feel useful helping the parents but now I'm eager to start work again in the resistance movement. I needed to rest and recover when I first arrived but now it is different. Hitler's propaganda is more forceful than ever for the unification of all German speaking people, thereby creating a greater Germany. We know that this will affect Czechoslovakia with nearly the entire German speaking minority in Sudetenland seeming to support Hitler.

I must look healthier, both mentally and physically as one of our leaders asks if I would be prepared to go and help our Sudeten friends in the struggle against fascism. At last, I am back to being really useful again. I have appreciated the break and fully understand that I needed the time to recover. Being twenty two years old and having been through such terrible experiences as a youth has had an impact on my psyche. Torture, solitary confinement in a concentration camp, being tried for High Treason against the German Reich, imprisonment for two and a half years and then there's the fear. Oh

---

[162] I wonder what happened to her

yes, the fear… I have needed these last few months to recover, but now I am ready to work for the movement again.

I say my farewells to my friends but for the usual security reasons give no information as to where I am going. I really cannot be sure if one of my new 'friends' is a Nazi spy – careless talk etc.

Although Sudetenland has not yet been occupied by the Nazis, the threat of such an event is real. My instructions are to organise the youth ready for an invasion. In Sudetenland I have the advantage over the locals as when I started in the resistance movement my friends and I very quickly had to learn how to organise ourselves without the knowledge of the Nazis. Also still being so young, I can understand the feelings and behaviour of the youth I am training.

We are hindered because the majority of the Sudetenland people are influenced by the Henlein Party (Nazis) and also listening to Hitler's propaganda. As a result especially being a German speaking part of Czechoslovakia, they listen to and believe in Hitler's call of "Ein Reich, Ein Volk, Ein Führer" which means "One Country, One People, One Leader". I really do not know how difficult my task will be.

I embark on a train to my new life and eventually arrive in the little mountain village of Čížkovice on the Czech/Sudetenland border. I'm met by Mr F Wehle who lives at Čížkovice 12 in the village. It is a relief that he welcomes me into his family. He has two sons and a daughter and all are employed at home producing earrings and small novelties made out of Czech glassware. It is an incredibly skilful activity and the articles they make are beautiful. These they sell to a wholesaler in the town of Goblenz.

They really are a wonderful family and make me feel very much at home, despite receiving no money for my lodging. I cannot pay them as I still have no personal money apart from the pocket money from the refugee organisation.

Čížkovice is just outside Sudetenland so it is a vital area of Czechoslovakia to set up the resistance. I spend most days walking into Sudetenland where many different Czech and Sudeten families provide me with meals and this gives me excellent opportunities to network. This often means me leaving the Wehle household early in the morning in order to walk over the mountains to arrive in time for lunch at another household. I shall always appreciate everyone's help as they are so friendly to me even when they did not have much food to spare.

A local traditional behaviour which somewhat disturbs me is observing the different status of women in society. I am not used to womenfolk not eating at the same table and not being able to take part in conversations around the table. I can just imagine what Mama would say if we had tried that in our home at Gertigstrasse 56! Despite this behaviour which is totally alien to me, I soon make many friends and take an active part in the anti-fascist youth movement. Artur Ulbrich and I soon become firm friends even though he is only sixteen years old. His father[163] is the Mayor of Sumburk-Jistebsko and I enjoy eating many meals with this family.

The lies and propaganda Hitler uses where he proclaims the ill treatment given by the Czech people towards Sudeten Germans increases daily and for me it becomes a certainty that sooner or later the region will be annexed by Germany. I work even harder with the resistance groups helping to improve their organisation. Even though they have been having problems with the Henlein people (local Nazis) they had not had the experience of fighting a fascist regime.

At regular intervals, I visit Gablonz. We make it a meeting point for German resistance fighters who are busy organising local people into fighting groups. We have all been active in our own allocated areas but it is good to meet each other in the upstairs room of a local pub. It gives us a chance to update each other with our progress and then discuss future strategy.

Gablonz an der Neisse is the second largest town of the Liberec Region and is known as a mountain resort of the Jizera Mountains. Eighty-six per cent of the inhabitants are Germans and the rest are Czechs, Jews and many other groups. There had been a large decline in the glass and jewellery industry during the 1930s which resulted, in unemployment and hunger. As with the situation in Germany, this has led to great support being given to the Nazi party. It's the same old story of history repeating itself. When will people learn?

---

[163] Herr Ulbrich, the Mayor, was sent to Dachau Concentration Camp as soon as the Nazis occupied Sudetenland.

Even being aware of this state of affairs we really feel quite hopeful that forming an active and militant defence of the Czech Republic against Hitler might work but will we have the support we need from Britain and the rest of Europe? Without outside help, Czechoslovakia will fall.

When I'm recalled to attend a meeting in Prague, I am told that my friend Siegfried has gone to Sweden in order to help reorganise resistance in North Germany now that so many of us have had to escape or have been arrested[164]. I'm asked if I would be prepared to return to Germany with a completely new identity and papers. They need so many volunteer replacements to reform the resistance movement. I know that numerous people have been arrested returning to Germany so new recruits are urgently needed. I am somewhat concerned, considering my observations whilst I have been in Prague, about the infiltration of the Gestapo. Somehow they seem to know about the people who are returning to Germany from Czechoslovakia. I feel that I cannot trust the system.

Despite my suspicions, I give my full agreement although I know it would be so difficult for me if they decide to send me to a different district of Hamburg knowing that I could not make contact with my family and friends. Perhaps I am to be sent elsewhere. Thankfully it all falls through because the situation in Czechoslovakia is becoming more precarious and they need me around the borders of Sudetenland.

It is summer 1938 and the Czech people are called up to defend their country. Defences are built everywhere in the mountains and it seems as if all the Czechoslovakian people finally realise that they are needed to protect their homeland. We hope that France and the U.S.S.R. will abide by their military agreements and come to our aid.

There are now armed clashes daily on the border with German troops. For weeks I dash about the area giving my advice and experience should underground resistance work be needed. More resistance groups are quickly formed. I've also been preparing to stay

---

[164] Unfortunately his return to Germany never materialised. Siegfried stayed in Sweden where he met and married his wife. After the war, Siegfried visited my mother to find out about my whereabouts. He was given my address but unfortunately we lost contact but I believe he moved to Hanover with his wife.

in hiding in some of the Czech family homes as by now I know enough people who would take me in. Trying to remain in Sudetenland would be impossible as there are too many Nazis there and I would not survive for long.

A conference is held in Munich concerning the annexation of the Sudetenland by Germany. It is unbelievable that the politicians of Czechoslovakia have not been invited or consulted. I hear Hitler promises never to go to war with France or Britain if there are no objections to his intentions. France and Britain seem to agree to these terms so they betray this wonderful country by surrendering the Sudetenland to Germany. The majority of the people in this part of Czechoslovakia seem to be taken in by the Nazi propaganda machine and await in quiet anticipation the arrival of German troops.

I have instructions to return to Prague as my organisation is trying to get me out of the country. I am in a quandary as I have so many letters from Rudolf and a photo album which contains pictures of his fellow International Brigade fighters. I am loath to part with such precious personal items. These are the only items I possess which have anything to do with my family apart from some letters from Mama.

I know the British Government do not particularly trust people within the International Brigade and if by some miracle, my organisation manage to get me to England, I do not want anything which might cause me problems in getting a visa. I decide to ask Herr Wehle if he could hide the items for me. He pauses at this request but eventually takes my precious items of my beloved brother. Will these items ever be returned to me I wonder? Perhaps he will hide them for me and one day I can return for them? Oh I do hope that one day I can have them back[165]. I pack my small bag and with a sad heart I say my goodbyes to such good people. I had hoped that perhaps this country would become my new permanent home. I do not find it easy having always to move onto pastures new.

Will anyone come to our aid? Knowing that I shall have to leave all my friends behind is very hard for me. They do not want to live

---

[165] To this day, these items were never recovered, so if anyone knows of the whereabouts of these items, my daughter and I would be eternally grateful to hear from you.

under fascism. I had suffered in Hamburg with the effects of Nazi domination so I know how they are feeling. I talk to them for some time encouraging them to stay behind to carry on the fight. I persuade them to work with the Czech and Slovak resistance workers using sabotage to prevent any further advancement of the troops into their country. This should be easier for them than it had been for us in Germany or even the Sudetenland as the thought of the Czech people losing their land to foreign troops and oppressors is abhorrent to so many of them.

I arrange to meet Artur Ulbrich in Turnau. As we sit having a cup of coffee together, he reminds me of the time when we were at the German youth group singing with powerful voices "Es rosten die starken Machinen" which roughly means "The strong machines are rusting". This brings back poignant memories for both of us. We always find singing a great motivator bringing ourselves together emotionally and that helps with our preparation to fight. Today I have brought a friend with me who will be Artur's new contact after I have left[166].

[166] Later Artur received a note from this person saying "the weather in Prague is not very good" which meant that the meeting was cancelled as the contact had suspicions that something had gone wrong. Artur decided to go all the same but no-one came. That night the Nazis entered Czechoslovakia. Had the contact become a victim of the Nazis? Artur never heard again from him after this cancelled meeting.

Artur Ulbrich was only seventeen when he took up resistance fighting. He wrote to me after the war telling me of his war activities and thanked me for the work I had done to prepare him for this event. He fought bravely both with sabotage and militarily until the end of the war. As Gablonz was only 8 km from the Russian border when the Russian prisoners of war arrived and as forced labour in the factories, he organised along with one Czech and one German comrade "Rote Hilfe" and supplied them with extra food, clothing and medication. In 1943 they started to supply the prisoners with passports and other documents. After arranging for many to escape, they helped the prisoners of war guiding them through the heavily wooded countryside and eventually handing them to his Czech comrades who took care of them. They found out the positions and took active part in destroying different SS formations and their ammunition stores in the area plus their defences etc. Artur Ulbrich eventually became the editor of a German newspaper in Prague (Prager Volkszeitung) until his retirement. He died in 1996.

After our chat, Artur is very quiet looking down, continuously stirring his coffee. I ask him what the problem is. Eventually he answers me.

"This will probably embarrass you Werner, but I shall really miss you with all your explanations of what is happening in Europe. I admire your beliefs in the socialist principles and you have stood up against the dangers and consequences of fascism. I am still only "half a child" but so were you when you started in the resistance group in Hamburg. I have learnt such a lot from you."

I can feel myself blushing at this point. Emotion is something I'm trying to avoid as life here is about to change for the worse. My colleague had been sitting quietly listening but seeing my embarrassment, tries to lighten the atmosphere, looks at me and slaps me on my back.

"Well Werner, it seems that I have a reputation to keep up."

The comment makes me smile and we finish our conversation making sure that everything will be in place when I have left.

To our disgust the German troops along with Polish troops who are allies of Germany also being a semi-fascist State march in and occupy the Polish speaking part of Czechoslovakia. The Hungarians who are also semi-fascist march into their Hungarian speaking part which they claim belongs to them. With the lack of response from the west, the annexing of the Sudetenland takes place and Czechoslovakia loses its defence fortifications which are on the Sudetenland side of the border. The transport system, roads and railways as well as telephone and telegraph systems are also disrupted. It will therefore be impossible to resist any invasion of Czechoslovakia itself. We feel betrayed by the democratic world.

I return to the capital in Prague which in autumn 1938 is the central point of our organisation. Most Jews, Czechs, Germans and anti-Nazis have left Sudetenland for the safer parts of Czechoslovakia. There is a feeling of unease everywhere I go. What will be our fate as we are all sure that it will not be long before the whole of Czechoslovakia will be under the German yoke and there is no country to escape to? We wonder if it will be possible to "disappear" in Prague and carry on the fight alongside our Czech comrades. We are certain that all our friends all over the world are trying to get us out of this dangerous situation but the odds are definitely against us surviving.

I move into an old abandoned factory which has become a large refugee camp. Sometimes in the middle of the night I notice some people quietly packing their few possessions and leave the premises. Perhaps they have decided to go to fight in Spain. I wondered if I should do the same, but I know that I could end up a liability to everyone not being able to bend one of my legs. In a fighting situation, I will be all but useless. That would put more stress on Rudolf as I know he would always worry about me and anyway, it looks as though Franco had all but won the battle for Spain. Many of our refugees are very young and were in youth groups. Some try to escape into Poland through Slovakia and others perhaps do not want to sit here waiting to be captured when the German army arrives. It's awful seeing many others suffering from nerves and frustration with the uncertainty of our future. Will we succeed in escaping the clutches of the Gestapo?

Christmas comes but with little festive spirit showing around our camp. Shortly after the event, the first few refugees are officially able to leave the camp. They each receive Czech passports in order that they are able to fly to France, England or Mexico. It is in our leader's hands as to who is in the greatest danger and has to leave first. This must be a terribly difficult decision for them to make.[167]

---

[167] Unbeknownst to me a Mr Geoffrey Masterman Wilson aged 28 – 30 years of age, who is a barrister-at-law in Chambers at 5 Essex Court, Temple signs a Form of Guarantee for me to come to England for the purpose of taking up residence either temporary or permanent. He signs a document stating that *"I the undersigned, being a householder and declaring myself to be possessed of sufficient means to carry out the necessary financial obligations do hereby unconditionally guarantee to hold myself responsible for their maintenance and upkeep during such time as they may be allowed to reside in this country"*.

This is a signed and witnessed document and Midland Bank confirms Mr Wilson to be respectable and trustworthy on 13th January 1939.

Quote from The Telegraph "A Quaker by upbringing and a protégée of the Labour politician Sir Stafford Cripps, Geoffrey Wilson was committed to the quest for a fairer world, whether in promoting the development of poorer countries or in opposing racial injustice. He became vice-president of the World Bank, chairman of the Race Relations Board and Chairman of Oxfam."

I hear rumours that I might be able to leave Czechoslovakia. This raises my hopes. Is it possible that I have a chance to be sent to a place of safety? I try to keep calm as I cannot stand the thought that I might be rejected.

On 27th January 1939 confirmation is sent to Miss Warriner at the Aleron Hotel, Prague that I have permission to enter Britain as a refugee for a period of twelve months. I cannot believe my luck. I have a chance to survive and start a new life albeit temporary, in Great Britain. Do they know anything about my background?[168]

---

[168] On 1st February a letter was sent from the Refugees from Czechoslovakia Organisation in England to a Mr Devonshire. Here are extracts of the letter. *"On behalf of Mr Frank Brown, I write to send you such information as we have concerning these ten young Social Democrats who are wanted by the Gestapo and who are now in Czechoslovakia… All the Refugee Offices and the Passport Department at the Home Office are overwhelmed with enquiries and the Czechoslovakian Refugee Office is moving its quarters, consequently it was almost miraculous that strings were pulled in London and Prague in time to save the men at all. Only by repeated visits and sometimes long waiting can information be obtained.*

However, I have this morning heard that the passports have been granted (confirming the earlier news that they would be) but that the men will "probably not leave Prague for a week or two." Judging by the experience of other refugees, I know that the "week or two" may run to several weeks, unless the authorities are now moving quicker than they were last month. We are in the very lucky position of being able to house all ten for the first few days after their arrival (whenever that may be) at the Clarion Youth Hostel, Hoddesdon, just outside London. They can travel at a time that suits their hosts.

They are all members of the German or Czech organisation corresponding to the Labour League of Youth. We have notes, in rather odd English about each one. Six have already served terms in prison or concentration camp and had to flee because they continued to oppose Nazi domination.

For each of the ten a guarantor had to be found to sign a promise to be responsible for his maintenance as long as he is in the Country. Of course this burden will actually be shared by branches of the Labour League of Youth and other groups of individual subscribers. As soon as the men arrive and we have some knowledge or their capabilities what they want to do, and how nearly we can suit possibilities to their needs, we shall begin to make plans for their future. Probably it will be emigration as the first certainty. Several may need a short holiday after recent hardships.

More than ten offers of hospitality have come in… You know I expect that no refugee may be employed in such a way as to displace a British worker or fill a place a British worker could take. There can be no acceptance of offers of jobs in the ordinary way… Yours sincerely Miss Margaret Macnamara"

Finally I get the news that my Czech passport is ready and that I have permission to enter Britain. Dare I raise my hopes that I might get away? I say goodbye to my many friends and try to cheer them up saying that I hope that they would follow soon.[169]

At Prague airport, I meet Gerard Heinz again. We chat about his theatre group in Hamburg called "Die Nieter" of which he was leader. It is nice to talk about something light after such a terrible time. However, I notice that his hands are shaking as well as mine. We know that we will be flying over Germany. What will happen if there is an emergency and we had to land there for some reason? Finally our plane ascends into the air and quietly, to myself, I say goodbye to Czechoslovakia. Flying over Germany seems to take forever, but at long last we leave the territory of my birth, childhood and teens and land at Rotterdam airport to refuel. We take off again for our final destination.

I cannot explain my feelings when on 25th February 1939 we descend and land in England, a place I do not really know much about, and a race of people who do not speak my language. However I am aware that they are a free thinking individuals, generally anti-fascist and that someone is brave and kind enough to sponsor me so that I can have a chance of survival. I will never be able to thank the people of Britain enough for giving me this opportunity.

I'm shaking with relief and also uncertainty as I descend the steps of the plane at Croydon airport. For the moment at the age of twenty three years, I am safe. Am I though? A 'storm' is still brewing in Europe and I only have a twelve month visa.

But where is Rudolf now that the war is over in Spain? Is he still alive? Has Ernst been arrested again? Is he safe? Is any one of us safe?

---

[169] Unfortunately many of my friends did not succeed leaving the country. Some went into hiding in homes with Czech friends, but I would hate to say how many were arrested by the Gestapo and lost their lives.

JEHO MANŽELKY
ET DE SA FEMME
Werner Stender
Podpis úředníka vydávajícího cestovní pas
Signature de l'agent délivrant le passeport

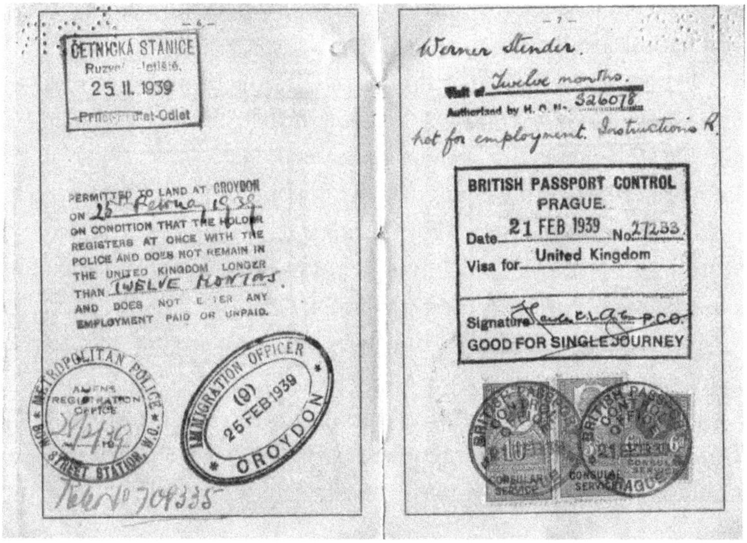
ČETNICKÁ STANICE
25. II. 1939
PERMITTED TO LAND AT CROYDON
ON CONDITION THAT THE HOLDER REGISTERS AT ONCE WITH THE POLICE AND DOES NOT REMAIN IN THE UNITED KINGDOM LONGER
THAN TWELVE MONTHS
AND DOES NOT ENTER ANY EMPLOYMENT PAID OR UNPAID.
METROPOLITAN POLICE
IMMIGRATION OFFICER
(9) 25 FEB 1939
CROYDON
Werner Stender.
Twelve months.
326078
Not for employment. Instructions R.
BRITISH PASSPORT CONTROL
PRAGUE
Date 21 FEB 1939
Visa for United Kingdom
Signature
P.C.O.
GOOD FOR SINGLE JOURNEY

CHAPTER 26

Rudolf from
October 1936 – February 1939

"Spain is not just fighting the nationalists – there has been years of interference from other countries".

Kurt makes this remark as we sit around the kitchen table one evening. I'm much more careful about conversations these last few months, but Spain seems more of a neutral subject which we all agree on so hopefully our conversation will not be reported to higher party members.

"Even the British, with a democratic government seem to put capitalistic ideals first in Spain so have too much influence in the financial status of the country."

I nod in agreement. "Many of Britain's wealthy have had financial investments in Spain and as far as I can see, feel threatened as they seem to think that the new republican government will freeze and nationalise British assets."

Hans became heated at this point. "If only thoughts can be put above personal greed and for the good of the nation as a whole."

We all laugh as this sounds like utopia. Hans looks sheepish. "I know but it makes me angry that any hopes of the republic trying to socially reform the country by educating, providing better health and working conditions for the poor, seem to be considered a threat to the stability of Spain according to the nationalists."

We have to agree with him over that statement. I add to the conversation.

"As it is, Britain is playing right into Hitler's and Mussolini's hands by obstructing the republic's naval defence from refuelling in Gibraltar or Tangier. How on earth can the republic fight the nationalists with such a hindrance?" I utter these words in despair. Why is politics always put higher on the agenda than the rights and freedom of the individual?

Otto joins in "I am amazed that Britain and France won't let the republican government purchase weapons. Once again, it seems that democracies are more frightened of communism than fascism".

I can understand his frustration.

"The wealthy seem to have more power, influence and even control on these so called democratic countries" adds Walter.

It always has been that way and somehow I think it will never change.

"I really must try to leave here and help our Spanish Republican friends" I add, my fist crashing on the table making all the articles on it jump up in the air. We all look at each other at this point and laugh at the disarray I have caused. Our conversations always are very serious and the vodka flows freely but now I keep my head not to say something which might be reported. Will I ever be able to leave this country and follow my beliefs I wonder. It seems that there's some underlying politics being played out at the moment. Some people in the Soviet Union are beginning to insinuate that there is a fifth column ready to infiltrate and destroy the established communist state and mistakenly are including us as part of the column. We had come for sanctuary after having escaped from fascist persecution. How wrong can they be!

So many of my friends have joined the newly formed International Brigade and have already left the Soviet Union. The idea of an International Brigade was first mooted last month in my adopted country. Yet here I am still going through the motions of getting permission to leave. I suppose the extra training I have been receiving will help the units when I finally can get to Spain, but this is all so frustrating. The strange thing is that I am being sent to Spain on behalf of the party. There's certainly a tug of war going on here between the hierarchies. I can't help but feel despondent and I must have shown this when one day I feel a gentle tug of my jumper.

"Comrade Nielsen as you seem to be heading outside I wonder if you would like some company whilst out for your walk."

I really will have to work hard at automatically acknowledging people using my new name. I seem to have had so many these last three years starting with Otto Kammers, Rudolf Rudolfovich, Karl Klug and now my new Norwegian identity of Sigmund Nielsen. I look at my colleague and take the hint that he needs to speak to me. As we walk around the grounds, he starts to talk quietly.

"Sigmund, I've been told that the EKKI[170] has no objections to you leaving the country but there's been a problem with Rose, the adviser of the organisation. You know how careful we have to be now and it's not advisable to talk openly."

I groan quietly. I know what is about to follow. He continues

"There have been concerns about Hanny Dünkel's books and then of course you haven't answered the allegations you made about Bredel".

"I'm just trying to keep a low profile about all of this. I really do not want to make any statements, even if it is the truth, which might incriminate other people. Even friends of ours are being arrested on such minor matters and I am sure some are trumped up charges. I'm all for spies being detained and imprisoned, but this is ridiculous."

"I know, I know" he replies consolingly. "Let's hope that they consider that you are of use away from this country fighting fascism in Spain".

I feel angry at this developing fear my friends and truly honest citizens are going through. I have no doubt that we are being watched even now. To waylay any suspicion, we try to say something to each other in a jovial manner making it look as though there has been no important content to our conversation.

Soviet army officers are starting to be arrested. I understand that they are being accused of collaboration with the German army in previous years. I'm aware that this is correct but only on the official orders of the government who were being paid large sums of money for providing armaments and poison gas during the 1920s. Who is really to blame here?

Finally to my greatest relief, Comrade Korniliev is told on 22nd October that I will be departing from the Soviet Union in the near future. At long last I can join my friends and colleagues already in

---

[170] EKKI – Communist International Organisation

Albacete. I finally say goodbye to my adopted country on 7th November 1936. I have mixed feelings about my time here as I believe in Marxism but is the present system complying with these values? Hopefully things will change here back to the true concept of communism and socialism. This country is one of very few who fought to alter completely the governing class system in order to give the working class a chance of a reasonable life so I have to cling on to the hope of it succeeding.

★

Our truck reaches breakneck speed along some pretty rough roads. We're all hanging on as best we can, singing and laughing as we're hurled around bends and almost jolted out of the long benches we're sitting on. At long last I belong to the International Brigade[171] and my fellow fighters and I are equipped ready to do what I should have been doing a long time ago – fighting the fascists. It's been a hectic few weeks, but we are on our way to Madrid having just left Albacete which is our headquarters. I think we all feel happy that finally we

---

[171] The International Brigade members were volunteers from all over the world. Many were political exiles from Germany, Austria and Italy but people came and joined from North America, Canada, Great Britain, France, Hungary, Yugoslavia, Romania, Poland, Finland, Soviet Union, Mexico, Czechoslovakia, Scandinavia and many other countries. Some had First World War experience, but many did not have any skills but were politically aware and wanted to stop fascism spreading. These men were untrained in the military sense until arriving in Spain where they received a short initiation of army training before facing the professional army and air force of Franco, the Moroccan Army (the Moors), the German Condor Legion, the Italian Aviazione and Mussolini's troops. During 1936 – 1939, some 35,000 International Brigade volunteers in total fought for the republican cause but at any one time, there were between 12,000 – 16,000 men. Alongside these volunteers were foreign medical volunteers including doctors and nurses who came to give their skills but risked their lives by being in the forefront helping the injured that had been fighting fascism. Also present were Quakers who were personally opposed to fighting but provided canteens, and helped with refugee work especially with regard to the Spanish children

will be fighting the nationalists and protecting the local population from the horrors of fascism.

I'd arrived in Spain on 18th November, the day that Germany and Italy officially recognised Franco's[172] regime. Now it is all out in the open, but will the free world jump to our assistance? Somehow I think not, but I will still keep hoping. Germany sent the Condor Legion[173] so now I know that we are fighting the Nazis from my own country.

As we near Madrid, the singing stops and the mood changes when we see so many civilians walking along the side of the road, trying to get to the safety of Madrid. It is a tragedy that these people have to leave their villages where they have lived in for most of their lives. Now they have lost their homes with the rapidly approaching nationalist army. The knowledge of reprisals which have been carried out by the Nationalists, the Falangist and other militia towards any left wing, trade unionist or supporter of the republican government is enough to make people leave their ancestral homes. Reprisals often mean a gruesome death and an unmarked shallow grave. If they have been lucky, the villagers will have had enough time to load up their carts with mattresses, household goods etc., their worn out donkeys struggling to pull the heavy loads. Most villagers try not to stop until

[172] When Franco was interviewed on 27th July 1936 by Jay Allen, a North American journalist, General Franco stated that he would save Spain from Marxism whatever the cost. Jay Allen mentioned that there was considerable resistance to his army trying to remove the democratically elected government and asked "And if that means shooting half of Spain?" Franco replied "whatever the cost." As a result mass executions and terror reigned over supporters of the republican government. Unfortunately wars are never "black and white" but a lot of shades of grey and so I have to say that retaliations took place to Franco's fascist thuggery. There were incidents of some republicans not having the same decent ideals of freedom and social justice and there was interference from Stalin. It is very difficult trying to explain in such a simplistic way for the uninitiated reader the history of the Spanish Civil War. I have therefore written about Rudolf Stender's experience during this turbulent history period.

[173] The Condor Legion was a branch of Hitler's air force. The cities and towns of Spain suffered mass aerial bombing from the nationalist side, courtesy of Franco's German and Italian fascist backers.

they reached the safety of the city. Sheep and cattle are herded along to some unknown destination by these frightened villagers. If we are in a siege situation later, these animals will become useful to the local population as well as ourselves.

The look on the faces of so many of the Spanish people's army shows us they have been through hell and back these last few months. One of the soldiers tells me that they have experienced relentless bombing raids, followed by being machine gunned from the air to where they had been sheltering in their shallow trenches. Some of these poor men look totally broken in spirit. The Spaniards have not experienced the Great War and have had no first-hand experience of such horrors in their own land. This has been a shock to the psyche of the nation. The citizens have been awakened to a concept of democracy and freedom of thought and now it's being snatched away by the fascists.

As we pass some of the Spanish soldiers, I notice women amongst their rank, some looking even more soldierly than the men. Their faces are etched with determination as they march along the road carrying their rifles as though they mean business. Other women are dressed in neat blue overalls, wearing make-up and with their dark hair oiled in the Spanish style[174].

I look round at my fellow International Brigaders. Yes, we have all been hardened over the last few years with our own bitter experiences of fascism. We have nothing to lose now. I think we all are aware that so many of our International Brigade colleagues are already dead[175]. They had marched through the centre of the city of Madrid to the cheers of the local population and then towards the sound of gunfire. After having fought bravely, many did not survive.

As so many of us have already suffered from the realities of fascism, there are times when we feel that our lives have already been sacrificed. The final battle is irrelevant for me personally but the remaining time on this earth is vital for our cause of stopping world

---

[174] Many such women are amongst the last to leave a battle scene so analysis of their character looking at their appearance can be misleading.

[175] In just one month of fighting nearly half of our colleagues who arrived on 8th November are dead.

domination of this evil. Other people deserve to live a life of normality. Our chance has already gone.

We've been briefed about the lack of natural defences here in Madrid which are unlike medieval town strongholds. This city is easily accessible from the surrounding countryside so will be a nightmare to defend. Only to the south does the city have any protection by the land sloping steeply down and which would cause problems to an attacker. There is also the old part of Madrid where the streets between Toledo Bridge and the Puerta del Sol are narrow and wind precariously for any potential attacker. Apart from this, it will be sheer grit and determination from the citizens of Madrid and the army who must risk death defending the capital of Spain.

The air raids have also shocked and terrified the local population of the city. They cannot believe that such horrors are being inflicted on them and their capital. It is distressing seeing the civilian population suffer in such a way. There are too many innocent people lying dead in the streets; men, women and children being piled on top of each other, many still clutching in their hands whatever they were doing at the time of their deaths. At night the bodies are removed to their last resting place and their families have little time to grieve as the sound of fighting continues in the near distance and the bombs explode around them.

It makes me angry seeing such sights. Whatever horrors happened in the Great War, it was a soldier's war. This is completely different. Incendiaries have been dropped on these poor souls, causing fires and death by burning as well as the normal destruction. On top of all this physical terror, the citizens received a leaflet drop one afternoon. The words of warning in the leaflets made them shudder. A quick translation from a colleague of mine explains that for every nationalist supporter who is murdered in Madrid, ten men will be shot. On their calculation 25,000 will be held responsible for the reprisals against the nationalists within the city. How disgusting for these civilians to receive such threats.

We have to prepare the defence of Madrid and orders are given for the civilians to fill bottles with petrol and to put cotton wool in the necks. They are told that should rebel tanks and armoured cars descend on their beloved city, they are expected to throw the bottles at the vehicles from roof tops and windows. Chains of women folk and children are formed as they pass torn up cobblestones and other items to their neighbour in order that barricades can be built. Reality has hit the citizens of Madrid with a very hard bump.

I have a Company of men who are my responsibility. There's only been a relatively short time to start building up their confidence, but as I have always led by example, I am sure we will do the best we can. The men in my Company listen very carefully to my instructions. I look at their faces listening to my orders. Some are inexperienced, but all have determination. It's a hard but true fact that many of these men looking at me now will not be long in this world. The omens are not good.

Straight away we're in the thick of a living hell at the University City campus. It's hand to hand fighting along with gruesome situations of throwing hand grenades into a room before entering. I yell instructions to fill windows with university books to protect ourselves from incoming fire. We are often in situations where we're pinned down without proper food to keep our energy up but our determination to defend Madrid from the fascists keeps us going. We have no time to grieve for our comrades as they meet their end, many of their wounds making them unrecognisable. Part of Franco's army consists of the Spanish Moroccan *regulares* who are renowned for their brutality.

"Sigmund – I must warn you to be careful". A messenger has managed to get through to our Company. I look at him with surprise at such a message being given in this dire situation.

"We've just heard that whilst the Moors[176] were occupying the research laboratories, they must have been having the same problem as us with the lack of food supplies. Apparently they'd decided to eat the monkeys, guinea pigs and other animals being kept there for experimental purposes. When we broke into the block to defeat these troops, we discovered that several of them were suffering from typhoid as the animals had been given that virus for experimental purposes".

I go cold hearing this as I have to admit that it hadn't occurred to me and we could have ended up with the same fate. I nod and

---

[176] Fierce and brutal army from Morocco

thank the messenger for this information and warn my Company not do the same as the Moors.

The weather continues to be appalling – we're cold, hungry and I can see fear on some of the young recruit's faces. So many of us older, more experienced men have been through too much horror already with the World War in 1914-1918, followed by being in the resistance against Hitler and his National Socialist Party. We try to encourage the youngsters hoping that it will help them to overcome their fear when we're under fire.

There is a mixture of artillery and aerial bombardments, and then bayonet and grenade fighting from room to room, facing the enemy eyeball to eyeball with the result that someone always succumbs to pain and then death, and not always the enemy. How many lives are destroyed in these battles? We mustn't be defeated otherwise fascism will be here in Spain and the revenge and punishments inflicted on the ordinary citizens will be horrendous.

Trenches and fortifications are dug when it seems that a siege situation could well be starting. Whatever happened to Franco's idea of arriving in Madrid without any problems? His General Mola had intended his army would enter the capital on 12th October, the day of the Feast of the Spanish Race. Mola would then drink a cup of coffee on the Gran Via. I smile at our small but significant victory that we have delayed his intentions. A notice has been put there on a table next to a cup of cold coffee reminding the locals of their victory.

The citizens of Madrid have been wonderful to the International Brigaders. They say that we have lifted the spirits of both the citizens and the local republican army. I'm grateful for some friends who can speak Spanish. I must admit that I am struggling at the moment to understand this new language but I shall have to start to learn. Unfortunately all the different languages spoken make us waste time when we are all trying to understand instructions but there are people from all over the world who have joined the Brigade.

How I hate war and the stench of death especially having lost so many old and new friends since I arrived in Spain. Day and night it continues and we suffer with lack of any proper sleep and food but finally I am allowed a few hours leave. We are allowed on the trams into the area where there are cafes still operating. Life feels almost surreal such a short distance away from the battlefield. We can have a drink, relax and also get some sleep. Relax – now that's a strange word in this hell hole with hand to hand fighting, throwing grenades at the enemy and trying to force them back from this lovely city.

A man had been quietly watching me as I sit with one or two others. It's always advisable to keep an eye on suspicious characters as we are aware that there are spies here. Eventually he wanders over to me and introduces himself. He's a newspaper reporter. Having introduced himself, in broken German he asks "You are obviously not Spanish so why are you here?"

I put down my drink and wearily look at the man. Is it worth answering that question when it's obvious to anyone who has any comprehension of the criminality and danger of fascism?

"I'm fighting for the freedom of the citizens of Spain against the tyranny of fascism. Isn't that obvious? As for me, I've lost everything I hold dear to me when I left my beloved home and family and now I am here so this does not happen to others."

A friend leans over and squeezes my shoulder gently in support and understanding. I look closely at the reporter's face. I'm not sure if he totally understands what is happening here. Why send someone over to Spain to ask such a ridiculous question. Perhaps he thinks that we have a subversive rather than altruistic reason for being here. So many people who are in the International Brigade are from all walks of life and from so many countries but all are here to risk our lives fighting fascism. If only these reporters could influence the people back home to convince their politicians to come to our aid. I shake my head knowing that it won't happen – politics is a strange thing with politicians having different priorities from normal people who want fairness and freedom.

I finish my drink, find a mattress and sleep heavily for a few hours before heading back to the tram and to fighting – something I know I am good at doing thanks to Hitler and his cronies. I have some wonderful young men who are waiting for my leadership back in the trenches at the battlefield. We have a bond of friendship and I shall fight to the end if the situation is needed. I'm just so exhausted at the moment but so is everyone else. The freezing cold weather doesn't help either.

We all joke though about the underground here in Madrid. At least if we get on a tram, we get off at the battlefront, but if the underground is used, who knows which side of the battlefield you get out at!

★

"We have to reform the units Sigmund".

My superior officer sits beside me as I am trying to eat a very belated breakfast. A short while ago during the end of November we had split from the XI International Brigade and we're now in the XIII International Brigade, although we're still known as the "Dombrowski" Division. With so many new arrivals to replace our lost friends, a decision had been made with the concept that it is easier to keep to nationalities. This seems to be disregarded in our division as we are still a mixed bunch of nationalities, but because many of us Germans learnt Russian, it's easier for us to converse with others who might know that language.

"Our new recruits are being trained at Tarazona de la Mancha. I have no idea why they seem to be spending so much time in parade ground duties and marching than preparing to go into battle. The Commanding Officer, Klaus Becker seems to think it more important." He stops speaking being deep in thought, then gives a shake back to reality. "That information is between you and me Sigmund" he adds quietly to me.

My surprise and horror hearing about Klaus Becker must have shown because he continues "When these new recruits are under your control Sigmund, I hope that you will be able to instil some of your knowledge and experience. These novices will need that before they are sent to the battlefield. It'll be a hard task bringing these raw recruits up to standard in such a short time especially considering they will be expected to fight against professional armies with German and Italian air forces assisting".

"I'll try to do my best" and then I ask "Where is Tarazona de la Mancha anyway? It would help to know where I am going!"

"It is south east of here" he says laughing.

"Is that part of the Albacete training grounds for the Brigade?"

"Yes, as you know there are training grounds in various villages around Albacete, and Tarazona is 37 km north of Albacete, but I gather that the XIII Brigade is about to be a mobile division and are being sent to Valencia ready for action. They will be taken out on exercises so hopefully they will be battle ready. You mustn't forget that some of these men have had no experience of any wars or action against the enemy" he reminds me again.

I pack the very few items I possess and head for Valencia. As I arrive at the camp, I say "salud" and at the same time raise my clenched right wrist to my right ear which is the republican salute and then I give the password for that day. It doesn't take me long to understand my superior, that the troops are becoming expert at parade duty but are they battle ready?

The Spanish troops eat in the same canteen as us and it is very obvious that there are problems with the different languages being spoken. Orders are given in French and German. To resolve this, interpreters from the battalion who speak two languages or more, especially Spanish, German, French or Russian are being asked to volunteer to become translators to help overcome the many difficulties of understanding each other. There are also requests for men to put their names forward who are qualified drivers, metal workers, electricians, tailors and shoemakers – all the skills to keep an army in good running order.

Machine guns have been placed in position ready for air attacks and guards prepare for duty. A rota has been set up so that each unit is expected to do their duty on a different day. There are written instructions given daily with a timetable for the troops and the military training plus the daily password to be used. We inform the headquarters of our battle worthiness with the numbers of troops fit and available for action. It seems as though the 8th Battalion will not be in Valencia for much longer.

The discipline and efficiency of the guards worries me as there are signs that the men do not fully understand their individual responsibilities. This does not bode well for us. If some of the guards are drinking, playing cards and gambling, then the barracks are insecure and weaponry can be stolen. This is appalling behaviour. We, the old soldiers fully understand the need for total discipline. I wonder if Klaus Becker is aware of these problems as surely he would insist that punishment be meted out. The commissars should speak to the men explaining the consequences of their actions. Surely the troops will comprehend the dangers due to the lack of discipline.

The battalion's training and manoeuvres however are becoming more intense so it seems that it won't be long before we're mobilised. The weather is deteriorating but compared to the Soviet Union, it's mild and anyway I have become immune to these hardships. I hear that the Soviet tank unit is ready for action and a machine gun unit. The Spanish, French and Germans also are ready. Someone has decided that explosive experts should be redeployed to a more appropriate company unit.

In mid-December, we start mobilising to Alfambra. So at last I'm back fighting the fascists. Schmidt, the Captain of the machine gun company, has taken over temporary command from Klaus Becker[177].

It is Christmas Eve. I wonder where my family is. What about Ernst and Werner – are they still in concentration camps? My poor parents do not deserve all this worry. What about Käthe and Rudi? Oh I feel so guilty about destroying my family. Hopefully Rudi, Erich and Gretel will cheer my parents up. When I think of all our wonderful Christmas Eves we used to have. Tears start welling up inside me. I shake myself back into reality. I have men expecting me to lead them and this weakness must not show.

A warning is issued from brigade headquarters that there is a high

---

[177] Is this the same Klaus Becker who was an officer in the Abraham Lincoln Brigade for a few weeks in July 1937? Klaus Becker is also mentioned in "The Owl of Minerva" by Gustav Reglar as being an artillery officer training troops in Albacete during late autumn 1936. Later in February 1939 when he was just about to cross the border from Spain into France Klaus Becker was about to annihilate a unit of men who knew something of his past but luckily Gustav Reglar's appearance prevented this from happening.

possibility of an air raid, but thank goodness we have four sub machine guns in position to protect us. The guns are pointing towards the surrounding mountains. Orders are given to ring the church bell if enemy planes are seen approaching. The tank division is ready for an air attack but some of the French soldiers are missing. When I report this to Schmidt he is furious to hear this news. He barks out instructions to find these men. Later he looks totally perplexed saying

"I can't believe this. I have discovered that some of our French comrades have disappeared to the market square and are drinking wine".

"This is ridiculous" I reply in horror.

"I have reported the situation to our commander but… " he then shrugs his shoulders in despair.

These are still early days of fighting so the full extent of the realities of war has not yet sunk into many of the new recruits. Most of them are civilians who have come to fight for a cause they believe in but their self-discipline is not in place yet. I just have to keep reminding myself of this fact and be grateful that so many young men are willing to fight with us.

On 25th December 1936 the company leader of the 2nd Company tells me that he has written to the battalion commander complaining that the tank division is now without both translators, one of which was Rowditch. These men have been recalled to headquarters. How on earth can the battalion expect to operate efficiently in war conditions with so many troops and officers speaking different languages. The company leader tells me that he has requested Martinez be returned immediately.

It isn't long before we've had enough of the soldier in charge of communications and sent him back to base from Alfambra[178].

A day later, we start preparations to take the city of Teruel which is in enemy hands. We have to stop the nationalists encircling Madrid which would cut off the route to France which we use for the reinforcement of equipment and men. This attack will also take the

[178] On 25th December the soldier sends a note to Klaus Becker before leaving Alfambra stating that he does not feel that this action was justified. He also stated that he appreciates Klaus Becker's decision to let him remain on the Staff and that he will "avoid" any questions which are asked about Klaus Becker.

pressure off our men still fighting to protect Madrid. Teruel usually
has the lowest annual winter temperatures in Spain and this year is
no different from normal. There is very little cover for the men and
the area is surrounded by rough gorges, mountains shaped like teeth
and twisted ridge fingers. Not an easy terrain to conquer. A mixture
of excitement and apprehension begins to pervade the atmosphere
here but deep down there is also fear but this is kept under control.

We try to hide from the men our sheer frustration when
insufficient lorries arrive at the base. How are we expected to get the
men to the battlefield? The artillery weapons and ammunition are
not sufficient and many are not usable. Where are all the sub machine
guns? What a disaster that we have to leave so much ammunition and
weapons by the roadside as they are useless. We have good established
soldiers here amongst the novices but this situation is so annoying. If
only we hadn't lost so many of my friends in Madrid as I am sure we
would have resolved all this mismanagement with our experience.
But as it is how on earth can we fight a professional enemy with such
difficulties? I've got to instil confidence in my men as it's no use going
into battle feeling defeated before we start. At least we have been given
240 hand grenades. Let us hope they work!

The doctor arrives and the field hospital at Villaba Baja is ready for
our casualties. Our battle orders are that all our formations including
the commando section are to be ready by 14.00 hours. There's a mixture
of excitement, nervousness and tension flooding through the 8th
battalion. We're given our battle objectives and at 19.00 hours we receive
food parcels so that we are ready to leave the camp by 19.15 hours.

Our first objective is to get into the valley, cross the River
Rambla, (which thank goodness is just a dry river bed) to attack
Gelzende on the other side and then on to Cerro de Cementerio.
This battle tactic is not one I would have chosen as it means
descending into a valley and we could end up in the situation where
we are just target practise for our enemy.

27th December arrives and battle commences. Before we start our
action, there is thirty minutes of artillery firing from our command
post at the railway crossover at Alfambra Strasse and this weaponry is
aimed at the Cerro de Cementerio. After this, the direction of fire

changes direction shelling at Santa Barbara for thirty minutes. Let's hope that this softens the enemy ready for our advancement.

We start our attack on Teruel. The Spanish Column is to attack Santa Barbara. We, the 8th battalion, are to head towards the right, the 10th to the left with the 11th to be held in reserve. At the meeting of all the units involved we are told that the first aim is to go beyond the River Rambla.

I grit my teeth and order my men into battle. My worst fears materialise as it becomes obvious that the battle strategy is wrong. The political commissars then give contradictory instructions to that of Klaus Becker and chaos reigns.

By the third day the French battalion appear to receive little instructions from their command, and then refuse to assist us which causes anger and hysteria by many within our battalion. This is really not good news. Falling out amongst the troops is no way to win a battle. We must support each other or more lives will be lost. How many of our officers have enough experience in a situation such as this? I try to calm my men and by example carry on, but holding position in a gravel pit with machine gun fire being sprayed around us is dangerous for all of us.

On the fourth day we manage to hold our positions. The mixture of raw recruits amongst experienced men makes it difficult to keep a solid formation. Crouching down, I see someone ahead and train the rifle in the direction of the target. Next second, something hot pierces my neck just below and behind my right ear. Involuntarily I've slumped over onto my left side with the force of what must have been a bullet. I can feel myself getting soaked perhaps in my own blood. A light headed feeling overcomes me but I have to keep conscious otherwise all will be lost.

I feel in a state of shock. Why hadn't I spotted the enemy on my right? I must have been a sitting duck. I look down a see blood pumping out of my body; so an artery must have ruptured. A colleague's hand touches my arm and I can vaguely hear him saying something but I can't understand him. Unconsciousness is beginning to waft over me. Come on Rudolf, just one last bit of effort otherwise you will be lost.

It is as though someone else is whispering, but I know it must be me giving instructions to my colleague on how to stop the flow of blood. Oh such terrible pain from my right ear to my left shoulder; and then my world goes black as I surrender to oblivion.

It must have been some time later when I weakly open my eyes to see some men looking anxiously at me. I can't see daylight only a ceiling but everything seems very primitive. Someone must have bandaged my wound and stopped the bleeding. Is this the battle field hospital? I feel myself slipping back into unconsciousness and the searing pain leaves me. My time has come and I have no will left in me to fight against it.

★

Voices seem to be in the distance but talking normally. Interspersed with these reassuring conversations are the groans of men, some crying in agony, some in fear and distress. Where am I? Is there an afterlife after all having no religious beliefs or am I still alive? What has happened to me?

I open my eyes and try to lift my head and focus on my surroundings. Pain shears through my neck and shoulder and I slump back again. Oh damn, everything seems to hurt and I feel so dizzy. This time I try to look to my left but that's impossible. I gently move my head to the right and can see that the room is full of beds with men in various degrees of mutilation. Someone must have seen me recovering as I hear him call "Nurse, he's awake".

What a wonderful sight appears before me as a blurred vision of loveliness looks down at me. She smiles in pleasure.

"Where am I?" My voice sounds strange and muffled. I try to lift my left hand, but the pain in my shoulder makes me wince. I try my right hand which moves but with acute pain in my neck. Somehow I manage to lift this hand to my face. There are bandages covering my right ear and below. I wince and look at the nurse again.

She gently holds my right hand and places it back to my side and then puts a cup of water to my mouth. I sip the delicious liquid.

"You're a very lucky man Sigmund. You were shot through your neck just below your right ear and the bullet came out of your left shoulder. How you survived we will never know, but the person who bandaged you on the battlefield saved your life[179]."

At this point, she seems to sound further away and I drift off into a deep slumber.

Voices disturb me from this wonderful peace of sleeping. Sleep is something most of us have been deprived of for so long. The talking continues. The person in the bed next to me must have died as I hear that they are to remove the body. I hear the orderlies saying that having lost both his legs and an arm and what with the disfigurement of his face from an explosion, life would have been so hard for him. Did he give up all hope of surviving with such injuries?

Perhaps with my wounds, there's a chance that in time, I might be all right provided that the bullet hasn't damaged my spinal cord. I can feel my feet moving but have I lost my legs? I remember in the Great War of people thinking that they could feel their legs, but these had either been blown off or been amputated. Am I feeling just the nerve endings misinterpreting the signals? The nurse did not say anything but do they wait until I am stronger before breaking such news? I can feel tears welling up inside me for a second or two before pulling myself together. I shut my eyes again and try to relax. Whatever happens, there's no point worrying about it as what has been done cannot be changed.

I know that I must have drifted in and out of consciousness after this but I am aware that nurses and doctors came and went, water and liquidised food is given to me but actual events and time I cannot remember. Finally my head clears and I feel strength returning to my body. The pain is still there, but somehow I feel more in control. A familiar face looks down at me and that lovely nurse looks really pleased.

"Well this is marvellous Sigmund. You really look so much better. The transfusion has helped enormously. In a funny sort of way, you are very lucky now that there have been so many medical advances learnt through horrific injuries inflicted on people. At least one positive outcome has come out of this dreadful war."

---

[179] The first aid bandaging was taught to Rudolf during his army days in the First World War and he writes to Werner later explaining that he had given instructions to someone to stop the bleeding

This lovely apparition in a nurse's uniform is indeed a welcoming sight to any soldier. We have experienced things no man should ever have seen or heard. She squeezes my hand and says that the doctor will see me soon and then she turns round to attend to the new occupant of the bed next to me. Shortly afterwards, the doctor arrives as promised.

"Good afternoon Sigmund. Your condition had us very worried especially as so many vital parts are within the neck area. I think that the worst is over and it is just a case for recuperating your body and mind. You lost a lot of blood when the bullet pierced your neck and shoulder and it will take a lot of effort on your part now to fully recover."

"There are no other injuries?" I ask with some hesitation.

"We do not know how much muscle and nerve damage has occurred until you start moving about, but you have two arms, two legs, a head, your trunk and your personal parts!" he answers smiling.

A wave of relief sweeps over me. I can see that there are many more patients here who are in far worse condition. I will make every effort to recover and hopefully return to fight those wretched fascists. My determination overrides the pain and my strength improves as does the capability of moving. By some miracle, the bullet has not permanently damaged any of my vital nerves, blood vessels, airway or gullet. The same could not be said for many of my colleagues here. The pain and stiffness gradually recedes as I persevere with exercising but the recovery is taking far too long for me. My left arm is in a sling during most of the day when I am not doing the exercises. Thank goodness I am right handed.

Benicasim Hospital[180] is in the area of las Villas de Cami Nou and the Hotel Voramar, near Valencia and is used for the

---

[180] This hospital was under the direction of The International Brigade from December 1936 until April 1938. It seems that the wounded and dying from the XIII International Brigade were the main occupants of this hospital but other units from the Brigade and Spanish republicans were nursed at Benicasim. During this period 7000 wounded and convalescent soldiers were treated here. According to Irene Goldin in "Womens Voices from the Spanish Civil War, *"Benicasim consisted of "lovely villas" and it was used as a convalescent centre for the wounded of the International Brigade."*

International Brigade. There are about fifty buildings in this vicinity including a convent. The smell of the sea and the mountain air purifies our spirits. We all tease and encourage each other as those of us who have some kind of future try to boost the morale of others whose outlook looks very bleak. There is a wonderful camaraderie in the International Brigade. This has been essential for us as we volunteered to put ourselves in extreme danger to fight a worthwhile cause, but we are still human beings with emotions.

On many occasions we even break into song. One of the songs guaranteed to get most of us singing is the *"Die Moorsoldaten"*[181] which was composed by Rudi Goguel and Hanns Eisler who were imprisoned in one of Hitler's Concentration Camps.

> *Chorus: We are the peat bog soldiers*
> *Marching with our spades to the moor.*
> *Up and down the guards are marching*
> *No one, no one can get through*
> *Flight would mean a sure death facing*
> *Guns and barbed wire block our view*
> *Chorus: We are the peat bog soldiers*
> *Marching with our spades to the moor*
> *But for us there is no complaining*
> *Winter will in time be past*
> *One day we shall rise rejoicing*
> *Homeland, dear, you're mine at last*
> *No more the peat bog soldiers*
> *Will march with our spades to the moor"*

Tears seem to appear from nowhere with the emotion of the song. There is solidarity amongst us Germans who have already been through so much whilst we were fighting Hitler in our old home country. As the last words are sung, we all try to look busy to cover any sign of weakness becoming lost in our own thoughts.

---

[181] *"Peat Bog Soldiers"* and the words are roughly translated into English. I recommend listening to the song on the internet especially the version by Pete Seeger

★

"Sigmund, is it really you?" I follow the sound of the voice which comes from one of the patients lying on a hospital bed. Heinz, one of my fellow XIII Brigaders is looking at me in amazement. "I thought you were dead Sigmund".

How lovely to see one of my fellow comrades but how unfortunate it is that we are both injured.

"No, I have too much to do yet Heinz before I finally leave this world. Franco's troops have to work a lot harder to finish me off." I sit on a stool by his bed and with my right hand grip one of his. "What happened in the end with our fighting to take Teruel?"

Heinz is silent for a while. I'm not sure if he has heard my question. I'm just about to ask again when he starts to talk to me.

"Sigmund, we lost that battle along with many of our comrades. It was a hopeless situation with Klaus Becker and the political commissars at logger heads. I know that the political commissars have written a report after the battle.

They complained that on the first day of the fighting, they realised that Klaus Becker didn't have the military qualifications which he said he possessed. If only there had been a more thorough preparation of the attack with its company leaders. It could have been more successful given the military situation. According to the commissars, Becker had the wrong attitude and therefore the instructions which he gave to the leader of the 2nd company made it impossible for him to fulfil the orders. As the military instructions could not be executed, success was impossible."

I keep quiet at this information as I have learnt that "walls have ears" and it is unwise to make comments. He continues somewhat bitterly.

"We all recognised that Becker had the spirit of someone always in a saloon and a commander of the parade. He saw that his major task was in preparing the troops for a parade rather than for active service. As for procuring sufficient weapons and articles of clothing… " He pauses deep in thought "Why did he not take sufficient weapons from Tarazona to Valencia when we became a mobile reserve?"

I try unsuccessfully to shake my head. It is impossible to shrug because of the pain in my shoulder and neck. I end up lifting my hands slightly to give some reaction.

"He is certainly not what I call a 'people person' so does not accomplish morale boosting confidence within the troops. Without this the company weakens in strength and will power. As you remember the troops were quite depressed knowing his lack of leadership qualities and as a result of his negative attitude everyone was demoralised. He wanted to retreat after three days and return to Valencia. Fancy him telling the leadership that he wanted to return to flying planes. If we had been thoroughly prepared for this battle, the last actions at the Cemetery would have meant success. As it was, I hear that he left the operation almost completely to the political commissars. He, according to the political commissars abandoned the combat area early without worrying about 80 comrades cut off between the enemy and our positions. He is supposed to have said that he is in a nervous and traumatic state of mind."

I am quiet for a while thinking about all of this information. I have no idea if my comrade Heinz is right in his analysis of the failure to achieve the capture of Teruel. It appears to me that people are busy trying to save their own skins and reputations. What I am sure about is that this lack of solidarity and leadership almost certainly caused the loss of this battle and the resulting loss of many lives. However, I have learned over these past years that it is very unwise to make any comment as there are people all too ready to report dissention.

"The way to look at this Heinz is to make every effort to recover from your injuries. There are so many International Brigaders including you, who are exceptionally brave and resolute in their beliefs of social justice and freedom. We will overcome these problems in the battlefield and communication difficulties so that we will win our fight against fascism."

Heinz face crumples into agony but he bites his lip and tries to smile. I had been so busy looking at his facial expressions that I had not noticed all his injuries. I look down and see that my poor friend's fighting days are over and may be his life. Blood is seeping through the sheets and I shout for the doctor. I'm pushed aside as Heinz is transferred onto a stretcher and rushed to the theatre. I know that I'll never see Heinz again. Yet another comrade has gone.

My recovery seems to be taking far longer than I ever thought possible. I can't believe how weak I feel and then there's the pain and stiffness in my neck and left shoulder. It's agony to try to lift and extend my left arm. How on earth am I going to use a rifle? I'm determined to recover and that needs perseverance with physiotherapy and exercising as much as possible. I know that I am needed back in active service. As time progresses, more and more of my old unit of the XIII Brigade are being brought in. This is really not good news. Surely there will not be yet another defeat for the Dombrowski Brigade?[182]

Normally there are one hundred and fifty beds here for the injured but at times there is a need for more and this is one of these occasions. By the end of February there are four hundred wounded here. The aisles are filling with dead men with not enough staff to remove them immediately being too busy trying to save some very badly wounded soldiers. The stench of blood, sweat and gangrene permeates the rooms. Some men are screaming in pain, others barely alive and are silent. Nurses and helpers rush around trying to assist. They have little time to stop and spend time with many poor souls who need comfort as they lie there waiting for death to take them away from their misery. Doctors are thin on the ground as they are busy in the operating theatre.

I have no right to remain here. There is a need for my bed even though I am not really battle ready yet. I must be able to do something to help fight this fascist army.

At long last I manage to persuade a doctor to release me from hospital. He also realises that with the large intake of badly wounded soldiers, there is a need for me to return to the battle field. I just hope that I'll be strong enough to be of use.

---

[182] During 6th and 27th February 1937, the XIII Brigade suffered 50% casualties. Nine hundred International Brigade men were injured during the Jarama Battle

This time my ability with explosives is much needed and my heart sings as I am put in with the German anti-tank division of the XI Brigade. The atmosphere is ideal for me as we have the same positive spirit of being there to fight these fascist 'bastards' no matter what the risk to life and limb.

While we take a short break from preparing for action, one of my friends is immersed reading something which looks like English. His ability to read and speak this language is very useful to us on many an occasion; at some point I must master the language myself. With his fluency in English he is able to keep us informed of British/American politics and events. I have to applaud some of the volunteers from these countries and have joined the International Brigade in order to fight with us; this is despite their government being complacent about the current situation here in Spain.

I look at the page again and ask him what he is reading.

"It's a copy of "The Nation" which is a left wing paper issued in England and New York." He pauses and then he continues "listen to this article by Louis Fischer – I'll translate it for you. It's called *"Can Madrid hold on"* and it is dated 16th January 1937." Then he starts to read *"If Great Britain called "Halt", Hitler would mend his behaviour unwillingly and Mussolini happily"*.

Initially murmurs of surprise are uttered and then as we consider these words, sounds of agreement fill the room. Otto is quick to evaluate the strange coincidence of the date by saying "Now that is interesting as that comment was written while Mussolini and Herman Göring were in Rome discussing how far they could go without having any adverse reactions from Britain. Do you remember being told about that meeting?"

"I do – as you say that is a strange coincidence. Another lost opportunity for the Spanish people. Who is this Louis Fischer?" I ask.

"He's a journalist whose reports are well thought through. I have read quite a lot of his articles. He has close contacts and friendships with people in very high places not only in Spain but in the Soviet Union and America. I guess by these connections he obtains privileged information and as such an insight in military and political situations. I know he has strong sympathies with our fight against fascism. He seems annoyed at the injustice of the western powers allowing the Spanish people to suffer. He writes for the left wing "The Nation" published in New York; also the "New Statesman" and "Nation" of London plus various other papers."

Wolfgang fumbles through some old newspaper cuttings he has kept, explaining what he is looking for.

"There is another article written recently on 27ᵗʰ March 1937 called "*Keeping America out of war.* Fischer explains to the reader how Germany and Italy can buy American arms and send them to Franco. I find that incredible when the Republic has no rights to rearm and to defend their people due to some stupid international law." He triumphantly holds up a scrap of paper. "He says *"the only way to guarantee peace is to stop the fascist aggressors who alone want war. It can be done in Spain. If Hitler and Mussolini are checked there, they will be weakened and sobered."*[183]

He read the last bit out for those who could understand English and then translated the article for the rest of us.

"Well isn't it good to hear him campaigning for our cause. If only an arms embargo could be put in place to stop supplies reaching Franco through Portugal – that would help" I remark.

Unfortunately I am becoming very cynical with regard to the west having any wishes to stop Hitler and Mussolini. Ignoring fanatical dictatorships often results in a more powerful extremist nation and a threat to humanity. I join the others giving a consensus of approval of Louis Fischer. I shall have to keep my eyes open for other articles by this man. It is good that we are still reading and debating albeit briefly in-between battles. It renews our will power to fight our enemy.

After a few days of training to adjust to the new unit, it seems we're about to become embroiled in a battle at Guadalajar. Much to my relief our Commander is completely different from Klaus

---

[183] Would this have changed the history of Europe and the consequences which lead up to the Second World War?

Becker. His name is Hans Kahle[184] who seems to naturally acquire unquestioning loyalty from everyone here. It feels like a great weight off my mind that I will not have to deal with internal squabbling as well as face the enemy; Hans and I have very similar past experiences, even being born in the same year, in 1899. Both of us feel angry at the events which led up to Hitler's 'triumph' in gaining power in Germany. Both Hans and I were in the German resistance and members of the Military Apparatus fighting against the rise of fascism. Just like me, Hans had to leave Germany in a hurry when the Nazis tried to arrest him, but he had escaped to Switzerland where he organised MOPR[185] to Spain.

He was initially a commander of the Edgar André Battalion but he is now commander of the XIth International Brigade (Thälmann Division). He has a marvellous reputation and I hope that despite the odds which are against us, we might manage to succeed. Hans Kahle has no compunction in ignoring inappropriate orders being given from Albacete. This is a relief to many of us German fighters. I have heard he re-evaluates these instructions to acceptable ones but ensuring that they are seen by those in higher places as obedience. Now that is clever. He then proceeds with assertion, taking into account and understanding the differences in the culture and the characteristics of the Spanish army, thereby managing to get the best out of them and the rest of the battalion. What a brilliant mind! Absolutely perfect for us seasoned soldiers as well as the fledglings.

I can't help chuckling to myself that this tall, heavy set man has similar qualities to the English "Robin Hood" as Hans takes pleasure in looting castles but hands the items over to the legal government to help with the war effort. Mind you, he has a fondness for a big china faience vase from Talavera which I hear he takes from one field headquarters to the next, all safely packaged in a case. He says that he wants to start a collection of Faience china after this war.

---

[184] Hans Kahle was a great friend of Ernest Hemmingway who was so inspired by Hans, that he characterised him in his novel "For Whom the Bell Tolls". Werner will also meet this wonderful man in another situation four years later

[185] International Red Aid supplying food, medical supplies, building and education equipment to Spain

I'm digressing with my thoughts and shake my head quickly to bring myself back to the present task. We have a battle to win but my heart has lifted being under the instructions of Hans. I know that I'm not really battle fit but with him in charge we have a chance of succeeding. The next battle will determine the future as if we lose, then it is possible that the citizens of Madrid will have to surrender. At the moment, although we failed at Jarama, the nationalists have also failed to gain control of the Madrid Valencia road. This means that we are still able to bring supplies of food and medical equipment alongside military weapons and men into Madrid. It seems now that their tactic is to encircle Madrid by attempting to win the area to the north east.

As we arrive at the station from our training ground, we cannot help but smile watching a troop train start to leave, full of men from our International Brigade. It is a train with many carriages and trucks providing all the requirements that a well-trained battalion will need. Men are packed in like sardines, scarlet scarves fluttering cheerfully from around their necks. All the men seem in high spirits with the long barrels of their guns held tightly by their owners. Some of the men are busy drinking wine but others responding to the cheers from the onlookers. Field guns are safely secured to the open trucks with men filling any free space. The International Brigade is good at boosting confidence to the Spanish people, putting on such a good show to the audience!

As they are leaving, I notice that they are being applauded by a train load of the wounded, being brought back for hospital attention. Despite many horrendous injuries, those that could wave their support to the out-going troops. Some were waving their crutches, others giving the republican red salute despite their bandaging hindering some. Morale is still high or at least we try to show everyone that it is.

This time we're up against 15,000 Moors and Carlists, plus 35,000 Italian fascists at Guadalajara. Number wise the odds are against us winning but we have many experienced fighters and a lot of people with sheer grit and determination to fight for the freedom of the ordinary Spanish population. Luckily we have some soviet tanks and aircraft at our disposal but it's going to be a tough battle. Our XI International Brigade is now more than 50% Spanish as we have lost so many of our original brave men fighting in the defence of Madrid. However with good leadership, we will have a chance of winning.

We prepare for battle but the lack of maps at company level always seems to hinder us experienced fighters and at times it does cause chaos. I have to keep asking myself if it would make much difference to battlefield strategy if the Spanish had been issued with them seeing that there is a literacy problem? So many of our Spanish colleagues are illiterate but it is not of their making. It seems unbelievable that the previous government of Spain considered it acceptable for a large stratum of the population not be worthy of an education. No wonder the republicans were so popular with the large majority of the electorate when at last they won power making it possible for education and literacy lessons to commence.

To our surprise and pleasure La Pasionaria[186] unexpectedly arrives to speak to some of our troops in the XI International Brigade. What an impressive lady she is, albeit dressed in male uniform and a soldier's cap, to see and listen to her talking to the soldiers in the trenches lifts our spirits. She stops and speaks to two of our young machine gunners who are only about sixteen or seventeen but these two young women are willing to die for the freedom of Spain.

Once again what appalling weather conditions we have to fight in. Never ending rain and mud and then snow hinders everything we try to do. The icy wind tears through our clothing like knives. Snow and mud makes traversing over land almost impossible at times so traffic jams and corresponding arguments of priority users ensue. At least I'm out of this being part of the antitank division. I scratch around my groin with anger and disgust. The lice which have

---

[186] Dolores Ibárruri was born 9th December 1895. She was a Spanish Republican leader before and during the Spanish Civil War. She is well known for her support during the Spanish Civil War and her famous slogan *"No Pasarán" (They shall not pass)* which she used during the battle of Madrid. At the end of the War she was exiled and only returned in 1977. She is one of the greatest orators of the 20th Century. She died on 12th November 1989.

invaded my uniform are part of my life now seeing that we have no chance of washing and putting on clean clothes. I notice that my friends have the same problem but none of us talk about it as it can demoralise the unit.

At one point the nationalists break a two kilometre gap through the Thälmann and Edgar André Divisions. Once again Hans Kahle's demeanour brings calm to the situation. This tall, heavily set man speaks calmly when panic ensues and despite the fact that we have less military equipment than many of the other units, he manages to instil discipline, obedience and respect from the soldiers and thereby overcoming the danger.

We manage to retake Trijueque which to our amusement makes Mussolini's Italians retreat in panic, leaving vehicles, rucksacks, weapons and cartridges lying around. As the troops of XI International Brigade and El Campesino's Brigade start marching along the road past these items I hear their officers instruct them to help themselves to cakes which have been found in the rucksacks and also to rearm themselves with grenades. It's amazing how they managed to do this without stopping and it's a lovely thought that the grenades will be used against the people who originally possessed them.

At least we have the advantage of a concrete runway at Albacete, whereas the opposing Legionary Air Force Fiats are unable to fly because of their water logged airstrip. For once we have the availability of 100 aircraft and 70 Russian tanks. Heavy sleet sets in shielding us from being viewed by the enemy but unfortunately it does delay us. We feel frozen but finally manage to destroy the enemy's tanks but amazingly the offensive succeeds with the Italian foes retreating in a panic.

The joy of respite from battle is immense especially with my previous injuries causing me so much pain and discomfort. Food is brought up on mules and even wine is issued. Some of the soldiers even though they are still in their trenches cook meals such as paella. Small pleasures can mean so much to us in this blood splattered, cold and wet territory. It's really bizarre how we are able to eat food and drink, when parts of bodies are strewn around us, but we manage to block our minds from this reality in order to survive these awful conditions. At least the stench of dead bodies is not so bad in winter. Alpargatas[187] are issued to replace many soldiers' shoes which have rotted due to all this partial mud, snow and ice.

I hear a mixture of sombre talk and then laughter as various tales are told of the battle. Again it is a strange thing how soldiers behave relating information of our victories, despite so many of our friends being killed. This camaraderie is vital though. Oh it's so good to be back with the International Brigaders. There's such a strong liaison between us even though language can be a problem. Our understanding of the psyche of the popular army members is better now that we comprehend and are tolerant towards each other's cultures. As our relationship develops there is a natural want to give cover when one of us leaves the security of a ditch or wall to advance on the enemy. It's hard to describe this feeling to anyone who has never been in battle.

I have never ending admiration for the women who have sacrificed their lives and have left the relative safety of their homes to join us in the horrors of war. One such person is Captain Encarnación Fernández Luna who commands a machine-gun company. A comrade enthusiastically relates an amusing incident he saw. The troops under her command who were present at the event managed to hold off a battalion of Italian Infantry until a counter attack could be organised with tanks and other reinforcements.

"She's a brave lady. I later saw Luna combing her hair looking at her reflection in a fragment of a broken mirror."

We all smile listening and picturing the event. Battle worn women seem to have an amazing ability to become feminine again as soon as the action is over.

The brief relaxation finishes and it is time to secure our boundary in a better manner than the temporary trenches which have been dug with bayonets and bare hands. The stoney Spanish earth and lack of spades hindered our earlier efforts. We build some defences by piling the stones from the fields into barricades. This also helps to protect us against the bitter winds. Many of the Spanish

---

[187] Shoes originating from the Pyrenees made with a rope sole from a tough, wiry Mediterranean grass

have so little clothes to keep them warm and only a blanket for sleeping and yet they fight so valiantly against the odds.

Something I find difficult to understand is our Spanish compatriot's attitude towards latrines. Being hardened campaigners with previous military service we know how to make life tolerable in general and essential during battle. However, many of the Spanish suffer from this lack of knowledge or incentive as they do not seem to bother digging latrines but simply live amongst the filth. Many of us Brigaders, having fought in the Great War, dig regardless of the difficulty of the terrain and the snipers who are ready to 'pick us off' but we cannot bear the thought of living in urinals. Mind you, our Spanish comrades probably think we are too fussy risking death just to avoid unpleasant smells! Then there is the problem of hygiene if we are not near a river, stream or lake. It is then impossible to keep clean due to the lack of access to water tankers and the scarcity of soap. I scratch again in disgust as the lice readjust their positions on my body.

To lift the spirits and tedium of our life style, books and writing material arrive and once again our Spanish colleagues have the opportunity of being educated. Reading, writing and arithmetic lessons recommence in the trenches. It really makes me annoyed that so many of the Spanish population have not received a basic education and are unable to read and write. The republicans became the democratically elected government and wanted to improve the lives of these people. Libraries have been created in villages and women started to be educated in thousands of new schools. In many remote villages there weren't even any pencils but now all children not in the middle of a war zone can go to school. Yet Franco with the support of Italy and Germany are trying to destroy these improvements to ordinary people's lives. It's almost unthinkable this lack of education ever happening in Germany.

"Rudolf?"

I jerk my head up in absolute horror. Who knows my real name? Someone is looking at me but I don't recognise him.

"No, I'm sorry but my name is Sigmund" I answer cautiously.

"Oh sorry I must have been mistaken" he hurriedly replies but comes to sit down beside me. He looks around to see if anyone is listening and then starts talking quietly to me.

"I don't know if you remember me but I'm Wilhelm Bahnik who worked in the resistance with your brother Ernst".

The face is very familiar but like me, he has aged too quickly in these harsh conditions and our previous life in Germany. I smile hearing this wonderful news. At long last I can speak to someone who knows my wonderful brother. Ernst is not only my brother but also my soul mate.

I ask questions about Ernst to make sure he knows my brother well. We all have to be careful these days. We talk for some time, after reminding him that I no longer use my real name. He nods in acknowledgement of this fact agreeing that for many of us, it is necessary. On no account must our names ever be reported back to the Gestapo. Who knows what would happen to our families back home. We all know what would happen if we are captured here! After an hour of catching up with our lives, Wilhelm[188] slaps me gently on my back and we part, never knowing if we will ever see each other again or come to that see our homeland again.

My body hurts: I'm cold and so exhausted. The healing inside from the bullet wound has reacted detrimentally. I am not sure if I have torn any repairs internally or if I have just overdone it.

"You cannot carry on in active service Sigmund or at least not for a while" remarks Hans Kahle who seems seriously concerned seeing my state of health.

"You'll end up dead, not having enough energy to see potential dangers. I'm recommending that you return to base to train our new recruits. You need to recover your strength. Your expertise in anti-tank warfare is needed there so that we have good, well trained Brigaders joining us ready to fight."

I know that he is right, but being removed from the front line is something I do not want. To disobey though is unforgivable so with reluctance I report myself to the Guadalajara[189] headquarters before I leave my brigade and head for Albacete. There's an unhealthy silence as I enter the room. The brigade staff are ashen faced and

---

[188] Wilhelm Bahnik fought bravely in the Edgar André Battalion and was to die in 1938 after being badly wounded in battle.

[189] This particular battle event is also known as the battle of Brihuega.

stunned which is surprising after winning such a hard and difficult battle.

"What has happened?" I ask in trepidation.

"The population of Guernica has been annihilated by blanket bombing. Those poor innocent Spaniards did not deserve such horrible deaths. Obviously this ancient Basque town and centre of culture has been destroyed" is the reply.

"Guernica?" I'm in such shock and disbelief that it is hard for me to talk. "But what is there militarily for the nationalists to justify such carnage towards these civilians?"

"That's just what we have been saying and this isn't the first time as you know that the enemy has blitzed a village or town. Vizcaya and the small picturesque country town of Durango suffered similar fates. It seems to me that Hitler is using the beautiful Spanish countryside and its population to practise aerial bombardment. The rest of Europe will suffer the same disaster unless we can stop these three dictators.[190] There are times when I wonder if we have any chance… "

The conversation peters out and there is silence for a while. No-one speaks as we are all thinking deeply about the future.

"What happened at Guernica?" I ask trying to bring everyone away from their personal thoughts.

"For three and quarter hours continual bombing took place from aircraft of the German Condor Legion aircraft[191]. Guernica has no anti-aircraft defence; it was of no strategic value to the enemy as we have limited equipment it was a defenceless town.

Not only ordinary bombs were dropped, but incendiary ones as well. The locals were in absolute panic and those who could, ran into the surrounding fields or the dugouts. These German murderers then flew their aircraft low over the civilian population and machine gunned the men, women and children. The surrounding villages have also suffered the same fate."

Silence ensues and then "It's the way it was done as well, meticulous in its cruelty."

---

[190] Franco, Hitler and Mussolini

[191] Please re-read the document "How is the situation in Spain" which is in Ernst's story – Chapter 24

He starts to repeat himself as though he has to be convinced that someone can be so callous.

"They initially used heavy bombs and grenades from groups of planes then the population were machine-gunned. Many of the civilians then ran back for shelter in the bombed buildings but their nightmare continued with about twelve bombers at a time dropping heavy bombs and incendiaries in the ruins to finish the population off. It's very similar to the actions that a cat plays with its victims before slowly killing them. It's a complete heartless and cruel act carried out on innocent people."

We look at each other in despair – it seems that there's nothing we can do to stop Hitler, Mussolini and Franco uniting against peaceful democracies such as Spain. We can give our lives to fight in the best way we can and hope that one day we will get support from France, Britain and America. Do these democracies really want fascism to take hold over Europe or is it the fear of communism which is preventing them from helping us? I am so tired and am beginning to feel old.

I give a "salud" clenched fist to my fellow Brigaders and head for my new military assignment and hopefully a chance to convalesce physically. On route to Albacete, I hear of in-fighting and hatred overflowing in the Barcelona streets. Communist fighting communist is a disaster especially at this time. Some belong to an organisation called POUM[192]. We cannot afford to waste time fighting each other. There are many things I disagree with here, but we must keep united to fight the fascists. Italy and Germany seem to be involved to an enormous extent with this war including personnel, military manpower and equipment and yet here we are fighting each other.

★

What on earth is going on here in Albacete? Once again it seems that the unfit and/or untrained but enthusiastic volunteers who arrive here are soon well trained at forming ranks, marching and turning.

---

[192] The Workers Party of Marxist Unification

I blanch knowing how so many of these keen men are ignorant militarily and yet are to be sent against the armies of Africa and Italy and the air force of Italy and Germany. Thank goodness some more experienced Great War veterans are also volunteering and are willing to aid the novices.

I am sure that it helps when the political commissars explain the reasons why we are all here and that there is a possibility that they may die fighting fascism. This is something which must help the men when facing our enemy. I was never involved in any battles during the Great War where it was explained what was happening and therefore believed in the reasons for us sacrificing our lives. Now we know why we are here but we need more artillery, weapons and planes. We are also in desperate need of experienced well trained armies from democratic countries in order to give us a chance to protect the citizens of Spain.

André Marty, the Brigade's controller is a short, stocky and surprisingly unfit looking man with a white moustache, oversized jaw, wears a black beret and is a man I can see who is not to be 'crossed'. I have seen how unwise it is to challenge him with contradictory or alternative ideas. He seems to be similar in his attitude to Stalin in believing that anyone with different opinions is a conspirator. There are too many people around with Stalinist ideas. This makes life very difficult for us as we desperately need the trust and commitment from the new volunteers who come ready to give their lives fighting for the republican cause.

I haven't got time for all these intrigue theories as we need stability and resoluteness from the men. I know that I have to make sure we do not deviate from our beliefs and that it is essential that I keep a close watch for any fifth columnists. In fact, it is my job to question new arrivals to check their authenticities. I have no problem with those instructions but some activities from my fellow compatriots are making me feel uneasy.

Some of the soviet intelligence activities are not always appropriate and too often saboteurs and internal enemies are seen everywhere. It is ridiculous making these assumptions should a person not have Stalin's 'political rhetoric' attitudes and speech.

How many more times will I find that the documents I have been given to read are inappropriate? I am not here to get embroiled in Stalin's indoctrinations and fears but to fight fascism. My fellow comrades in the Secret Intelligent Service or SIM have already intonated that I do not seem to understand the information and orders being sent. I give these reactions as to show objection to the policies would lead to my arrest.

I cannot carry out some of the instructions from the Soviet Union as my conscience will not allow me this luxury. I haven't lived all my life with honesty and dedication to justice and fairness to let things slip now. It's hard though being told that my political understanding is not progressing to the Soviet expectations. Showing ignorance or rather lack of comprehension of the latest policies is the only way forward at the moment as I still need to read and keep up to date with current events. This lack of enthusiasm for the new order will also mean no further promotion from my position as Teniente[193]. That is fine by me, but seeing how some men here being promoted only on their loyalty to Stalin and not their army expertise puts at risk our ability to win.

I feel uncomfortable about the way the Soviet Union is heading with a Stalinist form of government which at present seems to be a dictatorship and a doubtful form of communism. I just hope that this is a "blip" in the progression of a socialist/communist Soviet Union as I have given so much of my life to this belief since I was a teenager. When the revolution started in 1917 to remove the oppression of the working class and with Lenin as their leader, my heart had welled up in excitement and hope. I had thought at the time that perhaps it would be possible for Germany to become a socialist country, ending the way the wealthy abuse the working class. How unfair life has been for so many people just surviving above the bread line while the few with money experiencing their life of luxury. I want a democratic socialist government for Germany and its neighbours and I am willing to die for my belief. Our aims have been thwarted though with fascism on the rise.

As for Stalin, he must have a hidden agenda to which I am totally unaware and his present policies are temporary measures. I can't just

---

[193] Roughly equivalent to a lieutenant in the British army

abandon my lifetime beliefs because of some unpleasant activities that are starting to take place. If I do, it will mean that my whole existence has been a lie. I studied Marx and Lenin and yes I am a communist. My dreams are for the world to be a fairer place to live in. With so much poverty, starvation and exploitation taking place, the communist ideal seems the answer. There is wealth in the world, but only for the few at the expense of the many.

I still believe that socialist policies should be installed and I will fight for the rest of my life for these aims.

But what is happening with the Soviet Union? Am I putting my head in the sand, too frightened to admit that I have been living a dream? Could it be possible that my views are not the same as others here in Albacete and the advisers who seem to be everywhere? Is this the same form of communism that my friends and I have been fighting for whilst we were in Hamburg? We must keep true to our beliefs when we have fought so hard against the rich exploiting the poor in Germany.

I am only too aware that there are others here who are either under the spell of Stalin or are too frightened to speak out against him. Even I am wary with whom I speak to as according to some comrades here, my beliefs are heresy and I could be shot for disliking Stalin's extreme policy. It is worrying seeing the fear which he installs in people. However, all of us are a united front with our dedication to destroy fascism even though I despair at the ideas of the anarchists.

My time will come at a later date when I can show true feelings. To think that whilst in Germany I used to give speeches to rally the population into fighting for their social rights. It seems such a long time ago when the cause we were fighting was plain for all of us to see. There are times when I feel disheartened and disillusioned. I might be old (nearly 38 years old) and 'dry' as some of my comrade officers seem to be suggesting, but at least I still have my principles. I want a free democratic Spain and for the working class here to have the chance of education, jobs and healthcare. I certainly do not want to get involved in internal squabbling.

My military expertise in explosives generally and anti-tank experience in particular is useful for training the many keen new volunteers as well as the battle hardy troops.

Hatred, distrust and fear continue to seep through the streets of Spain especially in Barcelona. Arrests are being made of people who do not follow Stalin's beliefs. The leaders of POUM[194] are arrested at the beginning of June just as Franco's forces take over Bilbao. I feel very uneasy about all of this. I doubt if all these POUM soldiers and politicians are our enemies. Why arrest and in some cases sentence to death people trying to defeat Franco? We are losing good men with claims and counterclaims. I hear POUM soldiers are continuing to fight on our side in the battlefield and are only arrested when on leave. Internal bickering within the republican side might be our downfall.

Perhaps it's time to rethink my identity. If we fail to win this war, what will be my escape route? Where can I go where there will be sympathy to my belief in true socialism? At the moment Stalin is in power in the Soviet Union but how long before there's a new leader there or will Stalin revert to the original ideals of communism? Several of my friends are keen on escaping to Mexico as it is the only country recognising the republic. Perhaps they will take refugees from here. I decide to make Mexico my country should it be needed but as for now, we have a war to win.

Despite concerns about my 'lack of understanding' in the new ideas from the Soviet Union, I am made political commissar. They must feel confident in my abilities as a soldier and I will live, breath and die a loyal socialist and certainly never betray a friend. A political commissar has to promote the welfare of the troops, reinforce the reasons why we have all volunteered, listen to their complaints and worries and by doing all this uplifts the morale. These men are without doubt exceptionally brave to leave their homes and security for this place.

When we have some free time, the International Brigade people I am with join together with great gusto singing some civil war songs, ending of course with a rousing edition of "The Internationale". This never fails to cement our sense of belonging and comradeship.

---

[194] POUM – The Workers Party of Marxist Unification which is a group of main Catalan-based Marxist communists who were not part of the Comintern communists.

"Sigmonel, you are needed to report to headquarters".

My heart sinks. Have I been reported for some misdemeanour? As I walk into the room I give the clenched fist and "salud" to the officers on duty. To my relief they inform me that I have to report ready for action as I'm to take part in the battle to take Brunette. My body does now feel a lot stronger so I am pleased to be getting away from the politics and back to where I should be.

I have to smile at my name being changed, albeit slightly to Sigmonel. This is a sign that I am accepted into the Spanish fold and this pleases me. After all, we are fighting in Spain, for the Spanish and with the Spanish army.

This time we head for Navalcamero via Brunete, a village about 25 kilometres west of Madrid. This offensive will include all five International Brigades. The men know that I am always firm but fair and that I will put myself in as much danger as the rest of them should it be necessary. Orders have to be accepted in battle, otherwise we will be lost. This can be difficult though as some officers do not have battle experience. It's truly dreadful seeing such unnecessary slaughter. We need more leaders such as Hans Kahle.

If only we can have the use of really experienced commanders and less of the inexperienced Soviet advisers when in battle situations. Many of these advisers are sycophants to Stalin's political cronies. There are times when I wonder what sort of a country the Soviet Union might have become if Stalin hadn't obtained power. Perhaps whilst spending such a long time fighting fascism I have misunderstood the overall change happening in the Soviet Union.

As we are briefed for battle, it is obvious that we have a good chance of winning due to the surprise element. Also for a change, we have more troops than the nationalists. Let us hope our tactics are better and our commanders use their initiatives during the battle. Yet again, we have to draw our own maps. Surely we must have learnt from past battles?

Regardless of my concerns of our leadership's tactics, things start well and the 11th Division skirts around other skirmishes and advances on Brunete which has been badly defended. We are ordered to stop and wait for our colleagues. This is frustrating as we have the upper hand of surprise but now this will let the nationalists have a chance to reinforce this area. Before long my fears are beginning to be realised and with the lack of camouflage and the hard baked ground preventing us digging trenches, the German Condor Legion[195] have us as sitting targets.

"Hold your positions men. We must not let the republic down. Whatever fear you have inside you, we must stay and fight." I yell above the sound of shell and artillery fire. "We have to stop the tanks over there" pointing in the direction of oncoming enemy tanks.

"I've just heard that our lot are threatening to shoot anyone who's trying to retreat" squealed one of my men. "Guns have been positioned behind us – not trained on the enemy but on us."

"So hold your positions men" I yell again and continue to fire at the enemy.

Now is not the time to discuss and encourage as a political commissar normally would but it's vital to act with firmness and authority. The unbearable heat is making the dead bodies scattered around us blacken and become swollen. The smell is abhorrent. What a hell hole. The stretcher bearers are sitting targets as they bravely try to recover the injured.

Whatever or whoever has caused this disaster, it's no good dwelling on it. I know there have been some terrible decisions made by our leading commanders. We have failed to optimise on our surprise tactics right at the beginning and have let the nationalists reinforce their positions, but it's no good worrying over 'spilt milk'. Many good fighters have lost their lives already, but I have to keep the men calm, objective and ready to obey the commands.

"What's the point of being shot by our own troops for deserting our posts? We must continue." I yell as hard as I can at them.

Trust in me returns as I continue firing at the enemy and together my men hold firm but I can feel general defeat in the air. Realising that the nationalists will soon be sending more tanks in our direction, I quickly organise my men to dig and place anti-tank mines in position. Thank goodness they are now able to operate with only

---

[195] A volunteer unit of the German Air Force

the minimum of instructions. I think the brigades are beginning to realise the importance of anti-tank divisions. The damage these tanks can do against mere mortals is horrendous so they must be stopped.

Finally the new battle lines stabilise. We have gained about four miles along a ten mile stretch. Somehow I survive to live another day but this war is asking a terrible price on good people. We are losing so many brave men including many of my friends.

The morale after this battle[196] is extremely low. We have such continued beliefs in the just cause for which we are fighting but there is so much fundamentally wrong here in the hierarchy of our own organisation. How can it be put right? I really do not know. In the meantime honest brave men are dying through incompetence and also the lack of equipment. Stalin's conspiracy theories are creeping into Spain and are corrosive to all who have contact with them. This I fear might be causing problems in our leadership.

"Sigmonel you are needed in Madrid".

I look at my commanding officer in surprise. It's not normal to be expected to leave your unit but its better news than returning to Albacete. Once more my very few possessions are packed. I look at my fob watch[197] and realise that there's a chance that I can arrive in Madrid before nightfall as it is summer. It'll also be better travelling now that the strength of the midday sun has finally lessened. I manage to stop a truck heading in that direction, show my identity card and make my way to my next call of duty.

Hopefully I might have the opportunity of having a bath. That would be bliss as the human lice seem to have multiplied to almost unbearable levels. Short of burning my trousers it is almost impossible to kill them. The glistening white eggs resemble grains of rice and they remain in the seams of my trousers for a remarkably short time before hatching. Yes, a nice soak in a bath would be wonderful. My first dream is realised as I leave my unwanted companions behind and lay back in the warm water. This is a good move as I find out my duties are to help guard the incredible lady La Pasionaria[198]. What a privilege

[196] This is probably the bloodiest single battle of the war
[197] Which is now in the loving care of Ruth Stender
[198] Dolores Ibárrur

to be in the presence of such a powerful lady who believes in the same principles as me. This duty is relatively short-lived but a moment in my life that I shall never forget. Listening to her makes me decide that I should apply to be a member of the Spanish communist party. I feel more comfortable belonging to this organisation.

I know that my destiny is to take an active role in battles or to train troops in anti-tank combat situations. This time I have to head for Madrigieras and am in the 1st Batallon de Instruccion. It seems there has been a major change as to where we are training the recruits as Madrigueras used to be where the British were but now they've gone to Tarazona de la Mancha where we initially trained in the XIII Brigade. There must be a reason why but I have no inclination to find out. Here I bring up to standard the troops in anti-tank techniques and continue as a strong political leader at the camp. I shall always continue in my belief of Marxism even if I have to ignore some of the modern teachings and terror which can pervade the camp.

We desperately need more troops especially after all the losses we've had recently. Various mutinies have occurred which are a terrible admission for such an important cause but these men are mentally distressed at such futile slaughter. On 23rd September the International Brigade is incorporated into the Spanish Foreign Legion and we are not allowed more than 50% of our Brigades to be at officer level. Let us hope that this is a positive move. Two thousand of our men have typhus. What a waste of good brave men.

I put every effort I can to improve the fighting force; also to continue my intelligence work but it is a fine line I am treading here and my conscience will not betray honest men. Publicity to promote our cause means that photographers are encouraged to visit us but for me it's so difficult avoiding being photographed. Being a teniente of course makes this work easier than being promoted to a higher rank. This suits me in a place like this but I only wish the people with power would promote men with military experience and not on their politics. People often tease me that I am very serious and earnest, but it's hard to switch one's personality in the middle of a war and I am not sure who to trust; my fellow soldiers do admit that I am self-disciplined which I hope is a compliment. I am here for one purpose only – to fight fascism. Surely it is not a bad thing to be conscientious and being able to work on my own initiative. I really can't get involved in trivia as there is so much to do.

It's vital to question everyone who volunteers into our force. I willingly carry out the interrogation very thoroughly as it's extremely important to know who has volunteered and also of the situation back home – yes my real home – and to speak to anyone who might know what has happened to my lovely family. A new batch of volunteers has just arrived from various countries and on hearing that some of them are from Germany I can't help but feel excited.

"You say that you originate from Hamburg and your name is Schmidt[199]?"

He nods. My heart skips a beat with excitement and apprehension.

"Did you know either Werner or Ernst Stender?"

"Although he used a different name during our contact, I did know a Werner Stender" he answers.

At long last – someone knows my younger brother.

"This is someone you know?" he asks obviously having noted my expression. I nod unable to say who I really am as its vital I keep myself incognito especially in my job.

He continues. "Werner was one of my contacts in Hamburg but our group was infiltrated. All I could do was go to meet him at our allotted appointment and tell him never to return to his home under any circumstances as he would be arrested. I managed to put him in a safe house and we tried to cross the border together into Denmark. My sister, who was Prosche's girlfriend also needed to escape."

He stopped speaking for a few minutes. My heart again skips a beat. Surely Werner is alive and well. But he is so young to be involved like this. I think for a second or two. No he isn't too young I suppose as when I left Hamburg, he was a youngster and now it's nearly four years later. Will I ever see him again? Is he still alive?

"Carry on". My voice is rather sharp at this point.

"Both my sister and I managed to escape into Denmark as we had passports." He pauses, deep in thought. "I'm sorry but I must

---

[199] I cannot guarantee that this is his correct name

tell you that my sister is not to be trusted. She's got in with a bad lot." His eyes look sad and I can understand how difficult it must be to admit this about your own sister. It must have constantly been on his mind to blurt this out to me, but we need to know things like this as people like her can cause danger to our organisation. I thank him for being so honest and that I will pass on this information. I urge him to finish the information about Werner.

"All I can say is that I left him at the Danish border as our contact did not turn up and Werner didn't have a passport."

So my little brother is in trouble and I can do nothing to help him. This is a terrible scenario me being stuck here in Spain. Where is he? Has he been caught as there will be little chance of him surviving the Gestapo a second time round.

Where is Ernst? Is he alive or have they found out how seriously he has been involved in espionage. Has he been able to help Werner with his contacts or have they all been arrested? This is worse for me to endure than all the bullets being aimed in my direction. I thank him for the information and for trying to help Werner. Schmidt becomes a very useful member of our army.[200]

The answer as to the whereabouts of my little brother comes from an unusual source. Very rarely these days do I receive letters from the Soviet Union and addressed to me personally, but today is a very special day. As I open the envelope, I can feel my hands start shaking making it hard to read the contents properly. The handwriting is neat and tidy, which is totally unlike my scrawl and yes, there's the signature of young Werner. He's written to my friend in Moscow asking for my forwarding address. How did he know who to write to in Moscow? I can think of only one person who could have helped; the information will have come from Mama. She had the address which she knew she could write to in an emergency. I bet that information was hidden in the bottom of one of Papa's cigar boxes in his shop. Oh Mama what would I do without your love and strength keeping our family going.

Where is Werner now? I scan through the letter quickly before devouring it in detail. Well would you believe it, he's in Czechoslovakia! How on earth did he get there? Schmidt had said that Werner was

---

[200] He becomes a brave soldier and later dies fighting for the freedom of Spain

trying to get into Denmark and yet the letter is from the absolute opposite direction! Well, well, my little brother has really grown up. Tears well up and I kiss the letter with his familiar handwriting. My brother is alive. I'm missing such an important part of his life as he truly must be a man now and not a gangly, shy teenager. At least for the moment he is safe from our common enemy.

The hours slowly tick by until the day is over and I can disappear to my room. I reach for a pen and paper and start my reply. I usually hate writing but for once, it's a sheer pleasure for me. I had hoped and dreamed of writing to him these last few weeks when I knew he was trying to escape from Germany to safer lands. Czechoslovakia is not the safest of places, being surrounded by fascist states but for the moment he is all right.

I can just imagine the feelings Mama, Papa, Ernst and Lotte will have when they know that we are all in contact again. Werner will have to be the centre point not being able to write home myself. He will be kept busy writing letters to Hamburg and Spain but he was always better at writing than me. It's probably totally unnecessary to remind Werner to be careful, but I will all the same. It's essential that he uses my name "Otto" to everyone as I have no doubt that the Gestapo agents are still looking for me.

Oh the joy of personal happiness with contact of my family. I think I'll send Werner a photo album showing our life in the International Brigade. They show our existence in a positive light as I don't want him to worry about me in Spain. Hopefully when the fighting is over and fascism destroyed, Werner will be able to return the album to me when we are back together in Hamburg. If I do not survive, then my family will have seen the friends I have made and understand why I have risked my life here.[201]

Then the letter I have been dreading arrives from Werner suggesting that he joins me in Spain. I cannot even contemplate such an event. He has an almost straight leg so physically that becomes a liability in battle situations and then there's the personal one to deal with. How on earth could I carry out my work efficiently and without

---

[201] If anyone has found this album which was left in Čížkovice, our family would love to see it.

prejudice when someone who I love so dearly comes to Spain to fight? It will be an impossible situation for me and let's face it; Werner has to my knowledge never used weapons or had to kill anyone. To send him to battle with a high possibility of his death would finish me let alone our parents. If I ever survive and Hitler is defeated, how could I then face Mama and Papa? I know that I fight against our enemy and yes kill, but to expect my brother to do this? No I shall just ignore this letter. Hopefully Werner will read between the lines and accept that I do not want him here. He is too precious to me.

With pleasure I manage to meet my friend Wolfgang, who is able to understand English. He tells me that he has read another article written by Louis Fischer in *'The Nation'*. It is headed *"The Loyalists Push Ahead"*. He says *"the Spanish people are paying heavily for the privilege of fighting the world's battle against fascism, paying not merely in dead, wounded and captured, in the daily nervous strain, and in destroyed wealth but in unrelieved under nourishment."*

Without doubt he has managed to highlight the extraordinary deprivations which the Spanish people are suffering from. Surely something will be done to help them. There are about 25,000 war orphans in Barcelona alone, and so many of them have rickets due to poor nutrition. The death rate for the old and young has doubled this year.

"This journalist seems to have contacts and friendships with people in crucial positions. How can he have good relations and trust with the Spanish, Russian and American leaders even though their politics are at complete tangents to each other? Fischer seems to have such an understanding about the whole situation" says a comrade who had been listening.

"If only he could manage to get these leaders to pull together and help remove Franco from this country" I add to my friend's comments. I know that this is unrealistic now, but I still feel that I should say it.

It is time we start looking at the future of Germany. By some miracle, fascism might finally get defeated. We want democratic socialism and not Stalinism for my home country; of that I am certain.

In February 1938, some Germans colleagues from the XI Brigade form a committee. It's really good news that the membership includes both social democrats and communists. This way there's a consensus of middle to left wing members and this always makes a stronger union. During the middle of March I join many of my comrades at a conference of German exiles. It is time we reappraise the situation in Germany. If we can only persuade other nations of the evil of fascism and Hitler's regime, then there might be a chance of a democratic and socialist government being formed. On 13th March, we adopt a manifesto. During our time in Germany in the early 1930s, the social democrats and the communists were at loggerheads about the future of Germany. As a result fascism took hold when our two parties should have stood together against the threat of fascism. Now our manifesto is to stand united.

"We shall win if we are never again split, and are always united. Then the days of Hitler's dictatorship will be numbered and together we shall build a free democratic Germany, a Germany of peace, a Germany of freedom, a Germany of prosperity and social reform."

At last we are progressing towards a positive future for our country. There are bad omens for success in the near future as the previous day Hitler's men appear to have just walked into Austria. It certainly wasn't an invasion in the truest sense of the word, but is a step nearer Spain and come to that Czechoslovakia. Werner's position in his adopted country is somewhat precarious as it is becoming surrounded by fascists. I shudder at the thought of my little brother's danger. Perhaps I should have agreed to him coming here but in my heart I know that he would have little chance of survival here either.

I pack my small bag and head for Barcelona where the republican government is based. Negrín is returning from Paris where he has been meeting with French Ministers. There's to be a cabinet meeting at the Pedralbes Palace in Barcelona to discuss the future of the republic. However, my arrival is very badly timed as Italian planes which have been based in Majorca bomb the city continuously for three days. *Over 1000 women and children lose their lives during this carnage. I hope Werner will not have to support anyone suffering from the effects of bombs. My comrades here in Spain and I know too well how terrible it is for the civilian population²⁰².* It makes my blood boil seeing innocent citizens being annihilated or suffering such horrendous injuries. It's hopeless trying to help the injured as more bombs splinter every wall and shelter they try to hide in. In a battle, we don't see such concentrations of non-combatants being killed or maimed. What is Franco trying to achieve by these actions against his own people?

★

I've been given permission to re-join the XI Battalion special unit as the latest offensive against us is critical as they seem to be trying to split the republican zone into two by breaking through to the Mediterranean. This will be a disastrous situation if the nationalists succeed. The training of new recruits is becoming pointless being left with only the very young and old. My work in intelligence continues but I need to be out there fighting with as many loyal troops as possible. Is this the beginning of the end? We mustn't let it happen.

Once again I'm on the front line with my comrades fighting with everything we have in order to stop the nationalists. We have to hold on for as long as possible to give people a chance to retreat and regroup. *Franco sent all his overwhelming armaments against us. The bombs crashed with frightening regularity against us and about one hundred Batteries alone bombarded our defence in Gandesa. We had little to counter it and many good friends stayed in their positions regardless.²⁰³* The slaughter on both sides is terrible but I have little time to reflect on such matters.

Finally we withdraw from Gandesa, but retreating is a hard situation to accept. We have no alternative though with so little ammunition; food supplies are becoming virtually non-existent. Communications are difficult and it's becoming so easy for battalions to break formations. From the air enemy fighter planes dive down in our direction, strafing our exhausted troops with bullets and grenades. We try so hard to slow the advance but with little success.

---

²⁰² Section in italics translated from a letter to Werner from Rudolf describing the attack

²⁰³ Section in italics translated from a letter to Werner from Rudolf describing the attack

In less than a month we lose over 1000 officers and men in the 11th Brigade. In the Thälmann Battalion only 80 of the 450 men have survived just one battle and can continue to fight. So many good comrades have been killed including Artur Becker (Chairman of the Communist Youth League of Germany), the Battalion Commander Wilhelm Pinnecke, Hans Erbe (Fernando) who was our personnel department chief at Albacete, Commissar Wilhelm Glaser (Richard Schenk) and many others. All our efforts have come to nothing and we have to accept that so much territory has been lost.

★

So Franco succeeds in reaching the coast and now he's heading for Valencia and not as we initially feared, towards Barcelona. The weather again is atrocious with heavy rain which thank goodness reduces his airpower and has seemed to have slowed down his troops for a bit, but then the weather changes. We fight hard and our determination and strength pays off by withstanding the onslaught.

Fortifications from Sierra de Javalambre, across the Sierra de Toro to the heights of Almenara by the coast have been constructed in order to defend Valencia. These trenches and bunkers are known as the 'xyz' defence to take advantage of some of the most difficult terrain in Spain. This brilliant piece of defence is built to withstand bombardment by both the heavy artillery of 1000 field guns or 1000 pound aerial bombs. It helps to reinforce confidence within the troops and without doubt we need every bit of support.

I return to Barcelona and to my disgust I have to complete another form about myself. I'm sure my scrawl on the paper must indicate my feelings about paperwork, but there's no point fighting authority on trivia as it gets me nowhere! I put down about my time in Hamburg in 1924 when I was accused with 26 other people of being a member of an illegal party. I mention my friend Gustav Gundelach and then Morgendahl. Just at that point my patience and wariness snaps when I write the last name and add *"Morgendahl is a traitor"*[204]. There, I've written

---

[204] Taken from a document written by Rudolf and held at RGASPI Archives, Moscow

it so it's up to the authorities to query or action it. I never have written so openly before. I finish the report and as I look up, my good friend Gustav pops his head around the open door. He has a smile as broad as is possible. We don't see a lot of each other now as we have different roles in this civil war but it is just so good to see each other and to talk.

"Give my name as a reference" as Gustav looks over my shoulder to read the last part of the form I am completing. "You know that I am well known in the higher echelons of the party and I know that you have no other papers than Spanish ones."

I thank him and put his name down. Soon my business at the headquarters is over and we head out to a local hostelry where a bottle of one of Spain's great wines is opened and we spend a great time catching up with each other. As we clink the wine glasses together I couldn't help myself by saying "Spain has good wines and Germany good beer." Gustav laughed in agreement with me; it is so good enjoying a drink or two together after all this time.

But now it's time I returned to the battlefield; this time it is under the blazing sun of Lavante. This country seems to produce some extreme weather conditions and yet we carry on regardless. Life is really tough for all of us here. It is decided that our only possible hope for success is to cross the river Ebro and attack our enemy. Rafts are built plus pontoon bridges which will be needed to cross this mighty river. We give training to the men in minute detail in order to achieve a successful crossing. Many of the troops are being trained in mock situations and these are carried out in ravines, on rivers and by the coast. Our engineer corps are busy practising putting these temporary bridges over rivers and commandos have been crossing the Ebro overnight for surveillance purposes and obtaining information from the locals. La Passionaria's seventeen year old son is one of the commandos.

Our seriously wounded are to be sent to our make-shift hospitals. These volunteer nurses have given their time and in some instance their lives and most have left the comforts of their homes from all over the world. The doctors are also volunteers and they operate under horrendous conditions but in the hope of saving our troops who have been so horrifically injured. This time the hospital has been set up in a cave on our side of the river. They've managed to have lights which have been wired into the operating theatre and are using power generated from an ambulance. As for the rest of the temporary hospital, 120 metal beds have been installed and the ward is lit by tiny oil lights and tin cans with wicks in them. The cave is very low in height but is safe from the bombs. Those beds will be quickly filled and then the medics will have to cope until the injured can be transferred to better hospitals.

Finally in the early hours of 25th July, our plan is put into action with the commandos crossing the Ebro first in order to 'dispatch' the enemy sentries and to fasten lines for the assault boats. Six divisions manage to cross by boat and the using the pontoon bridges. I hear of a disastrous episode further down river close to the sea in which 1200 of our men in the XIV International Brigade died having been shot by the enemy or drowned trying to cross the Ebro. This event took place in just 24 hours; such terrible carnage. Those who had managed to cross were trapped and could not be rescued. This is not the time for us to weaken. We must continue to advance as quickly as possible as the element of surprise is important.

In our section within 48 hours we manage to liberate 600 sq kilometres. We head for Gandessa, where so many of our comrades died earlier in the defence of the town. Many of our troops suffer terribly marching with their feet covered in blood, but we walk 50 kilometres under the scorching July sun. Heat exhaustion causes many deaths but it's essential for us to make use of the element of surprise. We don't quite reach Gandessa when enemy planes attack us inflicting many casualties. We have only a few Russian tanks and where is our air cover? We need to have back-up.

I hear that there are problems back at the base as crossing the Ebro with reinforcements, weaponry and food is very difficult. During the day the pontoon bridges are being bombed and our engineers are trying to repair them at night which will explain why so little reinforcements are getting through to us. Once again dysentery and typhus becomes a problem; in fact it is another enemy against us with our men struggling to resist such debilitating illnesses.

Our injured cannot be repatriated to safety in daylight due to the aircraft attacks. If the wounded are lucky enough to survive the long day without medical attention, they are returned at night. The situation regarding our injured soldiers is serious but I'm so grateful to some doctor and nurse volunteers who've understood how hopeless it is to give immediate medical assistance to the very badly injured. These civilians help those who cannot be returned to relative safety across the river until after nightfall. Both women and men volunteers brave the bombs and strafing by the enemy and have set up a hospital at Santa Magdalena. At 2 am they had to leave as it became too dangerous and in darkness made their way to a tunnel at Flix. The grime from many years of soot and the railway line make life difficult for them. Despite this they manage to dig and clean the area as best they can to provide a further 65 hospital beds. I am told they have one lamp for three operating tables and initially a few candles in the ward. After two days when these are used up work is done by the light of matches. It's so easy to forget to mention these brave people helping us, but I find their caring very reassuring. After all, such people saved my life way back in December 1936. Who knows if they will be doing it again with all this killing taking place?

Oh these bomb attacks. There are times when it's hard to breathe and see with the dust and the noise of the explosions. One minute you have your comrades around you and then only parts of bodies. Some of the men put wood in their mouths to clench their teeth in order to stop yelling in fear. Bullets seem to be flying in all directions and it's so difficult to know if it is 'friendly' fire. At last I hear, just above the noise of war, the sound of our own aircraft defending us from the bombardment of our enemy. Even if it is six days too late, at last we can have some respite.

On 1st August, we're ordered to stop attacking but to defend. I've heard that we have lost 12,000 men and life for the remaining troops is becoming unbearable. The heat is increasing. It's 37°C in the shade and 57°C in the sun. I'm not built for being active in this heat. We try building stone shelters but this proves to be lethal when bombs explode around us as our initial protection becomes shrapnel for our bodies. The bombing and bullets directed at us seem eternal and the dehydration we all are suffering from makes our lives hell.

Eyes of men running, falling, screaming
Eyes of men shouting, sweating, bleeding
The eyes of the fearful, those of the sad
The eyes of exhaustion and those of the mad
Eyes of men thinking, hoping, waiting
Eyes of men loving, cursing, hating
The eyes of the wounded, sodden in red
The eyes of the dying and those of the dead[205]

The smell of death is all around us but we have to wait until dark before we can consider burying our dead. *What I will never forget is leaving a position under pressure and having to leave some comrades behind as they were wounded. It's bad enough having to do that but later reclaiming that same position, it's a terrible shock to find how our enemy has murdered our friends in the most cruel ways"*[206] It just shows us what we have to expect and what will also happen to the citizens who have supported the republican government should any be captured.

We're absolutely exhausted and I can see that the future of Spain looks very bleak. I've heard that Negrín has spoken at the League of Nations and that the International Brigade is to be withdrawn from fighting. For many of my friends, their fighting days are to be over and they will return to their home country and the security and love of their families. I only hope that they will not be victimised for their beliefs in coming to fight against the evils of fascism.

As for many of us who came from fascist countries such as Germany and Italy, our future is less certain. We have no chance of being repatriated to safety. Our only hope is to become part of the Spanish units and continue to fight to the end. The less fortunate will remain, unnamed in the soil of Spain.[207]

---

[205] Poem from an unknown soldier who was in the British Battalion of the International Brigade

[206] In italics from letter written from Rudolf to Werner

[207] So many unnamed volunteers are buried in unmarked graves. According to Ken Bradley's book *International Brigades in Spain 1936-39* those who sacrificed their lives in Spain consisting of approximately 3,000 of the 10,000 French and Belgian, 2,000 of 5,000 Germans and Austrians, 600 of 3,300 Italians, 750 of 1,500 Yugoslavs, 900 of 2,800 Americans, and 526 of 2,300 British

In order to comply with the agreement, we become Spanish citizens so no foreign fighters remain in the army. We continue to fight with everything left in our spirit as well as our body. We've been told to report to Barcelona as there is to be a parade marking the disbandment of the International Brigade. I owe it to my lost friends to be there and to hold my head up high, proud of our existence and our core beliefs. I wonder if the withdrawal of foreign volunteers from our side will be reciprocated by the nationalists as it has been hoped. I smile wryly thinking of this possibility. Somehow I think not as Hitler and Mussolini are determined to ensure a victory and now the world will continue to let fascism take prominence in the world of politics.

We arrive in Barcelona, ready for our parade down the Diagonal where we shall salute President Azaňa, Negrín, Companys and General Rojo along with many other of our leaders. It is a day I know that I shall never forget knowing that some 300,000 citizens of Spain are beginning to line the streets who just want to thank us. It will be a very proud moment when we parade along these streets and yet a bitter pill to swallow knowing that despite our sacrifices, Spain is to fall into the hands of our enemy – the fascists. I feel like going through so many "what if's but where is that going to get me?

"Britain, France, Germany and Italy have signed an agreement in Munich" the officer beside me mutters in frustration.

"What? What on earth are France and Britain playing at? What is this agreement?" I reply in horror.

"As it now stands, Hitler will be able to annexe Czechoslovakia's Sudetenland" is his reply.

What will this mean for Werner and his friends? Papa had been right that Werner will be surrounded. I just hope he'll have his wits about him; I am also in dire straits and cannot help him. What a mess the Stenders are in and all because no-one in the west is willing to stand up against these tyrants. Britain and France might yet regret their moves of placating Germany and Italy.

I grit my teeth with frustration but today will be a day to hold our heads high and be proud of what we have tried to do. We must remember our friends who are no longer alive and those too badly injured and cannot be here today to celebrate the existence of the International Brigade. I look at my comrades who are in the same situation as me. There has been no opportunity to smarten ourselves up, having come straight from the battlefield. This is not as we had planned the outcome of our sacrifice and beliefs. This is the end of the International Brigade and we have not succeeded in victory over tyranny. Many of our friends can now return to their homeland, their wives or girlfriends and possibly children. We must celebrate this if nothing else and also the comradeship between many of us.

Unfortunately politics and intrigue have thwarted us in many situations; battles have been lost which should not have been, but it's all too late now. I tried on so many occasions to avoid the political manoeuvring which I felt was detrimental of our aims of retaining democracy. I read so many papers and documents from Stalinist supporters and the Soviet Union which were not in keeping with our overall beliefs and I became so frustrated with trivia; all I wanted was for our men who had volunteered to fight against fascism not to be caught in the disputes but pull together in order to win battles. The cause is always more important than the individual.

It's no good thinking such thoughts today though as these thousands of Spanish supporters are now ready to view our parade to bid us farewell and to thank us for our help. My heart beats with pride seeing such love and support for us as flowers are strewn in our path. I hear the roar of aeroplanes and look up. So we are getting protection from our air force which makes a change. If only I could have smartened myself up a bit more for this occasion.

La Pasionaria starts to speak. *"It is difficult to say a few words in farewell to the heroes of the International Brigades, because of what they are and what they represent. A feeling of sorrow, an infinite grief catches our throat – sorrow for those who are going away, for the soldiers of the highest ideal of human redemption, exiles from their countries, persecuted by the tyrants of all peoples – grief for those who will stay here forever mingled with the Spanish soil, in the very depth of our heart, hallowed by our feeling of eternal gratitude.*

From all peoples, from all races, you came to us like brothers, like sons of immortal Spain; and in the hardest days of the war, when the capital of the Spanish republic was threatened, it was you, gallant comrades of the

International Brigades, who helped save the city with your fighting enthusiasm, your heroism and your spirit of sacrifice. Jarama and Guadalajar, Brunete and Belchite, Levante and the Ebro, in immortal verses sing of the courage, the sacrifice, the daring, the discipline of the men of the International Brigades.

For the first time in the history of the peoples' struggles, there was the spectacle, breathtaking in its grandeur, of the formation of International Brigades to help save a threatened country's freedom and independence – the freedom and independence of our Spanish land.

Communists, socialists, anarchists, republicans – men of different colours, differing ideology, antagonistic religions – yet all profoundly loving liberty and justice, they came and offered themselves to us unconditionally.

They gave us everything – their youth or their maturity; their science or their experience; their blood and their lives; their hopes and aspirations – and they asked us for nothing. But yes, it must be said, they did want a post in battle, they aspired to the honour of dying for us.

Banners of Spain! Salute these many heroes! Be lowered to honour so many martyrs!

Mothers! Women! When the years pass by and the wounds of the war are being staunched; when the cloudy memory of the sorrowful, bloody days returns in a present of freedom, peace and well-being; when the feelings of rancour are dying away and when pride in a free country is felt equally by all Spaniards, then speak to your children. Tell them of these men of the International Brigades.

Tell them how, coming over seas and mountains, crossing frontiers bristling with bayonets sought by raving dogs thirsting to tear their flesh, these men reached our country as crusaders for freedom, to fight and die for Spain's liberty and independence threatened by German and Italian fascism. They gave up everything: their loves, their countries, home and fortune; fathers, mothers, wives, brothers, sisters and children and they came and told us "We are here. Your cause, Spain's cause, is ours – it is the cause of all advanced and progressive mankind".

Today many are departing; thousands remain, shrouded in Spanish earth, profoundly remembered by all Spaniards. Comrades of the International Brigades! Political reasons, reasons of state, the welfare of that same cause for which you offered your blood with boundless generosity, are sending you back, some of you to your own countries and others to forced exile. You can go proudly. You are history. You are legend. You are the heroic example of democracy's solidarity and universality in the face of the vile and accommodating spirit of *those who interpret democratic principles with their eyes on hoards of wealth or corporate shares which they want to safeguard from all risk.. We shall not forget you and, when the olive tree of peace puts forth its leaves again, mingled with the laurels of the Spanish republic's victory – come back!*

Return to our side for here you will find a homeland – those who have no country or friends, who must live deprived of friendship – all will have the affection and gratitude of the Spanish people who today and tomorrow will shout with enthusiasm.

Long live the heroes of the International Brigades!"[208]

We're deafened by a massive uproar of cheering and shouting of approval from the local population to her long but wonderful speech. We all feel overwhelmed and I can feel a lump in my throat as I wander through the crowd of fellow Brigaders searching for my old friends who are to depart from Spain. It is such an emotional time. I have met some magnificent courageous people these last three years but have lost a great many more as they are now forever part of the Spanish soil.

Now is the time to say farewell to the living. I have nowhere I can call home; the fascists have taken power of my beloved country. There's no question about my decision to stay and fight with my Spanish colleagues. The battle of the Ebro is not completely over so that is where I'll go. Perhaps we can be of use to slow the advance and hopefully defend these citizens here in Barcelona where they have given us such a wonderful rousing farewell. What is going to happen to these republican supporters if we surrender? No I will fight for as long as possible.

I turn my back on my old friends and head for the battlefield once more. For those of us making this decision, we are only too aware of our future. I could write to Werner in Czechoslovakia, but what can I say to him? If I survive these next few weeks, I will try to contact him to see if he is safe. As for my parents, I think that it is better they know nothing about our situation.

We continue fighting during November but we cannot do anything but slow down the nationalist advance. Cold and hunger

---

[208] According to the International Brigade Memorial Trust, depending on the ability of understanding foreign languages, Spanish, English and French copies of this speech was given to all International Brigade volunteers in Spain.

is also another enemy and we lack weapons and ammunition. The very young and very old join us as they are conscripted into the army, replacing so many good colleagues. Finally our battle for the Ebro is over and it looks as though my fighting days here are at an end.

My body just sinks into this wonderful straw mattress as I pull a sheet and blanket up to my neck. Oh, it feels like heaven, having had a hot, albeit meagre meal with my hosts and *it is so nice to live with locals in their own home*[209]. I have no weapons to defend myself or my hosts but I have a roof over my head in the middle of winter.

Such small luxuries perhaps would not have felt so wonderful a few years ago, but after three years of fighting in Spain, I feel the stress leave me.

Deep down I know that this is not a safe place for any of us as it will only be a matter of time before the nationalist army arrives, but these pleasures are to be treasured. *We have no arms and we are only too aware that Franco's army is getting nearer each day. This small town, or should I say village of Bisaura de Ter*[210] *is about 60 km from the French border. It's beautiful here with lovely surroundings and there are cinemas and cafes to relax our tired bones*[211]. My jarred and tense brain is beginning to let go and I can feel myself beginning to enjoy these peaceful days. If only this was a real holiday and we could just live like ordinary people. Looking at my comrades, I notice their faces have hardened with suffering. We have all aged in these three years. My ears are hurting again which is not surprising after so many explosions landing close to me and the constant shooting. The damage done during the Great War and the resulting ear operation has all returned again with a vengeance, but I am still alive.

Some of my comrades have managed to retain their musical instruments; most of these items look as worn and dilapidated as us having been part of their owner's personal baggage from one battlefield to the next. Music is still important to many of us. As I had not brought my mandolin with me, I borrow one and before long we're all singing old familiar songs. Oh the joy of such small pleasures. *Our time at Bisaura de Ter comes to an end as we are given*

[209] Extracts in italics taken from a letter written by Rudolf to Werner
[210] Now known as San Quirico de Besora / St Quirze de Besora
[211] Extracts in italics taken from a letter written by Rudolf to Werner

instructions to leave in mid-January. The Spanish army needs to train new recruits here so it is time to vacate and leave our hosts.[212]

We are told to relocate to Palafrugell which is about 10 kms from Palamõs Again as we have no weapons to fight; all we can do is relax and await our fate[213]. The French border is shut to military aged men so what else can we do? News just reaches us about the ultimate in vicious cruelty. The little children in Barcelona, like their parents, have been close to starving. They thought that the Italian air force was being kind by dropping packets marked "chocolate" in Italian from their aircraft. These items in fact were anti-personnel bombs and many youngsters have had their hands blown off when they eagerly picked them up. It makes my blood boil that so heinous a war crime can be carried out on these innocent children. I had always thought that the Italians love children! I can feel the hate surging back into my body. I can't just take hearing this without doing something to help protect the people.

The onslaught of the nationalists is forcing the republican army into retreat and I can see absolute panic on the faces of some of the raw recruits. I cannot blame these youngsters who are hardly old enough to call themselves men. At the other extreme the men who are past their prime are expected to be physically fit. Both groups are expected to be ready to die for their country but for the youngsters, I feel such compassion for these youngsters as death should not be on the agenda for this generation. Even the soldiers who are trained properly are exhausted and almost unable to think straight.

Weapons are being discarded in the panic to see if they can get over the border into France. My friends and I have absolutely nothing to lose[214] as we will be shot without hesitation or even worse if we are captured by the nationalists. We are wanted men as far as Hitler's regime sees us.

"Should the International Brigade now become prisoners of the fascists without putting up a fight?" I yell at my comrades.[215]

"No, no, no" is the answer from nearly all present.[216] We shake each

---

[212] Extracts in italics taken from a letter written by Rudolf to Werner
[213] Extracts in italics taken from a letter written by Rudolf to Werner
[214] Extracts in italics taken from a letter written by Rudolf to Werner
[215] Extracts in italics taken from a letter written by Rudolf to Werner
[216] Extracts in italics taken from a letter written by Rudolf to Werner

other's hands and smile resolutely. We organise ourselves acquiring weapons mainly from the retreating army. Being refreshed after our stay in Bisaura de Ter, we are determined to give all we can in protecting the rear guard. Roads leading northwards from Barcelona are jammed full of horses, carts, cars, vans, lorries and buses. Both citizens and military throng the roads trying to escape the terror which awaits anyone who remains; that is unless you are a fifth columnist. These people I imagine are already wreaking their revenge on the poor souls unable to escape[217]. The situation is a humanitarian disaster.

And then there's the soldiers who are wounded and have been recovering in Vallcarca hospital. I hear that despite their injuries, many men who have lost arms and/or legs have been crawling along the ground begging not to be left behind and to suffer the fate of so many republicans who have been captured by Franco's army. Some soldiers who have lost their right hand and some who have terrible wounds to their right arm still show determination in trying to give the republican clenched fist salute.

My comrades and I decide that we have to do something to slow down the advance in order that the population, who desperately want to escape into France, have a chance of survival. Perhaps the French government will take a softer line and let the retreating army escape from the expected slaughter; if only they will open the border for them. They must relent with the numbers of the republican army marching in their direction; the only other alternative for the French is to produce and use machine guns against the Spanish republican army to prevent this mass exodus into France.

We pick up the discarded weapons[218], cleaning them as best we can whilst moving in the opposite direction of the masses. Defending these poor wretched souls is essential.

Will our rear guard actions delay the rapid offensive of Franco?

---

[217] When the nationalist troops entered Barcelona, they joined the fifth column men and women left in the city and between them, they carried out their revenge on those left behind. Approximately 10,000 people were murdered in the first five days during the so called "liberation" of the city. Information taken from Guillermo Cabanellas, *La Guerra de los mil dias, Barcelona,* 1973 *vol ii*

[218] Words in italics translated from a letter from Rudolf to Werner

How many people will we be able to save? All effort and lives given over the last three years is over and now all we can do is slow the enemy down so that Spanish men, women and children can escape from their own country to become exiles but at least they have hope of remaining alive.

None of us here wanted this outcome. I'm sure Europe and the world will live to regret their actions over Spain for this will not be the end of fascism – only the beginning. What fools these politicians have been. Can they justify their fear of communism or even socialism and the rights of the working class and risk the consequences of the tyranny of fascism?

Stop thinking like this Rudolf, this is not the time and place as we have people to save. I close my rifle up, discard the filthy cleaning cloth and hasten my pace towards the battlefield. Once again this is not an easy terrain for us. We can see the enemy approaching, but equally they can easily see us due to the lack of cover. The gently rolling hills is fine if we are fortunate to be on the high slopes but the nationalist weaponry and air power is far superior to ours thanks to the embargo placed on our side by the rest of the world. The Soviet Union tried to supply us but it has never really been sufficient; now is non-existent. I would also like to know the numbers of professional soldiers on the enemy's side compared to the professionals on our side. We have had to rely on so many inexperienced but enthusiastic civilians.

It's difficult fighting when there are so many people trying to flee. There is bound to be civilian injuries in such situations which I always find hard to observe. How would I be feeling if they were my own family? Thank goodness I ignored Werner's request for him to join me as I would be useless now as a soldier as I know I could not help myself from trying to protect him. But where is he now?

Once again I bring myself back to reality. Tiredness would be playing a part in all of my decisions if the adrenaline had not kicked in. *My present task is the defence of La Bisbal*[219]. For two days[220] there has been heavy bombing and what with La Bisbal being in a dip amongst

---

[219] Extracts in italics taken from a letter written by Rudolf to Werner
[220] 2nd and 3rd February

these rolling hills, it's so difficult to see our enemy. *Whatever happens, we've been ordered to remain where we are. Then realisation dawns as we discover to our misfortune that our enemy is not in front of us but they have skirted around La Bisbal in order to attack us from an unexpected direction. Despite our precarious situation we will carry on fighting. We must keep them at bay so that the retreat can continue. At the last moment before the enemy take us, we get the order to retreat.[221]*

I return to Palafrugell to pick up my belongings I had left with a comrade who had chosen not to join us in fighting. He and all my belongings have disappeared. I am sure I will meet this man again sometime, somewhere in this world![222]

Day and night we march in formation towards the border with France[223]. We've heard that at long last the French have opened it up to the remnants of the popular army[224].

We walk with heads held high and in good spirits knowing that we have done the best we can when we consider the circumstances.[225]

Once again I'm amazed at our medical support. Someone tells me of a civilian has been badly wounded civilian from the strafing of the enemy aeroplanes. He had been carried into a peasant's house by the roadside. As I pass by, inside I can see a doctor and a few women nurses, operating on a kitchen table where they are trying to save this wounded man. Despite everything, the medical units are still trying to save lives, which is an amazing achievement. How brave they are.

Finally on 8th February, our destination of the French border is reached[226]. We're almost numb with mental and physical exhaustion but I will not give anyone the pleasure of seeing how we're really feeling. I can hear sobbing from behind me as some of my German comrades go into delayed shock. I look back and see the land all along the Spanish side heaving with a mass of people heading in our direction. It looks

---

[221] Again words in italics taken from extracts of letters from Rudolf to Werner

[222] Again words in italics taken from extracts of letters from Rudolf to Werner

[223] Again words in italics taken from extracts of letters from Rudolf to Werner

[224] 5th February

[225] Again words in italics taken from extracts of letters from Rudolf to Werner

[226] Again words in italics taken from extracts of letters from Rudolf to Werner

as though the land itself is moving. I cannot even attempt to say how many people are here just inside France let alone the people attempting to cross the border. It's absolutely staggering to see such a sight.[227]

I turn my attention to my colleagues who are showing signs of having a mental breakdown so I try to lift their spirits[228]. As we are not in Germany, seeing the French Police guarding us on both sides of our formation is not the end of the world. I am sure these people will treat us fairly. We must keep calm. Every part of my body aches with hunger, thirst and fatigue but our woes are not over yet as we are ordered to march, who knows where. *Many of our men have little protection against the weather and all of us need refreshments.[229]*

We walk for a further 40 kilometres and still receive no food[230]. We're obviously heading for lower ground as very slowly the Pyrenees landscape changes to flat and softer looking territory. Where are we being taken I wonder? I try to keep the morale as high as possible but I can hear the footsteps of my compatriots becoming laboured. I look at their faces and can see deep ruts etched permanently into their young faces. Youth has left them forever. Grief is visible with those who have said goodbye to their homeland and to their families, perhaps forever. We're all filthy, not having had any opportunity to wash. And then there's the hunger, tiredness and thirst to overcome.

Sea salt and a bitter wind pitilessly pierce through our clothes making our weak bodies shiver. I think there must be a very wide beach in front of us but this is impossible to confirm as there are thousands of men huddling together and surrounded by barbed wire. Surely they are not going to imprison us on a beach in February and without any shelter?

"Be grateful that you are here. The camp we have just filled yesterday contains 180,000 people. There is 65,000 or 75,000 in this one" one of the policemen says nonchalantly.

Now is not the time to hesitate; we must show how proud we

---

[227] On 10th February, the border is closed

[228] Again words in italics taken from extracts of letters from Rudolf to Werner

[229] The words in italics are translations from letters sent from Rudolf to Werner

[230] The words in italics are translations from letters sent from Rudolf to Werner

are to have fought against fascism. We walk through the barbed wire gates as *Senegalese troops and garde mobile closely watch our movements, waiting eagerly for any of us to deviate from their orders. The coloured Senegalese guards treat us like dirt. They chase us with bayonets around the camp and nobody is allowed to protest. Some comrades lose their last belongings. Everybody has to hide their watch and valuables.*[231]

A congregation of fellow prisoners gather together so my inquisitive nature draws me in that direction. Oh thank goodness, there's a small stream so at long last we have some running water to drink. Surely though this can't be the only source of drinking water for all these thousands of prisoners. This bitterly cold wind whips over the vast sandy beach. We have no food; no shelter, no latrines and many of us have very little clothes to cover our weak bodies. The weather is appalling. The mortality rate will obviously continue to increase if this is the only hospitality we receive from the French.

There's no alternative but to start digging a hole in the sand as quickly as possible in order to get some protection from this wind. My exhausted body aches as I start using my hands to dig a hole. The wind continues to howl, hurting my ears; the sand particles sting my eyes. I finally slump into my new home and within a few minutes, I surrender my body accepting sleep.

Laughter of familiar voices fills me with joy. Mama and Papa smile indulgently at all of us as we tease Werner for being the last one to sit down at the dining table. We laugh together, picking up our cutlery and tuck into one of Mama's delicious meals. How lucky we are having such a close family unit.

My stomach aches with hunger forcing me out of my blissful dream and I feel ill. A lump in my throat makes it hard for me to swallow and a tear wells up in one of my eyes. Oh for those sweet happy times when we were all together. And now look at me! Werner is in danger as is Ernst. What will happen to all of us. I have lived through hell but am I now safe? Is my family safe?

---

[231] In italics translation from letters sent from Rudolf to Werner

Photo (right) found in the RGASPI Archives in Moscow which could possibly have been the photo taken as Rudolf left USSR in 1936 as we have a very similar photo of him (left) which was sent to Werner in England and taken during the Spanish Civil War.

Could this be taken whilst preparing an area for anti-tank mines? Rudolf is on the left of the picture.

Glossary

ADGB	Allgemeiner Deutscher Gewerkschaftsbund (Confederation of German Trade Unions in Germany 1919-1933)
AM Apparat	Military and political section of the resistance movement
Apparat	Divisions of the resistance movement
Article 48	Emergency decree signed by the president and gives him far reaching powers. Should only be used when security or public disorder threatens the country
Bezirksleitung	resistance leadership of Hamburg
Christlichen	Right winged trade union
Condor Legion	A volunteer unit from the German Air Force
DMV	Deutscher Metallarbeiter-Verband (Metal Workers Union)
DNVP	German National People's Party
Freikorps	Unofficial Paramilitary right wing reserve force: Forerunners of the SA and SS
Gestapo	Geheime Staatspolizei
I.K.K.I.	Executive Committee of the Commintern
KolaFu	Konsentrationslager Fuhlsbüttel (Fuhlsbüttel Concentration Camp, Hamburg)
KPD	Kommunistische Partei Deutschlands
Landsturm	Older class of reserve soldiers
MOPR	International Red Aid
NSDAP	Nationalsozialistische Deutsche Arbeiterpartei (Nazi Party)

OD	Ordnerdienster – organisation for the protection of left wing leaders from right wing paramilitary groups
POUM	Partit Obrer d'Unificació Marxista (The Workers Party of Marxist Unification)
Putsch	Attempt of a military coup of a government that depends on suddenness and speed.
Reichsbanner	A paramilitary organisation connected with the SPD
RFB	Rote Frontkämpferbund – a paramilitary task force of the communist party
Rote Hilfe	Solidarity organisation founded by Wilhelm Pieck and Clara Zetkin aimed at supporting workers families in dire need during the turbulent early years of the Weimar Republic. In addition Rote Hilfe arranged legal support and legal defence for workers who were under indictment for their political activities or views. By mid-1929 the Rote Hilfe had helped nearly 16,000 arrested workers with a legal defence and supported legal rights of another 27,000.
Rote Marinesturms	A military left wing division of the RFB
RM	Reichsmark
SA	Sturm-Abteilung – original paramilitary wing of the Nazi Party
SAJ	Sozialistische Arbeiterjugend
SPD	Sozialdemokratische Partei – social democratic party (right wing socialists)
SS	Schutzstaffel – a major paramilitary organisation under the command of Adolf Hitler. It became one of the most powerful organisations in the Third Reich. Responsible for many of crimes against humanity
Stahlhelm	Unofficial paramilitary right wing reserve force founded Dec 1918

Teniente	Possibly equivalent to Lieutenant in the British army
UDGB	Allgemeiner Deutscher Gewerkschaftsbund (Confederation of German Trade Unions in Germany 1919-1933)
USPD	Unabhängige Sozialdemokratische Partei – Independent Socialist Party (left wing socialists)
USSR	Union of Soviet Socialist Republic
Völkischen	A paramilitary organisation belonging to the Völkische Party which is a right winged anti-Semitic party
VVN	Vereinigung der Verfolgten des Naziregimes (Antifascist Organisation).

Epilogue

You will have to read my next book to know the outcome of the Stender family. I hope that you have enjoyed this biographical novel and in the process have had time to ponder about some of the similarities of the situation during the 1920s and 1930s to what is happening in the world today.

Hopefully you can now understand the trauma that my family went through in their fight against the rise of fascism. Our family is just one of many others who tried to prevent fascism from dominating world events and the subsequent slaughter of many innocent people. In the final book the family history starts in February 1939 and ends in 1950. I decided to split the story into two books when I realised that the personal and political information I have for this period is extremely complicated and detailed and to shorten anything would not give the reader a true picture of the world events and the intertwining life of the Stender family. I am not trying to say that my family are unique, but I feel that too little is known about families such as ours.

The information about my family is true except for some sections which I have been unable to verify. To be perfectly fair to the reader, I will mention below the situations which are not proven at the time of writing.

I cannot provide evidence that Ernst helped Rudolf escape via the docks but Ernst knew a great deal about Rudolf's activities and would naturally help his brother. Ernst also had a large number of contacts with the people who worked in Hamburg docks and would have the resources to help Rudolf at his time of need.

There is a list of new émigrés from Germany entering the Soviet Union in 1933 and on this list is Rudolf's name. By the side of his name is an asterisk and the comment that Rudolf was a specialist in explosives. This information is available in the Berlin Archives along with a note from the Gestapo that they were looking for Rudolf in

Berlin on 9th January 1935 and a warrant was made for his arrest in connection to an incident at the Berlin High Court. I can only assume that he must have been travelling between the Soviet Union and Berlin in his fight against fascism; he certainly did not return to visit his beloved family in Hamburg.

There is a document which has been included in my book which was confidential in the 1930s. It is a translation of a report found in Hamburg University Archives. It is a letter sent to people in high positions in Hamburg on the conditions of Fuhlsbüttel concentration camp and also the Gestapo headquarters in Hamburg. This was included in the story to explain to the reader the horrors of Nazism. It was never seen by my father until I brought a copy of it back to England for him to read.

The description of Rudolf's escape when the Gestapo arrived at our allotment to find and arrest him, is an accurate account of events; however I can quite understand any doubt as this incident seems so out of character to the usual cold and efficient behaviour of the Gestap.

I was indeed extremely fortunate to find and receive copies of Rudolf's personal file which is kept at the Moscow Archives. According to information written in Rudolf's own handwriting, the Dünkel family had been an enormous help to Rudolf in his resistance activities. Johann Dünkel had five children. We know that he helped Rudolf in 1923 by hiding weapons plus a typewriter. This last item sounds unimportant but typewriters were much coveted by resistance groups. Due to Johann's assistance in providing the availability to use his home, Rudolf and his organisation were able to carry out secretive work. One of Johann's daughter's married Hans Stender and we also know that Hanny Dünkel did some courier work for the resistance. Hilde Dünkel was involved in some political work for Rudolf at the Gross Einkauf Gesellschaft. Johann also offered his home to Rudolf as a 'safe house'. Another daughter was arrested in 1934 for her activities. However Johann's son was forbidden to enter the home in 1933 because of his political affiliations and possible connections with the extreme right wing. It shows how one family can have differing political beliefs.

As gratitude for Johann's help, my father believes that Rudolf gave his important collection of stamps to Johann but once again I have no proof. If this was the case, my father is pleased that Rudolf was able to thank him in some way.

With regard to Hanny Dünkel, all communications to her family in Hamburg finished when Stalin's 'Great Purge' started. Rudolf kept in contact with her until 1936. She had initially entered the Soviet Union for two years but decided to stay for a further period when she met her husband who was from the Soviet Union. Rudolf said that he was a very pleasant person. However, Hanny was never heard of again so we can only assume that she perished along with the thousands of others in Russia during this awful period. The file in the Moscow archives provided me with the information about the illegal books which Hanny brought with her from Germany. She probably thought that as there were shortages of educational books in the Soviet Union, that she was helping the new socialist country. The version of history being taught in a communist country is obviously at complete odds to a fascist Germany and therefore would be totally inappropriate and considered dangerous propaganda. I have also included details of the accusations being made against Rudolf including the comments he made about Willi Bredel all of which are held in the Moscow Archives.

Why did Rudolf leave the Soviet Union? When the fascists started to arrest German socialists and communists for their political beliefs and put them in concentration camps or executed them, many decided to escape to the Soviet Union for safety. As most readers are aware, the Stalin era of 'The Purge' during 1936 – 1939 meant that many émigrés started to be interned and worse; many were never seen again. Rudolf would have seen this start to happen and would have known that eventually he might have been arrested. Indeed, his departure to Spain was at risk because of the accusations being made about him. It is possible that Rudolf was aware that he could be arrested at any time. As republican Spain was in desperate need of people prepared to fight against the fascist army of Franco, his destiny once again changed. It is mentioned on many occasions in his personal file still held in the Moscow archives that during his period in Spain Rudolf did not like to get involved in trivia but held the bigger picture of fighting fascism, so perhaps staying in the Soviet Union would not have suited him. Yet again, none of this can be proved, but Rudolf's willingness to risk his life for his beliefs is well known; his fate was sealed knowing his talents could be put to greater use in Spain.

In the book "Eyewitness: A Memoir of Europe in the 1930s", Geoffrey Cox stated *"The men who were drawn to fight in Spain in 1936 had not grown up in the faith, but had come into it* [Communism] *either because of intellectual conviction or by hard experience. They were mostly strong, forthright individuals – which may have been one reason why Stalin was glad to see some 600 of them who had taken refuge in the Soviet Union depart to join this highly dangerous venture".*

I have made use of quotes made by Louis Fischer; I found these in a very useful reference book "We Saw Spain Die" by Paul Preston.

It is very hard to make black and white comments about this period but some facts are hard to ignore without feeling horrified. There are always rogue elements within organisations, but the majority of the men in the International Brigade went to Spain to fight fascism but they suffered great hardships along with their Spanish republican compatriots. According to the leaflet "The Volunteer for Liberty; organ of the international brigades" magazine and dated 17th January 1949 *"the treatment of the half-million patriots who escaped from northern Spain ten years ago represents an act of infamy that can never be erased from the conscience of the world. For these people, who three year fight within a blockaded country had aroused the admiration of the world, were permitted to die like flies. They died of their wounds, of dysentery, malnutrition, exposure and influenza in the French concentration camps of Gurs, Le Vernet, Barcares, Prats de Mollo and Argeles-sur-Mer.*

They died as slaves on the Nazi trans-Saharan railroad and in the labour camps and Dachaus of the Third Reich. They died in the F.F.I., fighting for the French Republic which had betrayed them and their republic when there was still a chance to win.

They have died since then of tuberculosis, overwork and semi-starvation in liberated France, in Mexico and North Africa." Approximately 10,000 Spanish Republicans did not return from the Nazi concentration camps.

For the republicans unable to leave Spain, tens of thousands were executed. In addition there were hundreds of thousands of men, women and children who were persecuted by Franco's regime by being incarcerated in prisons, concentration camps and labour camps. Young children and babies of mothers, who had been imprisoned, were removed from maternal care and were renamed, so that they would never know their parentage. These children were then placed in families who were supportive of Franco's beliefs. The children and older students' minds were corrupted by the "corrective" educational indoctrination of this dictator. Even professional middle class people with republican leanings were removed from office and were persecuted. I quote for Helen Graham book "The Spanish Civil War".

"While the Francoist dead had war memorials and their names carved on churches – 'caidos por Dios y por España" (those who fell for God and Spain) – the republican dead could never be publicly mourned. The defeated were obliged to be complicit in this denial. Women concealed the violent deaths of husbands and fathers from their children in order to protect them physically and psychologically. In villages all over Spain many kept secret lists of the dead. Sisters mentally mapped the location of their murdered brothers, but never spoke of these things. The silent knowledge of unquiet graves necessarily produced a devastating schism between public and private memory in Spain. It was a schism that would long outlive even the Franco regime itself."

Until 1963 any opposition to Franco's regime was interpreted as being punishable by a military court. During the late 1970s and early 1980s horizons began to emerge when at long last archive-based histories of the civil war were started but I understand that many documents had been destroyed by Franco's staff even up to his death. Unfortunately during the transitional period after Franco's death and the return to democracy, it had been agreed that there would be political amnesty, the so called "Act of Silence". No-one would be called to account for neither their crimes nor any truth and reconciliation cases such as in South Africa after apartheid.

I am concerned how little is known about the Spanish civil war by the post war generations both in Spain as well as in England and the rest of the world. The republican government was elected by a free democratic election in February 1936. It is very difficult to write in just one chapter the resulting horrific event of Franco's attack on Spain, so I have concentrated on Rudolf's involvement between the end of 1936 and beginning of 1939. I hope that the reader will then research about this period in history.

Would Stalin have had so much influence if democratic countries had supported the republicans against fascism? Would there have been a Second World War? How many lives would not have been sacrificed if only fascism could have been halted earlier?

At this point I must emphasize that I do not belong or ever have belonged to any political party. However, researching and writing this book I have come to realise how many wrongs have been done to our lovely world and its people especially the last one hundred years of European history and I now ask myself the reason why a government decides on a suspect foreign policy.

There are many excellent journalists and some good newspapers and for me there is an exceptional one. Their articles are well worth reading. I have never forgotten the advice of Ursel Hochmuth (author) who told me when she knew that I was intending to write a book, "always check your facts". I have endeavoured to follow her advice. It is always better to question the source of the information being given so as not to be manipulated. Hence, my research took many years before *"Gertigstrasse 56"* was completed!

The following is another quote from *The Volunteer for Liberty* which is a magazine of the International Brigades and is dated 17th January 1949 when the Second World War was over; the horrors of fascism still continued in Spain. The statement below I believe has a great deal of truth in it.

"These people – the Spanish people – those who survive today in exile or within the confines of the vast concentration camp which is still Spain, understand better than any other peoples the nature of fascism. And they also understand better than any other peoples the great secret weapon Hitlerism brought to such perfect flower: the weapon on anti-communism. For it was anti-communism that destroyed their republic. It was anti-communism in the name of Christianity that slaughtered a million and a half Spaniards from 1936-1939. And it was anti-communism that made it possible for the Axis

to conquer most of Europe before a shot had been fired in World War II…

But since they know these things so well, they also know that the enemy they fought in Spain – the enemy that still survives the Axis – is not nearly so worried about communism as it is worried about the extension of democracy. For it was not communism that was destroyed in Spain, any more than it was destroyed in Germany or Italy or Japan when fascism took power. It was democracy – the simple aspirations of the people for security, for decency, for peace."

Franco died 20th November 1975 and his body still remains at *Santa Cruz de Valle de los Caídos*. His body is in a named grave but how many of his brave opponents are still in unknown graves? On 20th November his supporters are still allowed to hold a requiem mass for this person. Where is justice?

I would like to mention my personal thoughts with regard to Czechoslovakia. It is a matter for historians to discuss the details and consequences of the decision made by the so called friendly governments towards the people of Czechoslovakia. On a more personal note I give a précis of events.

President Emil Hácha really had no choice but in order to avoid the breaking up of Czechoslovakia, he decided to suspend autonomous arrangements for the different areas but on the 13th March 1939 Jozef Tiso, the Slovak leader proclaimed Slovakia independent becoming a satellite state for Nazi Germany. On 15th March the Wehrmacht marched into Czechoslovakia, just over two weeks after my father had managed to escape.

Paul Preston makes the following comment in his book "We Saw Spain Die"

"The West had just effectively handed over to the Third Reich the substantial military resources of Czechoslovakia – more than fifteen hundred aircraft, over five hundred anti-aircraft guns, over two thousand artillery pieces and large quantities of machine guns, ammunition and vehicles."

He then put in a remark from Louis Fischer.

"any planes, tanks, and other arms produced, any divisions trained and equipped by Britain and France between the end of September 1938 (Munich) and 1st September 1939 when the war began, could not nearly match the power of Czechoslovakia's armed forces"

It is estimated that nine hundred German refugees and five

thousand Jewish refugees did not succeed in escaping and became victims of the fascists. This included Walter Beyer's brother-in-law who had twice managed to escape from the cruel hands of the Gestapo. This time he was "questioned" and died in a Gestapo prison in Brandenburg. I have no idea what happened to Werner's friends who had been left behind – that is apart from Artur Ulbrich.

However, I am pleased to say that the German army finally started to flee at the end of the war from many of the towns in Czechoslovakia where my father had worked in setting up the resistance organisations. Artur Ulbrich wrote and told Werner that he, along with other resistance fighters together with some 700 French and Italian soldiers who had been captives in the Gablonz prisoner of war camp all joined together in their fight for liberation.

The names of the people I have mentioned in the book who worked with Rudolf, Ernst and Werner in the resistance are their actual names. I have not embellished any information about them as all the details are in the Archives, apart from personal information told by my father. I feel justified in using their names as there is nothing detrimental in their characters – in fact many of these people have not lived to tell their story.

With regard to Ernst, please note that I have only written about what was 'extracted' by the Gestapo when Ernst and his colleagues were 'questioned'. I have no doubt whatsoever that these courageous people managed to successfully carry out far greater missions which were never discovered. Many of them, I can only find their pseudonyms as their correct names had not been discovered at the times of the trials so I would love to hear if anyone knows what happened to these people and what their real names are. If any relations of these brave individuals read this book, I hope that, like me, they will also feel proud of their relative's sacrifice to fight fascism.

My father closely observed his two eldest siblings and has no doubts that Rudolf and Ernst discussed resistance tactics; Rudolf was part of the military wing and Ernst was involved with a different aspect of the resistance, but these were interlinked. He knew how incredibly close his two oldest brothers were. Lotte, their sister spent many hours talking to my father after the Second World War about events from her perspective. Additional personal information was also obtained from Gretel, Ernst's daughter. Much of this will be revealed in the second book.

What I do know is that the Gestapo when they originally arrested Ernst, they only discovered the barest minimum about his resistance work despite the torture he endured and the terrible mental stress which the Gestapo inflicted on his wife. The documents of his original trial are held in the Berlin Archives. As more members were arrested much later, greater details were 'admitted' and as this included some of Ernst's activities during the early 1930s I have included this information within this book. I do not judge anyone confessing under such conditions.

Tragically, Ernst's resistance leader, Lux, had been so badly tortured that he did not survive. This is mentioned in the descriptive document relating to the conditions in Fühlsbuttel Concentration Camp. When Ernst was arrested Blöth, took over. He was mentioned many times during the later trials as 'deceased'. On enquiring to the Berlin Archives at what had happened to Blöth, I discovered that when he was arrested, rather than being tortured, thereby risking revealing information about the resistance and his colleagues, he decided to commit suicide by jumping out of a window in the Berlin Gestapo Headquarters. A very brave decision and as due to his sacrifice, many secrets were withheld from the enemy. Of course, for our enquiring minds, it also means that we have less information of activities and consequent bravery of these men and women.

The Gestapo's anger and their subsequent revenge when they discovered more about this group of resistance fighters will be in my second book.

If any visitor to Hamburg has time, there is a monument (Ehrenmal) at Ohlsdorf Cemetery which was erected for all victims of fascism. It is a sixteen metre high monument with 104 urns containing the earth of concentration camps and one with the ashes from an unknown victim from Buchenwald Concentration Camp.

On Memorial Day on 12th September 1948, the foundation stone was laid. The representative of Hamburg parliament and the Senate were present as well as the British Military Governor. Representatives from the V.V.N which is the anti-fascist organisation and the S.P.D. (Social Democratic Party) made many speeches. This memorial is a representation of the people's will to fight for freedom. Mayor Christian Koch informed the crowd that the memorial speaks to us. Germans never forget this. Amongst those present at this event were members of the army of occupation, the Senate of Hamburg Parliament, V.V.N., the Jewish Group, all political parties and Trade Unions and the Free German Youth. To the right of the Ohlsdordorf entrance is Ehrenhain which contains 56 gravestones of murdered resistance fighters.

Each May a ceremony is held at Ehrenmal to commemorate the end of the Second World War and to remember the victims of fascism. In May 2012, after speeches and songs including the "Moorsoldaten – Liedes" which prisoners sang in concentration camps, I walked with antifascist friends from Hamburg from Ehrenmal to Ehrenhain, Ohlsdorf and then I was asked to make a speech. I feel that both my speech and my father's should be added to this book.

My Speech

"Paul and I wanted to come and join you today to show our unity with all of you in order to celebrate the end of World War Two, the defeat of Hitler's Regime, the liberation of the Concentration Camps and to remember all the victims of fascism.

Over the years, I have been moved by the tragedy of so many people having lost their lives trying to prevent the horrors of the 1930s and 1940s and who are remembered in this Ehrenhain. My two Uncles and my father's best friend are just three people of the many brave souls here, who gave their lives for freedom and the defeat of fascism. However there are others who will probably never be recognised for their sacrifices made for our liberty and perhaps we ought to reflect for a moment concerning these individuals.

As some of you are aware, I have nearly completed my book of the three Stender brothers and their comrades who fought together against fascism and tyranny. Whilst researching material for the book I have come to the unsettling conclusion that there are too many similarities with regard to the present world crisis and with the social and economic conditions of the 1920s and 1930s. We are in a very unstable world and it is up to all of us not to let our forebears down by "burying our heads in the sand". If at all possible it would be nice if each of us, in our own way, will try to alert others of the dangers thereby stopping a catastrophe emerging from the political and economic crisis of today…

Finally, let us reflect on all the people whose names are forever etched on the gravestones here in Ehrenhain and to those unknown but brave souls who actively fought and lost their lives or even those who managed to survive but have suffered mental scars. We owe it to all these people that their sacrifices have not been futile. We must never let this happen again.

I would also like to mention before I finish that two weeks ago, Ernst Stender's only child, Gretel passed away after a long illness. She was just one of the many children of the resistance fighters who suffered as a result of their parents brave activities. I am pleased that Gretel's son, Holger and his family are here with us today, to commemorate the occasion.

Thank you for letting me express my thoughts. It is a pleasure to be amongst friends on a Day of Remembrance. I just wish that my father was well enough to be with us today but he sends his good wishes to you. Christine will read the message he has sent to you.

My Father's speech

Dear Friends and Comrades

Unfortunately out of health reasons, I am unable to take part on this Memorial Day. I am always well informed through the "Antifa" about the fight against the old and new formation of the fascists. We must warn again and again of the danger of fascism to all peace loving people and especially the youth. We have to make it clear that the old and new Nazis do not represent a political view, that these organisations always have been and still are crimes against the people of the World. We must never forget those victims of their crime! I am also pleased that the Jarrestadt Initiative is actively carrying on the fight against Fascism!

With antifascist greetings
Werner Stender

Photo used in Antifa Magazine Photographer Chodinski

Werner and Ruth Stender by the Alster, Hamburg – July 2014

Bibliography

Conspiracy of Silence by Alex Weisburg – Published by Hamish Hamilton

The Invisible Writing by Arthur Koestler ISBN 0-909-8030-1

Spanish Testament by Arthur Koestler

And I Remember Spain (A Spanish Civil War Anthology Edited by Murray Sperber *ISBN 0 246 10595 X*

The Return by Victoria Hislop ISBN 9780755332953

We Saw Spain Die by Paul Preston ISBN978-1-84529-946-0

Women's Voices from the Spanish Civil War Edited by Jim Fyrth with Sally Alexander ISBN 9781905007875

Antony Beevor's *The Battle for Spain*: *The Spanish Civil War 1936 – 1939* published by Weidenfeld & Nicolson, The Orion Publishing Group Ltd ISBN 0-2978-4832-1

The Spanish Civil War: A Very Short Introduction (Oxford, 2005) by Helen Graham ISBN 978-0-19-280377-1

Homage to Catalonia by George Orwell

Niemand und nichts wird vergessen: Biogramme und Briefe Hamburger Widerstandskämpfer 1933 – 1945 by Ursel Hochmuth ISBN 3-89965-121-9

Eyewitness: A Memoir of Europe in the 1930s by Geoffrey Cox. Dunedin: Otago University Press (1999), ISBN 1-877133-70-1

Defence of Madrid: An eyewitness account from the Spanish Civil War by Geoffrey Cox (2nd ed), Dunedin: Otago University Press (1999), ISBN 1-877372-38-2

The Illustrated History of the Third Reich by John Bradley – Bison Books Ltd

*Freedom Fighters or Comintern Army? The International Brigades in Spa*in by Andy Durgan

www.wapediamobi/en/International_Brigade

International Brigades in Spain 1936-39 by Ken Bradley, published by
     Osprey Books ISBN 978-1-85532-367-4
Disarmament and Clandestine Rearmament under the Weimar Republic by E J
     Gumbel
1918 "November Revolution" by Gilles Dauvé and Denis Authier
The Hamburg Revolution 1919 – Heinrich Laufenberg
Wikipedia
Anschläge – Deutsche Plakate als Dokumente der Zeit 1900 – 1960 Published
     by Langewiesche-Brandt 1963
"Einschnitte" Sechzig Jahre Mitten Mang über das leben des Hamburger
     Kommunisten by Tetje Lotz 1986
Neuengammen Concentration Camp Web Site
Crossing Hitler: The Man Who Put the Nazis on the Witness Stand by
     Benjamin Carter Hett ISBN 9780195369885
International   Solidarity   with   the   Spanish   Republic   1936-39
     (Leninist.biz/en/1975/ISSR389)
*Poisoning the Proletariat: Urban Water Supply and River Pollution in Russia's
     Industrial Regions during late Stalinism 1945-1953* by Donald Filtzer
The Great Crusade – Gustav Regler
     The Owl of Minerva – Gustav Regler
*Pears Cyclopaedia (War Economy Issue) Fifty-Third Edition*n A & F Pears Ltd
www.stolperstein-hamburg.de
Skandinavisiche Erfahrungen erwünscht?: Nachexil und Remigration by
     Michael F Scholz ISBN 3515076514
The Volunteer for Liberty: Organ of the international Brigades Magazine which
     is kept at the Abraham Lincoln Archives, New York (ALBA)
1984 by George Orwell ISBN0-547-24964-0 published by Secker and
     Warburg

Places of Reference

National Archives, London
Berlin Archives, Germany
SAPMO, Berlin Archives, Germany
Hamburg Archives, Germany
Hamburg University Archives, Germany
Home Office
MI5
Centro Documental de la Memoria Histórica, Salamanca, Spain
Ministerio de Defensa – Archivo General Militarde Avila, Spain
Associacion de Amigos de Las Brigades Internationales
Russian State Archive of Socio-Political History (RGASPI)
International Brigade Memorial Trust (IBMT)
Abraham Lincoln Brigade Archive, New York (ALBA)
Stender family archives